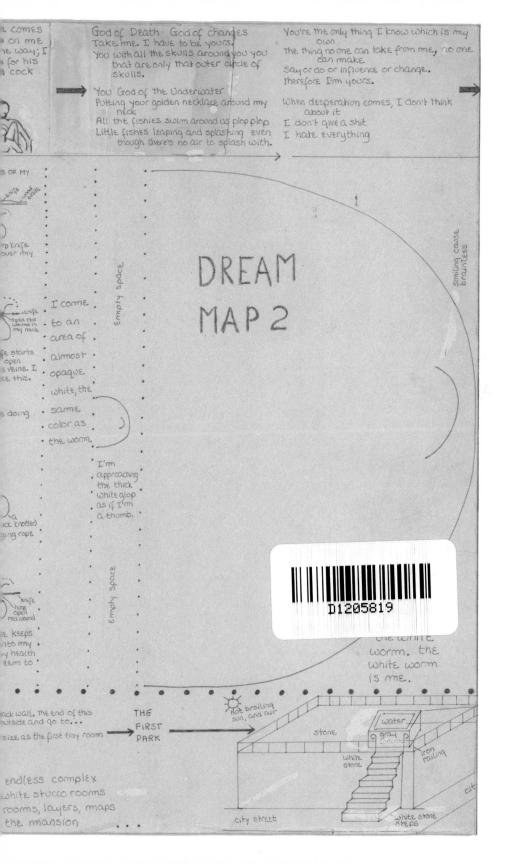

...COMES
...on me
...he way; I
...for his
...a cock

God of Death God of changes
Take me. I have to be yours.
You with all the skulls around you you
    that are only that outer circle of
    skulls.

You God of the Underwater
Putting your golden necklace around my
    neck
All the fishies swim around us plop plop
Little fishies leaping and splashing even
    though there's no air to splash with.

You're the only thing I know which is my
            own
The thing no one can take from me, no one
        can make
Say or do or influence or change.
Therefore I'm yours.

When desperation comes, I don't think
        about it
I don't give a shit
I hate everything

...S OF MY

...knife...blade

...p knife
...over my

...knife
open red
wound in
my neck

...e starts
open
...veins. I
...ke this.

...doing

...a
...k knotted
...ing rope

...knife
huge
open
red wound

...e keeps
...to my
...y health
...em to

I come
to an
area of
almost
opaque
white, the
same
color as
the worm.

I'm
approaching
the thick
white glop
as if I'm
a thumb.

Empty space

Empty space

DREAM
MAP 2

Smiling cause
brainless

...the white
worm. the
white worm
is me.

...ack wall. the end of this
...utside and go to...

...size as the first tiny room

THE
FIRST
PARK

Hot broiling
sun, and air

stone

water

gray concrete

white
stone

iron
railing

endless complex
white stucco rooms
rooms, layers, maps
the mansion

city street

white stone
steps

city

D1205819

EAT YOUR MIND

THE RADICAL LIFE *and* WORK
of KATHY ACKER

JASON McBRIDE

SIMON & SCHUSTER

New York   London   Toronto   Sydney   New Delhi

Simon & Schuster
1230 Avenue of the Americas
New York, NY 10020

First Simon & Schuster hardcover edition November 2022

SIMON & SCHUSTER and colophon are registered trademarks of Simon & Schuster, Inc.

For information about special discounts for bulk purchases, please contact Simon & Schuster Special Sales at 1-866-506-1949 or business@simonandschuster.com.

The Simon & Schuster Speakers Bureau can bring authors to your live event. For more information or to book an event, contact the Simon & Schuster Speakers Bureau at 1-866-248-3049 or visit our website at www.simonspeakers.com.

Interior design by Carly Loman

Manufactured in China

10   9   8   7   6   5   4   3   2   1

Library of Congress Cataloging-in-Publication Data

Identifiers: LCCN 2022021461 (print) | LCCN 2022021462 (ebook) |
    ISBN 9781982117023 (hardcover) | ISBN 9781982117030 (paperback) |
    ISBN 9781982117047 (ebook)
Subjects: LCSH: Acker, Kathy, 1947–1997. | Women authors, American—
    20th Century—Biography. | Experimental fiction, American—History and criticism. |
    LCGFT: Biographies.
Classification: LCC PS3551.C44 Z77 2022 (print) | LCC PS3551.C44 (ebook) |
    DDC 813/.54 [B]—dc23/eng/20220509
LC record available at https://lccn.loc.gov/2022021461
LC ebook record available at https://lccn.loc.gov/2022021462

ISBN 978-1-9821-1702-3
ISBN 978-1-9821-1704-7 (ebook)

CONTENTS

Preface   xi

PARENTS STINK
(1947—1964)
1

WHAT IT MEANS TO BE AVANT-GARDE
(1964—1976)
41

A NARRATIVE? NO, A VISION
(1976—1983)
147

TO LIVE FOREVER IN WONDER
(1983—1990)
223

THE SCHOOL OF THE SELF
(1990—1997)
287

Afterword   335

Acknowledgments   339

Illustration Credits   345

Notes on Sources   347

Endnotes   349

Index   373

About the Author   391

In my school called how can I live
in my theory of appearing
I lay out my costume.

—LISA ROBERTSON, "THE SEAM"

EAT YOUR MIND

Kathy Acker was that rare and now almost inconceivable thing: a celebrity experimental writer. Patti Smith with a post-doc, perhaps; Anne Carson, if she'd studied Greek during her breaks at a peep show; a Gertrude Stein in Gaultier.

When she died in 1997, at the age of fifty, she'd published thirteen groundbreaking novels, and had written screenplays, poetry, libretti, essays, and criticism; two novellas were published posthumously. These categories are sometimes useful, sometimes not. Often considered a poster girl for postmodernism—a word she was constantly ambivalent about—Acker abhorred limitations of all kinds, and she exploded the borders between novel and poetry, philosophy and journalism, art and entertainment. Most compellingly, between reading and writing. "Like Borges, I equate reading and writing," she wrote in the last year of her life. "To read is to write; to write is to write the world; to elect to neither read nor write is to choose suicide."

She was highly educated, a voracious reader with catholic taste, and she almost always wrote with other writers' books open in her lap or scattered across her desk or bed. Literature was both her life and her adversary, and it was impossible to judge her work by the standards we use to judge literary fiction. Very often, in fact, she deliberately wrote "badly" or "incorrectly," in defiance of literary authority and propriety, as well as conventions of logic, grammar, and beauty. Identifying language with knowledge and power, she sought, always, to disrupt language. Two of her best-known novels are titled *Great Expectations* and *Don Quixote*—she famously plagiarized scenes, phrases, characters, and ideas from texts both canonical and otherwise, collaging these with shards of her own diaries, sexual fantasies, gossip, political screeds, and blunt critiques of capitalism, liberalism, and patriarchy.

"Collage" suggests a degree of harmony, but Acker's fragmentary narratives are far more jagged and jangly than that. Her sentences are plain and direct, frequently aphoristic, punctuated by shifts into, and out of, the lyrical, the Gothic, the sentimental. "Names, identities, issues, emotions, everything evident is *fronted* compulsively," poet Steve Benson said of her work. The relentlessly hybrid, helter-skelter nature of her prose is reinforced by its frequent swerves into playscript, hand-lettered poetry, foreign languages. Lewd drawings and elaborate dream maps made by the writer herself often provide illustration. Reading an Acker novel is hardly like reading at all; you enter it, endure it, allow it to act upon you, like an acid bath. You can skip paragraphs, even pages, or open a book halfway through, and the effect more or less remains. You leave an Acker novel feeling scoured, stunned, ravaged, as if you've just emerged from a car crash or emergency surgery.

Acker's plots, such as they are, hinge on rape, revolution, and doomed, treacherous romance. Her writing suggests that love and desire are determined by culture, by various social and political premises that require constant negotiation, re-evaluation, and reformulation. Compulsively and hyperbolically, therefore, she wrote about sex, gender, and power, concerns that also consumed her everyday life. For Acker, sex and writing were as inextricable as writing and reading, writing and politics. Later in life, she often wrote while she masturbated, in the hopes of arriving at different kinds of expression. In a sense, her novels were written to be performed, and when read aloud, especially by her, they become even more incandescent.

Acker likewise performed her life as if she had written it. To borrow Judith Thurman's description of Colette, Acker lived turbulently and worked tirelessly. Raised in a privileged but oppressive Upper East Side Jewish family, she turned her back on that world as soon as she could, seeking a life of romantic and intellectual adventure that led her to, and through, many of the most thrilling avant-garde and countercultural moments in America in the late twentieth century: the births of conceptual art and experimental music; the poetry wars of the sixties and seventies; the mainstreaming of hardcore porn; No Wave cinema and New Narrative writing; riot grrls, biker chicks, cyberpunks. In all these scenes, she was alternately student and shadow, avatar, vampire, paladin. As this book shows, time and time again, Acker was not just a singular writer, she was also a titanic cultural force who tied together disparate movements in literature, art, music, theater, and film.

In her early twenties, she worked in live sex shows in Times Square, made porn films, and stripped in sailor bars in San Diego. Her refusal of literary propriety extended to a similarly flagrant contempt for conventional feminine identity. Though married twice to men, she preferred to identify as queer. She never had children. For her, monogamy was moot, and she had countless lovers, both men and women. Sex fascinated her, as a source of personal, complicated pleasure, but also as a way to understand power, gender, the self. "I threw myself onto every bed as a dead sailor flings himself into the sea," she writes in her novel *My Mother: Demonology*. Her legion of famous lovers included film scholars P. Adams Sitney and Peter Wollen; writers Rudy Wurlitzer, Hanif Kureishi, Lidia Yuknavitch, and Sylvère Lotringer; musicians Richard Hell, Adele Bertei, and Peter Gordon (her second husband); artists Robin Winters, Alan Sondheim, David Salle, and, allegedly, Sol LeWitt. "She really was like a librarian," Winters said, "and treated people like books. She wanted to read as many as possible." In turn, Acker often acted like *she* was a character in a book or myth. Another lover, the philosopher Johnny Golding, put it in related terms: "Kathy's 'fundamental' sexual identity was writer. Her sexuality was writing. She was having a sexual relationship with *that*."

All Acker ever really wanted to do was write, but she also wanted to be, and often was, much more than a writer: artist, rock star, philosopher, performance artist, cultural force. She was heavily tattooed and pierced, kept her hair extremely short and often dyed, adored outré, cutting-edge fashion. All of this provided a kind of dazzle camouflage that distinguished her entirely from her literary peers. Over the years, her appearance shifted dramatically: she could look like a deranged kewpie doll, a pirate from the future, an alien courtesan. "In a way, she was a clown," the writer Robert Glück said with admiration. "She would wear a ton of makeup, so different from everybody else in the room." Dodie Bellamy, the novelist and essayist, had a similar take: "She looked like a clown, but a totally confident, powerful clown." Author photos rarely appear on the front of books of fiction; in Acker's case, in the editions of her books that were published in the 1980s and 1990s, her well-known face and body were usually splashed across her covers, making them look as much like music albums as they did works of fiction.

The criminal and outlaw beguiled her, and in both life and work Acker assumed their defiance. She felt that art—or at least the art she was interested in—could itself be lawless, subversive, even antisocial; she signed the manuscript of a 1979 essay, "Miss Criminal." She possessed a contradictory charisma: seductive, funny, fiercely intelligent, and capable of extraordinary intimacy, she could also be agonizingly vulnerable, narcissistic, demanding, obdurate, and competitive. The fearless, ferocious persona that she projected masked a more fragile neurotic, and sometimes vice versa. She craved stardom, but buckled beneath its demands. Her disguises and performances were profligate, unstable, confusing. Even as she was regarded by some as a dangerous person, a kind of literary terrorist or "mistress of the obscene," as the *Times Literary Supplement* (*TLS*) called her, she reminded others of no one so much as their old Jewish aunts. She had "drawing-room manners," one friend said. Occasionally, she could reveal a surprising prudish streak: in a letter to Dennis Cooper about his book *The Missing Men*, she wrote that she found it "depressing," that he was too obsessed with sex. After seeing Stanley Kubrick's *Full Metal Jacket* with Salman Rushdie, she told a flabbergasted Rushdie that the movie's foul language offended her.

Her narrators are often child-women and she herself often behaved like a child, and a bratty one at that. She did what she wanted, when she wanted, how she wanted—no matter the cost. Friends and lovers could be dispatched for the most insignificant insult, perceived betrayal, or simply because they were no longer useful to her. At the same time, again perhaps like a child, she threw herself wholeheartedly into life, pursuing what she wanted with avidity, always eager to try the thing that was novel, unusual, even dangerous. It was no coincidence that the collection of essays on Acker's work that was published in 2006 was titled *Lust for Life*.

Acker's work inspired both admiration and anger, sometimes at once. The writer Gary Indiana, at various times a close friend and near nemesis, said of her books that her "indifference to whether her writing was good or bad . . . meant that a little of them went a long way." David Foster Wallace, sounding the underappreciative, confused note that Acker often encountered, described her early novels as "at once critically pretty interesting and artistically pretty crummy and actually no fun to read at all." In fact, they can be pretty fun, in various ways, and also funny, grotesque, titillating, profound, demented, recursive, shocking, baffling, monotonous, bilious, mischievous, and breathtaking. At the time, there was very little like Acker's writing in American literature. There is very little that resembles her writing in American literature now.

Especially for younger readers, and especially for young women, Acker was an icon of liberation, giving permission to read, think, and write differently. The writer Lucy Sante, who knew Acker slightly in the late seventies—"I nursed a distant and silent crush," she told me—felt that her being an emblem of emancipation had also, however, blinded readers to the particular delights of her prose. "Her public image and her function as a symbol for various kinds of 'empowerment' has overpowered the pleasure of the text," Sante said. "More pleasure in some texts than in others." The English novelist Jeanette Winterson summed up Acker's writing as, simply, "pioneer work of the kind that had hardly been attempted since Virginia Woolf's *Orlando* in 1928."

Acker didn't write to entertain, or to tell stories, or out of the impulse we heedlessly call "self-expression." Writing was far more serious than that for her, an occult tool of survival and transformation. "My life was very, very dark," she told *Bookworm's* Michael Silverblatt in 1992, "and has gotten relatively lighter as the years have gone on. I changed myself by using literature." She was an inimitable writer, but she found inspiration, nourishment, and community, for periods of time anyway, in cultural scenes from Black Mountain—the group of mid-twentieth-century avant-garde poets and artists that gathered around the North Carolina experimental college of the same name—to queercore, the punk LGBTQ movement that flourished in the late 1980s in Toronto, San Francisco, and elsewhere. She's most commonly associated with the brief moment in the 1980s and early 1990s when cutting-edge American literature was dominated by so-called transgressive fiction. In the *Los Angeles Times* in 1993, Silverblatt homed in on the hallmarks of the microgenre: a belief in the body as the locus of knowledge; a pervasive sexual anxiety; an obsession with abjection and dysfunction. Silverblatt lumped Acker in with provocateurs like Dennis Cooper, A. M. Homes, Bret Easton Ellis, Gary Indiana, Jeanette Winterson, and Lynne Tillman. Acker was close friends with a few of these writers, and shared with them a certain sensibility and aesthetic concerns, but her work had an intensity, formal experimentation, and ambition all its own.

There is an essential and luminous paradox in Acker's work and life: literature was liberation for her, but it could also be confinement. Literature showed her, over and over, new ways of being, new ways of thinking, and new ways of speaking. "Literature is that which denounces and slashes apart the repressing machine at the level of the signified," she wrote in *Empire of the Senseless*. But some books, often the literature that she first loved as a child, also reproduced or strengthened the repressive structures, the social codes, the *limitations*, that she struggled against. To write, therefore, was to constantly re-create the emancipatory potential of literature, to renew it, to provide herself and her readers with fresh tools of survival. To do so, she did three things—she explicitly revealed how conventional literature can reproduce those codes and limitations; she created a literary style and technique that evaded or attacked those same limitations; and she routinely confected fantasies of escape and rebellion: crime, piracy, magic. But usually, in Acker's books, the paradox recurs. As soon as escape or freedom is rendered and made possible, "reality"—abusive, politically corrupt, traumatic—inevitably intrudes. In her fictional worlds, the author makes the laws, but the laws of the real world are never far from the page. There is no redemption in an Acker novel.

Acker was, in a word, uncompromising. This was the theme of her life. She was a stranger to satisfaction. She was unable, or unwilling, to compromise over anything, from the incendiary subject matter of her books to the kinds of food she ate. This was, of course, both a strength and weakness. It enabled her to write the way she wanted, but it blinded her, occasionally, to the deficiencies of her work. It gave her entry to and prominence in rarefied cultural worlds, but it also made her paranoid, self-sabotaging, and impossible. Like all extremists, she was susceptible to caricature—of other people's ideas, of her own, of other people's images, of her own. As the philosopher McKenzie Wark put it, "Being Kathy Acker was not an easy thing."

× × ×

She was the first professional writer I saw read in public. It was the fall of 1988, and I was a sophomore at the University of Toronto. She read at what was then called the Harbourfront International Authors' Festival (now the Toronto International Festival of Authors), on a bill that also included, somewhat incongruously, the Trinadian-Canadian novelist Neil Bissoondath, the Cuban writer Miguel Barnet, and the Belgian writer Monika van Paemel. Based on Acker's books, which I had just started reading, and her pugnacious public image, I expected someone almost feral. She certainly looked the part. She was small, but wore a dramatic Vivienne Westwood armor jacket, and when she moved, the pin-striped pads of the jacket parted to reveal tattooed, sharply defined muscles. What writers had such bodies? Who, then, except bikers and convicts and rock musicians, really, had tattoos? Her voice had a honeyed menace, but when she read—from *In Memoriam to Identity*, a work in progress—she magicked her sharp, ferocious prose into something sublime. A few years later, when I saw her again, at a Grove Press party, I was struck once more by the seeming paradox of her public persona: she still looked forbidding, but also like she was

EAT YOUR MIND | xvii

having a wonderful time. She bobbed through the crowd, smiling broadly, her big eyes gleaming, happily chatting with everyone.

I was at an impressionable age, and completely bewitched by her fusion of sex and literature, the streets and the academy. In high school, I'd been an ardent fan of William S. Burroughs, both his writing and the dark, deranged character he played. Now here was someone who spoke lovingly of Burroughs's significance, who borrowed some of his methods, but was younger, and a woman, attractive but unearthly. Her fiction was shaped by the continental philosophy I studied and the other writers—Rimbaud, Faulkner, Stein—I was discovering and devouring. She seemed at once more accessible and more radical than Burroughs.

In much of her early work, Acker turned her own anxieties and ambivalence—about identity, sexuality, family, the body, language itself—into an engine. She dispensed with artfulness and craft, concerned largely with capturing the rolling boil of her own consciousness. She was a literal agent of chaos. If other writers told stories to "organize" the tumultuous slipstream of life, she made that tumult the story, and her writing could be as fumbling, angry, and ambitious as she herself was. "I remember Robert Creeley taught that a writer, a poet, is a real writer when he (or she) finds his own voice," she wrote. "I wanted to be a writer; I didn't want to do anything else; but I couldn't find my own voice. The act of writing for me was the most pleasurable thing in the world. Just writing. Why did I have to find my own voice, and where was it? I hated my fathers." Also, much later, in the introduction to *Bodies of Work*, an essay collection published the year of her death and which has only become more resonant and valuable since: "I trust neither my ability to know nor what I think I know . . . to write down what one thinks one knows is to destroy possibilities for joy."

Even a middle-class, white, straight, cis kid like me could identify with this. My life was relatively conventional and privileged, outwardly normal, but I was also a shy and anxious teenager, unformed really, with equally inchoate creative ambitions. I wanted to write too but had no idea what that writing could or should look like. What was my voice? Did I have one? Did I need one? What did I know? Don't we all, at some point, hate our fathers? I didn't want to write in, or with, the voice that I was *supposed* to write with; the identity, the category, foisted on me felt insufficient and, occasionally, intolerable. I craved freedom from that, and Acker provided it. I absorbed her oppositional energy, even if I didn't always know where to put it.

I wasn't alone in this, either. Like other cult writers, Acker inspires extraordinary and profound attachment. This is partly because Acker's narrators are outsiders, freaks, victims, and fuckups, pushing against an indifferent or oppressive establishment. Their broken hearts land them in the hospital or lead them to plot an insurgency. Anyone who's identified as such—that is, almost anyone who's been young—can see themselves in her work. Few novelists before Acker so nakedly paraded psychological damage, abuse, and masochism. Few so openly displayed their own vulnerability. She made trauma her subject long before it became an object of literary criticism or the routine plot of potboilers. This exhibitionism forged an immediate, if often uncomfortable, intimacy with her readers.

Despite her reservations, Acker *did* have a voice. It was one of the most distinctive in American fiction. Acker's friend the cultural critic and biographer Cynthia Carr described Acker's various, relatively interchangeable, narrators as "different names tagged to the sound of one voice raging—obscene, cynical, bewildered, and demanding to be fucked." This voice varied only slightly throughout her career. It possessed an ambient fury. It was an alarm. Most of the time, Acker paired it with a style that fell somewhere between hard-boiled crime fiction and fairy tale.

I heard Acker's speaking voice for the first time at that reading, which I attended with my closest friend, the writer Derek McCormack.* A week later, we went to get our own tattoos. I didn't know what I wanted, except for something that might make me look tougher than I was, as tough-looking, maybe, as Acker. I eventually settled on the only thing I could afford: a quarter-sized, monochromatic skull on my right shoulder. (Derek, meanwhile, got something even more in the spirit of Acker, and in supplementary homage to their mutual hero, Jean Genet: a colorful rose across his chest.) I never became a writer like Acker, but her influence—on my reading, on my ideas of writing and art—were as enduring as that tattoo.

x x x

---

* Many years later, Derek also recounted this Harbourfront reading, in Casey McKinney's online magazine, *Fanzine*. Reviewing a 2006 exhibition of Acker's clothes, curated by Dodie Bellamy and titled *Kathy Forest*, he described the Westwood jacket as something "Mad Max might have worn to the office."

In her 1984 novel, *Blood and Guts in High School,* Acker posts a warning to admirers and potential biographers alike: "Don't get into the writer's personal life thinking if you like the books you'll like the writer. A writer's personal life is horrible and lonely. Writers are queer so keep away from them."

She was half-joking, I think, but in any case, I obviously ignored this admonition. For years, I yearned to know more about Acker's life, and how her writing grew out of it. In the immediate aftermath of her death, there were new anthologies of writing by and about Acker, a symposium and a documentary, but Acker still remained a figure elusive and then, almost forgotten. This was partly because of fashion—her hairstyles, tattoos, and clothing were inextricably associated with the eighties and the early nineties. She was also similarly tied to philosophical and theoretical currents that some considered dated or passé: deconstruction, poststructuralism, etc. To some, she was the literary equivalent of Goth or emo, a phase that "serious" adults grew out of. Her representations of sexual violence and trauma, undeniably provocative to her contemporaries, became perhaps *too* provocative to later readers less appreciative of Acker's ironies and eager for transparent, even reassuring, positions on such topics. During her life, she was never given her adequate due as a serious, complex writer or cultural figure, and after she died, this seemed to be, frustratingly, even more the case.

But Acker was the most serious of writers, and as much as she was a product of her time, she was also, in so many ways, ahead of it. Her life and work, and the various artistic and political forces that shaped them, have become more relevant than ever, and shed ample light on our own age. Her work is so dense, and changes shape so frequently, that new generations of readers uncover new things in it all the time. Her magpie juxtaposition of found and stolen texts presaged the sampling and remixing of turntablism and hip-hop. Her quicksilver skip across time and space and genre hint at the way the internet compresses, expands, and elides history and culture. Her ongoing explorations of identity, gender, and ideas of post-humanity—with characters that regularly oscillate between male and female, animal and cyborg—anticipate the growing visibility of transgender and nonbinary people, and for some, her work can be read as an early form of trans lit. Acker was an enemy of both fascism and neoliberalism—political figures like Nixon, Reagan, and Thatcher are pilloried and parodied in almost every book—and in an era of ascendant authoritarianism, her work has even greater resonance. In her writing and life, she often started or took up complicated conversations around capital, colonialism, empowerment, and sex-positivity that continue today.

Finally, in her fraught, playful, recursive use of her real life, she made possible books by boundary-blurring, so-called autofictional writers like Chris Kraus, Sheila Heti, Jarett Kobek, and Tao Lin.* Acker's reliance on reworked autobiography, in fact, is a bright red line of tension throughout her work. While she warned readers to avoid her personal life, she herself used its details, with urgent frequency and for different effects, to pattern her fiction. She also simultaneously used that fiction to explore how identity is manufactured, distorted, and effaced. She was drawn to, and her writing deeply marked by, critical theory in which biography is considered little more than a Victorian relic, in which the author is dead. All of these contradictions arise in her description of her first "real" book, a collection of autobiographical prose poems titled *Politics*: "Autobiography is supposed to be the 'truthful' account of one's life. I quickly realized that the more truthful I try to be in language, the more I lie. One immediately comes up to language and learns either to be defeated or to let language fuck one, to fuck with language. To lie down. This is what I call 'fiction.'"

This is what we can call biography too. In both her writing and the numerous interviews she gave throughout her career, Acker dissembled, exaggerated, fabricated, mythologized, shaped, and reshaped and misshaped the facts of her life. Among artists and writers, she's hardly alone in doing so. But she was also always more truthful than she admitted, or cared to admit. In 1986, as part of London's Institute of Contemporary Arts' *Writers in Conversation* series, professor and cultural theorist Angela McRobbie asked her about the representation of mothers in her books, and a seemingly off-guard Acker said, "I hate to think I write autobiographically—and it probably comes roaring out."

---

* Chris Kraus's personal relationship to Acker is well known and explored later in this book. Heti's connection is more incidental. In June 1997, while a twenty-year-old intern at the now defunct Canadian culture magazine *Shift*, Heti emailed Acker to ask what she was then reading that "illustrates the way of the future." (Acker was among ten other writers, including Michael Chabon and Alberto Manguel, who were asked the same question.) While Acker's side of the correspondence has not survived, Heti's emails—in which her explanation of who she is and what she wants becomes increasingly wry, even combative—suggest that Acker was exasperated by the request and never did contribute. In any event, she was also gravely ill at the time and obviously had more important things on her mind.

In another interview, a couple years later, she claimed that a quarter of the material she used in her books was autobiographical.

But if she reflexively returned to the actual contours of her biography, it was also to frame that biography in terms both mythic and metaphorical. Her own life had its specific dramas, its unique twists and turns, but it also illuminated certain general aspects of sexual politics, the tyranny of the nuclear family, the blind spots of culture, and the slipperiness of subjectivity. Acker sometimes thought of her prose as journalism—"a writer is a kind of journalist, but a magic one"—but she also operated like a poet, unconcerned with whether her writing was fact or fiction. Another of Acker's friends, the conceptual artist Lawrence Weiner, argued that Acker's art didn't have its basis in facts—in what had happened—but rather, "it was about finding the thing that was *supposed* to happen." That gulf—between what happened and what was supposed to happen—was rich territory, an interzone in which Acker liked to dwell.

My primary sources for this biography were, of course, Acker's words themselves: her books, her writings about those books (in her private journals and published essays, in letters to friends, lovers, and colleagues), her public interviews, and a trove of legal documents and financial records. Given Acker's impulse toward self-mythologization, it's risky to rely on her own words—especially, of course, her fiction. But I also spoke with and corresponded with about 120 people who knew Acker, and while their memories, stories, and interpretations occasionally conflicted and were necessarily incomplete, sometimes even false, they also helped to corroborate and supplement Acker's own testimony. Perhaps more than most, Acker led multiple lives. She was governed by, and thrived on, contradiction. So, rather than rely on her reductive assessment above, it's better to keep in mind what Robert Glück said on the subject in his invaluable essay, "Long Note on New Narrative": "We were thinking about autobiography; by autobiography we meant daydreams, nightdreams, the act of writing, the relationship to the reader, the meeting of flesh and culture, the self as collaboration, the self as disintegration, the gaps, inconsistencies and distortions, the enjambments of power, family, history and language."

But there is glamour in maintaining mystery. Acker was devoted to hidden histories, alternative beliefs, the arcane and magical. She loved secrets and gossip, dress-up and disguises. She loved—and required—reinvention. She loved detective novels and mysteries, and she loved turning her own life into a mystery, for others but also, more importantly, for herself. As a child, Acker said, she dreamed of writing like Agatha Christie. Acker's mother—a larger-than-life, larger-than-death figure who would forever preoccupy the writer's work—kept Christie's novels in her library, and from the unlikely age of six, according to Acker, they captured her imagination. Her mother also owned a collection of porn novels, Acker claimed, and, less surprisingly, the precocious Kathy read those books too. In her young mind, sex and crime were twinned. Double books, double meanings, double lives. Much of her fiction had the staccato pulse of pulp. Her first novel, the posthumously published "pornographic mystery," was called *Rip-off Red, Girl Detective*, and for several months, she gleefully used that titular alias.

Despite our aspirations, no biography is ever definitive. Despite my best efforts, there remain certain unanswered questions in Acker's life, certain gaps and holes in the narrative. But, again, I think Acker would like this. She didn't seek to be solved. Holes are escape routes, openings. They lead to unknown possibilities. Her writing explicitly defied rationality and served as a harbor for the unknown; to a certain extent, her life did as well. In a notebook in which Acker sketched out her final work, an unfinished libretto titled *Requiem*, she wrote, "I'm giving you the clues, but as yet you don't know the clues to what."

PARENTS STINK

(1947–1964)

CHAPTER 1

———— × ————

I N THE SPRING OF 1995, KATHY ACKER RODE HER MOTORCYCLE FROM her Cole Valley apartment and across the Golden Gate Bridge for her first appointment with Georgina Ritchie, a spiritual advisor well known in the Bay Area. Acker was almost forty-eight, but looked both younger and older: she was short, with enormous but sunken eyes, full lips made even fuller by the bright red lipstick she once referred to as "cunt color after fucking." Her peroxided hair was cut into a Caesar, her ears heavily pierced. She wore an oversized black leather jacket, "GIRL" written across the back of it, which hid the tattoos and muscular frame that had long distinguished her. Her bike was a blue-and-silver Yamaha Virago, with tasseled handlebars and cowhide saddlebags, her helmet a matching gumball blue. As she sped through San Francisco's streets, she might have been a cobalt comet, blurry and burning up, hurtling, as always, toward uncertainty.

Something churned within her. She felt depleted, unsettled, ambivalent. After coming and going from the city for decades, San Francisco had finally become, for better or worse, home. Various local scenes provided creative nourishment and a sense of solidarity. But the queer community had been ravaged by AIDS. She was squabbling with the local writers who had been both her friends and admirers. While Acker adored her students at the Art Institute, she was tired of teaching as an adjunct—it was time-consuming, didn't pay enough. She still had to crank out book reviews, essays, and other journalism, work that she found intermittently interesting but which distracted her from the fiction that she considered her real writing. She was working on a new novel, *Pussy, King of the Pirates*, but spending more and more time immersed in the emerging digital subculture—her next project, she thought, might be released only as a CD-ROM. Meanwhile, her romantic life was unsatisfying, characterized by fleeting, meaningless affairs. She was considering moving to L.A., or maybe even returning to London, the last place where she'd experienced genuine love and where there had been, at certain points anyway, more affection for her work.

Acker was in enough turmoil that finally, her psychic, a garrulous ex–New Yorker named Frank Malinaro,* whom she spoke to several times a week, told her to go see Ritchie. Ritchie worked out of a houseboat in Sausalito, where her main clients were corporate executives. She specialized in pain and stress management, hypnotherapy, and, more controversially and compellingly, past life regression and clearing. Ritchie's father had been a doctor, but like Acker, she had developed a distrust of conventional medicine that led her along a much different therapeutic path. She was a devotee of Louise Hay, the bestselling, controversial spiritual writer who argued that we can transform our lives, and our health, through positive thoughts, and who claimed to have cured her own cancer this way. Ritchie told Acker that she'd seen healers in Mexico and Brazil perform psychic kidney transplants and brain surgery. Another healer, a professor at the Humanistic Psychology Institute at Sonoma State University, had taught Ritchie how to put patients into trances and lead them back through childhood and into their past lives. "The body remembers," Ritchie told Acker, "especially traumas. And holds these memories as scars, as wounds."

Ritchie didn't know Acker or her books. But soon into their conversation, she realized that Acker's body was scored with such scars. To Ritchie, her new client was in extreme stress and profound emotional pain. Past life therapy, she felt, would help her become "unstuck." Ritchie explained more fully: "I 'roto-root' the past. When a person goes through a regression, that person is able to stop obsessing about the trauma and is able to situate the trauma in the whole picture. For instance, take the blame off Mommy and Daddy [and] begin to see Mommy and Daddy as people situated in larger situations. All healing has to do with forgiveness. A healthy person is one who can say, 'I have no scars from the past that will keep me doing what I have to do today.'"

Their first session was held on April 10. Ritchie led Acker through a guided meditation, and, over time, her past lives slowly revealed themselves. To no one's surprise, trauma defined many of them. Together, Acker and Ritchie discovered that Acker had once been an Aztec sorceress during a time of political turmoil, and that, after protesting some abuse of power that she witnessed, she had been killed by someone she regarded as a friend. "You concluded

---

* Acker misspells Malinaro as Molinaro in her essay "The Gift of Disease," an error repeated in Chris Kraus's *After Kathy Acker*, among other places.

from this lifetime that the world was not safe," Ritchie told her. In two other sessions, held later that summer, they learned that Acker had also been a Native American who'd been raped and mutilated. Much more happily—and appropriately, given her longtime fascination with seafarers and pirates—Acker found out that she'd also once been a "mischievous" male Greek sailor. Knowing of the existence of this life, Ritchie suggested, could give Acker a "sense of limitlessness."

Acker later told an interviewer that Ritchie was "amazing," and that this regression process was akin to "working with fictions, working with myths." She claimed that she didn't care so much about these past lives per se, but she was beguiled by the idea that you could have relationships with both the living and the dead: "It's about an empowerment which is not some selfish 'I'm going to take control' but more like 'I'm going to learn to listen and find out exactly what I'm listening to.'" Just before Acker died, she told another friend, the culture critic Cynthia Carr, that the reason she and Carr had bonded so quickly was because they had been brothers in one past life and lovers in another.

Could there have been a more fitting therapy for Acker, or a more apt setting for it? Ritchie's houseboat may not have been a pirate ship, but it quickly became a life raft. Acker spent her whole adult life in a constant state of reinvention, and her writing was similarly obsessed with the productive mutability of identity. In her earliest published writings, she "became" other people, borrowing the literal words and identities of female murderers that had died long before she was born. In her writing, there are a number of different Acker surrogates or alter egos, and in her life too, friends talked often about the multiple Ackers they'd known. "She could zip herself into her Kathy Acker suit," said her friend the scholar and philosopher Johnny Golding, "and go and be Kathy Acker and all the 50 million personalities that that meant. There were different suits that she could wear."

Ritchie's teachings brought some of these worlds together. Acker was rigorous and analytical, a well-educated, devoted reader of very complex philosophy and literary theory. But she was equally enthralled with spiritual practices and belief systems that many of her friends and colleagues dismissed as fatuous: astrology, dream interpretation, Tarot, the Kabbalah. "I'm a New Ager," she once said. "I like any idealism." She similarly told her friend the novelist and poet Robert Glück, "I'm basically a New Age writer." She called paranormal phenomena her "area of play." In the last few years of her life, she regularly consulted Malinaro, whom she referred to as "an extraordinary medium."

In Ritchie's initial assessment, she assigned to Acker an enneagram, one of nine personality types popularized by the Russian mystic G. I. Gurdjieff. Acker was a *four*—the Tragic Romantic. "Fours remember abandonment in childhood," Ritchie wrote in the assessment, "and as a result they suffer from a sense of deprivation and loss. Their inner situation is reflected in the literary prototype of the tragic romantic who, having attained recognition and material success, remains steadfastly focused on lost love, the unavailable love, a future love, and a picture of happiness only love can bring. It has been characterized by Wolinsky as one who feels the only way to get love and control a situation is to feel pain.* In this structure, there is confusion between love and pain. Love = pain."

Ritchie had discerned a formula that had governed Acker's life. *Love = pain.* From earliest childhood, at least retrospectively, Acker experienced love as twinned with betrayal, abandonment, loneliness, resentment. Never mind the trauma of past lives, her more immediate past was, she insisted, just as traumatic. And no matter how desperately, how consistently, she tried to free herself from that past, it haunted her and her work. Contrary to Ritchie's exhortations, she could never stop blaming Mommy and Daddy. In her books and in interviews, she returned, again and again and again, to the stories of her family's alleged cruelty and neglect, making her parents, her grandmother, her half sister, into figures at once monstrous and mythic. So compulsive was this repetition, so lurid were these stories, that some friends and colleagues questioned their veracity.

Others, however, argued that this was beside the point. "Whatever happened to her made her who she was," her friend the editor Amy Scholder said. "Someone who felt abandoned easily, on the wrong side of power, and rejected for who she wanted to be."

× × ×

She was born Karen Alexander in Manhattan at 7:05 a.m. on April 18, 1947. From the outset, at least according to Acker, things were difficult—she was

---

* Stephen Wolinsky, author of *The Tao of Chaos: Essence and the Enneagram*, among other books.

born premature, underweight, ugly. But, as in a fairy tale, her difficulties, her pain, began long before her birth.

Acker's grandmother's family, on her mother's side, were the Greenfields, who arrived in New York from Austria in the 1870s or 1880s, and owned a butcher shop on York Avenue on the Upper East Side. Her grandmother, Florence (known as Florrie to friends and family, Nana to her grandchildren) was the oldest of three daughters, born on July 4, 1883. She married Albert Weill, a businessman who owned a glove manufacturing business in Manhattan. Acker's cousin, Pooh Kaye, believed that the family was affluent, upwardly mobile, bourgeois, and ambitious. But like many, they saw their wealth plummet when the stock market crashed in 1929. "We were the grandchildren of nouveau riche immigrants who lost most of their investments during the Depression," she said. Little else is known about the family's early years, and in Acker's own writing—a comprehensive but not always reliable record—some of those details are misremembered or obscured. In an early draft of her novel *Don Quixote*, Acker writes:

My father's and my mother's family're both from Alsace-Lorraine and Jewish. I know nothing else about my father's family. My mother's mother, her two sisters, and her mother and father came over to America when my grandmother was young, in about 1900. Though rich in the old country, they couldn't bring their wealth to America. (Am I making up these details?) I don't know why. Nana (my grandmother) must have detested being poor because in her late adolescence, she told me she's now inordinately (that's my word: hers is *very*) proud of having started a successful millinery shop. The millinery shop was in Brooklyn. Being in the shop introduced her, when she was 30 years old, to her first and only husband. (These dates don't match.) "I waited until I found the right man." The *right man* ran the American ladies' glove business.

According to Acker, Albert Weill died in 1950, and Florrie never remarried. But she was, and remained, a force: statuesque, commanding, intimidating. She was financially canny, a regular player of the stock market, but could also be miserly. When she was a child, Kaye said, Florrie would send her and her brothers just a single dollar bill for Christmas (a gift that later became $5, plus a box of Kathy's expensive hand-me-downs). Florrie's younger sister, meanwhile, sent Kaye and Kathy $50. According to Acker, her Nana disdained regular clothing stores because "other humans shopped in them," and she had her own dressmaker.

That Christmas was important at all suggests how little emphasis the family placed on its Jewishness. Acker would later say that she was "glad" to be Jewish—"I think we're intellectual, tough, funny," she told an interviewer, adding that she liked "the wandering business, not being nationalistic." But Acker's mother, Claire, did her best to downplay their faith; while she would be involved in various Jewish causes and organizations, according to Acker and other friends, Claire would have much preferred to be a blue-blooded WASP and acted accordingly—both the school and the summer camp that Acker attended as a girl were largely devoid of Jews.

Claire was born to Florrie and Albert on June 7, 1925. She was their only child and, Kaye remembered, adored and spoiled. At the same time, she seemed to live forever in Florrie's shadow, perpetually reliant on her mother's largesse and fearful of her wrath. Acker recounted one childhood memory of looking through drawers in her parents' closet. There she found a soft gray hat that she promptly put on her head. When Claire saw it, she snatched it away and slapped her daughter across the face. She told Kathy that it was her father's old hat and that Kathy was never to touch it again. Albert, Claire went on, was "the kindest man who ever lived," and Florrie the opposite. "You know what she's like," Claire said. "She still tells me what to do. You saw what happened with that dress I bought at the beginning of this week. She saw it on me and didn't like it. I had to take it back to the store. I'm 37 years old." In a prose poem that was part of Acker's first self-published chapbook, *Politics*, she claims that Claire inherited $250,000 from her father, but that she gave the money back to Florrie so "that her mother would still support her."

As an adult, Claire was physically beautiful: petite, with dark hair she kept short as she aged, and bewitching emerald eyes. Constantly conscious of her weight, she took "diet pills"—amphetamines—to keep it down. Her moods were unpredictable (the speed didn't help), and she could be narcissistic, arbitrarily cruel, extremely strict. She was intelligent but inhibited by the culture and the time period—she received no postsecondary education, became a mother at a young age, and never held a paying job. She did volunteer at the Jewish Guild for the Blind, typing books into Braille, as well as at an organization for "unwed mothers," according to her daughter and Acker's half sister Wendy Bowers, taking the young women to doctors' appointments. She shopped often and played mahjong once a week with the same group of women. Over the years, she had many dogs, always poodles, that she doted on. She usually dressed, Acker wrote, like a fifties "dowager," even into the seventies: tight cashmere sweater skirts hemmed at the knee, stockings, high black heels, small Gucci purse, bright red lipstick.

"She seemed bright, probably underchallenged in her life," said Peter Gordon, Acker's second husband. "She sort of had a little edge to her and a twinkle." Others recalled her a bit less kindly: "I remember Claire on one of the very few occasions that I was invited to their apartment as being detached and aloof," Kaye said, "more concerned about an upcoming session with her manicurist than being a good hostess." Bowers felt she was, on the whole, extremely conservative and saw everything as "black-and-white."

In the story that Acker would tell over and over in her books, and with only slight variation, Claire became seriously ill when she was twenty-one or twenty-two years old. A doctor told her that getting pregnant would somehow cure her. Claire did get pregnant, but the illness persisted. She wanted an abortion but was too frightened to get one. After Kathy was born, Claire was properly diagnosed with appendicitis. But before that, the man who had impregnated her had left both of them. "Let me tell you what is was like in that womb," Acker wrote in one of her last notebooks. "After my father walked out. Absence isn't absent; it's pain."

Acker's relationship with her mother would become extremely complicated, to say the least, but in these final notebook entries, she makes clear, yet again, how deeply she identified with Claire:

She was raw, a kid, with all the faults of a kid so now all she felt was rage, unadulterated fury. She would kill. She would kill that baby in the womb. She knew why he was leaving her—it was that kid in my womb—she had never wanted one anyway—the doc, he was a quack, he must be a quack, told her that if she got pregnant she wouldn't have this pain in her abdomen—she hated pain because she was a beautiful kid. What did she want with a brat since she was a brat? Get out of here. Get rid of it. Get rid of him too; he was walking out on her; she loved and adored him so much she would never love again.

Despite deep differences that would last for decades, Acker clearly had great sympathy for Claire. At the very least, her father's disappearance had united mother and daughter perpetually in rage and despair.

× × ×

This pain was retrospective, however—Kathy wouldn't discover this abandonment, or the name of her birth father, until she was a teenager. For the first few years of her childhood, she had no reason to think that the man who called himself her father and whose name was printed on her birth certificate was not her actual parent. Albert Alexander was known as Bud (perhaps to distinguish him from Claire's father and grandfather, all of whom shared the same name). His early adulthood was eventful if somewhat wayward: he dropped out of college at nineteen to run a clothing store; married, had a son, and then promptly divorced; was drafted into the army in July 1943, and spent the remaining years of World War II in the service. Nobody recalled how and where he might have met Claire, but when they did meet, she was three or four months pregnant with Kathy. They married soon after, and when Kathy was born, he raised her as his own daughter.

Bud was thin, short, balding. After her father's death, Florrie had taken over the glove company, and Bud worked for her there as administrator, seemingly continuing to do so even after the company was later sold. He made a good salary, Bowers remembered. Acker characterized him often in her fiction as a dissolute alcoholic, though Bowers recalled his drinking as no worse than the average consumption of the era—a beer or two every night when he came home from work. Robert Acker, Acker's first husband, described him as a "cipher," and indeed, his presence within the family, in the world, was almost imperceptible. "He went to work every day," Bowers said. "Did his job. On Sundays, we'd go to Rockefeller Center and go ice skating. Other than that, I mean, he was there. Was he a great father? No." Within Pooh Kaye's family, Bud's mild-manned remove registered as something worse. They considered him a playboy, ineffectual and lazy, undeniably reliant on his wife's money. "My father had huge contempt for Kathy's father. The family was not too fond of him." Kaye claimed.

In her writing, Acker is similarly scornful; the lightly fictionalized Bud character found in her books is consistently characterized as stupid, dull, his gentleness more a sign of weakness than virtue. His greatest sin is his indifference to art and literature. He also, it seemed, wished that Acker was a boy, and some-times treated her that way.

When she was born, Acker was named Karen, after Bud's sister. But Claire apparently despised the woman, and refused to call her daughter by that name, preferring, instead the nickname Kathy. "Karen" was so rarely used outside of official channels, in fact, that Bowers claimed to have never heard it. "She gave me this name she hated," Acker wrote of her mother. "Only when very drunk do I mention that name."

From the very beginning, then, Kathy's identity was literally up for grabs, and the process of naming, and the interpellation of women, would become a subject at the heart of her fiction. "As a girl," Acker would later write, "I was outside the world. I wasn't. I had no name." A name, she learned, could be both a privilege and a prison.

CHAPTER 2

U NTIL SHE LEFT NEW YORK FOR COLLEGE IN 1964, KATHY ONLY ever lived in one place, on the sixth floor of a nineteen-story, prewar building at 400 East 57th Street, at First Avenue. The building was located at the edge of Sutton Place, a highly affluent enclave just blocks from midtown and home, over the years, to such celebrities as Henry Kissinger, I. M. Pei, and Bill Blass. In 1956, Arthur Miller and Marilyn Monroe were the Alexanders' neighbors, occupying a penthouse apartment at 444 East 57th.

Kathy's home, however, was somewhat more Sutton Place adjacent— rent-controlled, relatively modest, on the small side. It had two bedrooms, two bathrooms, a sunken living room, a tiny kitchen. After Wendy was born, on July 1, 1949, the two girls shared a room, and would do so throughout their childhood and adolescence, a fact that forever vexed Kathy (she was still complaining about it with her psychic when she was in her late forties). In *Requiem*, one of her last works, Acker described the apartment thusly:

> A small apartment—its interior reveals that its inhabitants aren't all that wealthy. A narrow, dark green hall leads, on one side, to a large sunken living room, the largest room in the apartment. All the sofas and chairs in this room, of which there are many, have silk exteriors; the clear plastic that Claire explains are [sic] needed to protect the pale silks from stains are never taken off except when there are guests. There are a number of antiques including a captain's desk in which there are hiding places, a table whose inlaid pads are the color of ivy. A cabinet replete with china dogs supervises the large writing desk, of the same wood, beneath it. No one ever uses this desk.

Acker also recalled that she wasn't permitted to put up any pictures or photographs on the walls of her room, and that Claire, despite spending lots of money on her own clothes and furnishings, never changed the rose-patterned drapes or the green paint on the walls of her daughters' room. Even as they grew into teenagers, Kathy and Wendy still had the same single beds they slept in as children.

Kathy's refuge, as a young child, was the tiny park at the end of the street, beside the East River, where she sometimes went to play with her mother. For Kathy, the park offered possibility and solitude, as well as access to the natural world (as domesticated as it was), the sea, even other lands. In *Great Expectations*, this park is the site of a rare, enchanted, but ultimately fleeting, Christmas moment she shares with Claire: "I stay in this magic snow with the beautiful yellow sun beating down on me as long as I can until a voice in my head (me) or my mother says, 'Now you know what this experience is, you have to leave.'"

In all of her books, Acker describes the family home as a "prison," though, in many ways, it was far more ordinary and comfortable than that. Indeed, the outward conventionality of Acker's early childhood offers no hint of her future restlessness or iconoclasm. Bowers recalled that the family ate dinner together every night, then the girls would do their homework. Afterward, they would all retreat to Claire and Bud's bedroom, where they kept their only TV, and the family would gather on the bed and watch together. As she got older, Kathy rarely participated in this ritual, preferring to read alone in her room. The poodles were an ever-present feature of the apartment, both amusement and annoyance. Wendy and Kathy got along reasonably well, though even then they were clearly different—the former more athletic and less bookish. Both girls were extremely sheltered. Their early lives were a small, closed circuit: school, home, school, home. If they went anywhere else—to Broadway shows, Rockefeller Center, to the park at the end of the street—it was always with their parents or grandmother.

Among the many objects that Acker possessed at her death was an album of family photographs. It was large and pumpkin orange, its plastic cover smudged and tacky from decades of handling. Inside, glued to pages of faded, occasionally torn scrapbook paper, were just over a hundred black-and-white photographs of Kathy, Wendy, and other family members, some identified, some not. Here was baby Kathy at six weeks, held by Claire; a two-year-old Kathy, in Bud's arms, outside a Gristedes supermarket. In a photo taken in Westport, Connecticut, Kathy and Wendy pose in the grass with a nameless spaniel and their grandmother's African-American housekeeper, Grace Brown, who often served as their nanny. Aside from a photograph of Kathy talking on the phone, in which she looks to be about twelve, all of the pictures in the album are of her as an infant or young child.

"I tried to run away from the pain named *childhood*," Acker writes in *My Mother: Demonology*, "like you flush a huge shit down the toilet. I've been running ever since." But here, in these photographs at least, there's little evidence of this pain. There is, in fact, only its opposite: a smiling, tiny Kathy, perched on a pony, or beaming beside a Christmas tree, seemingly cherished by everyone around her. She looks like a sweet child, with plump lips and dark, expressive eyes. She doesn't seem to mind the camera, and in most of these pictures, smiles broadly (and much more frequently than Wendy, at least).

Of course, a single family photo album is a small, overdetermined, and unrepresentative sample. It shows little, proves nothing. But it was apparently the only trace of her family that Acker held on to throughout her adult life, and it remains the only real record of Acker's youth. It's easy to imagine Acker coming back again and again to these images as inspirational prods for her writing. Or perhaps simply to return to a bygone, relatively innocent time, reminding Acker of what she was like before the abandonment and death that would shadow her later years.

Many of the photographs show the girls at the beach. When Kathy was seven or eight, Florrie bought a summer home in Atlantic Beach, on the South Shore of Long Island. Thereafter, the family vacationed there every year, driving out as soon as school ended. Bud would still work in the city and would commute by train at the end of the day. The house was a block from the beach, and for some reason, Florrie was a member of one beach club, and Bud and Claire a different one. In any case, until they went to camp in Maine in their early adolescence, Kathy and Wendy spent every summer day at the ocean.

By all accounts, Kathy was always much closer to her Nana than to anyone else in the family. Where Claire seemed weak and dependent, Florrie was a confident, self-reliant survivor. "She saw Florrie as a tower of strength," Pooh Kaye said, "and someone who got her way." Kathy craved Florrie's admiration and respect, things that Claire also presumably desired but never seemed to receive. Florrie was more cultured than Claire as well—she was the one who took Kathy and Wendy to galleries and museums. When Acker first began to self-publish, she sent her chapbooks to Florrie, and, according to Kaye, her grandmother was "full of praise, much to Kathy's surprise and complete delight." Bowers concurred with this: "She understood what she was trying to accomplish with her writing. I think my grandmother understood Kathy better than my mother did."

× × ×

In Acker's writing, Claire is villain and victim at once, and above all, a black hole—all-consuming, unknowable. "I'm probably concerned with *my* mother in my texts," Acker wrote in an essay late in life. "I'm concerned with *the* father and *my* mother." The French feminist philosopher Luce Irigaray gave Acker some theoretical ballast here, arguing that, in a patriarchal culture, women are compelled to have a doubled, ambiguous relationship with their mothers: "On the one hand, my mother was or is my lover," Acker wrote. "On the other hand, my mother was a victim in the male-defined society. So, if I identify with her, I'm forced to define myself as a victim. So how do I deal with this double bind? Go mad? (Pun intended.) Irigaray says we, females, have to reinstate the mother as another person. I take that rather seriously."

It's frustrating therefore to have so little firsthand evidence of Claire's life and personality, other than, of course, Acker's words themselves. As the architect of her own myth, Acker was fortunate to have a family that did not keep records.* Outside of those published words, however, are the many notebooks and letters in which Acker worked out her fiction, drafted and rehearsed it, and the details within those pages are specific and consistent enough to constitute a portrait of some verifiable fidelity. "Most of it is true," Wendy Bowers averred, when asked of the novels' accuracy.

Bowers felt that she and Kathy had a happy early childhood, though Bowers also describes Claire as a "very strict" woman who completely controlled their young lives. "I think we agreed about a lot of things about our mother, but I was able to accept who she was," Bowers said. "I think my sister had a hard time with it." Indeed, the Claire that haunts Acker's writing is a complex and enigmatic figure, a mother both remote and authoritarian, malevolent and pathetic. From the beginning, when she gives Kathy a name that she hates, Claire makes her child an object of derision. She rarely expresses love or affection, never gives Kathy gifts, even at Christmas. When Kathy is very young, she has

---

* Pooh Kaye recalled that her own unstable mother cleaned out a trunk full of family letters and documents, including several letters from Acker to Kaye's father, Clifford, and replaced them, bizarrely, with McDonald's hamburger wrappers.

a beloved pink blanket, covered in appliquéd roses; at some point, Claire takes it away to get cleaned and then never bothers to return it. She is also capable of physical cruelty; a story Acker told several people, and repeated in her writing, was that, on at least one occasion, Claire ambushed Kathy in the shower and threw a glass of cold water on her, apparently hoping that her daughter would slip and fall. In another, darker version of the story, Claire tried to drown her. All of these injustices, from the minor to the grave, deeply marked Acker. She tallied all the above in one of the notebooks she kept for her novel *My Mother: Demonology*, summing them up thusly: "These are all the accounts of how my mother tried to kill me."

Above all, in Acker's mind, Claire hated Kathy because Kathy ruined her life. By getting pregnant, Claire lost Kathy's father and was forced to settle for a marriage to a man she didn't really love, to sacrifice herself to a life of compromise and dissatisfaction. "She tells him that he's worthless," she writes of Bud and Claire's marriage in *Requiem*. "He has a job only because he married into the family, all the wealth is on her side of the family. He tells her that he bought her her first mink coat. They go through this every single day." For Kathy, Claire never fulfilled her potential, whatever that potential may have been. She was a quintessential 1950s American housewife, a dumb stereotype slowly wasting her life, ultimately consumed by her own dissatisfaction. Her most important role, then, for Kathy, was to serve as a negative example. Kathy looked at Claire and determined that she would live as differently as possible. She would lead a purposeful, creative, self-directed life. She would never let anyone tell her what to do. "I have no sense of a person," Acker wrote of Claire, "I have a sense of my mother. My mother was a person; she stopped me from doing what I wanted to do. I wanted to get away from her." And Acker would not place anyone's needs above her own. For the rest of her life, she would never really take responsibility for anyone other than herself.

CHAPTER 3

———— × ————

T HE POSTWAR AMERICA THAT KATHY GREW UP IN WAS ONE OF UN-
precedented prosperity and stability. The population boomed, government spending boomed, and there was a sense that the country was, or would
soon become, almost entirely middle-class, both in terms of its values and its
economy. While capitalism seemed to have triumphed, and consumerism was
in ascendance, full employment and poverty relief were undeniably still goals,
taxes were high, and the country was still a limited welfare state. Benefitting
immensely from the countless European scientists, artists, and intellectuals
who had found refuge in the United States, however, and with its industrial
infrastructure intact and thriving, the country dominated global affairs. With
many great European cities still in ruin, New York City reasserted itself as a
global capital of commerce, art, and politics. A sense of conciliation and consensus prevailed.

At the same time, the U.S. simmered with anxiety—over Communism
and its spread both internationally and within the country's borders; over
the creeping corporatization of life and politics; over evolving ideas around
race, family, and gender. Millions of women had entered the workforce during
World War II, and while many returned to life as mothers and homemakers,
the sense of expanded possibility led directly to the emergence of women's
liberation the following decade. The development of the birth control pill,
which began in 1950, further amplified this shift. While mainstream society
extolled bureaucracy, conformity, and unity, a fledgling counterculture was
taking shape in opposition to these values. The best-known representatives
of this so-called Beat Generation were its literary stars—Jack Kerouac, Allen
Ginsberg, and William Burroughs—who first congregated at Columbia University and in Greenwich Village.

From the outset, Kathy was trained to do much more than keep house or
raise children. In 1952, when she was five years old, she started at the Lenox
School, an all-girls prep school located at 170 East 70th Street. The suffragette

and educator Jessica Garretson Finch founded Lenox in 1916. A Barnard graduate who felt that her education had left her with no practical skills, Finch had previously started the Finch School (later Finch College) as a secondary school to prepare women for the working world; Lenox was, in turn, created to prepare girls for Finch. Lenox's four-story Renaissance Revival limestone building was built as a carriage house and horse stable in 1902 and purchased by Lenox in 1925.*

By the standards of mid-century New York private schools, Lenox wasn't considered the finest education available, but it was unquestionably top-notch. Its head of school, Cecily Selby, was a renowned scientist with a degree in physics from Radcliffe and a doctorate in physical biology from MIT, and was working to make Lenox even more academically rigorous. Classes were small and intimate, and the teachers could be compelling, the curriculum strictly defined but ambitious. In grade seven, British history was mandatory; in grade eight, American. Students had to learn two additional languages, French and Latin. The school could be claustrophobic and regimented—classes of twenty were divided into two sections, "the smart and the not-smart," according to Linda Muller Vasu, one of Kathy's classmates—but there was also often, Vasu said, a pervasive atmosphere of joy in its halls.

Kathy was, apparently, a sterling student from the beginning: bright and bookish and hardworking. The cloistered, circumscribed life that she continued to lead—it was still just school, home, Long Island—might have been constricting, but it hadn't occurred to her yet to resist it. It's possible Kathy started writing during those earliest grades—she later claimed that she won a poetry contest in the sixth grade—but it's more likely her serious writing efforts didn't begin until high school, where she did, in fact, win a writing contest or two.

Kathy's classmates were awash in money and privilege. By the time she got to high school, her classmates included Faith Golding, a real estate heiress whose father owned Essex House on Central Park and controlled the Sterling National Bank, and who, at eighteen, married twenty-two-year-old Ron Perelman, later one of Wall Street's most notorious corporate raiders and New York's richest man; Sherry Frawley, whose father was the proprietor of Pete's

---

* Lenox itself merged with Birch Wathen in 1989 and is now the Birch Wathen Lenox School; the building became the home of the New York School of Design in 1993.

Tavern, the renowned Gramercy Park pub; and Betsy Kimmelman, daughter of hotelier Milton Kimmelman, who owned the Sherry-Netherland, the Ambassador, and the Barbizon, among many others. These were teenagers with their own chauffeurs and apartments. She and Wendy, on the other hand, took the bus to school. "I was born a rich kid," Acker would later tell an interviewer, but at Lenox she learned that there were kids born much wealthier and more advantaged than she.

× × ×

In "The Invisible Universe," an essay Acker published in 1982, she asks how a great writer comes into being. Her answer was characteristically overwrought, remarkable, and oblique, but in its run-on pileup of adjectives and nouns as revealing a self-portrait as any other she composed: "Hatred antipathy to human fear of everything selfishness inability to communicate deformed physical attributes chronic illnesses moods-like-demons in particular: epileptic escapism, thundering naïve desires?"

Books were a place for Kathy to engage that escapism, to satisfy her thundering naïve desires. She started reading at an early age, and found in literature not just a place to escape but a place for *everything*. Books were the most romantic, even sacred, of objects; they were time machines, genie lamps, merit badges, force fields. They provided insulation from the actual life she led, and opened up the possibility of other, more captivating lives; she could, literally, lose herself in books. "When I was a kid I always thought of books as more real than anything else," she told an interviewer. "I had a bad childhood and books really *were* my reality." To write books, then, to become a writer herself, was to create her own reality. She could summon love, exorcise hatred, and ultimately exact revenge on those who had rejected or hurt her.

She was a precocious reader too. While Claire read a fair bit also, mostly murder mysteries, Kathy told Wendy early in their youth that she was going to read "every single classic." At Lenox, her classmates recalled, she proudly carried around Modern Library editions of those classics, their covers always faced outward to advertise their contents. The first adult authors she read were Dickens, Blake, and Hawthorne. As this peacocking suggests, Kathy was competitive too, and books and writing were her preferred arena.

"Books are the only people who like me," she wrote, half-jokingly, a decade later. This wasn't quite true of her in high school. Kathy had her fair share of friends there, and teachers who openly adored her. But nevertheless, just as at home, she felt apart, different, lonely. If she was not exactly an outcast, to a large extent she considered herself an outsider. She tended to lean into this difference and strangeness, but in truth, she occupied a more in-between position, one she found herself in throughout much of her life, in fact—at once inside and outside, alienated and reconciled, blessed and cursed.

In grade seven, she met twin sisters Linda and Susan Muller,* who would become both good friends and fierce rivals. The Mullers were outsiders of a sort too. Though well-off, their parents were divorced, an anomaly at the time; the girls lived on Park Avenue with their mother. Kathy and the Mullers were all in the "smart" section of their grade, and would meet for study dates or talk about their homework over the phone. Linda recalled that their conversations were largely a blur of checking in and one-upmanship, particularly once they all got to high school. "Have you read this, have you done the math, what's your science project, what do you think about Gogol's *The Overcoat*?" They sometimes played bridge at the Mullers' apartment, staying up until two or three in the morning, then heading to Reuben's, a twenty-four-hour deli, for a late-night, early morning breakfast.

Linda remembered Kathy always wanting to be a writer, nothing else, and that she kept a commonplace book in which to chronicle her reading. But the Kathy she recalled was also an unabashed free spirit, physically unkempt and emotionally volatile. The Mullers were identical twins, and tall, blonde, and beautiful. Teenaged Kathy, in contrast, was small and somewhat gawky, with a mouth too big for her body, an effect she enhanced by not washing or combing her hair and often showing up to school in a grubby uniform. In retrospect, this seems like a deliberate, easy expression of defiance; it reinforced her sense of difference, her disregard for conventional behavior and appearance. To Linda, it suggested something more, that Kathy was virtually feral, basically unparented. "She never cared about how she looked," Linda said. "And most adolescents do. She was smelly. She was not particularly attractive. Nor was she friendly. She had the sorts of traits and values and mindset of a motherless female." In the classroom too, she was blithe about following rules, speaking without raising her hand, assertive and confrontational. Miraculously, her

---

* In another instance of Acker's poor spelling or faulty memory, she typically misspells Muller as Mueller in her books.

teachers usually tolerated such behavior; all was forgiven because of Kathy's academic brilliance and boundless curiosity.

Linda found Kathy refreshingly authentic, particularly for a teenager, but she was also somewhat afraid of and *for* her. This feeling became more acute when Kathy began to have sex, the first girl, Linda remembered, in their class to do so. "This was a huge thing in a girls' school," Linda said, "and she defined herself early on in that way." By the ninth grade, the three girls were going to weekend parties, and Linda recalled Kathy drinking and then disappearing with whatever boy took an interest in her. Kathy would later brag about these exploits, but Linda was alarmed by Kathy's abandon and apparent heedlessness. "She was sort of self-destructive," Linda said.

CHAPTER 4

———— ✕ ————

I N 1973, ACKER WROTE TWO BOOKS, *RIP-OFF RED, GIRL DETECTIVE* and *The Childlike Life of the Black Tarantula*, which sketched variations on an origin story that appears often in her work. *In Rip-off Red*, Acker includes several near-autobiographical paragraphs, such as this one: "My mother tells me my 'father' isn't my real father: my real father left her when she was three months pregnant and wanted nothing to do with me, ever. This husband has adopted me. That's all she tells me. I feel happy that none of my adopted father's blood is in me."

Acker suggests that this revelation occurred when she was eight years old, but according to her sister Wendy at least, this happened in somewhat different circumstances, when Kathy was thirteen. Sometime in the summer of 1960, the Alexanders were, as usual, vacationing in Atlantic Beach. Though Claire always tried to keep Bud's detested family away from hers, Bud's sister, Karen, and her daughter were also visiting. Earlier, somehow, the daughter had learned the truth about Kathy's parentage and had let Kathy in on the secret. Predictably, Kathy was shocked, then furious. As soon as she could, during dinner, she picked a fight with Bud, and when he tried to discipline her, she jumped up and screamed at him: "You're not my real father! You can't tell me what to do!" Wendy watched the scene, aghast. "Obviously, this was the wrong way to find out," she said decades later. "It had to be tough, really tough. It had a real impact on Kathy."

Indeed, it's difficult to overstate the gravity of this moment. Kathy's life was instantly capsized. She wasn't who she thought she was. But who was she? Who was her family? Why had her mother withheld this information from her? Claire had been abandoned but Kathy now knew that *she* had been abandoned too—before she was even born. To make matters worse, once the story was out, Claire also refused to tell Kathy who exactly her birth father was. She wouldn't talk about it. Bud had officially adopted her, Claire said; *he* was Kathy's real father. The identity of her birth father didn't matter. For Kathy, who despised Bud and who felt that Claire actually did too, this was wrong, impossible, and cruel.

Many children think that their parents don't understand them, or that they are simply not like them. Others believe, or fantasize, that they have literally been born into the wrong family. Kathy's cousin, Pooh Kaye, thought this definitely applied to Kathy: "She was like a cuckoo in the wrong nest. She landed in the wrong place." Such children must, therefore, they believe, be adopted—*that* would explain their alienation from the people they are supposed to love, who are supposed to love *them*. Their real families, the ones they're related to by blood—they must be more interesting and impressive, wealthier, more significant, than the one they've been burdened with.

Suddenly, this fantasy became real for Kathy. Throughout her adolescence and early twenties, she would speculate, sometimes wildly, about her true patrimony. "I began to think about my father," Acker wrote in a later notebook, "the one who made my mother pregnant. If he's alive, he'll treat me kindly. Why I have no reason to think this. No one treats me kindly; I'm a miserable kid. Why do I think my father'll treat me kindly (my mother didn't teach me this: she hates men)?"

At the same time, the knowledge that her real father, whoever he might be, had abandoned her, now provided license and justification. The seesaw of seduction and betrayal—others', but also her own—that characterized her childhood would now also shape many of her future personal and professional relationships.

This fact also immediately lent her life a literary shape. At times, she seemed to have felt that ichor coursed through her veins; at many others, she considered herself unwanted, rejected. In both interviews and her fiction, then, she cast her beginnings as equal parts *Hansel and Gretel*, *Moll Flanders*, and *Electra*. Jean Genet, modern literature's most famous foundling, became her idol. Rimbaud, himself forsaken by his father and raised by an authoritarian mother, became the subject of Acker's 1990 novel *In Memoriam to Identity*. Fictional orphans and near orphans—Jane Eyre, Pip, Jim Hawkins, Huckleberry Finn—would provide additional inspiration and models. "Kathy always struck me as somebody who was living in raw mythology," said her friend the comic book writer Alan Moore. "I think she experienced the events in her life in mythological terms; that this was sometimes to the detriment of her emotional relationships; but that nevertheless it was the essential fuel that powered her writing and her personality."

Everything seemed to change in this instant at Atlantic Beach. Kathy was, in effect, reborn. Her relationship with Claire, increasingly strained, fell apart. They fought constantly, and Kathy began to defy her mother any way she could. During the week, Kathy and Wendy wore their school uniforms, but even on weekends Claire forbade the girls to wear blue jeans. Kathy nonetheless stashed a pair in the apartment building's garbage room, and before going out, would sneak in there to change. She started to smoke and taught her cousins how to do so too. "Growing up, she was the apple of my parents' eye," Wendy said. "Then, all of a sudden, she started changing, getting her own mind. She just became determined that she was going to do what she wanted to do."

And, again, Kathy sought solace in books. In *I become Jane Eyre who rebelled against every one*, an abandoned project that she likely intended to become an additional Black Tarantula book, she writes: "I remember: the first time I remember exerting control over my being I decided to follow the things said in my books rather than my parents' hints and instructions. When I felt anxious doing experiencing something new, if I could find a precedent for the event in a book I liked I kept doing thinking feeling whatever."

Many books, of course, contained romance and sex, and it was here that Kathy most flagrantly rebelled. According to Kathy, Claire told her very little about sex, and what information she did impart was bizarre and inappropriate: That "petting" wasn't that bad, but that Kathy still shouldn't do it because it led to other things. That her menstrual blood was carrot or tomato juice. That Bud's penis was too small. As with Claire's behavior during Kathy's childhood, her having actually made these claims is impossible to verify, but their consistent repetition in Acker's fiction, notebooks, and correspondence suggest at least a kernel of truth. Acker later claimed she barely even knew any boys until the eighth grade, but from thirteen or fourteen on, she started making up for lost time. In both *Rip-off Red* and *The Childlike Life*, Acker writes, in the sub-section titled "Age 13": "I fuck and find out my mother's been lying. I know my mother lies about everything. We outwardly hate each other."

Two decades later, in a letter to her friend, the English writer Glenda George, Acker recounted that first sexual experience in exacting detail. Kathy was dating, she said, a fourteen-year-old boy named Dale Hemmerdinger, a student at the posh Riverdale Country School and the scion of a prominent real estate development family. In one of the buildings the Hemmerdingers owned, Dale had his own private apartment, one floor below his parents, where he would throw wild parties free of parental supervision. Possibly at one of these parties, or on a separate date, according to Acker, Hemmerdinger seduced her. Retrospectively, at least, the encounter was confusing, pleasurable, and illuminating, all at once:

> ... he's holding me like a baby and the fingers are inside my cunt and the next date or two dates later I don't remember I don't remember anything he's laying on top of me and rubbing and I like that a lot cause it makes me feel warm and we've got our clothes off and I'm sick of not doing things why I shouldn't do them I don't know and they feel so good and then he sticks this thing in me and I don't like it at all it doesn't hurt but it's uncomfortable and I can't figure out why he's doing it but it doesn't take too long and then he goes back to the cuddling so I figure if he has to do this weird stick-in thing so he'll do what I like that's O.K. and that night I go home and figure out while I'm lying in my bed that that's what fucking was somehow in my confused mind I thought men and women had babies by rubbing asses and sort of shitting together, it was confused, and my mother wanting to be WASP didn't tell me anything . . .

Hemmerdinger, who would go on to become a developer himself, as well as chair of the Metropolitan Transportation Authority, had no recollection of these liaisons and barely any of Kathy herself. He did acknowledge that he dated girls from Lenox; in fact, he married one, Elizabeth Gould, who was in a class ahead of Kathy. Gould, for her part, only remembered Kathy as "fast." It's possible that Acker, a couple decades after the fact, was confusing Hemmerdinger with another boy; it's equally possible that she made little impression on Hemmerdinger. Whatever the truth, in her letter to George, Acker acknowledged the narrative power that fucking could have: "Sex is terrific five years later when it becomes a story."

Indeed, this particular episode did become a story, a vivid one, in *Rip-off Red*. Some details were changed—here, the narrator is just ten years old, her paramour has the Dickensian name of Hammerblunt, the school he attends is called Riversmell. Acker's description of their sexual encounter hews closely to what she told George but takes on a more ecstatic tone: "We were both giggling madly, two waves, or sheets opening the nerves twisted upward from my cunt, I wanted him to continue . . ." The scene functions primarily, however, as an erotic tale that Rip-off Red recounts as a way to seduce her own sister, and then even this incestuous encounter serves largely as a pretext for Red's eventual escape and reinvention: "That night my sister and I, frightened out of our wits, split the city. My sister disappeared; I went to the coast, changed my name to Rip-off Red, started to starve. As far as I know, the police never searched for my sister and me: in New York they only care about pot-heads and political kids. I never saw anyone I knew in my childhood, again."

Elsewhere, and even earlier in her writing career, Acker put this a somewhat different way. Sex, she claimed, wasn't in fact all that pleasurable for her as a teenager, but being a "big tough sex queen"—that is, being regarded as someone adventurous, brave, and experienced—had a profound value all its own. In *Poems 5/71–6/71*, a typescript from 1971, she wrote, "the actual physical pleasure was of course minimal compared to the pleasure of becoming who I wanted to become . . ."

J UST AS KATHY WAS BECOMING SEXUALLY ACTIVE, SO TOO WAS SHE beginning to take writing more seriously. It's uncertain how old she was exactly when she started producing poetry and fiction, but 1960, as far as anyone knows, was the first year Kathy published any of it. That year, when she was in the eighth grade, the Lenox literary magazine, the *Quill*, printed a two-paragraph piece she entitled "Night." Less prose poem than vignette or sketch, thick with atmospheric description, it's set in a decaying English fishing village at an indeterminate time. In it, a young vagrant—variously, "a pitiful lad," "a pathetic youth," "the ragged creature," "the debilitated youth"—starving and despondent, drowns himself in the "waves that had been a mother to him for as long as he could remember."

The piece is assured, sophisticated, ambitious. It's intriguing that the subject is a boy—already, Acker is playing with gender—and that the setting and "plot" are so removed from Kathy's own lived experience. It's useful to remember that American poets were then enamored of their British counterparts, and there are echoes in "Night" of Dylan Thomas and John Cowper Powys, Kipling and Dickens. Kathy's own favorite poet was, at the time, Gerard Manley Hopkins. Many years later, she said that her teachers explicitly taught her that the English novel was *the* novel and that American novelists should be considered a "treat." Dickens and Blake were among the first adult authors she read; they "exploded open in my mind a visionary landscape called *London*," she later wrote. Other English writers—Austen, Trollope—provided a different lesson, showing how the traditional novel could reify the divisions of society. Such novels, she came to believe, mapped out hierarchies of class, gender, and species, and used language that mirrored this order. "The language of the novel had to be *proper*," she wrote, "elegant and ironic, even when the characters were depraved lower class hoodlums."

As an adult, Acker would regularly revolt against such dicta, but her juvenilia was deeply influenced by this. Throughout the next few years of high school, she published one or two pieces in the *Quill*, most of them in the purple prose poem style of "Night." In grades ten and eleven, she wrote two other poems—"Phantasmagoria" and "Variation on a Theme: Based on Romeo and Juliet, II, ii"—which, in their line breaks and meter, are more conventionally poetic and which won Kathy first place, two years in a row, in the school's poetry contest. As a prize, Kathy received a copy of *Final Harvest: Emily Dickinson's Poems*, originally published in 1961 and inscribed by her beloved English teacher Jean St. Pierre, who paraphrased both Walter Pater and Shakespeare: "To Kathy, In whom the gem-like flame of poetry burns brightly. For we . . . Have eyes to wonder, but lack tongues to praise. With love, Jean St. Pierre." Kathy kept the book for the rest of her life. Decades later St. Pierre reappears in her novel *My Mother: Demonology*, as a kind, protective teacher who introduces the narrator to Melville, Keats, Yeats, and *The Wizard of Oz*.

"Variation on a Theme: Based on Romeo and Juliet, II, ii" is especially compelling, if only for its hints of Acker's later methods. Here, Kathy takes a found text—a staple of high school classes around the English-speaking world—and reworks it to suit her own, somewhat inscrutable, purpose:

> So still the night.
> The moon has frozen all:
> So still black limbs of trees
> O'er which soar silent doves—
> black doves against a moon—
> And still these winter winds
> Which seep into my soul . . .
> Tybalt is dead! How can
> It be so cold.
> So still, so silent, deep?
> Yes Tybalt dead! O where
> Are black-plumed mourners
> Paid with icy thorns? And where
> The sound of that foul murd'rer's flight?
> A curse on him . . . on him who plunged
> My kinsman to ignoble dust, on him
> Who trampled careless on our love,
> A curse on this base pity . . .

The night is still
Wild doves have left
And black 'compasses all;
Tybalt is dead! But I care not . . .
Except his slayer's plight
Makes scared my struggling soul;
O Tybalt dead! That thought
Should bring new rage,
New incest to my mind; and yet,
In still of night
On barren lifeless rocks
I only fear for him . . .
Birth's bonds are severed—
Gaze with hate on my torn mind
O moon . . . for nought I care
A raucous fire leaves my soul,
Like winter trees,
Spent of all doubts. O soulless night
Be hushed, and icy winds; four nought
I care. This cruel live
Casts out all black and still.

In an interview several years later, long after Acker had become renowned for her appropriation, she would return to this poem as evidence of both the consistency of her literary vision and its early origins: "In high school, I was always imitating Shakespeare, redoing poems from Romeo and Juliet and so on. It's been that way ever since. What this comes down to, I think, is that I've never liked the idea of originality, and so my whole life I've always written by taking other texts, inhabiting them in some way so that I can do something with them."

× × ×

Shakespeare's play had personal resonance as well for Kathy, who was by then involved in her own fervid, forbidden romance. In the summer of 1963, she was taking courses at Trinity College's summer school in Hartford, Connecticut, a program that was open to students at the college, but also to high schoolers like Kathy who had excellent grades. There's no record of what she studied at Trinity, but those weeks would prove formative. In the dining hall one day, she met a freshman at the college named P. Adams Sitney. He was nineteen, three years older, an ambitious, snobby, self-styled intellectual, both an aspiring classicist and a devoted cineaste, and arguably even more precocious than Kathy herself. In high school in nearby New Haven, he'd formed a film society where he showed new and classic films and published a magazine that included the likes of Stan Brakhage and Anaïs Nin. He even managed to persuade Jean Cocteau to draw one cover. He favored three-piece suits and black-rimmed glasses and was extremely gaunt; Kathy, he said, weighed more than him at the time. A long red beard gave him a Mephistophelian mien. That summer at Trinity, Sitney was studying Greek and was obsessed with Ezra Pound, Propertius, and Charles Olson, heady poets who were largely unfamiliar to Kathy and which he gleefully foisted on her. He found Kathy highly intelligent, eager, and "slightly wild in a ragamuffin mode." Like him, she had Ivy League aspirations—Sitney would eventually transfer to Yale, where he would study Sanskrit—and he expected her to one day become a prominent academic. Her curiosity was a marvel to him, and he fed it with commensurate zeal. "She was a real live wire," he said, "filled with enthusiasm when she liked something. I was constantly pouring things on her." He gave her at least three Olson books (*The Distances*, *The Maximus Poems*, and *Call Me Ishmael*), and, for her seventeenth birthday, a copy of *La Femme 100 têtes*, Max Ernst's remarkable first collage novel.

Later that fall, Sitney temporarily dropped out of school and moved to a rooming house near Cooper Square in Manhattan, where he dedicated himself, more or less, to the underground and experimental filmmakers that lived in the city. This flourishing scene began with Maya Deren and Kenneth Anger and continued with Brakhage, Andy Warhol, and Jack Smith, just to name the most enduringly famous. These were fiercely independent artists who captured the convulsions of modern dance and religious ritual (Deren), who extolled the occult and homoerotic (Anger), who sought to depict visual perception itself (Brakhage), who upended the traditional star system and classical forms of acting (Smith, Warhol), who upended received ideas of filmic time (all of them). Jonas Mekas, the so-called godfather of this movement, had invited Sitney to become an editor at his magazine, *Film Culture*, when Sitney was still in high school, and after Sitney moved to New York, Mekas asked his protégé to help organize and tour an exhibition of new American films through Europe.

But until Sitney departed for the continent later that year, Sitney and Kathy saw each other almost every day. He took her to movies, of course, but also to plays, including the now legendary off-Broadway production of Genet's *The Blacks*, starring James Earl Jones, Cicely Tyson, and Maya Angelou. He introduced her to many of the cultural figures he knew—Smith and Mekas and the filmmaker and artist Carolee Schneemann, the poets Parker Tyler, Robert Kelly, and Jackson Mac Low, the Fluxus linchpins Dick Higgins and George Maciunas. He urged her to read Rimbaud and Mallarmé.

They frequently hung out at the one-room office of the Film-Makers' Co-operative on Park Avenue South, but as often as he could, Sitney took Kathy back to his room on East 4th Street so they could have sex. The place was cramped, furnished entirely with a desk and a bed, with a rope that hung across its length for drying laundry and a filthy toilet in the hall. Sitney eventually gave Kathy a key, though he was always fearful he'd be busted for squiring around an underage high school student. Not that the denizens of the rooming house would have likely cared or even noticed; Sitney's neighbors were mostly junkies and, at one point, the Beat poet Gregory Corso. On at least one occasion, Sitney brought out a Super-8 camera and filmed a nude Kathy in bed.

On Friday, November 22, 1963, John F. Kennedy was assassinated. Kathy was at Lenox and, she recalled, the students and faculty all gathered in the main auditorium, where a TV was wheeled in so they could watch the rest of the day unfold. Everyone was sobbing. Kathy was confused, uncertain about what had happened and why. In her confusion, she said, she fled the school and went downtown to see Sitney. They met at the Film-Makers' Co-op, and there too, people were mourning. But, Acker recounted, the filmmakers in that room weren't upset about Kennedy; they were mourning Jean Cocteau, who, Acker believed, had committed suicide because he was so distraught over the accidental death of his dear friend, the singer Édith Piaf. Cocteau and Piaf, in fact, died a month before Kennedy was shot, with the former already convalescing from a heart attack earlier in the year. But Acker's gloss on these events was in the service of a more personal, romantic lesson: "On that day, for me the child, there were two distinct worlds: the world of politicians political assassinations schools correct learning, and the world of artists. Artists were those who lived by and died for love."

In Kathy's 1961 yearbook, below a class picture, the name of each of the twenty students is accompanied by a motto, expression, or epigram. Whether these were chosen, bestowed, or both is unclear; some are glib ("Quarterbacks are her specialty"), others banal ("Laughter is the Best Medicine"). Kathy's motto was plucked from Virgil: *Amor Vincit Omnia*, or "Love conquers all." This sentiment would become much more complicated (and, to a degree, less positive) for Kathy over time, but it was largely true when she was a teenager. With Sitney, love—and sex—could relieve the oppression of parents, the dull expectations of society.

Despite Hemmerdinger and however many other adolescent flings, Sitney was Acker's first real love, in large part because he provided entry into artistic worlds that she was just discovering. SoHo and the Village were only a subway ride away from Sutton Place, but might as well have been a different galaxy. These worlds were at once delightful and dangerous, eye-opening and mind-expanding. "Growing up as a kid, given my class background, my religious background, or what not, I was expected to marry well," she wrote in a late essay, "or, when my parents realized I wasn't going to do that, I was expected to be a doctor or a lawyer or a scientist, and that was all that was allowed. I wasn't going to fit into any of those roles. So I found a sort of pocket. 'Bohemia.' At that time, there was something called 'Bohemia' and it made a lot of sense. I lived in Bohemia." How much she actually loved the brash, brainy, horny Sitney is uncertain—later on, when older, she'd dismiss him as a misogynist—but at the time, she revered, and desperately wanted, what he represented.

Sitney relished his role as an avant-garde Pygmalion, and Kathy in turn avidly absorbed his teachings and influence. While earlier she had dreamed of being a poet, now she knew real ones, and could see, up close and in detail, how one might become, and live, as a poet, a dancer, a painter, a filmmaker. In *My Mother: Demonology*, she writes, "This hint that it was possible to live in a community other than my parents', a community that wasn't hateful or boring, one of intellectuals, by opening up the world of possibilities, saved me from despair and nihilism." Kathy was suddenly in the company of openly gay people, drug addicts, geniuses, provocateurs, outcasts. She saw explicitly how art could be created in opposition or in parallel to a hegemonic, calcified culture. How communities and institutions—the Film-Makers' Co-op was formed in 1962—coalesced around that opposition. Here were filmmakers who had taken a commercial, even industrial, narrative form and thoroughly interrogated and subverted its materiality, its adherence to certain dramatic structures, its creative ambitions, who saw in it, who created *from* it, an art of endless visionary potential. For the first time—but far from the last—a historic cultural ferment swirled around Acker. In a story that she often later repeated, Jack Smith told her that he wanted to build a huge dome in North Africa, where people could come and tell him their dreams, and he would then turn these dreams into films that would be screened twenty-four hours a day. She was enchanted by this idea. In her future books, she would reproduce elaborate maps of her own dreams.

Acker would go on to describe this period with deep affection and gauzy exaggeration. She liked to refer to herself as a friend, or even mascot, to Smith and Warhol and this whole band of outsiders. The truth, Sitney said, was quite a bit different; she watched and listened, but said very little. She was shy, made no impression. But she *was* just a teenager. Still just a girl, still, indeed, usually dressed in her school uniform. What could she say to these men? How many of them even noticed her? Most of these artists were fifteen, twenty years older than she was, completely consumed by their work. When Sitney wasn't treating Kathy as a project or sexual plaything, he used her as a secretary, once having her deliver manuscript pages of Brakhage's *Metaphors on Vision*, which Sitney was editing, to Dick Higgins's loft in SoHo, where the book was being produced. But in her same essay about this bohemia, and obviously with hindsight, Acker writes that all of this was simultaneously strategic and necessary. This was how a young woman in the early sixties was forced to navigate the world, even the relatively liberated realm of the avant-garde:

> You know, one makes various compromises or rather, one puts on various masks, identic masks or identities, in order to survive. So, when I was in my teens, I hung around one of the forms of Bohemia, the poetry world; it was mainly guys there, a few women, but very few; you could see those women being on the edges of hysteria in order to maintain their position in that world. My position, as a teenager, was to listen to the big men and to keep my mouth shut. And I did it. That was the only way I could have done it.

x x x

Acker kept her romance with Sitney largely a secret. "I couldn't tell either my parents or anyone at my school about him," she later wrote, "for he was an artist. Artists are not acceptable boyfriends." She would sometimes tell Claire she was seeing a movie with friends, then sneak down to the Bowery. At other times, she enlisted a classmate's more presentable boyfriend to pretend to pick her up, then that couple would double-date with her and Sitney.

The tension between her two lives came to a head in late November. That month, the Jewish Guild for the Blind held its Thanksgiving Eve Dinner Dance, an annual benefit for the charity and society ball. Nineteen sixty-three was the fiftieth anniversary of the guild, and thanks to Claire's volunteering, Kathy was selected as one of twenty-seven high school girls presented as debutantes. The event was held near Times Square, at the newly opened Americana, then the tallest hotel in the world. This was a major event for Bud and Claire—it would be Kathy's "coming out" to society, essentially the announcement of her eligibility as a potential wife. They bought her a long, tight, white brocaded dress at Bergdorf's for the occasion.

Unsurprisingly, Kathy found the whole idea appalling, and though she couldn't skip out on the actual event, she did forgo the rehearsal in favor of meeting Sitney. Claire somehow discovered this and was livid. Her response was so violent that Acker felt compelled to record it in both letters to friends and in her earliest fiction. "One winter afternoon I manage to get out of the house," she writes in *The Childlike Life*. "I take the subway to 9th Street and Third Avenue to see my lover P. We spend the afternoon fucking. When I get home around 6:00 P.M. my mother asks me where I've been. 'Just walking around.' 'Why weren't you at the rehearsal for the Jewish Guild for the Blind Coming-Out Dance?' 'I'm sorry; I forgot.' She starts slapping my face as hard as she can. 'Whore. Whore.'"

At the event itself, Kathy was presented by Bud, who escorted her down a short flight of stairs and then paraded her around the ballroom before their first dance, a foxtrot. Kathy's date was a boy—his name lost to time—that she later described as gay. As soon as they could, he and Kathy left the dance, went to the ballroom's bar, and got drunk.

× × ×

At some point in their relationship—or perhaps after it had ended—Kathy told Sitney that Bud had once caught her in bed with a boyfriend (possibly her second husband, Peter Gordon). A version of this scene recurs repeatedly throughout Acker's work, from her early prose poem "Stripper Disintegration" to the libretto *Requiem*. In Acker's writing, however, the moment usually takes an ominous cast, with a Bud-like character banishing the boyfriend and then making sexual advances toward a Kathy-like character. He is pathetic and needy; he kisses and gropes her. He retreats only when Kathy telephones her mother and tells her what's happening.

While the scene is multilayered, with Acker using it emblematically, her frequent return to this moment does raise the possibility that Bud did sexually assault his stepdaughter. The unrelenting disgust with which Acker portrays him in her writing lends this even more credence. The frequency with which incest is represented too, even if portrayed figuratively or even ironically, only heightens this suspicion.

It's impossible to know if Acker was actually sexually abused as a child or adolescent, by Bud or anyone else. It's likely we'll never know. But she never spoke about it with friends, or in the many interviews in which she discussed all manner of intimate and personal detail. The writer Melvyn "Mel" Freilicher, who would later become one of her closest friends, said that she never told him about any kind of childhood abuse, adding that "it doesn't seem that she'd keep that kind of fact from her friends or the public at large." But other people who knew Acker at various times in her life—the poet Harris Schiff and the musician Jill Kroesen, specifically—who were themselves abused, recognized in her a shared trauma. "One can read Kathy's work as being very much the literature of an abused child," the poet Ron Silliman, another friend, also argued.

Ultimately, though, Acker wasn't dealing with assertion or information, but in ambiguity, ambivalence, and emotion. In a way, it didn't matter if her self-dramatization was factually true. The Bud character was no more real than the Kathy character, but both were expressions of larger truths about the oppression of women and children. "There are things that are just too bone-marrow awful," the artist Carolee Schneemann said of Acker's work. "And the culture doesn't really want to accept it."

CHAPTER 6

———— ✕ ————

SOMETIME IN HIGH SCHOOL, KATHY ACQUIRED THE NICKNAME CAS-sandra. Nobody remembers how or why. Was it a play on her name, or perhaps a nod to her interest in Greek? Or was she actually given, like the mythological figure, to prophecies of disaster that no one believed? Her later novels are, in many ways, prescient; even if the sobriquet itself didn't last beyond Lenox, the spirit arguably did.

The nickname is mentioned on her yearbook page in her senior year, part of the caption to an illustration of a headless statue, its foot planted on a box of books bound for India. Presumably, the books were charitable donations, and they are alluded to again in a paragraph that describes Kathy in rollicking, sardonic prose and which predicted her future literary success:

> Some people think that Kathy is a beatnik; others claim that she is an existentialist; but Kathy says that she is just plain Kathy. Whatever she is, she is different. She's more intellectual than many members of her class; she reads more; and she acts more avant-garde. She practices a studied nonchalance, taking things in her stride, letting trivial matters in one ear and out the other. Her close friends complain of her "stupid look." This look is the only facial expression that she uses when she hears the names of baseball players and television actors that she cannot recognize. It is possible that in the next shipment of books to India Kathy might be added to the cargo, for it is noticed that she often has unreasonable arguments with Mrs. Bacon. Despite Kathy's exotic, but sometimes esoteric mind, she might, one day, return to Lenox, as the Poet Laureate.

In the accompanying photograph, "just plain Kathy" does, indeed, look fairly plain: her hair is cut into a glossy flip that hangs just above her shoulders, her mouth agape in a slight, gap-toothed grin. Was this her "stupid" look? She's all head, all face, disembodied—below the neck, her shoulders and torso have been airbrushed into oblivion.

Sometimes, maybe, Kathy would have liked to have just been a head, a brain. Her body was, and always would be, incredibly important to her—a site of great pleasure, power, and knowledge. She would later write that she wanted to create, in fact, a "literature of the body," and she bristled against any theoretical separation of mind and body. "When reality is up for grabs," she said, "the body itself becomes the only thing you can return to." But she also often regarded her body as inadequate, ugly, and needy, a problem, a source of dread. It was something she strove to master and something to which she constantly submitted. Plagued by various painful illnesses for much of her adult life, it would betray her again and again.

× × ×

After Sitney left for Europe that winter, Kathy refocused on her studies. In her senior year, she was president of the U.N. Club and a member of the Dramatics Club. She had her sights set on attending Radcliffe College, Harvard's sister school and arguably the best university in the country for women. This was Claire's hope too. As Acker writes in her novel *My Mother: Demonology*, marrying a rich, old WASP was the best way for a young Jewish woman "to travel from the school into the world outside," and the only other acceptable path was to extend their education. "My parents and teachers, aware that I will not by nature marry a rich man, explained to me that by attending a top college I still kept the possibility of a rich or 'decent' marriage. If I was so evil that I couldn't even do that, I would at worst learn to be a top-flight scientist or lawyer."

But Radcliffe wasn't meant to be. And, again, the Muller twins, Kathy's enduring rivals, were partly to blame. They too had their hearts set on Radcliffe. But Radcliffe was a small school; it had quotas. There was no way it would take any more than two students from a single high school, and the principals at schools with students who wanted to apply had to carefully select which applications they would support. Cecily Selby, Lenox's principal, herself a Radcliffe grad, decided to back Linda and Susan. The twins had the same excellent grades as Kathy, the same perfect SAT scores. And they were more physically attractive and better behaved, more obviously appealing candidates.

Kathy was crushed. The rejection had even more sting because she had been excluded from the outset, barred from even attempting admission. She felt like an outcast once again. And, for whatever reason, she hadn't applied to any other similarly elite college—none of the other Seven Sisters schools, or Pembroke, or the University of Pennsylvania, all of which would have likely taken her. Her lone safety school was Brandeis University, a Jewish-sponsored, nonsectarian, coed liberal arts college also located in Eastern Massachusetts, which did accept her. The Mullers, meanwhile, didn't get into Radcliffe anyway; both ended up at Wellesley.

Grudgingly, Kathy went to Brandeis. But even once there, she couldn't stop talking about Radcliffe, and for the first few weeks of her freshman year, she let everyone know that she didn't belong there, that she deserved better. But Brandeis was arguably a better fit. Geographically, it was still close to Radcliffe, about a twenty-minute drive into the Boston suburb of Waltham. And from its contemporary architecture to its iconoclastic faculty, it also signified a distinct and appealing modernity. There were no Greeks, hardly any preppies. The student body was small, only about three hundred students per class, and many of them were Beatniks, artists, intellectuals, and misfits—the type of people that Kathy now felt more comfortable around. Leonard Bernstein had once taught there, and Irving Howe and Max Lerner were on the faculty when Kathy arrived.

The faculty's most notorious member was Herbert Marcuse, the marvelous, maddening Frankfurt School refugee. Marcuse had mashed up Marx and Freud, insisted on society's liberation from consumerism and capitalistic consciousness. An old man enthralled with the young, he was the guru of the New Left; his 1964 book *The One-Dimensional Man* was the unofficial handbook of Students for a Democratic Society, and two of his students, Angela Davis and Abbie Hoffman, would go on to become celebrities of the movement. He clashed frequently with Brandeis president Abram Sachar, who called him "corrosive" and "biting," "a rallying point in the offbeat youth movements, along with Ché Guevara and Mao Tse-tung." Contrary to the story that she herself later promulgated, Kathy never studied directly with Marcuse,* but his influence was undeniable. "Art breaks open a dimension inaccessible to other experience," he wrote in his last major work, *The Aesthetic Dimension*, "a

---

* Acker also claimed, in at least one interview, to have lived with Angela Davis, though there's no evidence that she actually did.

dimension in which human beings, nature, and things no longer stand under the law of the established reality principle." This idea, that art can serve as resistance to societal repression, would forever underscore Acker's writing.

Sitney had provided an escape, but Brandeis offered the possibility, finally, of complete reinvention. Going to college meant she would, at long last, be free of the Upper East Side, free of Claire and Bud and Wendy and Nana. Free to fully embark on scholarly and amorous adventure. More importantly, she might find out who she really was. She knew she was different. But how different could she, *would* she, be?

WHAT IT MEANS TO BE AVANT-GARDE

(1964–1976)

CHAPTER 7

————— × —————

B RANDEIS WAS FULL OF BRIGHT, ORIGINAL PEOPLE, BUT FROM THE
minute she arrived, Kathy was considered one of the brightest and most
original. Akin to her high school years, she seesawed between confidence
and insecurity, but her intelligence, looks, and intensity impressed almost everyone around her. She decided to major in classical studies on a campus in
which there were few classics majors. She called herself a poet, touted herself
an expert on avant-garde film. To friends and classmates, she seemed simultaneously vulnerable and experienced, feminine and androgynous. A fellow
freshman named Jeff Weinstein, who later became a food writer and editor at
the *Village Voice*, said, "She was one of the beautiful ones. She dressed hot, very
mod. She looked like one of the rich New Yorkers, and that's what I thought of
her until I met her and found out she was serious."

Kathy was so serious, in fact, that she ditched the first roommate she was
assigned because the girl partied too much and Kathy couldn't concentrate on
her studies. After requesting a room change, she was paired up instead with an
eighteen-year-old fine art major from Great Neck, Long Island, named Tamar
Diesendruck. This wasn't exactly a perfect match either. On their first day together, Diesendruck, who would go on to become an acclaimed composer, put
on a Robert Johnson record as she unpacked her books. Kathy was appalled.
She'd arrived with her own collection of jazz records, but she had never heard
rural blues music before. That didn't stop her from declaring it "garbage" and
demanding that Diesendruck never again play the album in her presence. "She
went ballistic," Diesendruck said. "She thought it was stupid and that I was an
idiot. I was very hurt." Months later, when a male classmate, who was a blues
harp player, expressed his enthusiasm for the same music, Kathy revised her
opinion and never complained about Diesendruck's records again.

Other women in the dorm had easier relationships with Kathy. "I remember her being kind and supportive," Debbie Anker, now a Harvard law professor, recalled. "Everybody thought of her as having this edge, but I saw this

other side of her. She was motherly." At one point, when the sixteen-year-old Anker was contemplating losing her virginity, Kathy was one of her most enthusiastic cheerleaders.

But Kathy wouldn't be spending too much time in her dorm anyway. On the first day of class, she had shimmied up a willow tree in the quad, where a sophomore named Peter Gould spied her. He was struck by her beauty and outfit—a pink tank top and jean shorts—and impulsively scurried up the other side of the tree so they could meet at the top. An aspiring writer, Gould had spent the previous summer in Guatemala and Belize, part of that time at a leper colony. But he was also shy and sensitive, a stutterer, from small-town Pennsylvania, and he felt that Kathy was, in many ways, his opposite: an urbane, wild New Yorker, more intensely emotional and imaginative than anyone he had ever met. But, as he would soon learn, she also loved books and literature as deeply as he did, perhaps more so. He was instantly bewitched. They chatted for a while in the willow, then descended and left campus, walking and talking along the banks of the Charles River for hours.

Two days after their initial meeting, Gould snuck Kathy into his dorm so they could have sex. It was his first time, and, fifty years later, his memory of that night was still vivid. They fell asleep, and then woke again just before midnight. Kathy got out of bed and Gould watched with delight as she paraded nude across the floor, bathed in the orange mercury light that leaked through the curtains. "Do you like me?" she asked. The question made no sense to Gould. Of course he did. All he felt was overwhelming gratitude. The next day, he ran into Kathy in the dining hall. Tentatively, he asked if he could see her again that Friday. "Of course, silly," she said. "Saturday too. We're going together."

They became inseparable that entire school year, their lives an alternating current of sex and study. Almost every night, Kathy and Gould shared a table at the library and read there, shoes off, their feet in each other's lap, until it closed around midnight. Occasionally, she shoplifted at the Brandeis bookstore, slipping books under her shirt that she later gave to Gould with the inscription "Love, Me."

That fall, student political activism, ignited by the civil rights movement and spurred on by the escalating conflict in Vietnam, roiled college campuses all across the country. Students for a Democratic Society (SDS), formed at the University of Michigan a few years earlier, was becoming a national force. At Berkeley, the Free Speech Movement was born, the first mass act of civil disobedience of the 1960s, and the progenitor of protests, sit-ins, and other demonstrations throughout the country. Malcolm X visited Brandeis in April 1963, and over time the student body became just as restive as those at Columbia and San Francisco State. In 1969, Black students occupied Ford Hall, Brandeis's main academic building, and demanded, among other things, the creation of an African and African American studies department. They were successful; Brandeis created one of the first such departments in the country.

Kathy was sympathetic to and supportive of this activism. But unlike her friends Debbie Anker and Mel Freilicher, a psych major from Yonkers, who faithfully, forcefully participated in rallies, marches, and organizing efforts, she would have been called an activist by neither herself nor anyone who knew her then. She would later exaggerate her affiliation with SDS, and her books contain an undeniable political dimension, but the barricades she went to were in her brain. "I didn't go down south and fight with the blacks," she said later. "I was always on the periphery being an artist."

Maybe not exactly being an artist, but at least someone figuring out how to become one. She was studying ancient Greek and, still under Sitney's influence, taking courses in the history of cinema. She continued to write poetry, efforts that Gould recalled as "imitations of Sappho." Only one piece from those days appears to have survived—an erotic ode titled "To Peter Lee Gould"— but it's braided with the classical references that frequently adorn Acker's later writing and opens with an echo of the poem that concludes her novel *Blood and Guts in High School*:

boy of the slim hips, alone on the windy shore
of Lesbos.
    what shall you dance
in the wind. in the seas.

too many poets have vowed on these shores
to the dim Attis.
and now
    we hardly remember.

too many feet have tread the measures,
dipping and rising

with the heaving dolphins,
silver on the black fish-scales.
    you, too, Orpheus
you were there, teaching the wild virgins
who sent you
        down to Hell ...

and here again, to guard this boy
in his first dance to the god.

may his feet touch the penis measures
his voice crazed with the winds.
    O first mother,
    black singer of Lesbos,
        rise in the boy erect!
let him ride your dolphins,
which few have ridden, down to death!

As at Lenox, Kathy continued to be a dutiful, conscientious student. But more culturally knowledgeable now, she also strained against the limitations of the curriculum. Brandeis's literature department, she felt, was "still living in the 19th century," and in the grip of New Critics like John Crowe Ransom, and Cleanth Brooks, who insisted that the only thing that mattered about a literary work was its formal elements, the words on the page; anything outside the closed system of the text—an author's intention or biography, historical context—was considered irrelevant to an understanding of the work. "Anything too passionate or conceptual was considered from crude to criminal," Acker said.

That November, an alternative suggested itself, when Allen Ginsberg visited the campus with Peter Orlovsky and Gregory Corso. Kathy and Gould joined five hundred other students and faculty crowded into Schwartz Auditorium to hear Ginsberg read the entirety of *Kaddish*, his 1961 masterpiece about his late mother. It was a historic event—Atlantic Records recorded the reading and released it the next year—though Acker would further embellish it in a portrait of Ginsberg she wrote decades later: "I remember that they walked on to a huge auditorium floor, dressed only in towels. I don't remember what either Allen or Peter said or read. I remember that one of them gave the other a blowjob." In fact, Ginsberg and Orlovsky were wearing Indian robes and, on stage anyway, there were no blowjobs. Many years later, Acker and Ginsberg became friendly, would in fact perform together, and that evening at Brandeis, she said, taught her more about poetry than any of her previous academic training: "I learned that poetry's only rule is that it is not about, it *is* joy. Poetry is all the treasures, the wonders that I believe sailors see and touch. Equal to and more than the pleasures of the flesh. That night I learned that all the dried-up professors in their dusty schoolrooms, whatever they taught, something about being a success in this culture, didn't begin to teach poetry."

Kathy constantly surprised Gould with the vehemence of her emotions, and several moments with her left him with lasting memories. On a trip to the Boston Museum of Fine Arts, for instance, the couple discovered in a quiet upper wing a reproduction of a tiny medieval Christian chapel room. Gregorian chants echoed from speakers around the space. Then, as Gould leaned in to inspect the frescoes, Kathy suddenly fell to her knees and started sobbing. "I want to be a nun!" she cried. "That's what I should be!" Gould was baffled at the time, but thinking about it later, deduced that Kathy had a very specific and romantic kind of nun in mind: a teenaged Spanish fourteenth-century beauty, forced into the convent by her father, separated from her young lover, and alternating between self-flagellation and masturbation. Kathy, he realized, was very capable of anesthetizing suffering.

She was also good at taking on, or channeling, different personae. A couple months after they'd been dating, he watched and listened as she called a well-known birth control doctor in midtown Manhattan to make an appointment. Her voice changed immediately, becoming, he remembered, "wealthier, older." They took the train to the city and dropped by her family's apartment, where Gould met Claire. They didn't stay long—not even long enough for Gould to form an impression of Claire—and traveled uptown to crash with a friend of Gould's, a Columbia student who left them alone for the night.

× × ×

Though clearly a product of the burgeoning counterculture, Acker was often ambivalent about it. In later life, she frequently pointed out hippie hypocrisies—that "free love" was largely exclusive to men, that class differences went unacknowledged, that their utopias were often grounded in retreat and separatism. Later, she denied even being part of that generation: "The Hippies were our parents," she wrote. "Our parents had had the good life and had taken too many drugs and we, their children, were abortions, mutilation. The Hippies had believed in LOVE and PEACE and we, their children, were mentally and physically misshapen."

But Kathy did revel in the era's anti-authoritarianism, and a so-called sexual revolution that, for all of its inadequacies, did unhitch sex from reproduction, did make birth control more accessible and abortion legal, did make divorce and homosexuality more broadly acceptable. When she arrived at Brandeis, Kathy said, "it was cool to fuck because that was the beginning of the hippie days." She described "prowling" with her girlfriends for men, sharing boyfriends, even keeping a chart that detailed the sizes of her lovers' penises. "We were really into sex!" she said. Kathy no longer went by the nickname Cassandra, but several Brandeis classmates did refer to her as "Lusty Kathy." She hung out with older students, theater majors who tricked out their dorms like opium dens—mattresses covering the floors, black curtains—and held orgies.

To Gould's chagrin, she also became friendly with a junior named Robert Acker, known as Bob. Acker was a history major from Queens, an intense, intelligent, volatile figure who, along with a few other students, had been busted for pot possession a couple years earlier and temporarily banished from Brandeis. To Gould, he looked like a menacing, skulking jackal, a character straight out of *Zap Comix*. By some, likely exaggerated, accounts, he exclusively ate steak tartare, studied in the library shirtless, and challenged townies to fights. Kathy's roommate, Tamar Diesendruck, recalled him once abruptly kicking Diesendruck in the groin, for some now forgotten slight. But Kathy adored his outlaw aura. In February, when Gould left campus to spend a weekend with an uncle in Connecticut, she promptly slept with Acker. He found her "smart" and "with all the guts in the world," but he was, by no means, as smitten as Gould was. Foreshadowing a persistent issue throughout Kathy's life, his interest was almost purely physical. "She was cute as pie," Acker said many years later. "But it was not the case of two hearts beating as one."

Gould was wounded by Kathy's infidelity, but their romance nonetheless trundled along. By the summer, they were living together in Boston, where Gould was house-sitting for a professor while working full-time at the Peace Corps' language lab on the Brandeis campus. Kathy, meanwhile, spent her days writing and reading. Every day, Gould would bring her five or six books from the library, and the next day she'd ask for more. On Saturday afternoons, they bought cheap vegetables, chicken parts for soup, and Spanish wine. It all felt very grown-up, but nonetheless, once a week, they had to drive to Cambridge to receive a call from Claire because Kathy had told her she was living there and looking for a job. Though Gould didn't recall what Claire and Kathy discussed, the conversations were evidently painful—afterward, Kathy would collapse into his arms, sobbing.

Gould was in love with Kathy, but he was also intent on becoming a writer. And becoming a writer, he felt, meant going to Europe and leaving her, temporarily, behind. In the fall of 1965, he went on an exchange to Scotland. Kathy, in turn, went back to Acker, who received her, more or less, with open arms. Months later, filled with regret for leaving her behind, Gould contemplated breaking off his trip and returning early. But Kathy had already moved on and quickly nipped this in the bud in a letter to Gould that was flush with characteristic melodrama:

> About your coming home—please please do not. It is a form of madness—madness that is fr. the gods—as is love, & pain, & the woods. But then we must live separated from the gods, & problems that sent you to Scotland will rouse themselves if you come home. The pendulum has swung: away from myself to your parents, your rightful ambition, your education, your need of geography other than Brandeis. Now I appear in the light of joy. But do you want to marry me now? Is your need and/or fear that powerful? For that is what shall happen—or what reason for an early return?

She was right—Gould wasn't ready to get married. Acker, however, was. He was about to graduate and move across the country. Brandeis had refused to renew Marcuse's contract, and the professor was decamping for the University of California at San Diego.* Several grad students planned to go with him,

---

* Several students, and the school newspaper, the *Justice*, maintained that Marcuse had been fired for his radical views. Abram Sachar argued that Marcuse's departure was much more innocuous. Retirement at Brandeis was mandatory at age seventy. In 1965, Marcuse was almost sixty-eight and had been offered a three-year appointment at UCSD. He chose the longer contract in San Diego so he could get an additional year of active teaching.

and Acker followed those students' lead.* Acker was still somewhat ambivalent about Kathy, but he also didn't want to lose her. As she would soon learn, he was more neurotic than desperado, more conventional than not. "I was a little scared," Acker said. "Not of her but of sex in general. People were getting abortions, people were committing suicide or trying to, people were going a little nuts. I hadn't been dinged yet but I thought, now I'm twenty, it's time to retire. Let's settle down." In a notebook a couple years later, Kathy would echo Acker's feelings: "We both needed someone to hang on to for life because we were scared and made schizoid." If they married, she could come to the West Coast with him. Kathy had never dreamed of becoming anyone's wife, but California was exotic and new, and she would be even further away from her family. It seemed like a worthwhile gamble.

Bud and Claire weren't especially happy about it. She was too young, they thought. They didn't want her to drop out of Brandeis. And who was Bob Acker anyway? What were his prospects? His mother was just a housewife, his father only a contractor for large construction projects in New York. Where was the money, the status? Acker was, Kathy would later say in interviews, a "Polish Jew," and her parents, being "high-German Jews" were appalled that she would consort with someone they considered so low-class. "They thought marrying a Polish Jew was the worst thing you could do," she said. The antipathy went both ways—Acker, who met the family only a couple of times, called Claire a "bitch on wheels." Confusingly, many years later, Kathy told an interviewer that her parents wouldn't pay for her schooling *unless* she got married. It's unclear, however, if they ever paid for her schooling at all, and most likely her grandmother did. She also said that she didn't want to get married, arguing that "I was a certain class and color. There were so many alternatives."

In any event, her parents' disdain did make Acker more alluring to her. In her 1984 novel *My Death My Life by Pier Paolo Pasolini*, she sketches a scene in which "Kathy" tells her parents that she's going to get married. They immediately assume she's pregnant and say they can help her get an abortion.

---

* Kathy and others later promoted the story that it was she who had followed Marcuse to UCSD, but in fact, she never took a class with him at either Brandeis or San Diego. Acker himself knew Marcuse and his grad student adherents, but, mainly because of scheduling, he had never studied with the philosopher either. UCSD was attractive to Acker not because of Marcuse but because it was cheap, easy to get into, and he simply wanted a school to hole up in, as he put it, "until the Vietnam War blew over."

She's indignant: "There are other reasons to get married!" "You might as well tell us if you're in trouble," her father says. Kathy responds by thrusting her scar-covered wrist in their faces. "Yeah, I'm in trouble," she says. Her parents recoil. Acker's narrator continues: "Each time I slice the blade through my wrist I'm finally able to act out war. You call it my masochism because you're trying to keep your power over me, but you're not going to anymore. This is the beginning of childhood."

In other words, marrying Acker was a way to start over. Maybe she could leave her childhood behind. She could create a family of her own, a better or at least a less oppressive one. "I was trying to get rid of my parents in my mind and feelings," she wrote in a notebook a half decade later, "and to have the calmness to do what I wanted." On September 4, 1966, the couple married at a simple ceremony at Florrie's summer house in Atlantic Beach. In one of the three photographs of the wedding that survive, Kathy looks unusually demure in white dress and veil, tanned and fresh-faced, with blunt bangs. But there's also the hint of a coy smile—at last, she's about to be someone other than Kathy Alexander.

When he heard the news of their marriage, Gould was crestfallen. He and Kathy had never really broken up, had never said goodbye. About three-and-a-half years later, he tracked the couple down in San Diego and showed up on their doorstep, stoned, looking for closure. He talked to Kathy for an hour, but the moment was thoroughly disappointing. She was frosty, and Gould discovered, to his surprise, that his own intense feelings had likewise cooled with time.

She would always be his first love, however, and he'd always remember her with great fondness. A few months later, he moved into a commune in rural Vermont where he wrote his first novel, a back-to-the-land fantasy called *Burnt Toast*. In it, the narrator, an aspiring poet named Silent, takes a lover named Kathy. In the scene in which she's introduced, Kathy is kneeling on a kitchen floor, looking at a raisin pie in the oven: "She was undressed, facing away from me, on her knees before the stove; the back and the top of her beautiful thighs were what I saw first, coming into the kitchen, and now that I was close to her I watched her breasts swing in the orange light of the fire (and the fire-shadow of her breasts on the thighs), her glistening lips, her white hands on the iron poker." Kathy's voluptuousness still clearly captured Gould's young imagination, the orange light he describes recalling that first night they spent together.

But the simplistic fantasy he conjured, that of the hippie earth mother, was one that she would never fulfill for anybody, and indeed, one that she would furiously reject. "I was turning around and going to the past," Gould said, of the different paths their lives took. "And she was plunging headfirst into the future. She was already launched in directions that I could barely understand or predict."

CHAPTER 8

———— ✕ ————

T HE NEWLYWEDS IMMEDIATELY HEADED STRAIGHT TO SAN DIEGO. Acker started grad school and Kathy continued her undergraduate studies, now in the literature department since UCSD didn't offer classics per se. Tuition in California was "half-nothing," as Acker put it, "and the faucet was open." The war in Vietnam was still on and he was happy to wait it out studying by the ocean. They found a cheap, two-story bungalow in Del Mar, a beach town on the northern edge of the city.

UCSD was only officially six years old by then, with close to six hundred students and 150 faculty members. Located in the hilly, affluent seaside neighborhood of La Jolla, about fifteen miles north of downtown San Diego, it had been established as one of the world's preeminent scientific research institutions, with an emphasis on oceanography. But the school's fine arts and humanities departments also grew quickly, and its philosophy department became the school's first functioning non-science graduate program. Over the next few years, a number of cultural pioneers would become instructors there: the conceptual artists John Baldessari and Allan Kaprow (creator of the "Happening"), the composer Pauline Oliveros (who, infamously, taught courses in Tarot and Indian cooking out of her home), and the iconoclastic film critic and painter Manny Farber.

Marcuse settled in relatively well. The poet David Antin, who arrived that same year, remembered him as a "sparkling and provocative figure in the philosophy department," who would wander down La Jolla Boulevard with his hands behind his back like "he was in some beautiful German city peering longingly into bakery windows." He would walk down La Jolla because it was the *only* street; there were no real streets in San Diego, or at least no street life. On the one hand, it could feel like the Wild West, but it was also a dull, homogenous, racist, deeply conservative city. Marcuse received at least one death threat from the Ku Klux Klan in 1968, and later, under pressure from the likes of the John Birch Society, the school's chancellor would try to force him out by introducing an arbitrary mandatory retirement policy. When Marcuse lured his best-known student, Angela Davis, out to UCSD for grad school, she recalled that when she first arrived, "it was weeks before I even saw another Black person." Bob Acker remembered being on a Greyhound bus, commuting to La Jolla, when news of Martin Luther King's assassination was announced; his fellow passengers erupted in joy. "San Diego was not only the furthest westmost place in the country," Antin said, "it was also the furthest rightmost place in the country."

But the overall political atmosphere of the place didn't often intrude on the Ackers' respective consciousnesses. Physically, at least, it was a beautiful and comfortable place to live. Any culture shock they might have experienced was softened by a cocoon that they formed around themselves. "It was delightful," Acker said. "I was in the water, out of the water, in the water. The air temperature was always seventy degrees, the water temperature was always seventy degrees." Acker made about three hundred dollars a month as a teaching assistant, more than enough to cover their expenses. Once Kathy married, her parents more or less stopped supporting her, and she supplemented Acker's income with small grants and what little she could make as an occasional TA herself. When they weren't at the beach, they hung out with Acker's fellow grad students, swimming, studying, partying. He and Kathy played cards, Go, chess. She was very good at chess and would play seriously for the rest of her life.

Kathy was somewhat less enamored of San Diego than Acker was. In a 1989 essay, "Blue Valentine," she recalled those SoCal days with bitterness: "I hated it. My life. The hippy years had begun when I had still been at Brandeis University near Boston and they were now into full swing. People around me believed that they and hopefully all other people could and would only feel only peace and love. Women wore granny dresses, became pregnant, and cooked healthy food. I felt isolated in this world, as if I was pitch black and everyone else, pastel."

Reading this essay for the first time, decades after Kathy's death, Acker accused her of an almost embarrassing level of embellishment—"her life fictionalized by her literary persona," as he put it. But he acknowledged that she was indeed far from happy at the time. Almost as soon as the Ackers arrived in San Diego, it was clear that the marriage was a mistake. They were probably too young, and their interests had never really aligned—Acker was a student of history, economics, and military diplomacy, while Kathy was almost exclusively interested in literature. Acker wasn't particularly fond of the poetry Kathy was writing either. Forty years later, he remembered it only as "nice" and "not really tasteful," and she, in turn, was dismissive of his feedback. "I'd listen to it, and every now and then I'd give her a suggestion," he said. "She'd give me this look—like, why don't you stick to things you know about?" Neither, it seemed, had the emotional maturity necessary for a conventional marriage.

To make matters worse, both of them were prone to debilitating anxiety attacks, which they referred to as "the hole in the head." Acker would often disappear into a depressive funk that left him unable to do anything but play solitaire for days on end—behavior that Kathy coldly captured in the first paragraph of her novel *Rip-off Red*: ". . . I got bored doing that Ph.D. shit and being frustrated professors' straight-A pet, especially being faithful to a husband who spent all his time in bed dealing out poker hands . . ." Kathy could play the hippie homemaker—she baked bread, sewed her own miniskirts—but wasn't capable of, and had no interest in, being Acker's caretaker. "She expected me to be the leader of the pack, the head wolf," he said. "She didn't want to be my mom." Nor did she want to be, as she put it in a later notebook, "a permanent Acker cock worshiper."

Kathy struggled from time to time with her own bouts of depression, even self-harm—at Brandeis, and possibly earlier, she occasionally cut herself. In the notebooks she kept a couple years later, she often referred to "the angels," which sometimes appear to be guardian angels but more often represent an ineffable, malevolent force that eluded description: "When I speak about angels I mean that there are many ways we experience we don't have language for most of them." The angels could play havoc with her emotions and behavior, their presence a particular form of torture: "the angels are making me into a distortion pulling out my eyes destroying my brains."

Kathy often spent whole days in the house, never getting out of her silk bathrobe. She was hardly idle, though. She read incessantly, kept writing poetry, and still made it to classes, where she continued to impress her teachers. She took courses in the philosophy department, and English courses with a sweet, Anglophilic Austen scholar named Andrew Wright, who later told people of Kathy that he "had never seen anything like her—intellectually and every other way." She dedicated one poem from those years, "Ode to Beautiful Women #2"—part of an unpublished manuscript titled *The Golden Woman*—to Wright.

It's the poems that surround it, however—"Ode to Beautiful Women #1" and "Ode to Beautiful Women #3"—that offer more obvious biographical insight and detail. "Ode to Beautiful Women #1" opens with the line "the imagination doesn't change anything" and then proceeds to damn, once again, the hollow lives of parents like her own:

> what are we interested in
> Today we finally broke with our parents
> the parents all over America
> taking amphetamine
> watching T.V. five to ten hours a day
> drinking two to ten martinis between 5:30 and 10:30 p.m.
> getting undressed in the dark
> getting up on weekdays between 7:00 and 7:30
> falling asleep at 10:30 in front of the television
> getting undressed in the dark
> going out to a Chinese restaurant run by a Jew from Long
> Island
> going to a French restaurant and eating Chateaubriand
> playing canasta the men playing gin rummy playing bridge
> with the girls […]

"Ode to Beautiful Women #3," meanwhile, is a more confessional, sexually explicit, and aggressive *cri de coeur*. It was a hint of the direction that Kathy's work would soon take but also of her incipient desire for extracurricular romance:

> I want to fuck you
> in a bed
> at night
> hold my legs open   while you move into   around in
> me
> I want to be alone with you
> I'm sick of shit   I don't want you once a week
> I want to eat with you
> work/ while you're working
> I want

to be with you
David's giving a reading
anybody's (friends') giving a reading
what sort of communism is this I want you
I'm sick of you wearing clothes sitting around in your
office/ your house pretending I don't know you
I'm sick of thinking about you and you're not here
I'm sick of knowing it's impossible
knowing that is not our poem it's the poem of an
old cliche when beautiful women returning through
our desire

In June 1967, the Ackers moved downtown, into a large, ramshackle six-room Victorian on Front Street that was ridiculously cheap—about $35 a month after they rented out the upstairs to other grad students. But it was also located right next to the highway and under the airport flight path. The interior was painted a kitschy lime green and pink, the kitchen infested with cockroaches, maintenance nonexistent. Bob and Kathy slept on a mattress on the floor, sat on cinder-block stools, ate at a plywood dining table that Acker built himself. But they had separate rooms to use as studies, and they did their own work there, mostly in isolation.

The relationship drifted, foundered. They talked theoretically about opening up the marriage but then never even got around to the swinging they thought could save things. The marriage would prove, retrospectively at least, an anomaly in both of their lives. In a notebook a few years later, Kathy dispatched the whole thing thusly: "Acker too straight me too woo-woo wanting a family a real wife I was a good actress for a year and a half I didn't even have to say that much which was incredible . . ."

× × ×

In 1968, everything seemed to change, everywhere. In Vietnam, it was the year of the Tet Offensive and the My Lai Massacre. In April, King was assassinated, and then in June Warhol was shot, and two days later, Robert Kennedy was assassinated. In May, violent student protests engulfed Paris, leading to a workers' revolt that nearly brought down the government. In the American literary world, John Updike released *Couples*, notable for its unusually explicit sex scenes, and innovative fiction flourished, with Robert Coover, John Barth, and even Andy Warhol publishing major novels during the year. In the *New York Times*, Martha Weinman Lear coined the term "second wave feminism." By November, Richard Nixon would become the country's thirty-seventh president.

Kathy graduated from UCSD that spring, and continued to write. Some of the poems she wrote during the period were propelled by the same violence and sex that animated "Ode to Beautiful Women #3." Others were gentler, like "Poems for Tamar 6. 7. & 8.," addressed to Tamar Diesendruck, her old roommate. This trio of poems swarms with allusions to Diesendruck's piano-playing, her Russian heritage, and Kathy's own biography: "it's raining all over the world: it's raining/on you and me: it's raining on the bed Acker/won't get out of." Others, like "Pornographic Poems," are peopled with yet more real-life figures—Wendy, Mel Freilicher—and oscillate between the oneiric and quotidian, the self-serious and self-parodic ("the murk of the dead within our fingernails up/the nostrils we have picked memories of beautiful childhoods").

Kathy obviously often longed for Brandeis, or at least for the friends that she had made there. Then that fall, to her delight and relief, they came to her. In September, Freilicher, Diesendruck, and Jeff Weinstein pulled up outside the house on Front Street. Freilicher and Weinstein had come out to California for grad school, the former at UCSD, the latter at UC Riverside (though a year later he'd transfer to San Diego); Diesendruck had followed a boyfriend out west. The crew crashed on the floor of the Ackers' house, curled up in sleeping bags, for days.

Kathy was thrilled to have them there, particularly Freilicher, who had abandoned his psychology studies and was now intent on becoming a writer too. Mere acquaintances at Brandeis, they became best friends in San Diego. A teddy bear with mercurial facial hair, Freilicher was gentle, funny, loyal, generous, self-deprecating. Kathy sometimes called him "Smelly Belly." They considered each other soul mates, bonding over books and boys and their mutual, romantic belief in themselves as misfits. "For hours, Melvyn and I would listen to Warhol's production of *The Velvet Underground*," Acker later wrote, "and fantasize about living in a society such as that of Warhol and his friends, a society in which the two of us weren't outcasts." When they weren't listening to Nico, they were at midnight screenings of underground films in East San Diego or hanging out on campus at the Anomaly Factory, a water tower that had been converted into a high-tech theater lab.

Kathy took a few graduate classes, including a Jonathan Swift seminar with Freilicher, which the two of them spent mostly making each other giggle. Freilicher ended up staying in San Diego permanently, teaching writing at UCSD and publishing cerebral, fizzy books like *The Unmaking of Americans* and *The Encyclopedia of Rebels*. Steeped in both literary and labor history, they blend memoir, criticism, and fiction, but wear their erudition lightly: historic personages like Margaret Fuller and Bayard Rustin mingle with the likes of Nancy Drew and Jimmy Olsen. In 1974, Freilicher started an experimental literary magazine, *Crawl Out Your Window*, which ran for fifteen years and where he published Kathy alongside the likes of Lydia Davis, Rae Armantrout, and Martha Rosler.

At Brandeis, Freilicher had participated regularly in student demonstrations, and in San Diego, he became even more of a firebrand. With Weinstein, he joined an antiwar group called the Radical Coalition, and later worked with artists' organizations, staging multimedia shows downtown. "What was going on," Freilicher recalled, "was the revolution. You'd go to class for two weeks, then you'd strike for two weeks." Alternative presses were flourishing, including the *San Diego Free Press*, whose offices, Freilicher remembered, were sometimes firebombed. SDS members served as Marcuse's bodyguards. Kathy, for her part, continued to remain above the fray. "She was completely with the program," Freilicher said, "but she wasn't into being at meetings and organizing stuff. She was more concerned with alternative lifestyles, squatters, that kind of thing."

Freilicher was gay but identified then as bisexual. Weinstein, meanwhile, was openly gay and occasionally taught classes in drag. He recalled, with some disbelief, that Kathy had told him he was the first gay man she had ever known. Even more surprising to him, she often asked him what he thought were naïve questions about his sex life—like, what do men do in bed together? The three of them all picked up a bit of money modeling nude for life-drawing classes. Kathy, Weinstein remembered, loved to take off her clothes.

CHAPTER 9

———— × ————

"**A**LL OF US COME FROM PARENTS**," KATHY WROTE. "MY PARENTS were not my biological parents; they were the poets." She was refer-ring to Allen Ginsberg, but she met her true poet-parents, the ones who meant the most to her, and who arguably had the most profound influence on her artistic development, in San Diego. If Kathy had hoped, naïvely, that marrying Acker was the "beginning of childhood," her introduction to David and Elea-nor Antin was, at last, the real thing.

The Antins were Jews from New York too, and though David was a poet and art critic and Eleanor a visual artist, they would both soon redefine their respective disciplines in various thrilling ways. David was thirty-six, tall, iras-cible, droll, and, thanks to a youthful case of alopecia, completely hairless. Eleanor, whom everyone called Elly, was three years younger, impish, and provocative. David had attended the City College of New York, where he met and befriended several artists and writers, including Jerome Rothenberg, Robert Kelly, and Elly (then Eleanor Fineman). He wrote criticism and poetry and told his students that writing itself was akin to engineering: "The technol-ogy is language. In order to invent something useful, you have to know what is needed now, but also you have to know the present state of the technology." In 1966, he received a master's in linguistics from NYU, and a year later, he served as the curator of Boston's Institute of Contemporary Art, before UCSD hired him as an assistant professor in the visual arts department. At UCSD, he taught critical studies and ran their art gallery. It was a good time to go: Elly thought New York had become dull and stifling, and Southern California seemed ripe with possibility. It was more financially advantageous too—at UCSD, David would get paid twice what he had received at NYU. "People told me it was a group of scientists standing with an open checkbook under a palm tree," he later said.

At City College, Elly had majored in creative writing and minored in art, while studying acting and philosophy in her free time, a combination of pursuits that led to a career of uncommon versatility and originality. Though she made paintings, sculpture, performances, and video, her creative shifts and the unclassifiable, capacious work led her, most often, to be labeled a conceptual artist. She thought that contemporary art could, and should, include different modes of personal exploration, fantasy, autobiography (and false autobiography). In a 1974 essay, "An Autobiography of the Artist as an Autobiographer," she called herself "a post-conceptual artist concerned with the nature of human reality, specifically with the transformational nature of the self." Her most renowned early work, *Blood of a Poet Box*, made between 1965 and 1968, consisted of a wooden specimen box filled with a hundred blood samples taken from poets that she personally knew. Her definition of poet characteristically elastic, the project included samples from her husband, Rothenberg, John Ashbery, Carolee Schneemann, John Cage, Yvonne Rainer, and Lawrence Ferlinghetti. She called these blood samples "portraits," and it was a good gag: reworked ready-mades that fused art and literature even as the work interrogated ideas of originality and community.

Elly and David married in 1961, and had a son in 1967 who they named Blaise, after the Swiss-French modernist poet Blaise Cendrars. In late May 1968, they drove across the country to arrive in California on June 8, a few days after Robert Kennedy was shot. They settled in San Diego's then depopulated northern outskirts, moving into a shabby, stucco-and-tile house in Solana Beach, on a bluff a hundred feet above the Pacific. From their terrace, they could watch whales and listen to coyotes. At UCSD, David taught courses on modern art, early Christian art, performance art, and a course called Strategies of Art-Making. "He was frighteningly intelligent," recalled one student, the artist Robert Kushner.

Because he'd published a couple books of poetry, David was also asked to teach a course on the subject. But he had never taught poetry before, and was somewhat dismayed to find that virtually all his students produced "late adolescent expressionist poems." Kathy's work was a bit different, he said—"verbally more complex"—but nonetheless he soon recognized a basic and common problem. Young writers, he said, always have to confront the fact that previous generations of writers have almost always beat them to the punch. That is, if they want to write about something, anything really, another writer has already done so. So he gave his students an assignment: they could write about anything they wanted, but first they needed to go to the library and find out if someone else had written about that subject already. Once they did that research and found those books, they could steal from them whatever they wanted. If they wanted to write about desert adventure, say, they could steal something from T. E. Lawrence. The work, David said, would be in putting those disparate pieces together. Within a month, David said, his students were combining Aeschylus with plumbing manuals, and creating "these wonderful, quickly shifting things," like race car drivers changing gears.

It was an unusual idea, maybe, when it came to poetry, but hardly new to anyone conversant with American visual art of the day. Artists as different as Joseph Cornell, Robert Rauschenberg, Bruce Conner, and Ray Johnson, to name just a few, had brilliantly used found (and sometimes copyrighted) materials to produce sculptures, paintings, and collages. Antin elucidated this thinking in the poem, "What It Means to Be Avant-Garde":

> and if you have to invent something new to do the work at hand you
> will   but not if you have a ready-made that will work and is close at
> hand and you want to get on with the rest of the business   then
> youll pick up the tool thats there   a tool that somebody else has
> made   that will work   and youll lean on it and feel grateful when
> its good to you   for somebody elses work   and youll think of him
> as a friend who would borrow as freely from you if he thought of it
> or needed to   because there is a community of artists   who don't
> recognize copyrights and patents   or shouldnt   except under
> unusual circumstances   who send each other tools in the mail or
> exchange them in conversation in a bar

Kathy would metabolize these lessons, and soon, famously, make them her own. She didn't technically enroll in any of David's classes, but she did audit them, and, at one point, told Freilicher that she was "apprenticing" herself to him. UCSD was new and small, and in some cases, instructors were barely older than the students they were teaching. Relationships formed easily, and both Kathy and Freilicher quickly became close to the Antins. They babysat for Blaise, went to faculty parties at their house in Solana Beach. Later, David would bring conceptual artists like Lawrence Weiner, Joseph Kosuth, and Dan Graham, for shows or to make new work in San Diego. As Kathy had done with Sitney and the New York filmmakers, she soaked it all up.

In 1969, the Fluxus artist Alison Knowles brought her installation *The Big Book* to UCSD. *The Big Book* was an eight-foot-tall "book," constructed from vinyl, wood, and metal, with pages on casters depicting an apartment complete with a stove, telephone, toilet, art gallery, books, and "other necessities of life." Viewers could move the pages but also move around and between them. Kathy was delighted by this literalization of literature's unending promise, of life as a book and a book as life: "I thought *this* is what a book should be," she later said. "It's so many pages and in all these pages everything can take place. It's the open realm of possibilities."

Kathy became so devoted to David that, for a brief moment, Freilicher worried they were having an affair. They weren't. David only ever thought of her as a kid sister or, even, occasionally, a daughter. "Elly and I were both very fond of her," he said. "She was a very charming person, very lively. She was very interested in new experiences. She was looking for liberation." That seeking, David felt, stemmed from a kind of distress in her, a woundedness. Elly, for her part, found Kathy "childlike, cuddly and sweet." That was part of her appeal, she said, that "she really wanted you to love her."

× × ×

At some point in 1969, in one of David's classes, Kathy met another poet from New York, named Leonard Neufeld. Known as Lenny, the twenty-five-year-old Neufeld was born in the Bronx, and had also attended Brooklyn College, where he studied linguistics and met Antin and Jerome Rothenberg. Around the same time as the Antins, he and his wife, the artist Martha Rosler, and their young son, had moved out to San Diego, where Rosler did her MFA at UCSD and Neufeld pursued a PhD. Neufeld was rail-thin, with long, kinky hair and a somewhat effete effect—in many ways, Bob Acker's opposite. Freilicher didn't much like Neufeld—he thought he was passive-aggressive and manipulative—but Kathy was immediately drawn to him.

Neufeld was similarly infatuated. "She was very attractive," he said. "Physically, intellectually, very up and enthusiastic." Neufeld was hardly a faithful husband, and he and Rosler had split up and come back together a couple of times already. When an opportunity presented itself, a few weeks after he and Kathy first met, they slept together. Neufeld thought Kathy's interest in him stemmed largely from his proximity to David and Rothenberg, whom she didn't yet know but whose work in ethnopoetics—which argued that the true roots of modern, experimental poetry were in ancient and indigenous cultures—she found compelling. This may have been true—her affection for Neufeld was erratic from the outset. She had little interest in exchanging one dissatisfying romantic relationship for another. But Neufeld, like so many of her other lovers, was also a conduit to a subculture and community that she wanted to learn about and become part of.

By now, Kathy's own marriage was teetering on collapse, and the affair only accelerated things. "As she got closer to the Antins," Bob Acker remembered, "she and I went further apart. She was simply going places that I wasn't following at all." Acker was hardly surprised that Kathy and Neufeld had hooked up, and, in fact, considered it a blessing in disguise. He had become convinced that their situation was "poison," and, still suffering from the paranoia that made him marry her in the first place, he was increasingly nervous that she would somehow "go off the rails," from drugs, depression, or something else. Never mind that Kathy was never a big drug user, and then only pot, speed, and the occasional tab of acid.

Soon, Acker moved out, and Neufeld, more or less, moved in. Kathy and Acker separated, and, a couple years later, officially divorced. Neither regretted the decision. "If I thought about it at all," Acker remembered, "I guess I felt checkmated. I didn't know what course of action had any promise." He quickly moved on, eventually becoming an attorney and staying in touch with Kathy only intermittently. In the early seventies, he went to a reading of hers in downtown Manhattan, and left after twenty minutes. When she sent him copies of her Black Tarantula books, he never bothered to respond. In an interview she gave a year or so before she died, Kathy referred to her first husband only as an "idiot." She kept his last name, however, for the rest of her life.

"Looking back on those days," Acker said, "the only surprising thing was that she and I had gotten together in the first place. When the suburban San Diego marriage broke up, she went back to New York and resumed her natural bent."

CHAPTER 10

———————— × ————————

B Y THE SPRING OF 1970, KATHY ACKER WAS TWENTY-THREE,* AND she had more or less lost interest in academia. "Dead men I don't want to be dead that way write a thesis on the Aristotelian 'e' flattery and pretending I'm whoever Prof. Garble wants me to be," she wrote. She was, however, much more serious about her poetry. All she wanted to do was write. She wanted to be surrounded by fellow writers, wanted to be taken seriously, and wanted to make serious, important work, even if she wasn't exactly sure what shape that work should take. While her relationships with the Antins, Freilicher, and Weinstein were rich and helpful, San Diego itself had started to feel too provincial and isolated. Neufeld, for his part, was floundering a bit, unable to settle on a dissertation topic, uncertain what direction his career should go in.

But he still had an apartment back in Manhattan. The rent wasn't bad—a hundred bucks a month—and, more importantly, it was a floor above the apartment that the poet Jerome Rothenberg lived in with his wife, Diane. Maybe they should move back home? To Kathy, of course, home had never signified safety, success, or comfort, but this would be different—it would be the first time living in the city without her family. It would be the first time living in the city as a practicing poet. Even if she wasn't completely sure about Neufeld, or didn't know what either of them would do for money, it seemed like the right way to go. They packed their bags.

The apartment was at 600 West 163rd Street, at Broadway just south of Washington Heights. It was a big place on the sixth floor, with five rooms that, soon after they moved in, they repainted bordello colors: the main bedroom a coral orange with large violet stars, the living room a deep crimson. They liberated some mismatched furniture from a friend's basement, filled the apartment with books.

---

* Given Bob Acker's almost complete absence from the remainder of this book, "Acker" refers to Kathy Acker here and hereafter.

The New York City that they returned to, especially compared to slow, placid Southern California, was a forbidding interzone, at once wild and filthy, depopulated yet loud. The city was nearing bankruptcy, and, as with other big American cities, increasing numbers of middle-class residents were fleeing to the suburbs in search of employment. Danger seemed to be everywhere: on the subway, in the parks, on your fire escape, inside your apartment. Between 1966 and 1971, the number of reported robberies almost tripled. In 1972, almost 1,700 New Yorkers were murdered—four times the number that had been killed less than a decade previously. The political unrest that continued to engulf the country was also, of course, present in the country's largest city: just a couple months earlier, a nail bomb in a Greenwich Village townhouse had exploded, killing three bomb makers, all members of the Weather Underground. For Acker, the city's chaos mirrored the uncertainty of her own life. "Days and days of anxiety each day," she wrote in a notebook from the period. "I hear only accounts of the collapse of the city through breaking pipes graft viciousness."

But New York was also, famously, in the midst of unprecedented artistic ferment. Manufacturing had collapsed and real estate had flatlined, but that also meant it was impossibly cheap to live there. "One could live an interesting existence on four hundred dollars a month," said the artist Duncan Hannah, who moved to the city in 1973 and would become a casual friend of Acker's a few years later. Budding painters, dancers, playwrights, musicians, filmmakers—especially avant-garde aspirants with little to lose and far more to gain—arrived in droves. The cultural world, or at least the one that mattered to Acker, was small but concentrated, intimate, and, above all, accessible. Warhol reigned. The Velvet Underground played their last shows at Max's Kansas City in 1970, and, in their wake, rock music took on new, unexpected forms: there was Patti Smith, the New York Dolls, Iggy Pop, Television, to name just the most famous. And not just rock—over the next handful of years, New York was the epicenter of loft jazz, classical minimalism, hip-hop, disco, salsa. Just a couple years prior, Ellen Willis had become the *New Yorker*'s first pop music writer, and in 1970, her cofounder of the radical feminist group Redstockings, Shulamith Firestone, published the groundbreaking *The Dialectic of Sex*. Kate Millett released *Sexual Politics*. That same year, Film Forum and Anthology Film Archives—run by P. Adams Sitney—both opened. The Stonewall riots a year earlier spawned a gay liberation movement. In SoHo, George Maciunas formed the first artists' co-ops.

Six years after Sitney had introduced her to some of these worlds, Acker took tentative steps back into them. She took dance classes with Meredith Monk, gobbled up Maya Deren movies. She and Neufeld got a pair of cats, Paul and Elizabeth, which she doted on. She went through a macrobiotic phase, and they sometimes ate at Paradox, on the Lower East Side, where you could get a bowl of rice and vegetables for a dollar. But mostly, Acker holed up in the apartment, writing, reading (among others during this period: Virginia Woolf, Henry Miller, Colette, Anaïs Nin, Burroughs, Paul Bowles, Joe Brainard), sleeping, and having sex with Neufeld.

Acker had been a relatively impoverished student in San Diego, but in New York, things immediately felt more financially desperate. She didn't want to depend on Neufeld, nor could she anyway—on top of the rent they split, Neufeld was paying $100 a month in child support and another $20 a month to a divorce lawyer. He was broke too. But Acker had never really held a nine-to-five job, and she wasn't about to start now, no matter how difficult things were. "... a job to me means adjustment the acceptance into the real reality I'm one of the unfits ...," she wrote in a notebook. This was at once admirable and adolescent. On one level, Acker had an undeniable sense of entitlement, and the privilege of someone who, up to that point, had never needed to work. On another, more interesting, level, she also possessed a persistent contempt for the conformity of the workaday world and an already unshakeable devotion to her art. A job was subservience and self-annihilation. Writing was work, to be sure, but it wasn't labor, it was thinking, play, make-believe, magic. Eventually, in terms of "straight" jobs, she would pick up part-time secretarial work and model for art classes, but she would never take anything that really disrupted the writing life she was trying to build—one that, for all of its precarity and uncertainty, provided at least a satisfying degree of autonomy. "I've spent the last four years of my life deciding the way in which I get money by refusing to do anything that would not let me over-sleep," she wrote, deadpan.

Neufeld didn't want to work either, or even really write that much; at twenty-seven, his greatest enthusiasm was reserved for sex. The libidinous freedom that Neufeld and Acker had granted each other in San Diego continued in Manhattan, and they both took advantage of it, though Neufeld far more frequently, and with far less anxious ardor. While Acker would have flings with various men and women and insisted on at least her *right* to promiscuity ("I must at all times have the same freedom a man would have," she wrote), sex had started to become extremely painful for her. Within weeks of arriving in New York, she was diagnosed with pelvic inflammatory disease (PID), a chronic infection of the reproductive system that's often a complication of chlamydia and gonorrhea. She sometimes dulled the pain with synthetic opium and Nembutal (medication that required yet more money), but the infection would persist for several years. "I was very sick," she later wrote a friend. "I had almost died." In a manuscript titled *Poems 5/71–6/71*, a single paragraph summarizes both her horrific health problems and the grim care she received (or didn't receive):

> I'm hemorraghing again today a week now Lenny fucked me last night I might have had a cyst that broke some doctor's talking about a health plan based on a desire for life and for the saving of life which no one in this country's going to want my right side now hurts around the ovary and I've almost fainted three times today in the last year every organ in my abdomen has been infected I had been told to take ampicillin by a richy doctor and fucked my intestines up a month ago started taking birth control pills again I immediately got a breast infection only nursing mothers are supposed to get then the hemorraghing the so-called doctor says no reason to stop taking the pills Lenny calls up why don't you call a doctor so I can get fucked up some more: stories about the death of the poor

When Acker reached out to Claire for help, financial or otherwise, she claimed that Claire rebuffed her every time. In a notebook, Acker writes that she called one day, convinced she was dying, and Claire told her that "the city will pay for your grave."

Neufeld's affairs could sometimes be agonizing to Acker, but she was more worried, it seemed, about her own ambivalent feelings toward him. Did she really love him, or was she just using him? Acker was terrified of becoming like Claire, trapped by economic necessity in a loveless relationship, and made crueler and more hostile for it. At some point, and to Neufeld's displeasure, she cut her hair into the quasi buzz-cut she would keep (with obsessive stylistic variation) for the rest of her life. It was obviously a small way to assert some agency over her own body and appearance and a denial of feminine beauty standards of the day. But ironically—or intentionally?—the style made her look even more like her mother. At the same time, Acker fretted, in frequent bouts of self-loathing, about Neufeld's feelings for *her*. On page 64 of one of her notebooks (undated but likely from 1971), she wrote the sentence "do you love me" eight times over.

It was a question she asked of many people in her life. Contact with her family remained infrequent and frustrating. According to Acker, they refused to give her money to pay for her medication ("they pissed on me when I was sick"). When Bud had a heart attack, Claire told Acker that she had caused it. ". . . I'm going to deal with them by not dealing with them," she wrote, "there are no more parents . . ." Nana, for her part, wasn't in Acker's good books either, demanding a certain supplication: ". . . my goddamn grandmother just sent me a valentine's card saying call me I should lick her ass . . ."

She turned instead to the Rothenbergs, looking, it seemed, for them to fill the parental role the Antins had. Well, at least Jerry. Diane, an anthropologist and writer herself, had little patience for Acker, who she remembered as "extremely self-absorbed and vain." But Jerry thought she was bright, adventurous, and attractive. He hired her and Neufeld to copyedit his anthology of Native American prose, *Shaking the Pumpkin*, and to serve as model/actors for his artist's book, *Esther K. Comes to America (1931)*. Occasionally, Acker and Neufeld would babysit the Rothenbergs' young son, Matthew. They hung out with the couple's more interesting friends, poets like Jackson Mac Low and Diane Wakoski. The Rothenbergs were about fifteen years older than Acker, and, like the Antins, showed how a couple might make a rich and creative life together.

Despite the age difference, Acker often felt attracted to Jerry, even confiding in her notebooks that she was actually in love with and wanted to sleep with him. Though more often, she recognized him as a mentor and, unwilling to upset his marriage, stifled her desire. In one of her notebooks, *Diary 1*, she writes, "I don't know how to put down my feelings about Jerry very upset since I speak to few people none as fully as him though that's not fully at the point when I could go closer to someone I feel abstracted scared? I feel like I've been to bed with Jerry it's stupid to pretend that's fantasy because it's literal truth (though not now)." After the Rothenbergs left New York for San Diego in January 1971, Acker sent these pages to Jerry, with an accompanying letter that contained a half-hearted apology—"please excuse the personal stuff I should have talked about it to you before this but I didn't know of course I have no intention of publishing or publicizing any of this that could hurt anyone without full permission etc.? do I have such?" There was also a hint of her growing ambition—in the same letter, she asked if she could use his name as a reference if she submitted the work to the Dial Press.

Jerry also brought Acker to the Poetry Project at St. Mark's Church-in-the-Bowery at East 10th and Second Avenue. The Poetry Project, cofounded by the poet and translator Paul Blackburn, was arguably the most significant forum for American poetry in the twentieth century. St. Mark's Church had a long history of social activism and support for the arts. Throughout the 1960s, it was home to free jazz concerts, screenings of banned underground films, and experimental theater workshops. Blackburn read solo at the Project's first official event on September 22, 1966; a month later, Lawrence Ferlinghetti read to an audience of twelve hundred people, with five hundred turned away at the door. The community that gathered at the Project was fractious, incestuous, and eclectic, comprising loose- and tight-knit gangs of poets that would later be labeled Beats, New York School, Deep Image, Black Mountain. At the time, regular participants and audience members comprised a pantheon of innovative American poets: Rothenberg, Diane Wakoski, Robert Creeley, Ted Berrigan, Alice Notley, John Ashbery, Anne Waldman, Charles Bernstein, and Ron Padgett. The Project dissolved the oft-mundane concept of the poetry reading, staging day-long, celebrity-studded marathon events and multimedia bacchanalias like the one John Giorno hosted in 1969, complete with fog and light machines, music, acid-spiked punch, and hundreds of joints. "The Poetry Project burns like red hot coal in New York's snow," Ginsberg said.

In Acker's early writing life, it provided a similar heat, as well as regular inspiration and solidarity. It was a place where she developed the early style that characterizes her first published works, where she experimented with and cultivated different voices and registers, where she finally, openly, declared herself a poet in front of people other than her friends and lovers: "by reading these poems relations of emotions publicly I assert their worth my blood the way in which I live reading them publicly is the complement to this private writing down and is a complete act . . ."

× × ×

Sometime in the late 1960s, though probably even earlier, Acker began to keep regular, voluminous notebooks, the contents of which provide the most detailed, sustained account of her early adulthood and first attempts at becoming, if not yet a professional writer, then a serious one. Acker often refers to these notebooks as "diaries," but the word isn't quite apt or sufficient and, indeed, on the cover of at least one notebook, the "title" *Diary* is struck out and replaced with the word *Poems*, a putatively more capacious category. "Logs" might be a better term too, cataloguing as they do the steady formation of Acker's sensibility as a writer.

In lined, spiral-bound notebooks of various sizes, in handwriting that is loopy and almost childlike, Acker chronicles the ups and downs of her relationship with Neufeld, other sexual affairs, her half-hearted attempts at employment, gossip about writers, her own fragile mental and physical state, her dreams, her cats, books she's reading, her thoughts on writing, compositional methods, memory, and representation. Even when broke, she usually used, as she would for the rest of her life, a Montblanc fountain pen. For the most part, these entries are rapid, raw, and intimate, a punctuation-free stream of consciousness, where one event or thought suddenly gives way to another, and subjects and subjectivities shift without warning or signpost. Seemingly factual events butt up against, or run headlong into, fantasy and dream. As in her later writing, friends, lovers, and colleagues appear frequently, their names unchanged.

It was as if, now definitively and publicly identifying herself as a writer, Acker was either permitting or forcing herself to keep her eyes and hands moving, to keep writing and writing and writing, to get *everything* down—or out. Did she have a choice? Her consciousness was less stream than geyser or cataract. The scholar Claire Finch describes the notebook entries as "a succession of gasps."

Most diaries are pocked with performance, half-truths, and the misdirection of memory, but Acker's notebooks are this and something more—early experiments in the juxtapositions and collage of her later fictions. Acker spelled out her method, to a certain degree, in a 1971 notebook titled *DIARY DREAMS II*:

> I want also to be able to put down on the spot how I experience each event even these words make it seem like there's an inside experiencing mechanism and an outside event because I constantly change lie forget the lie was a lie invent on top of that I want a record of the way in which I remember and distort or refind experience through time

though that's my private shit since my life can't be this fascinating to
anyone else something pleases me about putting trivial incidents down
as they happen one by one I don't know what I don't care if I remember
properly in fact I remember none of my pre-school childhood . . .

In another instance, she wrote "this diary is about the destruction of myself
and everyone else I know as the destruction is taking place from day-to-day."
A few years later, on the cover of another notebook, she scribbled, "I'm not
sure what I'm doing. A messy sloppy account & diary. I try to figure out what I
know." In a letter to the artist Alan Sondheim, she describes the notebooks as
"my attempt to map at that time my total prsent [sic] consciousness . . ."

The notebooks were a place to process the tumult of everyday life, but also
a kind of laboratory—how could she turn this tumult into writing, into art?
She was just beginning to explore how, and why, a self is constructed on the
page, and what at first seem to be pages of immediate, confessional musing are
in fact a fragmentary, emotionally excessive blend of reportage, dreams, fiction,
and memoir. "Fantasy, sensorial perception, dream mixed," she wrote.

Soon, she would take chunks of these diaries, some short, some long, rewrite them explicitly as poems, and type them up. Like other female poets
of the time—Bernadette Mayer, Anne Waldman, and Alice Notley—all of
whom she would soon meet at St. Mark's, she was taking the conversational,
quotidian qualities of New York School poetry and giving them an eroticism
and sense of duration and perception that were subversive and unabashedly
feminine.

Acker also gave this formal slipperiness a kind of ontological weight, for
the reader of the notebooks the effect can sometimes be simple confusion.
Where does reality begin and fantasy end? What makes a dream different from
a memory? How does memory produce a self? What is a fact? What is truth?
These are questions she would repeatedly ask in her later fiction and, indeed,
the errant, indeterminate nature of the events she describes in her notebooks
confirms what Acker later argues in her novels: that language is inadequate and
truth irreducibly complex and unstable. Binary divisions between fantasy and
reality, dream and memory, she maintains, are false, simplistic, and unproduc-
tive; all these different things inexorably fold in on each other.

For the biographer, though, it means regarding these notebooks, to a certain extent, as enclosed in quotation marks. It means relying on these entries

as evidence—of actual events, of Acker's thoughts, desires, and beliefs—only up to a point, and a point that is in constant motion. At the same time, the fact that Acker fills these pages with such banal incidents, and that her observations usually appear deeply personal, suggests that reading these pages as an approximate factual representation is not unwarranted. The young woman that emerges is herself in flux, and appears, by turns and at once, petulant, defiant, earnest, seething, self-sabotaging, fearful, isolated, longing. From time to time, and especially when discussing her cats or her writing, there are eruptions of elation, even ecstasy. She feels too much, doesn't feel enough. She has a difficult time meeting people, she hates people. She loves her body, hates her body. She loves New York, hates New York. In one moment, she is completely convinced of the value of her writing; the next, it's worthless. She craves authenticity while struggling to define what that even means.

Above all, she is constantly questioning—what she thinks, what she does, what she writes and feels and remembers and desires. Even as the entries can feel hurried and harried, for Acker, writing seems to be a way to slow down her pain, to snatch at and examine it.

There are countless moments in the notebooks that are impossible to authenticate, but many others that, when pressed, release a compelling essence of veracity. In one vivid example, Acker recalls Freilicher and his girlfriend at the time, Wilma Korevaar, visiting New York just before Labor Day of 1971. The two young couples get drunk, ride bikes to Central Park, gossip. It's a welcome visit, but in her notebook, Acker complains about Freilicher being "in his usual depressed and ambivalent state," and then, worse, trying to cajole her and Neufeld into having sex with him and his girlfriend. In her account, Acker bails on the orgy but then, trembling and upset, listens as the three of them have sex in the next room. Decades later, both Neufeld and Freilicher remembered a much different scene. Neufeld claimed that he was never attracted to Freilicher and nothing sexual ever happened between them. Freilicher, for his part, recalled Neufeld nefariously luring everyone, Acker included, onto their waterbed, where they removed their clothes and then, before anything really happened, quickly put them back on. Freilicher distinctly remembers Acker's violent trembling. Korevaar doesn't remember Acker being there at all.

In any case, Acker wrote incessantly, filling notebook after notebook throughout 1970 and beyond, later typing up extracts that she called poems. She wrote so much that a tenant on the floor below complained about the incessant clatter of her typewriter. Writing was pleasure, possibility, perversion; she was devoted to it, obsessed with it, addicted to it—"this writing is getting to be like junk I'm going crazy doing it want more." When she wanted to show Freilicher just how much writing meant to her, she drew a circle and said, "*This* is the area of freedom—writing." Then she'd point outside the circle and say, "*This* is the world." (She made similar claims in other places, including in her novel *I Dreamt I Was a Nymphomaniac!: Imagining*: "This is the realm of complete freedom: I can put down anything.") But in the pages of these notebooks, "writing" and "the world" form something more like a Venn diagram—the two overlap, creating something altogether new. Writing, for her, was alchemical, the freedom to rearrange and reimagine the world. Even decades later, in a letter to the film theorist Peter Wollen, another writer and friend, she still held on to her belief in the transformative liberation of writing: "... it's only one fucking life one life to do everything to do everything to the hilt. I am stupidly romantic, and writing is one way, no possibility left of hiding lying keeping shut. I don't like being in pain, but I'll take pain any day over prison. Every day what writing for me is my fight against the prison..."

CHAPTER 11

———— X ————

B RANDEIS, BOB ACKER, AND SAN DIEGO HAD ALLOWED ACKER TO
ostensibly shed much of her Sutton Place background. Coming back to
New York with Neufeld let her break, for the most part, the new bonds—
marriage, the academy—that she'd acquired out in the world. She wanted to
go even further. As she put in *Rip-off Red, Girl Detective*, the novel she'd start
working on a couple years later, she was ready to descend "to the more interesting depths."

About five months after they had been back, Neufeld came across an ad
in the *Village Voice*, placed by Robert Wolfe Studios, which was looking for
actors for pornographic films. Throughout the sixties and seventies, Robert
Wolfe, more commonly known as Bob Wolfe, produced thousands of silent,
B&W 8mm film loops, so-called fuck films that were shown in peep show
booths. The peeps themselves were an innovation pioneered by Wolfe's boss
Marty Hodas, a vending machine operator who had the idea in 1966 to outfit
old coin-operated movie machines with loops that showed the kind of fron-
tal nudity then commercially unavailable in New York. He then distributed
the machines to the rapidly proliferating adult bookstores in Times Square.
With Wolfe, Hodas became a zealous producer and distributor of such films
himself—he was called "King of the Peeps" or "Lord of the Loops"—and he
began buying up leases on storefronts up and down 42nd Street and Eight Avenue, converting former camera shops and pinball arcades into porn bookstores
and peeps. The King of the Peeps was also a loathsome human being—sexist,
temperamental, violent. He beat his wife and children so badly that the family
dog pissed the floor every time he came into the house. Bankrolled allegedly
by the mob, which he consistently denied, Hodas also soon came to own several profitable movie theaters in the Deuce, whose screens he quickly dedicated to hardcore porn. While Wolfe worked with future stars of the industry
like Linda Lovelace, his actors were mostly amateurs: young, attractive, horny
hippies out to make a quick buck, usually $75 to $100 a film.

Neufeld was intrigued by the possibility—"It felt adventurous and exciting and a way to have more sex," he recalled. So was Acker. To her, porn could be performance, material, and experience, all of which would feed her writing. They soon headed down to Wolfe's 14th Street basement studio, which turned out to be a cramped, fetid place furnished only with a stained bed. The films were made mostly at Wolfe's place, but on at least one occasion, Acker and Neufeld shot films for another producer in their own apartment. At the latter, another pal of Rothenberg's, a baby-faced photographer from Long Island named Larry Fink, dropped by to take some pictures. He was a few years older than Neufeld, a disciple of Lisette Model's and a colleague of Diane Arbus and Garry Winogrand. While later better known as a society photographer, he'd also have one-man shows of his photojournalistic work at the MoMA and the Whitney. Fink was both attracted and repulsed by the whole scene, and found Acker, in particular, a puzzle: "My interpretation was that she couldn't feel real emotions," he said. "She was so droll and blasé that to me the only way she could feel was to abject herself." Fink would later shoot the stills for Rothenberg's *Esther K.* book and Neufeld got Fink to shoot him and Acker for the cover of his own 1972 poetry book *Theory*. In that black-and-white image, they look almost like a gender-reversed John Lennon and Yoko Ono—Acker stands in the foreground, her hair cropped, wearing Lennon-like granny glasses and a see-through white shift while Neufeld, his long dark curls framing his face, peeks shyly over her shoulder. "Everybody had a little *vie bohème*," Rothenberg recalled, "but theirs was a special version of that."

The couple's porn career didn't last long. Neufeld turned out to be more self-conscious than he'd expected; he often had trouble performing. And for Acker, what was at first a lark soon became something more parlous. "Kathy was always kvetching," remembered Diane Rothenberg, "complaining how imposed on she was because she had to participate in these sexual things. I remember her telling me she went to an audition at a producer's office without Lenny. And you know how a producer sometimes comes on to an aspiring actress and sometimes the actress runs out of the room? Kathy didn't run out of the room." Neufeld's memory of the incident is somewhat different—he said that Acker showed up alone to a shoot where there was no one but a cameraman and that the cameraman told her he was going to have sex with her and film it. While Neufeld maintained that Acker simply didn't appreciate this "being sprung upon her," and was hesitant to say that she was raped, or even forced into the act, Acker detailed a similar scene in her 1982 novel, *Great Expectations*, which strongly suggests that she was. Toward the end of that book, an Acker alter ego answers a want ad and travels to a West Village basement apartment, where a photographer sexually assaults her. "While the big man was shoving himself into her," Acker writes, "the girl lay as stiff as a log and wouldn't allow herself to feel any pleasure because this was the main way her fear would allow her to express anger."

In Acker's notebooks, her disgust for the experience, for the whole porn-making endeavor, in fact, quickly becomes apparent. She writes often of her "hatred of men." She starts having nightmares. She thought she was being followed or stalked. Finally, she just stopped going to the studio.*

But sex work was still nonetheless preferable to any number of mind-numbing straight jobs. That December, when Hodas offered Acker and Neufeld the opportunity to perform in a live sex show at Fun City, a magazine shop and theater on 42nd Street, they took it.† They usually did at least six half-hour shows per shift, though they were expected to be on call at the theater for up to fourteen hours. Acker was paid $20 a show. It was more than enough to pay their rent and, more importantly, it gave her the whole week to write.‡ The theater seated about a hundred men; the audience was always men, and often tourists, each paying $10 to $15 a ticket. The sex was simulated, and Neufeld and Acker devised scenarios and characters around the phony fucking: Neufeld might play Santa Claus and Acker an excited young girl on Christmas morning, or he a therapist and she his randy patient. "It was my only venture into playwriting," Neufeld said. Their "set" was a lone chair and a wobbly single bed, covered with

---

* None of the loops seem to have survived, but a half-dozen years after they were made, the poet Ron Silliman stumbled across one of the films in a San Francisco porn shop. The thing he remembered most about it was a scene in which Acker is flogged—with lettuce leaves. Acker later claimed, half-jokingly, that this was her first experience with S/M.

† That's the name that Acker used or remembered, though the actual name may have actually been the Avon 42nd Street or the Fake; no one really remembers. In a notebook, Acker writes that the theater was the only theater in New York to offer a live sex show, and in his *Tales of Times Square*, Josh Alan Friedman reports that the first to do so was the less felicitously named Mine-Cine. By which he's probably referring to the Mini Cinema on Seventh Avenue and West 48th Street.

‡ In a March 1976 interview Acker gave to *Only Paper Today*, the Toronto art magazine, she said she performed six days a week, but entries in her notebook—"I'm working in a live sex show for bread it gives me six days of leisure"—contradict this.

a filthy green blanket. Acker often forgot her lines and, with the shows considered on the edge of legality, was constantly afraid of being busted by the cops. Occasionally, to fill time, she would do solo stripteases, listlessly pretending to masturbate or simply opening her legs so audiences could ogle her.

Acker was of two (maybe more) minds about the work and often threatened to quit. She described the job in a notebook as "the lowest way to make the basic bread," but also later told an interviewer that she was "into it," adding that "I don't draw hard categories you know." A few years later, in *The Childlike Life of the Black Tarantula*, she returns to these days, in a molten account that flickers between the comic and the contemptuous, horror and hilarity, capturing her overall ambivalence about the job before arriving at its dagger-like final sentence:

In one of the acts in my sex show I become a young woman who is talking to a psychiatrist. I tell the psychiatrist how Santa Claus fell out of the chimney told me I should always be a good girl I talk baby talk I should always do what he tells me I slowly start taking off my blouse and rubbing my right hand over my right breast, I have to believe in Santa Claus. Suddenly, as I'm about to kiss my nipple, I stop; I see hundreds of men watching me. I've delusions: men follow me, men want to hurt me, men want to have sexual activities with me without my consent and desire to. The psychiatrist laughs at me. The men who are watching me as I writhe around on the bed start talking to me I joke back with them. The psychiatrist tells me I've hearing delusions; I cut off my hair; I'm Joan of Arc. I lead soldiers in drag and kill everyone. I become hot: I rip off my clothes, I begin to masturbate men make me ooo soo hot. The psychiatrist fucks me we both come five million times. OOOO O yes yes that's it no no? o please o yes o please o come on faster. . . . faster give it to me now NOW ooo (low) ooo (higher) oooo oooo oah auahhh oahh. eha. (down again). All my diseases are gone.

Around this time, Acker ran into P. Adams Sitney on Broadway. He was now teaching at NYU's new cinema studies department. While Acker referred to him in a notebook as a "goddamn woman-hating fucker," she found herself still attracted to him. Sitney was somewhat surprised to find she was now enthralled with the writers he'd introduced to her as a teenager, but also appalled that she was eager to become part of the New York art scene, which he more or less reviled. She later called him and had him meet her at the apartment. Neufeld was there, but he soon left, and she and Sitney had sex. To Sitney's surprise, however, Neufeld returned shortly after and was eager to join them; Sitney reluctantly agreed. Later, he went to see them both at Fun City, a spectacle he found degrading and pathetic. "The drama was awful," Sitney said, "the acting phony."

x x x

There was other, more compelling, drama backstage, that Acker was faithfully capturing in her notebooks. In the dressing room, and on breaks when she would grab a table at nearby Tad's steak house or a greasy spoon called Embers, Acker filled page after page with scenes, observations, and dialogue taken from the days and nights at Fun City. Much of this was inspired by her fellow performers, whose lives were more difficult than her own, tawdry and titillating psychodramas replete with hard drugs, crime, and sour romance. One of these performers was a future porn star named Marc Stevens, nicknamed "10½," and later photographed by Robert Mapplethorpe.* She often hung out with him and his boyfriend, Mickey, the couple's frequent spats a regular source of material. She later claimed that Warhol superstar Joe Dallesandro was friends with the guy who cleaned the Fun City peep booths, and that she and her fellow performers were all basically waiting for Warhol to discover them. "We weren't entirely joking," she wrote, "but we were hoping."

Acker had also then discovered the pioneering writing experiments—the cut-up, the fold-in—that William Burroughs and Brion Gysin published in the *Evergreen Review*.† "All writing is in fact cut-ups," Burroughs and Gysin wrote. "A collage of words read heard overheard. What else? Use of scissors renders the process explicit and subject to extension and variation." Following their lead, Acker took the stories she heard at Fun City and collaged them with her own diary and dream material, sometimes transposing these stories to first

---

* Acker usually misspells his name as "Mark," and he was occasionally credited as such in later films he made.

† Acker often credited Burroughs and Gysin's *The Third Mind*, which collects these experiments in one book, with influencing her early writing. She, in fact, considered *The Third Mind* Burroughs's most important book. It wasn't published, however, until 1978, long after she'd started publishing.

person. The result, not unlike her notebooks, was jagged, breathless, largely free of punctuation, with Acker shifting swiftly and deliberately from subject to subject, image to image. "I really love doing cut up like destroying everything and making music of it," she later told Bernadette Mayer.

For Burroughs, the cut-up and fold-in were means to reveal the codes that construct the world, to, as he famously wrote in *Nova Express*, "storm the reality studio" and "retake the universe." For Acker, they were ways to think against every repression, to overturn the worlds, and words, of parents, gender, the academy, authorship itself. They could subvert the strictures of identity. They could anatomize sexual power. If Burroughs was a satirist, Acker was a kind of metafabulist.

Acker loathed the theater on 42nd Street and the men who ran it ("the shits," she called them), but the work and the environment provided what she, retrospectively at least, considered a productive and profitable radicalization. While she was certainly no naïf, up until that point she had been a more or less "good" middle-class girl. Now, suddenly, she was not just part of the working class, but a sex worker, surrounded by other sex workers. It was akin, perhaps, to Simone Weil going to the factories. She acquired a new, deeper understanding of capitalism and feminism. Stripped of her own class privilege, so to speak, she was now confronting, every week, the violence of male privilege and the male gaze. If she had only ever been a casual observer of the protests that roiled the campuses at Brandeis and UCSD, here she was fully *engagée* in the sexual revolution, literally putting her body on the line. "In my life politics don't disappear but take place in my body," she would write a few years later in *Blood and Guts in High School*. In several later interviews, Acker would credit this period in her life with utterly transforming her perception of power in the world:

> It changed my politics . . . the 42nd Street experience made me learn about street politics. It's not that I was that interested in sex. It more gave me a viewpoint of whatever goes on in actuality through the kind of sexual perspective. I think Genet has the same perspective. You see people from the bottom up, and sexual behavior, especially sex minus relationship—which is what happens in 42nd Street—is definitely bottom. Then you see it in a different way, especially power relationships in society. And I think that perspective never left me.

This perspective was complex, however. At the same time, she told Sitney, with pride and glee, that she had become a "whore." When not working, she favored short skirts and, occasionally, transparent dresses with nothing underneath. While she was learning up close how sex could be central to female oppression, how it served as a tool of control, she was also taking pleasure in exhibitionism and performance, and in the idea—as staged and debased as it was in this context—that desire could, potentially, be a site of resistance. The tricky, maybe impossible, reconciliation of these things would preoccupy her future writing.

In a sense, Acker was slumming. Many years later, those months in the sex industry would continue to establish her bona fides, and remind readers that, no matter how close she skirted to the literary mainstream, once upon a time, she was an up-from-the-streets wild child.

In March 1971, as Acker had feared, the vice squad raided the theater. Acker and Neufeld were arrested for public lewdness. They spent a night in jail, with her bosses finally bailing them out. Acker and Neufeld eventually had to appear in court multiple times, and in her notebooks, Acker bristles with equal contempt for Hodas, the lawyers, and the cops, conjuring a conspiracy of profit in which the only losers were her and her fellow workers: "it's the ass-hole [sic] of the shittiest bureaucracy that will exist we're the ones who sit in the court became criminals if who don't show up for 12 hours each month if we don't take whatever shit anyone decides to hand out . . ." Acker would later glamorize criminals and lawlessness in her fiction, but the real-life hoodlums that she worked for were, she knew, hardly romantic figures. As she wrote at the time, "I admire criminals in my head knowing they're shits businessmen motherfuckers like everyone else."

CHAPTER 12

———————— ✕ ————————

A MONTH BEFORE THE BUST, ON FEBRUARY 10, ACKER AND NEUFELD went to the Poetry Project to see Patti Smith and Gerard Malanga read. Ever since high school, when she first saw his poetry at the Gotham Book Mart, Acker had idolized Malanga (and fantasized about sleeping with him). She had never heard of Smith. Not many people had. But just a few months older than Acker, she'd already established herself as a rock critic and an emerging, electrifying poet, and was an intimate of two other soon-to-be-titanic cultural figures, Robert Mapplethorpe and Sam Shepard.

For Smith's very first public reading, Mapplethorpe had convinced Malanga to let her open for him at St. Mark's, and Smith exploited the opportunity as fully as she could. She tapped an acquaintance at the Chelsea Hotel named Lenny Kaye to punctuate her reading with bursts of electric guitar, the first time the instrument had ever been played in the church. She wanted to perform her poetry, she said, the way she had learned from Jim Morrison and Jimi Hendrix. February 10 was Bertolt Brecht's birthday, and she opened her performance with a rendition of "Mack the Knife," while also dedicating the reading to "criminals from Cain to Genet." She read from poems like "Oath," whose opening lyric, "Christ died for somebody's sins/But not mine," would also serve as the opening lines, more or less, of "Gloria," the first track on *Horses*, her debut album four years later. Poets John Giorno and Joe Brainard were in the audience, and, thanks to Malanga, the church was packed with Factory folks: Lou Reed, Rene Ricard, Brigid Berlin, Warhol himself.

For Acker, who'd long dreamed of joining Warhol's world, it was an exhilarating evening. Smith mesmerized her. Lots of rock stars fancied themselves poets, but few poets tried to turn themselves into rock stars. And even rarer and more thrilling—a *female* poet, a *female* rock star. Smith was self-possessed, fierce, beyond androgynous. She reminded Acker of no one so much as herself, five years earlier, at Brandeis—or at least how she wanted to be and wanted to be seen. "She's gorgeous half male though she comes on very tough at the point of exploding into total femininity," Acker gushed in her notebook before, characteristically, turning on herself: "I really like her have no way of meeting her of course I won't I probably like this being all shut in myself safe in the 42nd half fantasy real underground god forbid I should actually talk to someone who also writes . . ."

Three months later, though, Acker would make her own Poetry Project debut, as part of an open mic reading on May 7. She had just turned twenty-four. It was her first public reading in New York. Acker read from her notebooks, and while her performance was considerably less theatrical than Smith's, she was thrilled by the enthusiastic response, especially from the women in the audience. In a letter to Jerome Rothenberg, she wrote that the night was ". . . very beautiful I feel all religious all these women were coming up to me afterward and saying your stuff was really great it really moved me so I'm feeling terrific . . ." She realized then that she was in fact largely writing *for* women, and hoping that they would feel, hearing or reading her words, the same connection to her work that she felt when she read certain female poets or saw movies made by women.

Women were a dominant force at the Poetry Project by then. Many of its earlier luminaries had achieved some mainstream success or moved to other parts of the country, but a younger generation was thriving at the church, largely influenced by the innovative work and thinking of poet Bernadette Mayer. Slim, radiant, beetle-browed, and irreverent, and just a couple years older than Acker, Mayer was considered a second-generation New York School poet, though her work was more overtly conceptual. In 1971, with Anne Waldman serving as the Poetry Project's director, Mayer began teaching weekly writing workshops that became renowned for the intellectual rigor she brought to them and the heterodox literary methods she espoused. Gathering as many as twenty poets at a time in the vestibule off the church's main sanctuary, she encouraged her students to read widely: everything from *Curious George* to Ludwig Wittgenstein. With the students, she devised a playful, generative catalogue of writing games, exercises, and prompts, such as "Write a soothing novel in twelve short paragraphs," or "Write as you think, as close as you can come to this, that is, put pen to paper and don't stop. Experiment writing fast and writing slow," or "Rewrite someone else's writing. Experiment with theft and plagiarism." She recommended workshop participants keep a variety of journals: of their dreams, food they ate, tenant-landlord situations, skies they saw, times of solitude.

While Acker never actually participated in these workshops herself, she was aware of their lessons, some of which resembled things David Antin had taught her. She already wrote as she thought, or as close as she could come. She already stole stories and images from other books and people. But she admired Mayer from afar, enchanted by her beauty and intellect. The two women, it turned out, shared a number of affinities. Like Acker, Mayer had endured a difficult childhood and had studied Greek and Latin. Like Acker, she had strong ties to the conceptual art world—from 1967 to 1969, she co-edited a magazine of avant-garde writing with performance and video artist Vito Acconci (who was also married to Mayer's sister, the celebrated artist Rosemary Mayer), and Mayer's first major work, *Memory*, which she began in the summer of 1971, was a hybrid piece that combined photography and recorded narration. Mayer ignored the confines of genre and published everything from sonnet sequences and short stories to translations of Catullus and guides to science writing. Even within single works, she oscillated between poetry and prose, and she peopled her writing with both real-life figures and literary characters. Much of her work is a relentless interrogation of gender, interpretation, narrative, and authority. She revered Gertrude Stein. She experimented with the epistolary. She was a devotee of the stapled, mimeographed literary magazine, enthralled with its speed, immediacy, and democratic production. Ultimately, she offered a liberating literary model for Acker, and even if Acker later rarely mentioned Mayer as an influence, at least publicly, that influence was undeniable.

Though Acker referred to Mayer in a notebook as "a standoffish person," in December 1971, she also wrote, in a notebook dedicated to "GERTRUDE STEIN & ALL LESBIANS" (and subtitled "DIARY TO FIND OUT WHAT'S HAPPENING"), that Mayer's work "touches reality" and made her question her own. Later that month Acker gave Mayer one of her notebooks to read but almost immediately regretted it: "she probably won't like it and I was wrong to do that I didn't know how else to get to her." More than forty years later, Mayer didn't remember reading that particular notebook or having that particular encounter, but she did recall Acker as a "lively, vivid presence." The two women eventually became friends and later, for a brief moment, roommates.

After that first open mic reading, Acker was at the church at least a couple days a week. She continued to read from her notebooks, and while the work had obvious kinship with Mayer's and Waldman's, which also involved collaging her diary writing with snatches of overheard found "verse" from the streets and the radio, Acker's writing was more aggressive and bluntly sexual. All three were obsessed with accurately and unapologetically representing feminine experience, but Acker went the furthest in complicating what was considered feminine. Even then, there was tension in the persona she projected in her writing: it was vulnerable, even abject, but also angry, tough, streetwise.

Acker later claimed that the Poetry Project crowd was dismissive or hostile toward her, partly because she worked in the sex industry—"They thought I was some kind of pervert," she said, and "I realized I'd never be one of them"— and she would tend to minimize St. Mark's importance in her development as a writer. But Mayer, retrospectively at least, thought Acker was extraordinarily gutsy, taking an exotic and precarious path no other writer she knew had dared to take. There was also a poetic resonance to it, Mayer said, that informed her work: "Her writing was as schizophrenic as the life she was leading, going from philosophy and poetry to sex and back again. It was breathtaking."

Waldman, for her part, came to consider Acker a "hero," and said, decades later, that her writing was "amazing, headstrong, important." Also a couple years Acker's senior, Waldman felt that their writing lives had been almost en-twined, that they bounced off the same literary influences, and that they were united in producing neither "left verse poetry with the usual tropes and epiph-anies" nor *New Yorker*–friendly short fiction. "There's a naughty, exhibitionistic girl-child at the center of it," Waldman said of Acker's work. "It's un-subtle in interesting ways, revealing too, which makes it more democratic and honest. What other women were doing this?"

If anybody, it was certain male poets at the Poetry Project that may have been grousing about the exhibitionism of Acker's work. During one evening, Harris Schiff, who was assistant organizer of the reading series and with whom Acker had a brief affair, read a poem that criticized what he considered the overreliance on sexual content in the poetry of the day. Acker, who felt that Schiff didn't take her work seriously anyway, went on stage immediately after him, and proceeded to read some of her raunchiest passages. They never dis-cussed the evening again.

× × ×

In late 1971 and into early 1972, Acker took the notebooks she filled at Fun City and Embers, her life in the more interesting depths, and began to slowly turn these pages into what would become her first chapbook.* Acker said that the book, titled *Politics*, was written under certain rules, "rules which any academic poetry class would condemn as severely as the Spanish did the Jews." She wrote as quickly and badly as possible. While increasingly interested in narrative, she had no interest in traditional novelistic concerns. There were no "well-rounded" characters. She would not rewrite.

This may have been true of her initial notebook compositions, which are relatively free of redaction or revision. (Specific dream sequences are, however, occasionally labeled as such.) But when the notebook entries were selected, typed up, and collated, Acker did, in fact, rewrite and reorder portions of the text. She framed the extracts from her 1971 notebooks with more abstract, less autobiographical pieces titled "Ghost Story" and "Political Desire," as well as additional, untitled fragments or vignettes that do seem to also describe parts of her life. These fragments were also part of a larger typescript Acker titled *Portraits*, though it's unclear if she intended *Portraits* to be published as is, or if this was just an ongoing file of writing that she kept.

In one of these fragments, for the first time in her published writing, Acker recounts the defining wound of her early childhood: "I don't know who my father was. I don't know if my mother was married or not. I don't know if she wanted to have me or not. I don't know if she showed me she wanted me or not when I was a child but I presume from irrational beliefs deep within me that she didn't." This piece, which Acker titled "Velvet Awareness" in a different, separate typescript, ends with an all-caps pronouncement that Acker might have used as an epigraph for virtually every one of her future books: "DOWN WITH THE FAMILY THE FAMILY IS THE WORST EVIL/IN THIS COUNTRY IT IS THE CAUSE OF EVIL EVERYWHERE."

Acker later described *Politics* as "little prose poems," but the central diary material—perhaps because of the biographical window it opens, its reportorial snapshot of Times Square in the early seventies, or because it's littered with characters, as deliberately sketchy as they may be—has an overt narrative

---

* It's not quite clear how much of her work her family actually read or even saw. Wendy remembered Acker giving Claire "her first book," which may have been *Politics* but was more likely *The Childlike Life of the Black Tarantula*. "I don't think my mother got into it, didn't want to get into it," Wendy added. "'You want to write about your family?' For my mother, that was the end of it."

momentum that Acker would later explore more directly. Divorced from its diaristic context, however, the section takes on a seething, and almost dream-like, texture.

Politics was thirty-two pages long, including a title page indicating it was published by Papyrus Press in May 1972. According to Neufeld, there was no Papyrus Press—"it was just a name for her own self-publishing efforts"—but he had no recollection of where the name came from. Acker made photo-copies, between two and three hundred, stapled the books herself, and then she and Neufeld distributed them to bookstores by hand and mailed them to friends. Among the poetry communities on both coasts, the book became a small sensation, with one poet likening it to Diane di Prima's frankly erotic *Memoirs of a Beatnik*, published three years earlier. Acker was delighted: ". . . my desire to be seen and understood is naïve but i [*sic*] am pleased it feels so exciting when i know my writing is in the world and not just trapped in my mind or these pages . . ."

At the same time, she worried she might have made a mistake in focusing on what she called the "sensational material." Anticipating similar struggles she'd have later in her career, Acker feared that the book's explicit sex would either give readers a distorted impression of her intentions or result in an un-wanted kind of notoriety. "I didn't want to become real famous," she later said, with some disingenuity. "Not that I would, but I didn't want to chance it. Be-cause I thought it would ruin me. It would have messed up my head." When publishers like Black Sparrow Press and Dial Press expressed interest in possi-bly reprinting the book, she was wary, and ultimately refused. "The 42nd street shit that's only 1 part is NOT what my writing's about," she told Rothenberg.

Even two decades later, in an interview with Sylvère Lotringer, at various times her lover, mentor, and publisher—and who would publish the sex show section of *Politics* in the Acker miscellany *Hannibal Lecter, My Father*—she was still struggling with this conundrum.

"I was very scared," she told Lotringer, "and thought if this gets published in a big way and people pick it up and listen to the sensationalism, because it's about the sex show, I'll never be a writer, that's it. You know, they'll put a frame around me, and that'll be it. So I didn't do it."

"But you have that anyway," Lotringer said, referring to her career at the time.

"Yeah, but I think this would have been worse, Sylvère, I think it really would've been bad. Do you know what I mean? I couldn't have handled it back then. I was 20 years old.* You know, I don't know, this media hashes people up."

× × ×

Politics opens with an untitled fragment, a scene really, of an unnamed female narrator having sex with another woman:

> I'm lying in bed with her I touch the visible scalp in the center of her forehead then I run my hands slowly down her long and messy locks we meet kissing for a long time feeling the texture of mouths then of the skin and the position of our bones the inset of the eye and the thinness of the ears the tenseness and warmth within our bones especially within the small of the back forces us to our and each other's sex: breasts and hair and smell for a very long time we arouse each other always with a minimum of caress warm heavy breasts salty bitterness of the hair under our arms that cats adore to lick we have our arms around each other's shoulders our bodies barely touch we look at each other her long brown hair very white skin she has a thin mouth that opens wide when she smiles brown eyes I like mine my hair is almost gone my face looks long like a child . . .

This description, tender and tame, goes on for a page, becoming increasingly graphic and ecstatic. While the next piece or poem—a caustic, partial portrait of Claire, seemingly—sharply interrupts this opening moment, Acker returns a couple pages later to flick again at another, possibly different, sexual relationship with a woman.

The hot-and-cold equivocation of this sequence aside, Acker's sexual interest in women was growing. As Acker's relationship with Neufeld cycled through love, indifference, and antipathy, she yearned for more satisfying, and less oppressive, romantic relationships. She believed that she could find these with women and, as the notebooks suggest, started to make deliberate attempts to cultivate them. "I'm getting involved in womens lib actually lesbians

---

* Unless Acker meant that she was twenty years old when she first began keeping the notebooks that comprised *Politics*, she was fudging or misremembering. She was actually twenty-five when the book was first published.

lib to be honest," she wrote Rothenberg. Her notebooks and typescripts from the period are emblazoned with titles and subtitles like "KEY WORD LES-BIAN" and "Diary: Warm Cat Fur/Lesbian II"; one notebook is "dedicated" to "GERTRUDE STEIN & ALL LESBIANS." A paragraph in *Poems 5/71–6/71* consists entirely of the word "lesbian" repeated sixty times. In a large, brown, spiral-bound notebook, titled "Concrete Poems," she filled entire pages with the words "myself," "lesbian," "angelic," and "holy," repeating them in rows starting from the outermost edges and working inward. With some nervousness, she attended dances hosted by the Daughters of Bilitis, whose New York chapter was located in a loft on Prince Street; became infatuated with a couple of different women; flirted with other female performers in the sex show. "Liking women means liking I'm a woman," she wrote in a notebook, though she later scratched this sentence out.

She knew she was indulging, to a certain degree, a fantasy—"hopefully lesbians have more sense I don't enter that society because it's the only one left to idealize"—and once she started spending more time with gay women, she found herself as often confused and frustrated as she was giddy. She didn't agonize over her sexuality, per se, but she did agonize over what that attraction meant to, or for, her sense of self. In theory, being gay could mean ditching men once and for all, but, as she quickly learned, lesbians had their own specific hang-ups and complications. Most significantly, Acker insisted that she was bisexual, and she was irritated when other women insisted on more rigid categorization. In a notebook entry from January 19, 1972, she wrote:

> . . . go to gay women's poetry reading read parts of earlier diaries mainly about self & cultural destruction no or hostile response perhaps because I mentioned word "gonorrhea" I made them uptight because I was pushing them to be conscious of their individual strangeness (unsureness) all other women read about being lesbians & got terrific responses. Feel old confusions because I'm not sure if I'm lying by reading at a lesbian gathering I don't want to deal with my self-image the way the group presents its image . . .

Acker would eventually find more gratifying sexual relationships with women, and would solve this problem of self-image by insisting she was "queer." But for the moment, anyway, being with women did little to assuage her loneliness. Neufeld continued to conduct multiple affairs and, even worse, Acker felt he wasn't a serious artist. Seeking more intellectual stimulation, she went back to grad school, starting a joint program in classics and philosophy at CCNY and NYU. She quickly realized that academia still bored her, though, and soon dropped out.

× × ×

With so much in disarray, from her domestic life to her sense of self, against her better judgment, Acker took a job. After they left the sex show, Neufeld had found work with Burt Lasky, whose small Riverdale firm provided editorial services, proofreading, and indexing to various New York publishing houses. After a while, Lasky hired Acker too, as a secretary. It didn't last long. While Lasky was, in Neufeld's memory, "a very liberal guy," Acker was "a little too unconventional and didn't fit in well at the office." Once again, straight work was anathema, and office life, to her mind, almost as sexist and demeaning as the sex show. She and Lasky yelled at each other constantly. In her *Poems 5/71–6/71*, she sourly summed up her opinion of all work that wasn't writing: "Secretarial work shit file clerk work shit upper eschelon [*sic*] proofreading copy-editing publishing work shit advertising fashion money work shit unemployment work shit ass-licking work shit sex dancing work shit Medicaid work shit rich gynecologist reporting work shit government work shit richy work shit all university so-called learning work shit." She briefly went back to sex work, performing as a go-go dancer in New Jersey, but was appalled again by the men she worked and performed for. She was appalled by herself. "I'm perpetrating the domination by men of women," she wrote.

Even if writing was the only thing that wasn't shit, her relationship to it was changing. While she still called herself a poet, she also felt more and more estranged from the Poetry Project, which she now considered elitist, and the scene there dull, self-indulgent, and insular. At the end of *The Burning Bombing of America: The Destruction of the U.S.*, a book she started working on right after *Politics*, she writes, "ALL POETS BECOME OTHER POETS SAME THE SAME LINES ST. MARK'S CHURCH IS A REVOLUTIONARY CRUISE-JOINT."

To her mind, even the form itself was unduly limiting. Prose seemed to offer greater possibilities, creative and otherwise. But, as she did with parts of *Politics*, she wanted to write prose the way that poets wrote poems—explicitly engaging with language at the level of the sentence, and conceptually, using what she called a "process." William Burroughs, whose work flickered productively between fiction and philosophy, had shown her how to do that, as had Gertrude Stein. But there were other examples, all around the world. The effects and influence of the *nouveau roman,* as conceived by writers like Alain Robbe-Grillet and Nathalie Sarraute, were still being felt in North America. Latin American literature was booming, with books as different as *One Hundred Years of Solitude* and *Hopscotch* finding avid English-reading audiences. In American fiction, postmodernism—a term that would soon, to Acker's chagrin, be reflexively associated with her own work—was in ascendance. Since the mid-sixties, experimental writing by the likes of John Barth, William Gaddis, and Thomas Pynchon had turned mainstream literature on its head while still, often, finding mainstream acceptance: in 1974, to cite just one major example, Pynchon's *Gravity's Rainbow* shared the National Book Award with Isaac Bashevis Singer's *A Crown of Feathers.*

Acker read all of these postmodernists, and loved some of them. But all of their writing showed her that you could write formally challenging, even difficult, fiction and it would find an eager audience. Maybe even more than that. Stein and Burroughs and Pynchon had all become, in their various ways, celebrities. Who knew how far she could go?

CHAPTER 13

───── × ─────

F ROM HER EARLIEST DAYS AS A WRITER, ACKER'S AMBITIONS WERE almost entirely shaped by avant-garde, innovative, and experimental models. She had no interest in writing lyric or confessional poetry or middle-brow fiction. While she read widely, keeping a close eye on her contemporaries, she had little desire—or arguably, the ability—to produce work that was agreeable, expected, or docile. This was motivated by a familiar *épater la bourgeoisie* and an elemental contrariness: "I have a natural imp tendency to want to destroy." But it was also driven by idealism, a desire to make work that was nothing less than visionary, that could itself remake the world. "Writers should present the human heart naked," she wrote, paraphrasing Edgar Allan Poe, "so that our world, for a second, explodes in flames." She wrote to figure out why she acted in certain ways, why she thought in certain ways, how her memory worked, how experience was perceived and processed and represented, particularly the experience of reading, which remained perhaps the experience that most defined this most bookish of writers. She wrote to complicate herself.

Unsurprisingly then, for the first many years of her writing life, she likewise spurned the traditional routes of publication, rarely submitting poetry or short fiction to major literary journals, or her novel manuscripts to agents and publishers. She instead formed her own spaces and channels, establishing her reputation first in the non-literary worlds of art, music, and performance. Her earliest books were self-published, and her work appeared only in alternative and small publications like David Meltzer's *Tree*, Lucy Sante's *Stranded*, and Mel Freilicher's *Crawl Out Your Window*. She would eventually coax the mainstream book industry toward her, though she would never shed her resistance to prevailing literary codes. Sylvère Lotringer said that he never thought of her as a "natural" or "easy" writer, adding that she became one by "hook or by crook." "She's a different kind of writer," he said. "She became a writer in spite of writing."

Early on, Acker also renounced what many consider the very foundation of writing—voice. For the vast majority of writers, developing or cultivating a literary voice is a natural part of becoming a writer; it's not an easy, logical, or always conscious process, but it is generally regarded as an essential and inevitable one, as routine as the creation of an individual personality. Your distinctive perspective, your worldview, your vocabulary—all contribute to a writer's voice. And a significant part of this process is absorbing and then discarding the influence—the voices—of other writers.

Almost as soon as she started seriously writing, Acker was suspicious of this very idea. It felt presumptive and oppressive, and she had zero faith in it. To begin with, why *one* voice? She didn't have a single voice. She constantly felt scattered, atomized, even schizophrenic, and shouldn't her writing reflect that? Like everyone, she had variable and multiple voices, registers, personalities, selves. "A biography is considered complete if it merely accounts for six or seven selves," Virginia Woolf famously wrote in *Orlando*, "whereas a person may well have as many as a thousand." Just as significantly, Acker found the idea paternalistic and patriarchal. To her mind, it privileged certain political perspectives and worldviews—male, Western, white, heterosexual ones—and naturalized them, made them universal and authoritative. There were, to use theorist Judith Butler's phrase, "regulatory fictions" that kept in place the idea of a subject that was unitary, transcendental, and rational. "I was brought up in this poetry world where the idea was to express yourself," Acker said, "and the last thing in the world I wanted to do was express myself." Acker preferred, she said, to "pick everyone else's viewpoint, mush it all together." She didn't limit her attack to poets either, mocking the totalizing ambitions of establishment writers like Norman Mailer, Philip Roth, and John Updike. "All those novelists have this thing about the great American novel. You have to write the Great American Novel. This perfect novel." She much preferred someone like the protean and prolific Jean-Luc Godard, whose ethos she described as "just churn it out and if it's bad one time it's good the next." While the work of Mailer, et al., purported to represent some kind of universal experience, she considered it in fact "superfluous." As a woman, as a poor person, as someone in pain, she didn't see herself in it at all.

In the spring and summer of 1972, Acker was "churning out" writing that swerved between verse and prose. She collected several of these pieces in a kind of novella she titled *The Burning Bombing of America: The Destruction of the U.S.** Like *Politics*, it uses reworked diary material and includes familiar figures—Neufeld and Mayer, Jerome Rothenberg and Harris Schiff all make appearances. But the book is composed of several sections or chapters, with titles both austere—"Communist Aesthetics," "Communist Story II," "Abstract Essay Collaged with Dreams"—and absurd—"Outer Space Messages Total Chaos!"—and with a corresponding tone that shifts abruptly and frequently, from apocalyptic science fiction to revolutionary tract to alienated American yelp.

At the end of the *Bombing Burning* typescript, Acker left a note to herself, presumably directions on how she should read the book aloud: "read softly, evenly, like a story. 2 minutes per page." But *Burning Bombing* barely resembles a conventional story, or even a coherent one. If it does tell a story, it's that, perhaps, of the curdling of the counterculture. ". . . Bob Dylan shits out money," she writes, "notice where the money lies you'll find out where the killers lie the men who are annihilating the universe . . ." When Acker looked around New York, around America, all she saw was corruption, chaos, and alienation—a society fractured, a country in turmoil, the debris of utopia. The previous couple of years had been marred by Altamont, the Manson murders, Kent State, the splintering of SDS, and the rise of the Weathermen. Acker, like others, remained appalled by the sexism and racism that had undermined the revolutionary movement.

Though there's no such explanatory note attached to *Burning Bombing*, a note that prefaces a group of poems Acker titled simply "Works Done 1968" helps frame her use of "communist" in the novella: "By the word 'Communist' in these poems, I do not mean the Communist Party. To some extent I had them or some party in mind when I wrote many of the poems; I have found some of their members to be fascist pigs. By 'communist' I remind of 'communal' an imaginary communist group or world which I have not found yet to exist, the nearest being certain relations between women." Indeed, while *Burning Bombing* is often bleak and horrifying, it's enlivened by moments of exhilaration. Things fall apart, but can be rebuilt in new and better ways. Other worlds are always possible.

---

* The typescript of *Burning Bombing* reverses the order of the title and there is no colon between the two separate titles—i.e., *The Destruction of the U.S. The Burning Bombing of America*—but I have preserved the order as it appears in the Grove Press edition from 2002.

Burning Bombing of America was never published in Acker's lifetime—it doesn't seem like she tried to publish it or even wanted to—but Grove Press released it in 2002, with a note by editor Amy Scholder suggesting it was written "after Pierre Guyotat's *Éden Éden Éden*." Guyotat was one of France's most daring and controversial novelists, a darling of renowned thinkers like Michel Foucault, Jean-Paul Sartre, Simone de Beauvoir, and Jacques Derrida. His first novel, 1967's *Tomb for 500,000 Soldiers*, was a hallucinatory, psychosexual account of his time as a young soldier in the Algerian War. He was an extremely important writer for Acker, and would remain so for her entire life.

Éden Éden Éden was published in France in July 1970, though also prohibited from being sold to anyone under eighteen, and not translated into English for several years. In fact, Acker would translate it herself about nine years later. Set in Algeria, it's written in a lexicon and style—visceral, incantatory, taxing—quite distinct from conventional French prose. It consists of a single, unending, 256-page sentence, punctuated by colons, slashes, dashes, and swarming with repetitive, corporeal images. Bodies sweat, ingest, shit, gleam, bleed, quiver, fight, fuck. In its fusion of the avant-garde and the classical—the book is really a kind of epic—it was tailor-made for Acker. For her, Guyotat was trying to "get beyond human psychology" in his novels, to arrive at a material reality uninhibited by neurosis and idealism.

Burning Bombing was perhaps written less "after" *Éden Éden Éden* and more in dialogue with it. Acker's America was broken and malevolent, but it was not the war-torn Algerian desert. The writing borrows the aggression, acceleration, and, to a small degree, Guyotat's typographic innovations, but it is still gentler, more overtly domestic and personal. The book's opening lines and pages—"armies defect first in the woods and polluted lakes the cities small towns are covered in the blood of God in the burrows and hidden alleyways of unknown anarchists criminals buggering and fucking for ages . . ."—most strongly echo Guyotat, but, as in her later books, that appropriation is soon abandoned or juxtaposed with other styles, other appropriations, other texts.

× × ×

Acker dedicated a couple of sections of *Burning Bombing* to Neufeld, but their three-year-old relationship was more or less over by the time she had finished the book. In the fall of 1972, she typed up a poem, "Breaking Up," culled from longer entries in a notebook titled *Household Objects*, that seemed entirely composed of conversations between the two of them. Though none of the poem's lines is explicitly ascribed to either person, sentiment like this, which comes near its end, can clearly be attributed to Neufeld: "you don't accept responsibility/you use men/you fear men" and "I've done everything/you're entirely irresponsible/you're unable to care for anyone but yourself."

The end of the relationship was hastened, however, by a new romance that Acker began about a month before she wrote "Breaking Up." In August, unemployed and at creative loose ends, she flew out to San Diego to visit Mel Freilicher and the Antins, hoping, it seemed, for some guidance and comfort. It wasn't a long trip and Acker left her stuff back in Washington Heights. When she found out that Jeff Weinstein had agreed to deliver a car cross-country to New York, she asked if she could tag along. Weinstein said sure, but that they would have another passenger with them, a buddy of his named Peter Gordon.

Gordon was a twenty-one-year-old UCSD music student and aspiring composer, four years Acker's junior. He was gentle, generous, and cherubic, with full lips that matched Acker's own. If the small, wide-eyed Acker appeared childlike far into adulthood, Gordon looked, some said, like a giant baby. He was born in New York, spent his childhood in Virginia, and then his teen years in Munich, where his father worked as a journalist for Voice of America. In Germany, Gordon learned to play clarinet and saxophone and received an eclectic musical education: he watched the Munich opera perform Anton Webern and Arnold Schoenberg, and in clubs caught the likes of Duke Ellington, James Brown, and Ray Charles, even performing once himself with Chuck Berry. After Germany, the family moved to Los Angeles, where Gordon, then a senior in high school, ended up befriending a neighbor, Don Van Vliet, aka Captain Beefheart, and hung around as Beefheart recorded *Trout Mask Replica*, the landmark double album that launched a thousand avant-rock acts. While at UCSD, Gordon had a band, one of many he would form over the next few years, that transformed pop hits into free-form improvisations, and similar to Acker's feelings about contemporary poetry, he considered the art music of the time "elitist" and sought to make music that was "hedonistic but also brainy."

He and Acker hit it off. Too well, at times, for Weinstein—they were soon having sex in the back seat of the car while he, somewhat exasperated, chauffeured them across the country. Weinstein was a bit surprised that they became so close so fast—they seemed like very different people to him—but Gordon was undeniably smitten. "She was fascinating," Gordon recalled. "She had this incredible energy: a certain self-centeredness, yet sort of an inherent naïveté, which was charming." He found her funny too, and affectionate, warm, and vulnerable. By the time they got to the East Coast, he had more or less fallen for her. Though Neufeld was still living in their apartment, Gordon ended up crashing there with Acker too. Neufeld didn't begrudge him anything—he blamed Acker entirely for their breakup—and he and Gordon eventually became reasonably good friends.

After a week, Gordon returned to California. Three weeks later, and much to his surprise, Acker showed up at his apartment with her books and cats. They hadn't really discussed moving in together, and Gordon had never before lived with a girlfriend, but he nonetheless received her with open arms. (Not the cats, though—he was allergic, and they were soon re-homed.) Gordon lived in an apartment in Solana Beach, the first neighborhood where Acker had lived with Bob Acker, and she was grateful to be living by the ocean once again. She reconnected with her old San Diego friends, joining a women's meditation group that Pauline Oliveros ran, planning a new literary and art magazine with Mel Freilicher. She seemed grateful for everything, in fact, especially for the chance to start over again. In a letter to Harris Schiff, who had decamped to New Mexico himself, she wrote, "Split w/ Lenny & couldn't stand NY raped every night lungs couldn't function . . . anyway also there was this musician in S.D. I love—so I split to S.D.! and! here! am I! . . ." To Bernadette Mayer, she described San Diego as "paradise."

She and Gordon would occasionally drive to L.A. to visit Gordon's family or to catch a concert, staying overnight. While at first Gordon's parents "didn't know what hit them," Acker fit in surprisingly well. His father wrote plays and he and Acker bonded over literature. She even showed him her writing, which he gave her feedback on (but which he kept hidden from Gordon's mother, a psychotherapist). Acker often joined her and Gordon's grandmother in the kitchen and helped them cook. Before she moved out west, Acker had repeated in a letter to Gordon the "DOWN WITH THE FAMILY" couplet that she'd included in Politics, but the Gordons, it seemed, were the Jewish family that she wished she had—or at least a family she felt comfortable and connected with. She soon started to refer to Peter as her brother; it was, she told Schiff, "a sacred relationship."

But as usual, she was broke (and now, after airfares, $500 in debt). Gordon had a grad school fellowship and his parents were also still helping to support him. He happily shared that money with Acker, but it wasn't a lot. To make ends meet, by that fall, she had started stripping in sailor bars around San Diego. It was a return to the sex industry, but a far cry from Times Square. "It was performing," Gordon said, "not like turning tricks. It was a show." She adopted a pseudonym, Target, and worked a circuit of different joints, sometimes performing for sailors just about to head off to Vietnam. Dancers supplied their own music, and Acker danced to the Velvet Underground or jazz musicians like Ornette Coleman and John Coltrane. While other dancers employed popular dance moves, Acker would call upon her classes with Meredith Monk and, Gordon said, "dance interpretively, bringing out the angst, as well as the erotic joy." Full nudity was illegal in the city, so Acker wore a wig and various costumes; Gordon's grandmother, a lover of vaudeville, helped sew sequins onto her outfits. "It's a nice place to work as a stripper," Acker later told an interviewer. "You didn't get much money but sailors turn out to be very nice people."

× × ×

Through that winter, Acker read Henry James, Wilkie Collins, and Malcolm Lowry, and while she continued to write poetry, by the spring of 1973, she had also begun a novel. Titled *Rip-off Red, Girl Detective,** it was a far different project than either *Politics* or *Burning Bombing*. It had the veneer of conventional, representational fiction—a semblance of plot, loosely drawn characters, suspense—and Acker even gave its typescript a kind of pulp fiction cover: a partial line drawing of a reclining woman, captioned with the expression "'Nuff said!?!," Stan Lee's familiar Marvel Comics sign-off. It included a dedication too: "For my brother Peter Peter." Acker didn't use her real name as author, however, preferring to use Rip-off Red as both pen name and titular character.

Peter Peter is also the name of a character in the book, secretary and partner to Red, who describes herself as a "superdetective." At the novel's opening, Red is planning to go from California to New York and "rip off the money" from the city's anarchists and junkies. On the plane there, Red meets a woman named Sally Spitz, who's trying to figure out why her father, a jeweler, keeps vanishing every night for several hours. Red takes the case. Before long, however, Spitz

---

* Again, there's a slight discrepancy in the title. According to the typescript in Acker's Duke archive, the title eschews the hyphen and a colon is used instead of the comma: *Ripoff Red: Girl Detective*. I have again, however, deferred to the style of the 2002 Grove Press edition, *Rip-off Red, Girl Detective*.

is murdered while at her parents' place, an apartment building at 57th Street and First Avenue, Acker's childhood address. Red vows to avenge her death.

While Spitz may have grown up in Red/Acker's apartment, and has Acker's own daddy issues, it's Red herself who explicitly shares parts of Acker's biography. In the novel's second part, a flashback takes Red to her early childhood and teenaged years where, as the daughter of "Oiving" and "Clear," she shuttles between wealth and poverty, travels through various New York boroughs, and forms a preposterously named criminal gang, the Banana Followers, with Harvey the Bagel and Weirdo the Rat. They rumble with a rival gang called the Tomatoes. Young Red learns to masturbate, to have sex, to hate her parents, to dream, to flee, to change her name. After this interlude, Acker returns to the plot, which speeds, with knowing absurdity, toward a conclusion that anyone familiar with Acker's work will find unsurprising: Spitz was murdered by her father. Acker described the novel as "basically about illusion vs. illusion very abstract."

Many of its pages are spent describing the sex that Red has with Peter Peter and various other men and women. The passages are detailed and breathless, raunchy, and repetitive. Acker wrote these pages for her own titillation, but also to make the book commercially appealing. She knew that other serious writers—the Scottish novelist Alexander Trocchi, the poet Diane di Prima—had written porn novels for money, and she thought *Rip-off Red*, if sold and marketed as such, could bring in a few hundred dollars. (Grove Press, she told Gordon, would be the "perfect publisher.") In a letter to Bernadette Mayer, she called it a "pornography mystery" and likened it to the cult anti-Western film *Billy Jack*: "You're so entertained so much sex you don't know you're being blurped on the head until you fall down WHOOM."

Acker spent eight hours a day working on it, off and on for six months. It never did make her any money, and like *Burning Bombing*, would languish, unpublished, among her papers for several years after her death. But it was her first long investigation into actual narrative, her first experimentation with genre conventions, the first inklings of the staccato, hard-boiled style she'd employ in her future writings. The book's final lines—"I'm no longer a detective. I'll decide to become someone else."—would also herald the next significant chapter in her evolution as a writer. As a pseudonym, Acker would hold on to Rip-off Red a bit longer, but she would soon also adopt a more enduring and life-changing alias—The Black Tarantula.

CHAPTER 14

—————— ✕ ——————

ORDON'S SOLANA BEACH APARTMENT WAS JUST AROUND THE COR-
ner from the Antins' house, and when Acker returned to California in
late 1972, a more purposeful and experienced writer than when she left, that
friendship became even more important. The two couples frequently met for
breakfast, and she and Gordon occasionally babysat the Antins' son, Blaise.

The Antins had been experimenting with new forms themselves and had
arrived at methods and ideas that would, in ways subtle and significant, influence Acker's next artistic steps. David had already introduced Acker to the use
of found materials, collage, and appropriation. But he added to that a different
notion of how a poem might be written and performed, reversing the order of
that process in fact, or turning it inside out. In April 1972, David was invited to
give a reading at the art department of Pomona College, a couple hours north
of San Diego. Rather than reading from notes or a published book, however, he
simply cleared his throat and began to speak, improvising a lecture on art and
art-making that was by turns witty, profound, and bracing. On the drive home,
he and Elly listened to a recording of the talk, and Elly said, with characteristic
certitude, "That's a poem."

David typed it up, and that talk, "talking at pomona," became the first of
what he would call "talk" poems. *Artforum* published it later that fall, and he
also included it in his Kulchur Press book *Talking*. The talk poems became
David's renowned, beloved signature, his own microgenre. It was speaking as
thinking, talking as writing. The poems illustrated the power of improvisation,
how capacious poetry really could be, and the pleasurable friction produced
when combining the high- and lowbrow—he moved deftly and sometimes
comically between Wittgensteinian language games and quasi–Borscht Belt
routines about his mother. But David was quick to say that he wasn't an enter-
tainer, and unlike, say, later examples like Spalding Gray or Garrison Keillor,
he didn't "give a damn if half the audience walks out." He was a master of meta-
phor, a master of the emblematic story, and his talk poems swarmed with both.

A bit earlier, but continuing into 1973, Elly had started her own equally winning conceptual art project, *100 Boots*. She placed a hundred black rubber boots on the beach below their house, facing the sea, and took a photograph of them. At David's suggestion, she made more pictures, all while moving the footwear from location to location—outside a church, in a field, at an amusement park, at a Greek nightclub—with, over time, the boots traveling from California to New York, where they made their way to MoMA. Over two-and-a-half years, Elly made fifty-one such pictures, which she turned into postcards and mailed to a list of a thousand people and institutions around the world. The boot's adventures became more fantastic—they committed a crime, had a love affair. She first thought of the series as a picaresque novel in the vein of *Huckleberry Finn* or *On the Road*, and then more as a set of stills from a movie serial like *The Perils of Pauline*. The project, Elly said, was conceived to "circumvent some of the spatial and temporal limits imposed on an artist whose work is shown in a gallery setting." It became a key piece in the relatively new medium of mail art, made most famous by Ray Johnson and various members of Fluxus.

But Elly was busy with much more than her boots. Continuing her earlier investigations into identity, gender, and race, from the early seventies on, she created and adopted several fictional "alternative selves," the performances of which she documented in several photographs and videos over the next couple of decades. She donned a fake mustache and beard, wig, floppy bucket hat, cape, and boots and became the King, a valiant, if impotent, monarch raging against the wealthy landowners of Solana Beach. For several weeks, she also assumed the identity of a fictional Black ballerina from Sergei Diaghilev's Ballets Russes, a blackface performance which Elly said she intended as a show of solidarity but which was later criticized as exploitative, ill-advised appropriation. Less problematic were two fictional white nurse characters, Nurse Eleanor and Eleanor Nightingale, both of whom appeared in videos she made in the late seventies. "I consider the usual aids to self-definition—sex, age, talent, time and space—as tyrannical limitations upon my freedom of choice," Elly famously declared.

These performances were part of a small, pioneering, contemporaneous wave of such work from women artists. In New York in 1973, Black conceptual artist Adrian Piper applied her own fake mustache, along with sunglasses and an Afro wig, for a project called *The Mythic Being*, in which she took diary entries she'd written as a teenager and presented them (in both *Village Voice* advertisements and live on city streets) as a physically different person. Suzy Lake's series of large-scale photographic self-portraits—*Transformations*, from 1973 and '74—depicted her "becoming" other women, men, and children. In San Francisco, the artist and filmmaker Lynn Hershman Leeson created a fictitious alter-ego named Roberta Breitmore, whom Leeson "played" in a series of actual real-life activities-cum-performances—getting a driver's license, renting an apartment, undergoing psychoanalysis.

There was a certain hybridity to all this work, with each artist borrowing and blending tropes and techniques from film, photography, and literature, all to make a new kind of conceptual art obsessed with role-playing, biography, perception, and gender. With *Rip-off Red*, Acker had attempted something similar, fusing noir, philosophy, and porn. The more time she spent with conceptual artists—and also musicians, thanks to Peter Gordon—the more that both visual art strategies and methods of musical composition illuminated new directions for her fiction. Though she would later reconsider and dismiss this idea, she learned from the conceptualists that what mattered most in making art was knowing *why* you did what you did. For a writer, she now felt, it was not enough to blindly, automatically use the language and methods given to you, which is what she believed most English-language novelists unthinkingly did.

The conceptualists were also cannier about the circulation of their art, or at least had developed multiple ways to get it in front of people, to make a lasting impression. Elly's mailing list was one way, but there were also, of course, art galleries of various size and description, public spaces, magazines, even TV. Elly had a theory about the art world too, and it was something that Acker took to heart—to get them to pay attention to you, you have to do the same thing over and over. "It was not cynical," Mel Freilicher recalled. "It was like, this is what you have to do. You have to make certain moves. It's not a question of pandering or doing what will sell. It's being emphatic."

× × ×

In June 1973, Acker started a new notebook, a UCSD-branded spiral-bound one, working out in its first few pages De Morgan's Laws, the rules of logic named for the nineteenth-century British mathematician Augustus De Morgan. Several of her notebooks from the period, in fact, (as well as brief passages in her earliest published books) are dappled with her musings on epistemology, perception, logical forms, memory, and language, influenced by her reading of philosophers like Henri Bergson, Gustav Bergmann, and Wittgenstein. At one point, she "interviewed" David Antin, with her purported questions and Antin's answers a collage of her, or their, own words and sentences cribbed from Wittgenstein's *On Certainty*. "Do you care whether you can *know* I want to fuck you?" Acker asks, tongue somewhere near her cheek.

After dozens of pages of exercises and truth tables, however, the real work of the notebook begins. At the top of a page, Acker writes, "Intention: I become a murderess by repeating in words the lives of other murderesses." Below that, in caps: "THE CHILDLIKE LIFE OF THE BLACK TARANTULA." Acker repeats this on the front of the notebook, writing above it with typical self-deprecation, "A Minor Work."

This "minor work," would, in fact, be a major breakthrough. Taking the autobiographical second part of *Rip-off Red*, Acker expands it, combining it with vignettes describing her daily life (set off in parentheses) and, most significantly, plagiarized, reworked extracts from historical crime books like Edward Hale Bierstadt's *Enter Murderers: Eight Studies in Murder* and *Blood in the Parlor* by Dorothy Dunbar. She continued this work into a second notebook, this one with the title *THE BLACK TARANTULA DRIVES HERSELF INSANE: A DOCUMENT*. Here, she writes "by The Black Tarantula" and, at the top of the notebook's cover, "THE BLACK TARANTULA HAS ALMOST ELIMINATED HER IDENTITY. SHE BEGINS TO ELIMINATE HER FEAR." Between the two notebooks, she composed about thirty pages in this style. The piece's final sentence reads, "I'm hysterical start screaming louder and louder," but in an accompanying note, Acker wrote with apparent satisfaction, "calm end 'poetic.'"

In letters and on manuscripts, Acker would soon regularly be calling herself The Black Tarantula, TBT for short. But who was The Black Tarantula? *Why* The Black Tarantula? If Acker ever had a good reason for the pseudonym it's been forgotten or she never publicly divulged it. "It's just another name," she told a friend at the time, "and I like black, very sleazy." Years later, she told Sylvère Lotringer that, back then, "everybody wore make-up, everybody dressed up all the time and everybody changed their names. So I made up a name for myself. I liked tarantulas in those days, and I probably like them now. Mexican kids keep them as pets." She went on, seemingly also talking about how she saw herself: "Everyone thinks they're horrible but they're really sensual, really soft and furry. They're not terribly dangerous. The worse thing they do is sting like a bee."

But the name obviously had a number of alluring connotations. It conferred anonymity and secrecy, suggested danger and death. It could have been the name of a superhero, or a spy. It made her something other than a woman, other than human. It again, immediately, placed her identity in quotes and up for grabs. "Being a poet and working with language is a lot like being a spider," David Antin wrote in "The Structuralist"—a talk poem that offers some clues to Acker's work—and "working with silk because the language comes out of your mouth much the way thread comes out of a spider so that it looks like you've made it but only in a way . . ." Acker would later sometimes sign letters with just a hand-drawn, almost abstract, tarantula: a black dot with eight filament-like legs that curve outward like a sun's rays.

As for the writing itself, what was this thirty-page whatsit supposed to be? Another prose poem? A story? The first chapter of a novel? Acker later said that she had the "idea of doing like a Dickens novel, a serial where I'd send out chapters every month," though it's not clear when this idea occurred to her. There were other cultural examples of serials, of course—pulp novels, on radio, in the movies—and the tenor of Acker's piece hewed closer to the spirit of these.

When she showed the work to the Antins, Elly suggested that Acker send the serials to everyone on the mailing list she made for *100 Boots*. The two women had become closer—"I've never opened up to anyone before so much about my work," Acker said—and she leapt at the idea. Acker soon began sending the chapters—typed up, then mimeographed at a local newspaper office and stapled together—often without identifying herself as their author, to artists and writers she did and didn't know: among them, the Rothenbergs, Sitney, Jackson Mac Low, Ed Ruscha, Barbara Barracks, Vito Acconci, Carolee Schneemann, Lawrence Weiner, Robert Duncan, John Perrault, Ron Silliman, Grove Press's Barney Rosset. "That list in the pre-internet days was gold," the poet Eileen Myles wrote. "You could actually reach out and touch the inside of all these people's mailboxes." Gordon helped her, stapling pages, stuffing envelopes. Acker tucked in the envelopes her own small, wry card, which read: "You are on the enemy list of The Black Tarantula."

Some recipients were puzzled, others intrigued, even thrilled, by the work. The format was modest, even primitive, but the writing was both anguished and aggressive. Her web grew quickly. "She became the darling of the art world," Elly recalled. (Though not without a hint of retrospective rancor—after Acker became well known, she regularly gave David Antin his due as a major influence, but almost never mentioned Elly.)

"It was about setting up friendships," Acker said of these early pamphlets. "As if they were little letters to people that I sent out." The communication, in some cases, went two ways. In 1974, for example, Schneemann, a multidisciplinary artist best known for experimental performances and films like *Meat Joy* and *Fuses*, published *Cezanne, She Was a Great Painter*, an artist's book comprising letters and fragments from Acker's notebooks, manifestoes, and performance scripts. Included was a poem titled "For The Black Tarantula," which argues, midway, in all-caps: "OUR CIVILIZATION IS TO SPEAK TO EACH OTHER/CIVILIZATION IS THOUGHTS OF OUR BODIES."

× × ×

"I'm sick of not fucking knowing who I am," Acker writes in *Politics*. *The Childlike Life of the Black Tarantula* was a way, she said, of figuring that out. But her method, as she outlined it anyway, was quixotic. Of all the things she knew and didn't know about herself, she knew, definitively, that she had never murdered anyone. So she raided the crime and law sections of the UCSD library and checked out all the biographies and autobiographies of famous female murderers she could find. She copied out sections from these books and then essentially inserted them into and alongside autobiographical sections that detailed her troubled family history, her money and health concerns, her current sex life and affairs. It was a real experiment, with these autobiographical sections serving, she said, as the "control." In a letter to Jackson Mac Low, she described this technique in depth:

The Black Tarantula series (one's coming out a month) is basically my way of making myself schizophrenic, schizophrenic w/out the censor (identity, superego, causer of similar patterns) I half make up my own words, half use other people's jargon which slightly fits . . . the idea that if I'm do [sic] this slowly and don't scare myself by sudden shocks I'll be able to deal w/ other people more honestly & directly, evolve new ways of being with people, better ones, I'll break thru my overwhelming paranoia—crack up the old identity god. So I copy texts (get rid of style, expressionism in writing) + become the people of the texts . . .

In the second installment of *The Childlike Life of the Black Tarantula*, Acker writes, "I want to read books about schizophrenia, especially Laing's books and the books from Kingsley Hall. I'm getting sick of pornography and murders which is all I used to be interested in." And, indeed, Acker had immersed herself in such literature, reading books like Mary Barnes and Joseph Berke's *Two Accounts of a Journey Through Madness*. She was particularly fascinated by R. D. Laing, the radical Scottish psychiatrist, and the ideas around schizophrenia that he explored in *The Divided Self* and *Sanity, Madness and the Family*. For Laing, madness was liberation and renewal, mental illness more theory than fact. "Insanity is a perfect response to an insane world," Laing famously wrote. In a 1984 essay on Goya and Caravaggio, Acker reformulated this statement: "The only reaction against an unbearable society is equally unbearable nonsense."

Later in her life, as Acker's behavior became more erratic, narcissistic, and paranoid, Gordon and many other friends would suspect she suffered from undiagnosed borderline personality disorder, even possibly dissociative identity disorder. Certainly, qualities that she exhibited throughout her life—a fear of abandonment, impulsiveness, disproportionate anger, frequent mood swings—are symptoms of borderline personality disorder. But a posthumous diagnosis is impossible, of course, and risks pathologizing behavior, or thinking, that, as extreme as it could sometimes be in Acker's case, is hardly uncommon. More important is the fact that Acker zealously repudiated psychotherapy and analysis her entire life. She never had a conventional therapist, never sought, as far as we know, any course of psychiatric treatment; she had no interest in being "cured" or "fixed." When she learned that Bernadette Mayer was seeing the celebrated analyst David Rubinfine, for example, she was horrified, arguing that Rubinfine was "brainwashing" her. "I told Kathy it was none of her business," Mayer said. "But she didn't approve of anything that so smacked of the bourgeoise." Perhaps. But Acker's attitudes may have stemmed from her many years of poverty, when she received inconsistent, even slipshod, treatment from various free clinics. She was also extremely suspicious of all authority, medical or otherwise. Gordon thought there was yet another reason, that Acker "saw psychological pain as being her source of creativity." To interrogate this heartache then, with the aim of somehow reducing or altering it, could, theoretically anyway, destroy it.

But there was more to it than that. The antipsychiatry of Laing—and later, Deleuze and Guattari's incendiary, anti-capitalist critiques of Freud and Lacan—was revolutionary for Acker. These philosophers offered a more productive, even joyful, way of slipping the confines of self and social order. They showed how fruitful paradox and contradiction can be. In *The Childlike Life*, the narrator constantly fractures or refracts, almost ecstatically describing an ever-shifting physical appearance and worldview. Now they are a woman, now they are a man, now they are a spider. Now they are Kathy, now they are Silver Gold Lamé (another alias), now they are The Black Tarantula. Now they are a node, a network, a nothing.*

"I look at my body as if it were a web," Acker writes in one of the loveliest passages in her early work, "solely a way of asking people to touch me. My body doesn't exist. I watch myself: I'm now heavy and even more beautiful: huge curves of thighs zooming into the valleys around my belly I begin to love myself as if I'm someone else no I realize my attractiveness coldly, I basically couldn't care how I look; I can see anything in a set of shifting frameworks. I'm interested solely in getting into someone else. I find the heavy flesh sensual, as if it were permanent. I'm not sure if I think of myself as a person."

Maybe, contra *Politics*, it didn't matter so much if she didn't know who she was. Maybe it was more important that her identity didn't remain settled or fixed, that she was always becoming someone, or something, else.

x x x

Acker worked tirelessly on *The Childlike Life*, tallying up the words on the inside back cover of her notebooks. She typically wrote three to four thousand

---

* Nineteen seventy-three was also the year that Flora Rheta Schreiber published *Sybil*, her explosive, controversial account of dissociative identity disorder (then known as multiple personality disorder). Acker never publicly mentioned the bestselling book, but it's interesting to note how she was exploring, in a much different way, related ideas around trauma, the formation of self, sexual abuse, and the malleability of memory. The writer Stephen Beachy touches briefly on this in his 2007 essay "JT LeRoy and Narratives of Abuse," which compellingly situates the case of the fictional writer, JT LeRoy, against the backdrop of such books. Many figures in Acker's later circle, including Ira Silverberg, Dennis Cooper, and Eileen Myles, were duped by LeRoy's creator, Laura Albert.

words a day. Writing by day, stripping by night—it was a considerably more relaxed version of the life she'd had in New York. Not without its difficulties, as she notes in this exemplary paragraph, but it was relatively stable: "I live quietly I change my way of life I eat grains vegetables some dairy products because I have an ulcer I'm too poor to see a doctor about once a month I fall in love with someone at the same time I live with Peter who I love I rarely form friendships I deal awkwardly with people I fall in love with."

She still also struggled from time to time with severe depression, and Gordon would do his best to help her. "You knew there was a dark side," he said, "but it took a while to see how deep it could really get. She would have these descending spirals of darkness that couldn't be stopped." This darkness manifested itself in harrowing ways: Acker would fixate completely on things, or utterly withdraw, becoming practically catatonic, and retreat to her "cocoon-like" bed. She still occasionally cut herself, and in letters over the next few years, there was the odd mention of suicidal thoughts. In *Rip-off Red*, Acker suggests that she even tried to hang herself once, though Gordon has no recollection of this. During these bouts of depression, he would cook and feed her miso soup, try to nurse her, but sometimes, he said, nothing consoled her, and they both just rode out the episodes. It's impossible to know how much this was bound up in Acker's relationship to her family. But, obviously, she repeatedly dredged up old offenses and indignities as she wrote, and this process inevitably affected her mood. As distant as they were from her physically, her extended family was never far from her psychically. Gordon recalled a road trip to Tijuana, where Acker bought an embroidered blouse with a high collar. "I look just like my mother in this," she said. She wore it with pearls given to her by Nana.

Around this time Acker also started to get semi-regular abortions. An early piece titled "Murderers-Criminals Join Sunlight," which was part of a short sequence of poetic exercises and subtitled: "Exercise #1: Create Music Through Repetitions of Own Sounds," lists the dates of two of her abortions before the poem begins: 10/28/72, 11/2/72. The dates line up with what she told Bernadette Mayer in a letter from the same time, that she had one unsuccessful abortion and then a second one four days later ("which I hoped worked because I'm broke").

While some women find the abortion procedure deeply difficult, emotionally painful, and frightening, Acker tended to treat these operations with relative ease. She seemed to attach little psychological baggage to them, and she was publicly dismissive of their difficulty, treating abortion, more or less, as a form of birth control. "She dealt with them very casually," Gordon recalled. Indeed, Acker seemed to almost revel in the act, as a defiance of certain societal norms, but also as a refusal, again, to have her body policed by anything or anybody. In the early nineties, in San Francisco, she went straight from an abortion to a photo shoot with her friend the philosopher Avital Ronell. Ronell was shocked, and when she expressed concern, a cavalier Acker waved it off—"Why are you being such a girl?"

In her writing, abortions would signify other things. In *Blood and Guts in High School*, she writes, "Abortions are the symbol, the outer image, of sexual relations in this world." A graphic scene in an abortion clinic opens her *Don Quixote*, with the operation portrayed as an enlightening, even generative, process. In *Memoriam to Identity*, her feelings about the procedure are just as complex and political: "When a woman's body turns into a baby-wanting machine and if the woman doesn't want a baby, she has to wage war against herself." And a few pages later, "Since life and death are inextricably mixed, you can't condemn abortion. Maybe that's why I had so many abortions."

Clearly, for all of her professed love of Gordon, she didn't want to have kids with him. Nor was she interested in a monogamous relationship with him. At the beginning of June, at the Antins', she met a writer and artist named Dan Graham, whom she quickly developed a crush on. Graham was five years older, and already an instrumental figure in the conceptual art world. She liked his work and his ideas about art, and he was friends with Bernadette Mayer too, another endorsement. He also had what she called "a body I like: heavy enough to run into and feel its weight on me." But their romance, such as it was, was brief and unsatisfying. In *The Childlike Life*, Graham appears as D, a character who sleeps just once with the narrator and then promptly ghosts her:

> I call up D in Los Angeles do you want to sleep with me with me when and where there why don't you spend a few days with me I'll call you tomorrow. No call three days later I'm maniacal I have to see D I don't know him hello I've got a ride to Los Angeles lie I'm not sure I know where we can stay should I not come up come up. We don't touch talk about anything personal spend night together I have to be at Irvine in the morning I'm busy call me Friday. Do you want me to call you yes. I call Friday call Saturday Sunday this is Kathy O uh do you want to

spend a night with me again are you too busy I'm too busy uh goodbye have a good time in New York uh goodbye.

In real life, the day after this dispiriting interlude, a tortured Acker wrote to Mayer asking for any information she might have about Graham. It's not clear what Mayer told her, if anything. But the D character floats through several chapters of *The Childlike Life*, a ghostly nonentity who is emblematic, finally, of an indifferent art world, cruel and unthinking men, and Acker's own vulnerability. Later, in a letter to Jackson Mac Low, she downgraded Graham to simply "this artist creep" who "doesn't talk about anything but art."*

Gordon more or less shrugged off these infatuations, which he saw as almost performative. "It wasn't like I loved the idea but it was a funny thing," he said. "It was almost like exploring different characters or something for her." He appreciated too that she was open and honest about the affairs, and never tried to deceive him. In any case, he enjoyed his own occasional dalliances and was also preoccupied with his own burgeoning career. By that summer, he had grown tired of the music program at UCSD and its emphasis on "rigid, post-serialist modernism." He decided to transfer to Mills College in Oakland. John Cage had taught there, and, in his wake, it became an epicenter of experimental music: Terry Riley and Robert Ashley were on the faculty; Steve Reich, Trisha Brown, and Laurie Anderson were all, at one point or another, students.

Acker agreed to join him. She didn't really want to leave San Diego, but she didn't think she could make money there any other way than stripping, and that lifestyle had become wearisome. Despite her ambivalence about the poetry community, she craved again the company of a wider circle of writers. And both of them wanted to live in a big city again but not necessarily New York. In July, she and Gordon drove up the coast and headed to Haight-Ashbury.

---

* To the best of my knowledge, Graham has never spoken publicly about this fling with Acker. He never responded to my repeated interview requests.

S AN FRANCISCO WAS A NEW CITY TO ACKER, BUT ALSO A FAMILIAR and welcoming one. It had been a beacon for the Beats; home of San Francisco Renaissance poets like Kenneth Rexroth, Robert Duncan, and Jack Spicer; the cradle of both the New Age movement and the sex industry. An enormous gay and lesbian community flourished there—the Daughters of Bilitis, whose dances Acker had attended in Manhattan, and their male counterpart, the Mattachine Society, had relocated there from Los Angeles in 1955. In 1969, there were fifty gay organizations in the city; by the time Acker and Gordon arrived, four years later, there were eight hundred. The Cockettes, an anarchic, gender-bending theater troupe that emerged out of a commune in the Haight, and which Acker often credited as an influence, had more or less disbanded by 1973, but their spirit lived on in the equally outrageous Angels of Light. "Everyone goes around saying love all the time (really!!)," she told Jackson Mac Low, "it's like a cloud of nuttiness covers this city..."

Acker and Gordon settled in the ground-floor apartment of a three-story Victorian at 46 Belvedere Street. The apartment had two separate parlors, with Acker using one as a writing room and Gordon using the other as a studio. Missing her cats, Acker replaced them with other animals: two hamsters, named Art and Revolution, and a pair of parakeets, Jackson Mac Low and John Cage. Around the corner were a few other friendly musicians, all of whom were loosely affiliated with Mills and all of whom had adopted their own winsome stage names: "Blue" Gene Tyranny, Clay Fear, Phil Harmonic, Rich Gold. They shared a house they dubbed the Honeymoon Hotel, and Gordon and Acker soon became close to them.

It was an age of aliases. Aside from Lynn Hershman Leeson's Roberta Breitmore, San Francisco was also home to a Canadian mail artist named Anne Lee Long, who had refashioned herself as Anna Banana when she moved to the city and founded *Vile* magazine, a parody of General Idea's *FILE*, itself a parody of *LIFE*. Several months after Acker's arrival, a group of militant revolutionaries calling themselves the Symbionese Liberation Army, who had previously murdered Oakland school superintendent Marcus Foster, kidnapped heiress Patty Hearst from her Berkeley apartment. Two months later, Hearst claimed to have joined the group and changed her name to Tania. SLA leader Donald DeFreeze's nom de guerre was Field Marshal Cinque, and other members had aliases like Mizmoon and Yolanda.

Acker's own appearance shifted frequently—she'd grow her hair out a bit, then cut it very short again. Sometimes she wore lots of makeup, other times none. Gordon himself occasionally went around in drag, going by the name Art Povera. When Acker listed her name in the phone book, she used both The Black Tarantula and Rip-off Red.

At first, life in San Francisco wasn't all that different from life in San Diego. "Basically I eat, shit, fuck etc, read and write," she told Harris Schiff. To Mac Low, she was more effusive: "Even tho I still haven't gotten over the jolt of entering another new environment, & that swirling in my head, I feel I can live here . . . artists are so open here." As always, though, money was extremely tight, especially as Gordon's father had by then stopped helping them out. Acker still refused to get a job—"I've made the final decision not to work unless the work concerns my writing, I'd rather starve"—and Gordon was compelled to support them both, taking various night and day jobs to do so while still attending classes at Mills. One of those night jobs was working at a porn bookstore, where Freilicher would cruise when he came up to visit. To save money, Gordon cut Acker's hair. She frequently skipped meals, preferring, she said, to use what little grocery money they had to pay for the printing and mailing of The Black Tarantula serials.

Late that summer or early fall, for a payment of a hundred dollars, Acker agreed to do a new translation of Aristophanes's *Lysistrata* for a colleague of Rothenberg's named Charles Doria. She soon gave up, however, finding the play dull—"too much of it came off as women's lib cant which I guess I've heard too much of or something." She offered instead to translate another of Aristophanes's plays, *Thesmophoriazusae*, which she'd seen performed by the Angels of Light, and which tells of a group of Athenian women who plot to kill Euripides because of his misogyny. Acker also proposed including an introduction that would, in effect, be a meta-translation, accounting for both her research on Greek society of the period and her experience writing the translation: "I have to translate autobiographically and that means including the ideas I read think express feel act on etc. that preceed [sic] my actual translation of words of play." At the end of an explanatory letter to Doria, she added a handwritten postscript: "The obvious idea of Aristophanes: that politics should be determined by sexual and individual needs, not vice versa, is important to me." She included a copy of this introduction ("a TARANTULA of ideas," she called it), which, in keeping with her writing from the period, juxtaposed frank, even miserable, descriptions of her daily life with snatches of, among others, Aristophanes, Plato, Yeats, and W. G. Forrest's *The Emergence of Greek Democracy*. What Doria thought of Acker's proposal is unknown, but it clearly wasn't what he, or his publisher, had bargained for. He would eventually publish an anthology of newly translated classic work in 1980 and Acker's *Thesmophoriazusae* would not be part of it.

At the same time, she continued to produce new installments of *The Childlike Life*, turning out a new one every month or so. A third installment was titled "i move to san francisco. i begin to copy my favorite pornography books and become the main person in each of them." Those pornography books included *Thérèse and Isabelle*, Violette Leduc's notorious tale of adolescent lesbian love, which Acker mashed up with half-remembered, half-fantasized scenes from Lenox. A fourth installment used *The Carnal Days of Helen Seferis* by Alexander Trocchi—"my favorite pornographer," she said of him, "I've never seen a man so well understand female sexuality." In a fifth, she "becomes" Yeats. "I'm trying to become other people because this is what I find interesting," she explains. "I'm trying to get away from self-expression but not from personal life. I hate creativity. I'm simply exploring other ways of dealing with events than ways my lousy habits—mainly installed by parents and institutions—have forced me to act. At this point, I'm over-sensitive and have a hard time talking to anyone. I can fuck more easily." In the sixth and final installment, she immerses herself in the words and biography of the Marquis de Sade: "sometimes I think he's horrible, sometimes I think he's great, but he always makes me question." On the last page of the typescript, Acker wrote "This will be the last TARANTULA for a while," but by May 1974, she'd started making notes toward a follow-up she called *I Dreamt I Was a Nymphomaniac!: Imagining*.

In a preview of the censorship Acker would run into later in her career, some printers refused to print the books because they found them morally offensive. More bothersome to her was the rejection of printer-publisher Noel Young, to whom Kenneth Rexroth had referred Acker. Young was the founder of Capra Press, a celebrated micro-publisher in Santa Barbara that published short, offbeat books by the likes of Henry Miller, Ray Bradbury, and Raymond Carver, and he felt Acker was simply not in their league ("too green"). Even worse than this, however, was the criticism she received from old friends like Bernadette Mayer and Harris Schiff. While Mac Low had praised the pamphlets—"the use of abstraction and philosophical self-analysis is brilliant"—Mayer had characterized them as polemical, boring, and didactic. Whatever Schiff's actual comments were—they're lost to time—they clearly stung too. In December, Acker wrote him a forceful defense that summed up her perspective and intentions:

> If you have something to say about the TARANTULAS say it, and I'll reply if I think a reply's necessary. I basically don't care about criticism because I'm more interested in ideas than in whether I've said something nicely or whatever, but I'm really interested in talking about the ideas which are the TARANTULAS. Re: "how come I write mainly about myself?" and "why don't I make up new people?": I don't write mainly about myself though I use the word "I" rather than the second or third person. I use basically found material, material written by other people; about one fourth of the TARANTULAS, if that much contains autobiographical material. I'm interested in my relations to other people, my possibility of getting outside of myself. Since I'm interested in this as a real problem, I don't make up people, because then I'd still be dealing with only my own thoughts, I try to use the thoughts etc. of real people. I'm not interested in self-expression (perhaps you misunderstood some of the ideas, or I haven't been expressing them clearly enough) . . .

If Acker was discouraged, that feeling didn't last for long. In *Nymphomaniac*, she doubled down on her ideas. Continuing her excavation of self, she still used diary material and still gave characters the names of her friends and lovers—the title itself was a nod to Elly Antin's *I Dreamt I Was a Ballerina*. Peter Gordon appears as an SLA agent and "the most gorgeous fag in town," sometimes male, sometimes female. "I assured her I would never stand in the way of her work," Acker writes of this quasi-fictional Gordon. "I mainly needed to be financially supported, left alone, fucked, told I'm a wonderful writer." Acker continues to shift abruptly between dream narratives, plundered passages from other books, and her own eccentric reimaging of current political crises like the Attica prison riots. In *Nymphomaniac*, though, she abandons the reader-friendly signposts she'd used in *The Childlike Life*: the parenthetical demarcation, the lists of plagiarized books that punctuated each installment.

For astute readers, however, the source material was hardly hidden. Most apparent, perhaps, was Blaise Cendrars's 1926 novel *Moravagine*. An underground classic, the book chronicles the exploits of its titular anarchist and murderer, who, released from a hospital for the criminally insane by a sympathetic and obsessed psychiatrist, embarks on a global reign of atrocity, terror, and revolution. Cendrars, a name that was itself yet another pseudonym, argued that Moravagine was his double. "What an incredible fucking writer he is," Acker said of Cendrars. "The speed at which he goes!" Acker transposed sections of the novel from Russia to an unruly, politically fraught America, renamed Moravagine for Gordon's teacher Bob Ashley, and substituted figures, like the anarchist Peter Kropotkin, with Patty Hearst.

Just as she's been for many other writers, artists, and filmmakers, Hearst was a seductive subject for both Acker and Gordon. As with the Weathermen, the SLA's radicalism held an undeniable (if temporary) romantic charge. Acker and Gordon were intrigued by what Hearst's outlandish story said about racial politics, capitalism, the possibilities and limitations of revolutionary activity, and, as always, the refusal to be, in Acker's words, "an enclosed individual." There was a material appeal too for Gordon. The SLA communicated their demands through cassette tapes that the group sent to local radio stations. Gordon recorded these communiqués and, in the studio, edited and blended Hearst's voice with those of friends like Tyranny and Phil Harmonic, who repeated her words. He called the piece "Greetings from the SLA."

The true subject of *Nymphomaniac*, however, was Acker's philosophical investigations, the concentrated representation of which was almost unheard of in American fiction, mainstream or otherwise. "Ideas are most important," she told Mayer, "don't cover over ideas with fancy writing." Still concerned with investigating or exploding an authorial "I," she now wanted to see how memory and imagination shaped subjectivity. In a notebook, she mapped out, more or less, what she was trying to do in the book:

use myself changing as model for change.

Change → changing memory

(can't get rid of memory)

but remembering concerns changing past in terms of present: present
    desire rel for future.

Making this clear/find more about remembering in terms of changing
    myself

Remembering involves repeated time (Kubler)

what if imagining
involves this time?
what if repeated time
becomes revolutionary?

Q: How does (my) remembering differ from my imaginings?

Kubler was George Kubler, the art historian and author of *The Shape of
Time*, a study of formal and symbolic ideas of duration. But Acker was also
reading Sartre and the Austrian mathematician and philosopher Gustav Bergmann, whose knotty writings on ontology she found particularly useful. *Nymphomaniac*, unsurprisingly, was a more challenging project than *The Childlike
Life*, "a messier work on the whole," and more difficult to write. "I was searching for something," Acker told an interviewer.

But what? What did she hope these experiments would help her find? A
way to process the painful memories of her childhood, or to determine which
were true? ("My first remembering is my desire not to perceive events as they
are," she writes.) Or a way to, again, figure out who she was and what she really
desired? ("Intention: escape this horror as I know it and made by it. How can
I (I being a model of any individual) change? Assume the relativist theory of
time accurately maps time in the world. 'I change.' What do I mean by 'I'?") Or
was this just a way to make fiction that felt sufficiently rigorous, even revolutionary? ("My mission is to reveal the uncertainties, unimportances, and final
equivalents of all identities.") All of the above, most likely. "Why shouldn't
writing be everything?" she wrote to Mayer.

But if *Nymphomaniac* was a more difficult book to write, it's also a more difficult book to read. It's often bewildering and occasionally muddled; Acker's refusal to revise gives it an often inhospitable shape. When Acker's work is described as "raw," critics and readers are usually referring to the emotion and sex in her books, but here too, the overt philosophy could be called raw, or, at the very least, lightly processed. Mayer was right to call it dull, at least in parts. While Acker could, and does, subtly weave philosophical ideas into her work, large sections of *Nymphomaniac* are also clotted with chunks of academic deliberation that wouldn't be out of place in the grad school seminars she had recently fled:

I write down a certain number of words repeat those words again. Does the first unit of words mean the same as the repeated unit? That is, either events in time (as for time, for space) are isolated, or mutually dependent with regard to meaning not existence. (For a moment, skip the problem of meaning and existence.) If the meaning(s) of the writing events depend(s) at least partially on the temporal relations of the writing events, the relativist theory of time seems more accurate.

In the book's most notorious sequence, Acker relates a dream that encompasses her family, the art world, and sex. The dream ends or fades out: "As we're fucking, her boyfriend enters the room and stops us because we're not supposed to act sooo" Then, the dream sequence begins again, word for word, concluding with the same fade-out. Like a musical refrain, she repeats it again, two more times, and the chapter ends. Such repetition occurs frequently throughout the first half of the book. "I wanted to see if repeating would change things," she said. "If time was basically made up of moments. If it was qualitative or quantitative." Also, perhaps, the repetition of moments, particularly the harrowing ones of her childhood, offered a chance to start over. Perhaps she had in mind again Gertrude Stein, who wondered if repetition existed, or whether it should just be called *insistence*?

Acker shuffles subjects, ideas, and perspectives with the kind of speed that she admired in Cendrars, but then often slows down, and even runs aground, on the reef of her ruminations. Nonetheless, the novel would find fans among Language poets like Barrett Watten, whose essay, titled "Foucault Reads Acker," describes *Nymphomaniac* as a "liberationist text [which] records an undoing of self at a historical moment of political crisis that Acker wishes to perpetuate by textual means," and the New Narrative writer Robert Glück, both of whom would become close to Acker. Glück first stumbled across the book at the Small Press Traffic bookstore in San Francisco before he had ever heard of or met the writer. At first, he recoiled from Acker's refusal of readerly pleasure or even stability, then enthusiastically embraced her strategies: "Rather than drawing conclusions, developing identifications or thematic connections, that is making judgements that lead to knowledge, Acker creates a reader who is lost in strangeness." For McKenzie Wark, who credits Acker with helping her transition from male to female, Acker's almost nonchalant insistence on gender fluidity in *Nymphomaniac* and her other books was literally life-changing: "A mythic world opens in which genders and sexual orientations emerge together, mutate together, differentiate together."

× × ×

Though Acker described herself at the time as a "bloody hermit," she ventured frequently into San Francisco's literary and art scenes. Most Tuesdays, she swung by Intersection, a performance and poetry space then located in an old Methodist church in North Beach. When the Empty Elevator Shaft, a print-shop-cum-bookstore in Noe Valley, started its own short-lived reading series, Acker attended that too and had some of her Black Tarantula serials printed there. As she finished additional installments, she continued to diligently disseminate them through her mailing list, while also taking them to bookstores like Berkeley's Sand Dollar, where she sold them on consignment. (Acker stayed in touch for decades with the Sand Dollar's owner, Jack Shoemaker, later the founder of the venerable North Point Press, publisher of Guy Davenport and Juan Goytisolo, among many others.)

At least once a week, she also accompanied Gordon to Mills, where she became friendly with faculty like Robert Ashley ("wonderful nice to me," she told Jerome Rothenberg). Ashley, then forty-three, was a renowned composer and creator of conceptual theater, sometimes called the greatest genius of twentieth-century opera. His enthusiasm was legendary, his innovations myriad, his influence on American musicians like Laurie Anderson and David Byrne profound. His most famous work was arguably 1983's *Perfect Lives*, a cryptic, sui generis television production that ostensibly chronicles two musicians staging a prank bank robbery in a small Midwestern town and which has been called variously the first American opera, a performance novel, and a magpie nest of language. Though no fan of opera herself, Acker later credited Ashley with showing her how to create writing that was more of an "environment" rather than centralized, meaningful narrative—a "de-narrative," she called it. At one point, she and Ashley contemplated writing a movie together ("a saga about the Midwestern U.S., of sorts, and the pathology of everyday living"), a project which, alas, never came to fruition. In a letter to Bernadette Mayer, Acker wrote that her male "art stars" were Ashley, Gordon, Lawrence Weiner, and David Antin; the female ones were Mayer and Elly Antin. (Dan Graham was "on outs.")

When Acker and Gordon first arrived in San Francisco, they started hosting a weekly three-hour show on KPOO, a local community radio station. The couple were told they could do whatever they wanted, and they did, with Acker reading work by Antin, Mac Low, de Sade, or her own writing. Gordon played music by the likes of Arthur Honegger, invited Ashley and Terry Riley on as guests. "I don't know if anyone listens," Acker wrote to Mac Low, "but it's fun." Soon, however, they learned the station's managers were not quite as permissive as they had first thought. At some point on-air, Acker told a story about how she lost her virginity, and on another occasion, Gordon had Ashley present a talking piece. The first violated FCC regulations; the latter KPOO deemed too boring. The show was dropped. "It was very repressive and very demeaning," Gordon told the *Berkeley Barb* at the time.

A few months later, though, they debuted another show on Berkeley's KPFA, the first listener-supported broadcaster in the country. *High Art in Its Highest Glory* was essentially proto-talk radio, a three-hour program during which Acker and Gordon (and later Ashley) would chat about various topics and ideas, then take calls from listeners, who could talk about whatever they wanted. Gordon mixed and layered the various voices, creating an alluring soundscape. Acker, Gordon recalled, "had no filter." At one point, someone with whom she'd been having an affair called in, and they broke up on the air. Soon enough, they received an admonishing letter from the station's program director, and that show was canceled too.

Gordon's cohort at Mills was tiny and tight-knit, and he quickly befriended a classmate named Jill Kroesen, who also went by the stage name Fay Shism. Kroesen was a lissome, dark-haired musical daredevil who, like Gordon, mingled rock and pop with avant-garde experimentation. Her MFA thesis at Mills was built around a song she composed, "Fay Shism Blues," which reimagined Hitler as a femme fatale. Gordon performed on that, and the pair would collaborate frequently over the next few years, including on Ashley's *Perfect Lives*. Kroesen loved Gordon, calling him years later "the greatest guy in the universe."

Her feelings toward Acker were more complex. While acknowledging that Acker was smart and charismatic, she also thought that Acker "didn't care about other people's feelings at all," and Kroesen never found her particularly friendly. This might have had something to do with the fact that Kroesen and Gordon ended up sleeping together. It was a fling, and only lasted a couple of weeks, but as Gordon had learned by that point, Acker's attitudes toward monogamy didn't exactly extend to her partners—she could be extremely possessive.

Kroesen also had a difficult time with Acker's writing. She had endured her own "horrible" childhood, had been sexually abused, in fact, and found any violent or pornographic art extremely upsetting. She was amazed that Acker would willingly revisit her own childhood memories in her books. "In her work, it was like she was running like a mad person away from the pain," Kroesen said, "but leaving this trail of information to figure it out." Still, Kroesen was captivated enough by Acker to write several songs about her over the next couple of years, ditties both affectionate and acerbic, like "Don't Steal My Boyfriend," "Please Don't Hurt Me," "Lenny and Kathy," and "Pelvic Inflammatory Disease Blues." "Prince Charming Blues," which Kroesen dedicated to Acker, borrowed a refrain from the Rolling Stones' "(I Can't Get No) Satisfaction," sandwiching it between verses like "I had a boy with a penis as long as a kitchen knife/When he tried to fuck me I thought I'd lose my life/I left him for a gorgeous man whose prick was short and fat/But oh my god he comes too fast." Kroesen, who was also a talented graphic artist, ended up designing a cover for the first printed edition of *The Childlike Life*—a collage with a stylized spider splayed over Acker's face. Acker never really cared for it, and ditched the image in all subsequent editions.

× × ×

As Gordon became intimate with Kroesen, Acker continued to seek out her own extracurricular romances. "Lots of street sex, bang, bang, bang," she told Mac Low. For a while, she had a standing weekly liaison with Honeymoon

Hotel resident Rich Gold, and there were other brief encounters, including a one-night stand with the poet-novelist Andrei Codrescu.

In February 1974, she embarked on an affair of more lasting significance with the conceptual artist and writer Alan Sondheim. The relationship was fraught and, from the start, bound up in Acker's messy family history. That month she flew to New York to collect a small trust fund that her maternal grandfather had left her: $300 in cash, as well as an additional hundred dollars' worth of stock dividends. As Acker told it, this money had been kept secret from her, with her parents forging her signature and keeping the dividends for themselves.

How exactly Acker learned about the trust is unclear, but what made its existence even more dramatic was the fact that the check was made out to someone named Karen Lehman. Here, at last, was her *actual* birth name. Her biological father, she had finally discovered, was someone named Harry Lehman, Jr. She learned that he was the scion of the family that founded the Buffalo-based Wildroot Company, a hugely successful purveyor of hair tonics, shampoos, and other products. (Ronald Reagan appeared in their advertisements; Colgate-Palmolive bought the company in 1959.) Acker was stunned and disoriented. At long last, at twenty-six years of age, she was close to tracking down her real father.

Or was she? While she suddenly had the information she'd long sought, she didn't quite know what to do with it. What did she want from this father she had never known, and who supposedly hadn't wanted her? The discovery briefly paralyzed her. While she would travel to New York and briefly visit Claire and Bud, she wouldn't, it seems, actively try to find Lehman for over a year.

Instead, as she'd been doing her whole writing life, she'd once again transmute his abandonment into art. On February 18, she read at the Poetry Project alongside Mel Freilicher and Ed Bowes. Alan Sondheim was in the audience. Sondheim was five years older than Acker, thin and nebbishy, with a nimbus of thick, dark hair. He was a prolific polymath who'd already produced a thicket of book-length essays, spoken-word performances, and experiments with new technology, and Acker, who'd heard about his work through David Antin, was curious about him. A couple days after the reading, she had dinner with him and his wife, Beth Cannon, at their apartment on 17th Street, where Acker said, they "talked for twelve hours." Acker returned to San Francisco a couple days later, but their connection was intense, and they decided, over the course of several letters and phone calls, that they would make a videotape together "exploring sexuality." Sondheim scrounged some money from the Rhode Island School of Design, where he was a guest artist, recruited a student named Emily Cheng to operate the camera, and flew Acker back to New York at the beginning of March.

At his apartment, they ended up making two tapes, though the second one, a satire of the first—an "inverse, both sexually and in terms of mood," in Sondheim's words—was lost for several decades. The first, however, became a small sensation. Over the course of fifty-four black-and-white minutes, Acker and Sondheim engage in a kind of dispassionate verbal jousting, trying to define both themselves and their relationship to each other. Or, more accurately perhaps, perform this act of definition. Acker's hair is buzzed short, and she's wearing rimless glasses, dangly earrings, a dark cotton scarf around her neck. They talk haughtily about control, about perception, about power. With Lehman fresh in her mind, Acker says she regards Sondheim as a father figure—her "perfect father"—or as a kind of analyst, using him to get to memories that were too painful for her to access any other way. Sondheim, for his part, thought Acker was his "soulmate." He calls her a "powerful person," and says, to Acker's evident delight, "You're gonna kill people, baby, you really are."

Much of their conversation, however, or their respective monologues, occurs as they are having actual sex. Cheng's camera captures, with intermittent focus, Sondheim stroking Acker's clit and her rimming him and sucking him off while he struggles to narrate his thoughts and sensations. Sondheim later remembered Acker acting "suicidal" during a break in the taping, though Cheng only remembers Acker's self-confidence and her "utter lack of self-consciousness with her body and emotions." Chris Kraus situated the tape in the lineage of confrontational conceptual art that included Vito Acconci's *Seedbed* and Chris Burden's *Shoot*, but the overall effect is something like an early Chantal Akerman film rewritten by Woody Allen.

"We pushed things as far as we could," Sondheim later wrote. "I felt needy. I hated myself." The tape was later shown at St. Mark's, Yale, RISD, and the Whitney, among other places, titillating, amusing, and repelling its various audiences. Eventually, Acker and Sondheim agreed not to show the tape without their mutual consent; they both considered the experiment a failure.

Acker never talked publicly about the two tapes, and only rarely, as she became a better-known writer, did she ever mention Sondheim. It seemed she would have preferred the whole experience be forgotten. But over the years, the first tape, which was never formally titled, became known as *The Blue Tape* and, when it was rediscovered a few years after Acker's death, took on the aura of an archaeological treasure. It was a glum artifact of the New York art world in the early seventies, with its dubious gender dynamics, sexual gamesmanship, and intellectual braggadocio on full display. You can practically smell the bodies. The emotional vulnerability, performative or not, is oppressive. For Acker devotees, however, it was a rare, unedited glimpse of her charm and difficulty, and, above all, the lengths she would go in the name of self-determination and knowledge.

CHAPTER 16

THE RELATIONSHIP WITH SONDHEIM WAS INTENSE AND DESTABILIZ-
ing, but it died down as quickly as it had flared up. By that summer, Acker
had become disenchanted, calling him "a shit" and "a schmuck." She'd also
found a different focus for her romantic energies. At the Empty Elevator Shaft,
where he was giving a reading with Barrett Watten, she met Ron Silliman, a
poet whom David Antin had suggested she look up. Silliman was about a year
older than her, and had been raised in Albany, California, just north of Berkeley. Then, and throughout his career, Silliman moved between quite different
spheres—after registering as a conscientious objector during the Vietnam War,
he worked for the Committee for Prisoner Humanity and Justice while also
writing and publishing several books, organizing readings himself, and serving
as executive editor of the *Socialist Review*.

Silliman became one of the best-known Language poets, a group of formally adventurous poets in the Bay Area and New York whose name was
derived from the *L=A=N=G=U=A=G=E* journal edited by Bruce Andrews
and Charles Bernstein. The Language poets, as the Acker scholar Georgina
Colby usefully defines them, rejected the "processural" poetics of Charles
Olson, which had once influenced Acker, and "attacked the instrumental value
of language put forward and sustained by a capitalist society." Their number
included Rae Armantrout, Clark Coolidge, Carla Harryman, Bob Perelman,
Hannah Weiner, and Lyn Hejinian, among others. Silliman's essay "The New
Sentence," published in 1977, was a landmark Language manifesto and he remains one of the movement's most compelling, if controversial, theorists. In
2002, Silliman started a popular blog, which quickly became a vital, comprehensive online repository of innovative American poetry.

At their first meeting, Acker handed him the latest installment of *Nymphomaniac*. Silliman was impressed. It was clear that she was writing fiction,
not poetry, and while Silliman was a self-professed snob about novels—*why*
would you want to write one of *those*, he wondered—he was delighted by the

foundational questions she was asking about fiction-making. "She was really trying to figure out, 'What is a character?' 'How do you make a character?' 'How does a character acquire a voice or is it the voice that generates the character?' 'How do you get a character through the door given that the door is simply an imagined construct?' She tore fiction down to its very core." He found it quaint and somewhat romantic too that she was writing her book, or books, one installment a month, and he found himself deliberately going to readings hoping to bump into her and get the next one. They would eventually sleep together, but she'd always value him more as a friend and confidant.

Her appearance and contradictory affect beguiled him. She was the first woman he'd seen in San Francisco with hair so short, but he loved her "good smile," and thought she made a point of being attractive and off-putting all at once. Despite her "very hard-edged physical presentation," and unlike just about every other poet and visual artist he knew, who lived in predictable bohemian squalor, he thought she valued what he called "a positive, supportive environment around the house." (On Belvedere, that meant old-school comfy hippie trappings: a waterbed, plenty of printed cloth, the pets with their amusing names.)

The attraction went both ways. Silliman appears frequently as a character in *The Adult Life of Toulouse Lautrec by Henri Toulouse Lautrec*, the third and final Black Tarantula book, where an Acker alter-ego named Giannina calls him "my closest friend in San Francisco." They started going to readings together, taking the Geary Street bus and then disembarking at a mutually convenient intersection where they would stand and talk and flirt for hours. She was one of the few people he knew in the poetry scene, maybe the only one, who was also interested in what was going on in art and electronic music, and she sometimes took him to those events. For the final section of *Nymphomaniac*, she took some documents that Silliman had from his job at the Committee for Prisoner Humanity and Justice, lifting its bureaucratic catalogue of penal procedures and grievances, substituting inmate's names with those of her friends, and essentially publishing it verbatim.

On one occasion, Silliman and Acker were invited to read together at a restaurant on Telegraph Avenue in Berkeley. It was an important reading for Silliman, the public debut of the first section of his book-length poem *Ketjak*, but Acker, with precocious aplomb, decided she wouldn't read at all. Instead, she had Gordon, Rich Gold, and Phil Harmonic go up on stage and instructed them to talk about what The Black Tarantula was like as a lover. "I think Kathy had something more salacious in mind," Silliman remembered, "but they were all perfect gentlemen. They all recounted what she had told them to talk about, but they were really not going to talk about their love lives with her." Nonetheless, and with no hard feelings, Silliman quickly realized that he'd been upstaged by Acker's "marvelous sense of self-mythologization and theater."

Acker would soon abandon such stunts, but her readings would always be characterized by that sense of theater. She treated every reading as a real performance, and she deliberately avoided the expected. If there was a microphone, she might not use it. If there was a lectern, she'd stand in front of it or sit on the stage. At the Western Front in Vancouver, whose performance space used church pews for seating, Acker told the audience that she didn't want anyone to sit in the pews, but rather to come up and sit on the floor with her. "I'm a performance artist," she said, "I'm not going to just read from my book." Lynne Tillman, the novelist and critic, first saw Acker read in New York in the late seventies, and remembered one occasion, at a now forgotten restaurant on Third Avenue. Acker sat on a table in the middle of the room, with people all sitting around her. She pressed her mouth against the mic, whispering "sinisterly," an effect enhanced by the fact that she was reading about people who were in the same room. "She did what she wanted to do," said Tillman of Acker's reading style. "She took these great liberties." Inspired by that particular event, Tillman started working on a novella she called *Weird Fucks*.

Many other writers, including Dennis Cooper, Leslie Dick, and Kevin Killian, claimed that Acker taught them how to read their own work in public. "If she thought she was losing her audience," Killian said, "instead of speeding up, as you have a tendency to do as you're up there dying, she would slow down to a crawl. The audience, even if they're bored, says, 'Am I missing something?' and they really focus in on her. She would just do it until she had every last person in the room. No matter what part of the story it was. It was a trick I learned for the rest of my life." In their novel, *Inferno*, Eileen Myles similarly captures Acker reading in Germany late in her life: "Each of us was to read for 8 or 10 minutes and Kathy would read for 21. And miraculously she didn't kill the room. I'd watch her going on and on same fucking story. I'd think how can she do this. Deadly. But she was okay. More than that. People were riveted."

x x x

As Acker's career started to take off, Gordon was also moving on to more lucrative creative pastures. While still enrolled at Mills, he began playing sax in a band called Butch Whacks and the Glass Packs, a "50s rock-and-roll genre revue" that toured North America, sometimes opening for the likes of the Doobie Brothers. During a three-week stint at the Cave in Vancouver, in an ardent, lonely letter, Gordon told Acker about his increasing musical confidence. "It's strange," he wrote, "I could be big in rock if I worked at it. It's really a matter of getting into the drag." That drag would only fit for a short while, though, and he stayed with the band for just six months.

Acker had little patience for that particular scene, burrowing instead into her own work. She gave a reading with the poet Jim Carroll at Intersection that November, kept working on *Nymphomaniac*. Writing the book was exhausting, though, and she found distraction reading Bertolt Brecht and playing with her animals.

By that point, Jill Kroesen had moved to New York, and Acker was starting to think that maybe she should return to the East Coast again too. "I now need the input," she told Mac Low. Though she still loved Gordon, she said, their sex life was nonexistent, and it often felt like they were on the verge of or in the midst of a real breakup. Acker asked Bernadette Mayer if she could arrange a reading for her at St. Mark's, and after some back-and-forth, Acker booked a flight to New York to coincide with the opening of an Eleanor Antin gallery show in mid-January 1975. Around the same time, Gordon would be in Chicago, where the Glass Packs had a three-week residency at the Playboy Club.

Just before Acker was to leave, though, in December, she received an unexpected letter from Ted Castle and Leandro Katz, the founders of the Vanishing Rotating Triangle Press (TVRT), a tiny New York–based purveyor of poetry by the likes of John Ashbery, César Vallejo, and Gerard Malanga. They had been on the Black Tarantula mailing list and wanted to reprint *The Childlike Life* in a TVRT edition. Katz admired "the leaps of language" in Acker's work and likened her appropriations to the pastiches in the outrageous plays Charles Ludlam produced with his Ridiculous Theatrical Company. Acker was excited by the offer, but wrote back saying her "old stuff seems dead to me" and tried to persuade them instead to publish a new Rip-off Red book titled *I Become a Revolutionary*. Castle and Katz stuck to their initial plan, however, and while TVRT editions normally had miniscule print runs—three hundred copies or so—*The Childlike Life* would be their largest production to date, about a thousand. It would be a loose arrangement, though; TVRT bought no rights and would pay Acker only in copies of the book. Still, they were a legitimate publishing house, and Acker was understandably elated. "This was special," Gordon recalled. "They were her first publishers."*

× × ×

Arriving in Manhattan that January, Acker quickly realized that Castle and Katz weren't her only fans. She now had a certain notoriety in downtown art and literary circles. In a letter to Silliman, she wrote, "in SF I thought no one gave a shit about my books here I'm some kind of star."

Or, for better or worse, The Black Tarantula was. An aura of mystery, danger, and sexual aggression clung to the pen name. Eileen Myles, freshly arrived at St. Mark's themselves, recalled that the Poetry Project was abuzz about "the legend of The Black Tarantula." At one point, the poet Bill Berkson tried to pick Acker up, telling her that he'd read her writing and knew "what she wanted." "My books made everyone think I'm Ms. Cunt," she told Silliman, her dismay colored by an irrefutable pride. Acker would always be equivocal about fame: craving it on the one hand ("that was her goal," Gordon said), but frustrated that she couldn't completely control how it affected her work and life. Even later, as she more strenuously stage-managed her public image, it always threatened to undermine how seriously her writing was taken, or obscure it completely.

If Acker was becoming an underground star, like many an underground star she was also still broke and alone, with nowhere, really, to live. She ended up crashing at Mayer's apartment on Second Avenue for more than a month. It was a somewhat fraught arrangement to begin with, given Mayer's regard for Acker's recent writing and complicated further by Mayer's own domestic

---

* With Printed Matter, TVRT later copublished different editions of both The Childlike Life and Toulouse Lautrec, with covers created by Katz and William Wegman, respectively. Katz believed the arrangement was the result of an affair between Acker and Sol LeWitt, a cofounder of Printed Matter, a rumor almost impossible to substantiate. (I asked Lawrence Weiner, who knew LeWitt well, and he could neither deny nor confirm, saying only that "Sol was a Don Juan and Kathy had round heels.") In any case, TVRT received no compensation from this collaboration, and Katz felt that Acker never cared enough to intervene on TVRT's behalf. Because of this rift, he wouldn't speak to her for years.

dramas (she'd had an affair the previous summer with Anne Waldman and was now involved with Waldman's ex-husband, Lewis Warsh).

Acker was also now between books, somewhat bored with both herself and her writing. Her first week back, looking for some other artistic outlet, she started attending workshops with Simone Forti, a pioneer of postmodern dance. She was soon consumed by the work. It felt good to be out of her head, working with her body, and she supplemented these classes with ones taught by Trisha Brown and Kenneth King, until she was dancing about five hours a day.

In one of Forti's classes, she met Pooh Kaye, a twenty-four-year-old dancer, choreographer, and filmmaker, and also Acker's cousin. (While growing up, Acker had known Pooh by her birth name, Louise, and it would be years before they realized they were related.) Kaye had just graduated from Cooper Union and was then making a series of Super 8 films in which she performed, nude, a series of task-like dance movements in a variety of environments. They became close, and, for a while, Kaye idolized Acker. "I was trying to figure out what I was doing," she recalled, "but I was pretty unformed compared to someone like Kathy." They went to openings and parties together—dancer and artist parties being better than dull poet parties—hung out at places like the Locale on Waverly, which Mickey Ruskin opened after departing Max's Kansas City. After staying with Mayer, and before she found her own place, Acker couch-surfed all over downtown. She went from staying in Richard "Rip" Hayman's apartment above the Ear Inn, a beloved literary-minded dive in the lower Village, to living in the Spring Street loft owned by Dick Higgins and Alison Knowles, which Kaye occasionally cleaned to pay the bills.

Acker told Silliman that Kaye was her "best girlfriend," but soon, she had also befriended another female writer whose work hewed closer to Acker's own. Constance DeJong was working on her first novel, *Modern Love*, which she would also start serializing that fall in five installments (and to a mailing list of five hundred) out of the Westbeth office of Performing Artservices, Inc., a nonprofit artists' management firm founded by Bob Ashley's wife, Mimi Johnson. DeJong, who was dating composer Philip Glass at the time, and who would write the libretto for his *Satyagraha*, was also keenly interested in the performance of her writing and would later become renowned for readings where she recited her prose from memory. *Modern Love* was elliptical and dissonant, part detective story, part postmodern historical romance, both a downtown cousin of Renata Adler's *Speedboat* and an American version of the *nouveau roman*.

DeJong lived near Tompkins Square Park in the East Village, and she and Acker began meeting regularly for coffee and to talk shop. They were very different people, with very different backgrounds and personalities. DeJong was less social, more reserved, but she spent most of her time with composers and performers, and was delighted to find another prose writer with whom to discuss technical aspects of the form—verb tenses, narrative construction, and the like. "It was not a conversation I had with anyone else," she remembered. "We were people of language and people of words." DeJong thought Acker's "polyphonic voice" was entirely unique, that she was "doing things with language that other people had not done." She was equally impressed with how devotional Acker was to her writing. "She was a dead-serious person. Writing was everything. And she was always working. It wasn't as boring as, 'Oh, she had a work ethic.' It was much more driven than that—she was an extremely driven person." Acker similarly gushed about DeJong to Silliman: "an incredible writer [who] I feel I can learn a lot from her writing it's incredibly precise i.e. so transparent." They shared their respective literary enthusiasms (Acker: Burroughs, Genet; DeJong: Stein, Duras, late Woolf), and at one meeting, Acker gave DeJong a copy of Violette Leduc's gossipy, self-abnegating memoir *Mad in Pursuit*. DeJong could see immediately what Acker had gleaned from the French writer—"the relentless voice of the struggling, self-obsessed Leduc persona, hyperbolizing her encounters."

Acker and DeJong were united as well in their opposition to what, decades later, DeJong called "the gatekeepers" of commercial publishing. "Kathy and I were like, 'Fuck the gatekeepers.' The gatekeepers of what? Some old-fashioned idea of what the novel is? I know I wasn't going to seek that approval or wait for it. I was acquainted, as was Kathy, with a number of artists who were older than we were and who were very can-do people very good at finding a way to have visibility. The music people did that. The dance people did that. The film people did that. Steve Reich and Philip Glass were not waiting for Lincoln Center to come calling. They went out into the world."

The world those artists went to, or more often ushered into being themselves, was a rapidly expanding array of artist-run centers, performance spaces, and nightclubs that bloomed throughout the drear hothouse of 1970s lower Manhattan. Nineteen seventy-five was the year that New York officially teetered into economic chaos, when President Gerald Ford famously told the city to "drop dead," denying it federal bailout money. It was, as DeJong writes in *Modern Love*, "a city lost and beaten and full of emptiness." But the ubiquity of massive, cheap work spaces, lack of police and bureaucratic oversight, and a seemingly insatiable hunger for artistic collaboration led to an unprecedented surge of cultural activity. It helped too that the art world was relatively small and concentrated—a grungy, scrambling, and interbred village. "There are two hundred thousand artists in New York now," Sylvère Lotringer said. "Then there were two hundred. The news went very fast."

The Kitchen, a performance and video art space, had opened in 1971 in the literal former kitchen of the Mercer Arts Center and by 1974 had moved to its own digs at Wooster and Broome streets in SoHo. Richard Foreman, the legendary experimental playwright and impresario, formed his own theater in a narrow loft at Broadway and Broome. Burgeoning institutions like the Franklin Furnace, Artists Space, Printed Matter, the Franklin Street Arts Center, and the Institute for Art and Urban Resources (later P.S.1), all of which opened their doors around the same period, provided emerging and alternative artists with money, company, and a home.

With some excitement, Acker told Silliman about 112 Greene Street, a six-story, 24/7, art laboratory-cum-gallery created by artist Gordon Matta-Clark and a sculptor and self-described anarchist named Jeffrey Lew: "this guy named Jeffrey Lew is setting up a downtown Lincoln Center one floor of which will be devoted to printing & he's promised Connie [Constance DeJong] she will have full control of the printing press which means I can too." While formerly desolate SoHo was being transformed and redefined by visual artists in the mid-seventies, the denser and more impoverished East Village and Lower East Side, meanwhile, nurtured a more literary and theatrical pedigree. As Alan Moore and Jim Cornwell put it in *Alternative Art New York*, those neighborhoods constituted a "poet's district . . . thick with the forms and attitudes of previous cultural moments." In other words, as Edmund White wrote of the period, "Then, there were only possibilities."

Those possibilities would later be mythologized to the point of cliché, but many of the artists who imagined them, who nurtured them, who lived through them, do nonetheless recall the time with affection. "It was such a playground," Pooh Kaye said of the city. "It was so bankrupt, so formless. Anybody could put their own ambitions on top of it. You could make art anywhere." Lynne

Tillman, who had just returned from several years in Europe and would soon befriend Acker too, was similarly intoxicated. "I think we are all very interested in what was happening at that moment," she said. "There was a lot going on. There was a lot of stuff to go to see. There was a lot of loft parties. There was a collision of people downtown." With New York largely broke too, the market didn't really dictate what kind of work was being made; there was no real market, no pie to fight over. Artists woke up, had an idea, then grabbed their like-minded friends and cobbled together enough resources to make it. Then they moved on to the next thing. The writer Lucy Sante summed it all up perfectly: "1975 is a new world, somehow [. . .] the year is a laboratory."

Acker, for her part, was of two minds about all this. "There never was a better time," she said, with genuine nostalgia, many years later. "The community was absolutely strong. All my friendships have really come from that time." But in the moment, she alternated between enthusiasm and revulsion for the scene. She found the attention she personally received both thrilling and confusing, and she wasn't quite sure how to navigate the social dynamics of the art world. The male artists, whom she often derided as macho cowboys, were sexually aggressive. Though many people were interested in her work, she didn't always feel that enthusiastic about theirs. To her mind, artists like Vito Acconci were more or less over, and the new art that she was seeing in SoHo—the gallery stuff, at least—was tepid: "none of it dangerous or with any social implications."

She also claimed to hate the overweening competition of the art scene, what she called "the Protestant work ethic, the real a-political coldness of the artists." But even she knew this was disingenuous. After just a short time back in New York, she had become even more conscious of the art world's hierarchies, the shifting strata of cultural capital, and how this shaped both the content and reception of art. Acker herself gleefully participated in this pecking order. She and Mel Freilicher "graded" the St. Mark's poets as A, B, C, or D and, at one point, even wrote out a flow chart detailing how these people could help them become famous. "It involved befriending (sucking up to) x-number of A-list people," Freilicher remembered. "You were allowed—even required to—alienate a small number of people on the B- and C-lists but only after fulfilling A-list requirements. It was a lot of fun." Acker also worked just as hard as anyone else, probably harder. It was a matter of "survival," though, she told Silliman. "Here art is ART WORK IMPORTANT. There ain't nothing else."

Where else was she going to go, though? There weren't a lot of places for a writer like her. She told Silliman he should move there. And then, she went and got an actual job. Taking tickets a couple nights a week at the Kitchen, she made $15 a week. It was, she said, "about the only job I've ever had that I like."

CHAPTER 17

———————— × ————————

G ORDON VISITED NEW YORK IN FEBRUARY, BUT RETURNED TO CAL-
ifornia soon after; he'd continue to go back and forth while he toured
and finished up his MFA. At some point, he and Acker had officially broken
up, but they would still remain a couple, sharing an apartment again many
months later.

Acker was pleased with herself, though, that she hadn't, as she'd done
in the past, immediately traded one heavy relationship for another. She was
still meeting and getting involved with people—for sex, for company, for
connections—but none of these relationships really had the intensity or
drama of her previous ones.

While still living at Mayer's, Acker hooked up with a twenty-three-year-
old musician named Rhys Chatham, who also worked at Tin Pan Alley, a
Times Square bar popular with jazz musicians, strippers, and artists, and was
the Kitchen's first musical director. Chatham first met Acker at St. Mark's and
was, like others, initially cowed by The Black Tarantula's fearsome reputation.
While he soon got over this first impression, calling Acker in hindsight "an
absolute sweetheart," he remained somewhat shocked by what he considered
her libertinism. Even in an era of unbridled sexual promiscuity, Chatham felt
that she "really did sleep with everyone," and had a particular fondness, he
said, for younger men like himself. At the time, Acker was still, for better or
worse, largely dependent on Gordon for financial and emotional support, both
of which allowed her to write, but Chatham thought she also required fresh
infusions of romantic adventure to fuel her work. "She was a poet," he said.
"When she fell in love with one person or another, she was inspired to write."

Her female friends, who were sometimes collateral damage in her carnal
pursuits, were more curt. They didn't care that she slept around—that was
practically a given in their circles—but they didn't appreciate her open disregard for their feelings or attachments. "She slept with every man I knew," Pooh
Kaye said. "She'd co-opt people's boyfriends, husbands, lovers, anyone they

had crushes on. It was a thing she did. At a party, she went after a guy I was interested in right in front of my face. It was unreal." Another friend, the artist Aline Mare, who was dating sculptor Richard Serra at the time, had a similar recollection: "I'd see her at parties, where she just zoomed in on someone. It didn't matter if they came in together, and they were obviously a team. She would just direct her sexual and intellectual prowess. Like an animal, almost." Even the poet Eileen Myles, then still, in their words, "actively heterosexual," experienced Acker this way. "For several years," Myles said, "I was fucking people who Kathy had just fucked." One night, the two of them were at Arcadia, a pizza joint frequented by the poetry crowd, sitting in a booth with two men. Myles, who was relatively friendly with Acker, recalled her refusing to even meet Myles's gaze, essentially treating Myles as if they weren't there.

Acker wasn't particularly enraptured by Chatham—"he's more idiotic and childish and selfish than me," she told Silliman, "[though] we get along well"— but she did scribble this note to herself on the back cover of the first notebook she used for *The Adult Life of Toulouse Lautrec by Toulouse Lautrec*: "Reality: I admire Rhys because he has power . . . I don't fall in love w/ men just who are nice to me. Power = able to survive." What power did Chatham possess, in her mind? A sexual power? Perhaps she meant the cultural and social capital he had, owing to his role at the Kitchen and his growing reputation in the downtown music scene. As Chatham had divined, several of Acker's relationships, as is the case with so many ambitious people, had been driven, and would continue to be driven, by how useful a lover could be to her. Or how they helped her discover and cultivate different parts of herself. Ron Silliman concurred: "It was clear that she really treated sexual relationships, instrumentally, career-wise."

Power and sex too were inextricable for her. "I think they were utterly connected in her mind," said her friend Betsy Sussler, the editor of *BOMB* magazine. A few months after her relationship with Chatham began, Acker would watch filmmaker Kathryn Bigelow, a close acquaintance when the latter was in the graduate film program at Columbia, publicly pursue the older French intellectual Bernard-Henri Lévy at a Semiotext(e) event. When a somewhat appalled Acker asked her why, Bigelow smiled and said, "Power, baby, power." It was a story that Acker loved to tell, though rarely, if ever, acknowledging that she might also be talking about herself. "She was a skilled tactician around power," Eileen Myles said. "That's what she was interested in." Sussler, who during their friendship found Acker heartbreakingly lonely and vulnerable, thought that Acker's relationship to, or understanding of, power was more complicated than that, particularly when it came to her sex life. "She wanted to be sublimated, subsumed and consumed," Sussler said, "and yet she wanted to have power over [men]. She wasn't a femme fatale."

As all this testimony suggests, sex was of profound, complicated, and sometimes confusing importance to Acker, and would remain so for the rest of her life. On the one hand, her fascination was crude and simple—as she would put it, she really liked to get fucked. And she could become bored quickly by her lovers. But it didn't end there. As literary territory, sex was incredibly rich, a limitless zone within which she could theorize about bodies, desire, performance, affect. Sex was her favorite topic, she said, describing herself as a "fanatic." It contained both narrative—expectation, tension, release—and poetry—seduction, rhythm, fluidity. Its pleasures could be transcendent and its disappointments crippling, a dialectic that Acker never tired of revisiting. It was also, finally, the corporeal expression of love—irrational love, fascistic love, devotional love—which never stopped being her great subject. "These writings are the fuels of love," she wrote in *My Death My Life by Pier Paolo Pasolini*. "Each statement is the absolute truth—and an absolute lie—because I'm always changing." Acker's love life, at many points, could seem almost indiscriminate. Her lovers were formidable intellectuals and accomplished artists, but just as often they were feckless poets, sycophantic students, and middle-of-the-road journalists. Physical attractiveness wasn't always a big deal to her either; some friends thought she had terrible taste.

Boyfriends, husbands, and lovers were useful as material. In almost all her books, Acker includes figures based on real people, with various degrees of fidelity. Acker, however, never pretended that her characters were anything more than textual playthings, configurations in a composition within which to situate ideas or simulate voices, reliable shorthand to specific emotional effects. In some cases, these characters bore little more than their real-life analog's name; at other times, they were lightly drawn facsimiles. Silliman became a character in *The Adult Life of Toulouse Lautrec*, as did Chatham. Chatham was delighted to be used in such a manner, but Silliman had a somewhat more complex reaction. He first thought that Acker's description of him as "gentle" was, for her, an insult. Years later, though, re-reading lines like "Ron's a great poet: His varied sensuous language reflects and questions itself," he would come to see how affectionate this thumbnail portrait was. "She made me out to be a better person than I was," Silliman said.

Acker started *Toulouse Lautrec* in May, around the same time TVRT was publishing *The Childlike Life*. The new book was less about herself, or about Acker trying to excavate herself, as human being, text, or author, and more about an exploration of genre and "myth." Throughout Acker's career, "myth" would be a complex, mercurial word in her vocabulary but which mainly meant a kind of overarching discourse or narrative. Aside from Silliman, Chatham, and, again, Peter Gordon, the book teems with historical, real-life figures: the titular disfigured French painter; Van Gogh; Jacqueline Onassis; James Dean; Janis Joplin; Henry Kissinger. Dean, according to Acker, represented the "myth" of the 1950s, Joplin the '60s, and Kissinger the '70s. It also churns through several familiar narrative modes and styles—art history, Agatha Christie mystery, fable, porn, Hollywood film, tabloid newspaper, and crime biography—while also employing Acker's now signature maneuvers: shifting genders, appropriation, the incessant emphasis on power and sex. Acker wanted to figure out, she said, how to engage a hegemonic, mainstream culture, which she called "the jailer," and transform its meaning or its relationship to "us"—us being the marginalized, the poor, artists. "I'm all excited by my new book," she told Silliman, "which everyone will hate it's what I've always wanted to do."

While still far more concerned with ideas, she was also becoming, in her own way, more interested in the usual architecture of fiction: story and plot. While dismissive of mainstream contemporaries such as Joyce Carol Oates, she raved to Silliman about writers like Thomas Pynchon: "God Pynchon's a good writer! I see how much I have to learn. I'm still so awkward & slow & uncourageous. I do things too slowly. I mean he has such a range!"

She found further inspiration in a more unlikely source—bestselling schlockmeister Harold Robbins. As always, she scorned any distinction between so-called high and low culture, and happily read (and borrowed from) writers and genres—porn and pulp fiction, most obviously—that her more snobby colleagues tended to shun. Robbins knew the power of a good story as well as the power of a good fake biography—he famously concocted his own outlandish rags-to-riches backstory. And, similar to Acker, albeit to much different effect, he stole his epic plots and larger-than-life characters from real life, fictionalizing everyone from Frank Sinatra to pornographer

Larry Flynt. As Acker told Silliman, reading Robbins was positively revolutionary for her:

> Took to reading J. Suzanne[*sic*] H. Robbins I. Wallace the last week with the idea that I've been reading everything the avant-garde's done and everything by dead writers but I have no idea what non-avant garde stuff's been done in this country in past 25 years ... Robbins turns out to be the main interest and a large one: his use of fact/fiction business, especially not especially actually in everything I've read so far, the conception of writing as its existence based on audience: reaction so the dealing with anticipation, expectation, maneuvering, etc. all this in relation to American politics and existence, use of story narrative as myth (a source of common energy information) that again has politics advertising conceptual basis, and the information! A range that no avant garde person has touched, and a new way my writing opens.

Acker lifted four pages from Robbins's 1974 potboiler *The Pirate*, itself loosely based on the life of flamboyant billionaire arms dealer Adnan Khashoggi, and folded them into *The Adult Life*. Whether in tribute or merely, as she said, for "the information," the gesture was both innocent and inspired. "Robbins is really soft core porn," she later said, "so I wanted to see what would happen if you changed contexts and just upped the sexuality of the language. It's a very simplistic example of deconstruction." As entirely different as Acker and Robbins's aesthetics and ambitions may have been, the two writers were united, improbably, in their attempts to capture the unstable interplay of the real and the imaginary and the grotesque machinations of the culture. Robbins had figured out how to make himself rich off of such attempts. Acker, meanwhile, was, in her words, "just some nut who piddles around with these problems to amuse and teach herself."

× × ×

In the spring of 1975, Gordon moved back to New York more or less for good, and he and Acker sublet Constance DeJong's apartment while the latter spent the summer in India. Acker had her own room, which she decorated with books, vivid yellow-and-orange Mexican fabrics, and a foam pad draped with a white silk quilt. "This slum will have to do," she told Silliman.

She told him too that there were "about four guys I sleep with now and then." One of these relationships was more meaningful than the rest. Through Aline Mare, she had met the writer Rudy Wurlitzer, a friend of Richard Serra's and Philip Glass's. Wurlitzer was a novelist and screenwriter with an appealingly gnomic aura. By that point, he'd already published three acclaimed books, each a distinctive, haunting blend of minimalism and psychedelia, as well as the original screenplays for Monte Hellman's *Two-Lane Blacktop*, the entirety of which had been printed in *Esquire*, and Sam Peckinpah's *Pat Garrett & Billy the Kid*. Acker was clearly drawn to his fame—he was another example of someone who had found success on his own terms—but their romance was agonizing from the start.

Acker referred to them as "best friends," and she clearly wanted more from the relationship than he did. But every time they slept together, usually at Wurlitzer's run-down apartment on East 23rd, Wurlitzer would "freak out" because Acker was still living with Gordon and then he would distance himself from her. "He's been burned before," she told Silliman. In Wurlitzer's recollection, however, they were little more than fuck buddies. Decades later, he said that, while he admired the "passionate integrity" of Acker's work, he never thought of them as a couple, nor was there ever the promise that they would become so. The attraction for him was almost purely erotic—"We both seemed to hit each other's windshields at the same time."

Their correspondence, however, suggested the relationship was considerably more intense and intimate, at least in the moment. When Wurlitzer later decamped for Cape Breton, Nova Scotia, where he was living with Robert Frank and collaborating on his film *Keep Busy*, he wrote Acker several letters— long, pained, portentous discussions about what their romance meant and didn't mean, his distaste for the New York art and literary worlds, his own spiritual anomie.

About to turn forty, Wurlitzer could be as much of a drama queen as Acker. For her part, Acker seemed to crave his literary and intellectual guidance. She would occasionally dismiss her own writing and was for the moment obsessed with Japanese writers like Yukio Mishima and Yasunari Kawabata, told Wurlitzer that she aspired to their elegance: "simple paragraphs, each paragraph an image. 1, 2, 3. The flow absolutely like a straight line." Acker applied for a grant from Creative Artists Public Service (CAPS), administered by the New York State Council on the Arts. If she got the money, she was thinking of using it to head somewhere warm, either Florida or Haiti, and then, the following summer, to Nova Scotia and Wurlitzer. That latter trip would never happen; by then, Wurlitzer was spending more and more time in Paris and Hollywood. In the early eighties, he would give Acker a copy of his novel-in-progress, *Slow Fade*, and though it wasn't her style—"he sets Hollywood bland language deals against Tibetan-Indian gorgeous searchings"—reading it, she said, felt like she was "touching Rudy's naked body." Soon after, though, and to Acker's dismay, Wurlitzer lost all contact with her. "We disappeared into separate worlds," he said.

Romantic angst rarely interfered with Acker's writing, however, and she worked throughout, further prodded by the example of Harold Robbins's productivity. "Even a hack novelist works an eight-hour day," she said. All her labor began to pay off. In July, she received her first real press coverage. In the July 4–10 edition of the *Berkeley Barb*, Loren Means published a glowing review of the TVRT edition of *The Childlike Life* headlined "Kathy's Genius."* The review compared and contrasted Acker's book with Andrei Codrescu's *The Life and Times of an Involuntary Genius*, concluding, "So Andrei will probably be a star—his work is fun, and doesn't threaten. And Kathy will probably remain as she is—pissed off and brilliant, and so scary."

On July 21, Acker and Gordon performed at the Poetry Project, and the Project's newsletter advertised *The Adult Life*: "The Adult Life of Toulouse Lautrec is the most recent outgrowth from the overactive cranium of the Black Tarantula, alias Kathy Acker. This adorable little sex & mayhem pamphlet is available for a dollar, change, c/o The Project." To Acker's delight and surprise, even the *New Yorker* took notice of this reading, including her in an August 4th "Talk of the Town": "The Black Tarantula, a young white woman with short brown hair, read excerpts from her new novel to fifty people at St. Mark's In-the-Bouwerie Episcopal Church. There's a murder in the book, which takes place in Montmartre in 1886. The characters include Vincent van Gogh, Toulouse-Lautrec, and Hercule Poirot, left for dead hours earlier at *Publishers Weekly*." Later that winter, in the December 29, 1975, issue of the *Village Voice*, Richard Goldstein listed Acker in a roundup of the year's best writers,

---

* The paper listed the publisher as Viper's Tongue, which was essentially Leandro Katz's imprint at TVRT (conceived originally in Peru in 1961). After TVRT's demise, he would continue to use the imprint—"my seal," he called it—whenever he published anything of his own.

with an accompanying photo and blurb which read "she has produced a stream of seminarrative prose, culled from raw data and her own sense of melodrama."

At the bottom of the same page was none other than Andy Warhol, whose *The Philosophy of Andy Warhol* had come out earlier that year. At last, she was in the company she had so long craved.

CHAPTER 18

———— × ————

Ａᴸ FTER DEJONG RETURNED FROM INDIA THAT FALL, ACKER AND Gordon found their own place, at 341 East Fifth Street, between First and Second, near the police station. A quintessential East Village railroad apartment, it was dark and cramped, with a kitchen and bathtub in the back, two corridor rooms, and a main bedroom in the front. Acker took the front bedroom, filling it with manuscripts and so many books that a friend joked there were "about seventy-two thousand." Roaches were such a routine nuisance you couldn't open a book or the fridge, which just barely worked, without a couple scurrying out. At one point, when Freilicher was visiting, the ceiling in the main room collapsed, sending plaster and dust everywhere. The East Village itself was a dangerous ruin, prostitution and drug use rampant, the membrane between bohemia and underworld exceedingly thin.

Their rent was $150 a month, something they still found tough to make. While Gordon was gigging and trying to put together his own bands and projects, he worked in radio production, cutting tape and other audio work. Acker's paycheck from the Kitchen was still small enough that she was eligible for food stamps, and in a letter to Silliman she enumerated the meager contents of their fridge: "eight eggs, a bit of butter, a carrot, tea, and half a daikon." At some point, Lawrence Weiner—"one of the nicest artists around," as Acker called him—gave her an emergency thirty-five bucks.

Just as Acker had, Gordon threw himself into downtown's various cultural scenes. Despite Chatham's initial jealousy toward him, the two became fast friends and collaborators. Gordon also reunited with Jill Kroesen, who was working with Arthur Russell, a pop-art musician and composer who'd been a lover of both Allen Ginsberg and Kevin Killian. Since coming back to New York—in an illustration of just how small and incestuous the scene really was—Kroesen had fallen in love with and married Acker's ex, Lenny Neufeld. The same month that Acker and Gordon appeared at St. Mark's, Kroesen and Neufeld performed there too. With Chatham, Russell, and other like-minded musicians, Gordon began forming ad-hoc ensembles, playing the Kitchen, Artists Space, and other venues, eventually forming the Love of Life Orchestra, a renowned conceptual pop band that included Kroesen, Chatham, Russell, David Van Tieghem, "Blue" Gene Tyranny, Laurie Anderson, David Byrne from time to time, and Acker herself. The band's first record, which they released in 1978 on Mimi Johnson's label, Lovely Music, was the wryly titled *Star Jaws*.

As Gordon found his footing in the art-music world, Acker was finishing up *Toulouse Lautrec* and thinking ahead toward bigger projects. She was still sending the serials to subscribers on her mailing list—it now numbered about five hundred people, she said—but she was weary of scrambling for printers and the money to pay them. "I want to do a big novel," she told an interviewer. "I've changed." She felt she'd arrived at the end of the intellectual puzzles she was exploring in the book. "The problem of identity had become too complex," she wrote a decade later, "and, at the same time, had resolved itself. I realized that identity is made, the legend of Daedalus is true, and perhaps of Icarus, that when one writes, one doesn't express true or false identity, truth or falsity, one makes identity."

The identity that Acker was making, or at least asserting, was one that was increasingly aggressive, even cutthroat. Her former complaints about the competitiveness of the art world started to sound hollow, as she began to see other writers, particularly young, female writers exploring similarly innovative terrain, as an existential threat. Even mutually beneficial alliances could be sabotaged, or heedlessly discarded.

In January 1976, she and DeJong persuaded the Kitchen to allow them to perform on a double bill later that month. Heretofore, the venue had had no literary programming, welcoming only performance artists, dancers, and musicians to its stage—its official name at the time was the Kitchen Center for Video and Music—but Acker and DeJong argued that they too were performers of a sort. "It was a big deal," DeJong recalled. "A lot of people would come to the Kitchen." Acker decided to stage a candlelit reading, with Laurie Anderson and Jill Kroesen, of a new short story she'd titled "Florida," a loose adaptation of Maxwell Anderson's play *Key Largo*, which had been turned into the John Huston film of the same name. She'd written it, she said, when a PID flare-up left her in bed for three weeks. "I had a strong, undeniable urge to read the script for *Key Largo*," she remembered. "Such a script was not to be found, at least by me in my bed. So I did the next best thing, I wrote this script according to my memory. A memory of holes, like those landscapes I love the most." DeJong meanwhile performed sections of *Modern Love*, accompanied by prerecorded musical elements and another person voicing one of the characters.

In the Kitchen's press release, Acker was listed first and DeJong second. But just before the 8:30 event was to start, Acker took DeJong aside and said that they needed to talk about which order they would go on. The thought hadn't occurred to DeJong, but it was clearly something that Acker had given ample consideration to. "I'll just tell you that you don't want to go second," she said to DeJong. "Because what I'm doing is so amazing, you *cannot* follow." DeJong was shocked. When did her friend transform into her rival? The floor, she remembered, seemed to open up beneath her. Suddenly, she saw the dark side of Acker's drive. "That was Kathy's first move to winnow me out," DeJong said. "She just had to exclude me from her existence in this kind of totalizing, brutal way."

Whatever Acker's reasons, it was apparent that she didn't just need attention, she needed *all* the attention. After that reading, the two women never really spoke again. When they were in the same room, Acker would look the other way. On the road, when people would ask Acker about DeJong, in a what-happened-to-her kind of way, Acker would lie and say that DeJong had given up writing. Even worse, she would tell people that she, Acker, had taught her everything she knew. A couple years later, when the *Village Voice* was promoting a reading that she and DeJong were to give on behalf of photographer-writer Anne Turyn's *Top Stories*—a popular series of downtown chapbooks ("a prose periodical") by women writers published between 1978 and 1991— Acker refused to participate in an accompanying photograph if DeJong was also going to be included. Even after that, at another event, DeJong, intent on burying the hatchet, approached Acker and tried to talk to her. But Acker was capable of sustaining hostilities for a long time—she turned her back on DeJong again. Decades later, the rejection and animosity still rankled and perplexed DeJong. "When you maintain a whole constellation of grudges and enmities and make enemies of people," DeJong said, "that's a lot of burden to hold around in your head."

What compelled such abruptly hard-hearted behavior? Was it borne out of a misplaced sense of self-preservation, a matter of, as she so often put it to Silliman, survival? Eileen Myles, who could be, by their own admission, a relatively driven person, even "manipulative," recognized the possible necessity of Acker's cunning, even as they found it noxious and vaguely preposterous in the relatively genteel poetry world. "Rock 'n' roll, art, theater people—they're all unabashed ambition, all about winning, and getting it," Myles said. "Kathy had that. She was on a climb. She was such a cunt. But the fact is, she got up every fucking day and wrote. It was her religion. That's why she was here. That's awesome. That's awesome for a woman. It's awesome for a woman to say, I have that, and then deliver."

Other people, of course, took a more dim view. "I think she felt intellectually superior to other people," Pooh Kaye said. "And she'd just drop them. They'd become uninteresting." Jill Kroesen saw something even more insidious. Even though Acker had ditched Neufeld and obviously had her hands full, sexually speaking, once he and Kroesen married, Acker still made attempts to seduce him again. "I think she was dangerous," Kroesen said. "It was just take, take, take, take, take. And if you really let her, she just would hurt you." But Kroesen came back, again, to Acker's childhood, blaming her "abandonment" for what she considered an almost sociopathic cruelty. "I think that her pain was so severe," she said. "I think she was doing whatever she could to get rid of the pain. She was desperate." Acker was so often conflicted about her own writing—entirely convinced of its importance one day, self-deprecating about it the next—that perhaps the only position she could consistently sustain was one of embattlement.

It was also maybe the professional analog to a pattern that Freilicher saw play out in her romantic relationships. In the early days of a new romance, she tended to idolize a paramour, catering to their every need, acting, in her words, like a "geisha." Soon, however, she would turn self-protective and selfish. Her work, as always, would again become her first priority; her needs would take absolute precedence. "She felt like she was kind of deceiving people about who she was," Freilicher said, "and made it impossible when they found out because they wanted her to be the geisha."

Whatever the case, the break with DeJong was only the first such rift that Acker would have with her literary peers—mostly women, but occasionally men too. As her career unfolded, there would be several other rivalries, grudges, and quarrels, often over the most trivial differences or slights. With other female writers, she was often at first solicitous and supportive, helping them to secure publishers, providing blurbs for their books. But she could retract that support as soon as she felt imperiled. As her own fame grew, it seemed that the only other writers she could tolerate for long were young, emerging, and preferably fawning ones, or those who were more famous or powerful than she.

Sometime in the early to mid-nineties, Acker drew up a document, seemingly never published, that she titled "Ten Out of Many Women Writers." The list, which actually included eleven writers, opens with this preface: "This is a list of writers who are female whose work matters to me. It isn't a list of the women writers whose work matters the most to me, for I don't think nor feel in that way—so absolutely and judgementally. And it's a list of the writers, rather than of works, for it's the writer's work throughout time, a lifetime, the process rather than any individual work that interests me." She divided the list into two categories, "The Older Ones" and "Contemporaries (briefly)." The older ones included (in order) Jane Austen, George Sand, George Eliot, and Gertrude Stein ("the mother of us all," Acker wrote also, alluding to the title of the Virgil Thomson opera for which Stein wrote the libretto). On the contemporaries list: Hannah Arendt, Simone de Beauvoir, Luce Irigaray, Christa Wolf, Marguerite Duras, Maya Deren, and Emily Brontë ("for wildness").

Despite Brontë's eccentric inclusion, Acker obviously meant contemporaries in a temporal sense. But it was telling that, unless you count the naturalized Arendt, only one of these contemporary writers was American (Deren), and none were, in any real sense, *her* contemporaries. Literary success, to Acker, was a zero-sum, take-no-prisoners game.

A NARRATIVE? NO, A VISION

(1976–1983)

CHAPTER 19

———— × ————

Around the time of the Kitchen reading, Acker found out she got her CAPS grant—$7,000. It was the first and only such grant she would get in her lifetime. The money enabled her to travel to Haiti that June. Acker had wanted to visit the country, for years, probably because of her interest in both vodoo and the country's revolutionary history—it was the first country to be founded by former slaves and the first independent Black nation. Silliman suspected she was influenced by the Afro-Caribbean poet Aimé Césaire—"how to be a French, avant-garde, Black, Third World person was an interesting question for her." Pooh Kaye believed it had something to do with the political traumas the country had endured: "The daddy and son, that iconography," she said, referring to the despotic Duvalier dynasty.

Acker was exhilarated upon arrival, writing Silliman from the cheap, family-style Pension Brise de Mer in Cap-Haitien that she was surrounded by missionaries and sailors, and that Haiti was "wonderful and interesting." She planned to stay until August, she said, and was writing lots. "Now going out to talk to local 10-year-old boys roosters climb up trees here people ask me for hairs from my skin . . ." In the novel she started on the trip, *Kathy Goes to Haiti*, she described the country as "beautiful," further saying "Everything is very slow here. There's no tension." That early excitement gave way, though, to more equivocal emotions: "When I was in Port-au-Prince, all the time these guys would follow me . . . the first day I was in Port-au-Prince, I got seven marriage proposals, not to mention other propositions." "It was terrifying for her," Kaye recalled of the trip. "It was in the midst of the Papa Doc shit and she was being hassled continually. She said guys were knocking on her door at night, and she felt very unsafe. She came back very shaken."

While Acker later played down the autobiographical nature of the book, *Kathy Goes to Haiti* opens with a paragraph as truthful and plain-spoken as any she would ever write:

Kathy is a middle-class, though she has no money, American white girl, twenty-nine years of age, no lovers and no prospects of money, who doesn't believe in anyone or anything. One summer she goes down to Haiti. She steps out of the American Airlines plane and on to the cement runway, her first example of Haitian soil. She's scared to death because she doesn't know anybody, she doesn't know where to go in Haiti, and she can't speak the language.

From there, Kathy travels through the country, meeting and sleeping with several men, including a drug dealer named Roger. The menace that Kaye spoke of is transformed into a hallucinatory, ruefully ironic narrative of libidinal and ontological desperation, the country's oppressive history and politics a vivid backdrop for Acker's exploration of power, misogyny, and race. With its intentionally naïve, sometimes cliché or discordant language, and bursts of graphic sex, the novel feels, at times, like Anaïs Nin doing her best Jane Bowles impersonation. It ends with an emblematic description of a vodoo ceremony, which Acker called "the most documentary" section of the book. "It's like real theater," she said, of vodoo. "Our culture is deprived of anything that good."

Still perhaps under Robbins's spell, Acker set out to make *Kathy Goes to Haiti* an accessible novel. "I wanted to prove I could do a conventional book," she told the *East Village Eye* a few years later. She also described it as "a genre piece"—a pastiche of Nancy Drew and stable porn—"and therefore not simple, not a novel at all." On the typescript, she subtitled it "A Piece of Trash," with a handwritten note to whoever would become the book's production editor: "to be designed as a children's book."

As with *Rip-off Red*, Acker thought that the book could have some kind of commercial life as a porn novel. She included a sex scene every twenty pages or so. That wasn't enough to keep her interested, however, so, characteristically, she gave herself further constraints. She "mathematically" composed the book, with every other chapter a porn chapter, and each chapter, except for the central one, mirroring its facing chapter; mirrors, Acker noted, are of great significance in vodou. In an introduction to *Young Lust*, a British omnibus edition of her early work published in 1988, she elaborated:

Having been trained as a poet, I was, and still am, interested in verbal architecture, in language and how language works, rather than in telling a story. There seemed to be many stories in the world, some of them quite complex, and I saw no need to add to them. A novel, I had been taught, was composed of a plot and believable or well-rounded characters. I decided to write a novel that, while seeming to have a story, had none and whose characters were so deprived of psychology as to almost not exist. I wanted to stick a knife, a little one, up the ass of the novel . . .

But, like *Rip-off Red, Kathy Goes to Haiti* attracted no commercial interest. There was barely any interest, in fact, among literary and small-press publishers. After Acker completed the novel, it languished for more than a year, with one now forgotten press after another either abandoning the project or going bankrupt. "I don't know what the hell to do with it," she wrote Lafayette Young, an old friend who owned a bookshop in San Diego. "I'm sure it'll never get out into the world and it's probably not good anyways but I enjoyed writing it and I love Haiti, so I've decided my work is totally uncommercial all I'm going to do is send it to friends whenever I can get someone to make me a free xerox copy. What a long ridiculous sentence."

While the artist Robin Winters was originally going to create illustrations for the book, Acker instead approached Robert Kushner, a former student of David Antin's she bumped into from time to time at St. Mark's. Kushner liked the book and came up with the idea to accompany most of the novel's sex scenes with small, graphic, black-and-white block print illustrations.

Kushner and his wife also hosted regular meditation sessions at their Tribeca home, using techniques and chanting that they'd learned from Swami Muktananda, whose Siddha Yoga teachings emphasized self-realization and the "divinity" within oneself. A year earlier, Muktananda had established an ashram in Oakland, which Acker had visited, and she started attending the sessions at Kushner's place too. Six to ten adherents gathered each day, and meditation began at 5:30 in the morning, followed by chanting and a simple breakfast. Acker wrote all night, Kushner said, and would come by in the morning for the sessions, then return home and sleep during the day. "It was a sweet time," Kushner said. "I always noted that we were starting our day with that program and she was finishing hers."

Peter Gordon remembered that Acker was always interested "in the power of different systems," and she explored, with varying degrees of fascination, tarot, Kabbalah, and Tibetan Buddhism. After reading Lama Anagarika Go-vinda's *The Way of the White Clouds*, a now classic Western account of Tibetan spiritual traditions, she told Silliman that the book reminded her of the par-adoxes of language she'd been exploring in her own writing. "The book has really smacked me whumped me open," she wrote. "Suddenly I'm thinking of LANGUAGE AS TRUTH, which is incredible to me . . . Could one book tell the truth?" While Kushner didn't get the sense that Acker's interest in Muktananda's teachings was an abiding commitment, Acker would, in fact, maintain a regular meditation practice for the rest of her life. Especially as she got older, non-Western and esoteric spiritual practices became a growing source of succor.

At some point in her life, probably when her travels made it too diffi-cult to keep real-life pets, Acker started to collect stuffed animals, which she carted from apartment to apartment, home to home. Over the years, some of them acquired names: Ratski, Woolfie, Witch or Bitch. In one of those toys, a scruffy, well-loved creature that might have been a ferret, she kept a slip of paper on which she had written a mantra: *Amadam Ham Maduram Ham*. Sometimes called the "mantra of mantras," the Sanskrit phrase roughly translates as "I am immortal, I am blissful," or "I am eternal and free from the struggle of body born, body changing and body dying." The slip of paper was still in the toy after her death, but when exactly she had chosen or been given the mantra was uncertain, and it was impossible to know how long it had been secreted there.

× × ×

That fall, after Acker had returned to the East Village apartment, she was talking to Ted Castle at TVRT, when he mentioned that he was originally from Buffalo. Still casually on the hunt for her birth father, Acker asked him if he knew anyone named Lehman associated with the Wildroot Hair Tonic Com-pany. As it turned out, he did—his father had had business dealings with Harry Lehman, the company's late founder and, seemingly, Acker's grandfather. He had died in 1959. Acker had booked a reading at A Space, an artist-run center in Toronto, in January, and on September 30, she wrote poet Robert Creeley, then teaching at the University of Buffalo, a couple hours southeast, to see if he could arrange a "reading/whatever" for her there too. "Not only would I love to give a reading, but I'd also love an excuse (and some money, that possibility) to stop in Buffalo so I could try tracing down my father."

Whether that reading came through or not, two months later, again through Castle, Acker appeared to have tracked down her father—seemingly named Harry Lehman, Jr.— in California and wrote him a letter on November 23 (misspelling, as she would, his name as Lehmann):

Dear Harry Lehmann, Jr.,

You've never met me (I believe) and you'll probably think it weird [*sic*] to hear from me so I'll explain as much as I can:

My mother is Claire Weill (Alexander) and I believe I am your daughter. I have always wondered who my father is. My mother and her mother refused to tell me who he is or what his name is.

A year ago I received a small trust fund my grandfather (on my mother's side) had set up for me. This trust was made out for Karen Lehmann. A few months later I met an uncle (my grandmother's sister's son) Clifford Kaye who informed me that your parents came from Buffalo and that they do or had owned Wildroot Cream Oil. He remembered that your last name is Lehmann.

About a month ago, one of my closest friends, Ted Castle, happened to be talking about Buffalo. Ted's parents come from Lockport—which I gather is near Buffalo. I asked Ted, Lord knows why, if he knew any Lehmann's in Buffalo who were associated with Wildroot Cream Oil. To make a long detective story short, Ted's father had business dealings with your father and is friendly with Pansy Fairburn (who's now Pansy Fairburn Cass). Pansy Cass gave Ted's father your address in California.

Since I've never really had a father, I have no idea what relations between fathers and their children are supposed to be— if that matters at all. I would like to meet you. However I have no wish to impose on you; I can understand if you would rather have nothing to do with me. By the way—I'm sure it doesn't matter— my desire to meet you has nothing to do with my mother or her side of the family; actually we're not very friendly. Just for myself,

I'm curious who you are, what you're like, I've been so for a very long time.

I'm coming to California in February (I'm a writer have to give some readings). Perhaps we could meet sometime? [...]

Yours, Kathy (Alexander) Acker (Karen Lehmann)

P.S. Even if you don't wish to see me, any information you can give me about yourself and, if possible, though recalling the past can be a nuisance, about your marriage with my mother etc. would be more than welcome.

It's unclear if Acker ever even sent this letter, but there's definitely no record of her receiving a response. The evidence surrounding her contact with her apparent birth family is scant and opaque. Peter Gordon remembered her father being named Donald, not Harry Jr., and that Acker did, in fact, track him down, possibly in Florida. Wendy too claimed that Acker did find him ("somewhere in upstate New York") but had little other knowledge of their reunion other than "it was okay, but not great."

The only firsthand accounts of Acker having any contact with the Lehmans were, again, her own terse, somewhat confounding, reports, the first of which she included in her 1982 novel *Great Expectations*, her most nakedly autobiographical book:

My aunts Martha and Mabel greet me. I've never met them before.

They're very wealthy and they're so polite, they're eccentric. They tell me I'm going to meet my real father. I don't want to see him, I do I do. I know he's handsome.

Aunt Martha tells me he's away at the moment.

We stop, walking in front of a picture of my father. At least it's a picture of him. "Your father," Aunt Mabel comments, "was too adventurous. Wild . . . headstrong . . . Your mother was his first wife and you were his child."

"Who's his new wife?"

"He's had three. Last year he killed someone, shot him, who was trespassing on his yacht. The family got him off on psychological reasons. After his six-month stay in a rest home, he just disappeared."

"Aunt Mabel's scared, dear," Judy's commenting on Punch, "that you have some of your father's wildness."

Despite my politeness, they know who I am.

"I really don't know very much, Sarah. But I don't think you should have anything to do with him."

"Your father," Aunt Mabel interrupts her sister, "acts unpredictably. He can be extremely violent. We have no way of telling how he'll act when he sees you. The family has decided to help you as much as we can, but we can't help you with this."

I don't know what I'm going to believe.

He—for there can be no doubt of his sex, though the fashion of the time did something to disguise it—was in the act of slicing at the head of a Moor which swung from the rafters. It was the color of an old football.

The last, gruesome paragraph of that passage was plucked from the well-known opening of Virginia Woolf's *Orlando*, itself, of course, a blend of fact and fiction, biography in the guise of a novel (and vice versa), with a narrator both ambiguous and unreliable. A couple pages later, the narrator does finally meet her father, but he is hardly the romantic "sexually magnetic daredevil" that she had conjured in her mind. Kind and gentle, he's already endured five heart attacks; his greatest physical pleasures are booze and a half-pint of coffee ice cream before bed. He blames the narrator's mother for "his hard life," and the narrator, in turn, is understandably disappointed: "I watched everything and I swore I'd never marry a man I didn't love and I'd never live for security."

Several years later, however, in a talk Acker gave in 1993 titled "The Killers," she has revised the "plot" of this moment while still retaining some of its more dubious details:

I never met my father. Though he was married to my mother, he left her when she was three months pregnant with me. When I was twenty-six years old, through an accident, I traced my father's family. I wrote to them and they wrote back that they would accept me into their family and we arranged to meet. I thought that I was going to meet my real father, but I only met the first cousin. He told me (and I think he was a little crazy—well, not crazy but eccentric, because rich people are never crazy) that perhaps I should not meet my father. Why? Because my father had murdered someone who was trespassing on his yacht. After he had remained six months in a lunatic asylum, the state had excused him of any murder charge. My father then disappeared. No one knew where he was, said the first cousin. And so I abandoned my search for my father, for my life at that time was hard enough and this new trouble was simply not worth it.

As always, the negative space of her past, with all its gaps and contradictions, remained a bottomless source of images and provided a kind of prefab pulp fiction. The mystery of her birth father, that particular hole, was a lens through which to examine a number of things: class, patriarchy, memory, even the caprices of storytelling and narrative. In "The Killers," Acker travels from her murky childhood to various loose ideas about identity and realism, with detours into works by Melville and Julio Cortázar. As ever, Acker is opposed to mimetic narrative, which she argues is a reductive, phallocentric "control method." Far more preferable for her are narrative structures that permit chance and the unknown, the dangerous, the magical, the limitless: "To play, then, both in structure and in content, is to desire to live in wonder." The real facts of Harry or Donald's life, the real facts of Acker's relationship to him, were obstacles to that wonder. Better to just turn those facts into art, and then vanish into it.

The Lehmans were just one affluent, esteemed Jewish dynasty that Acker claimed connection to. She also often said that she was related to the Ochs family, former owners of the New York Times. The writer Sarah Schulman argued that Acker was "from the kind of family known to New York Jews as 'Our Crowd'—her family, the Alexanders, along with the Lehmans, Loebs, Ochs, et cetera were the best educated, wealthiest, and most sophisticated Jews in the world." But this was again only a partial truth: Acker was related to the family quite distantly, and only through marriage; the documentarian Jacki Ochs was a distant third cousin. Her romanticization and exaggeration of these family ties was another way to give her life a mythic texture. Pooh Kaye said of Acker's birth father, "She used to fantasize about him being some rich, important guy," as a way of explaining why he didn't want to stay with

Claire, implying obviously that Claire was, again, not worthy of either father or daughter. Freilicher, on the other hand, saw a different kind of longing in Acker's attempts to overstate her social status. It was a way to reassert her value, to claim what she rightfully deserved. "Nobody was offering her a place at the table," he said. Schulman, who was a great admirer of Acker's, and who benefitted from the older writer's generosity early in her career, still saw in this a somewhat unpleasant exercise of privilege: "Her background and financial cushion gave her a sense of entitlement that was unreasonable."

× × ×

With a sad symmetry that would now start to characterize Acker's life, just as her real father had seemingly emerged, her stepfather passed away. On January 12, 1977, Bud had a heart attack and died at Lenox Hill Hospital at the age of sixty-one. One can surmise that Acker hardly mourned at all. In an early draft of *Blood and Guts in High School*, she included a scene in which her surrogate, Janey, visits her dying father in the hospital after a heart attack. "Janey's mother had come home the night before and told Janey not to be upset. It was nothing serious. Her father had just had a heart attack, but now he was over it. Janey wasn't crying, was she? Janey couldn't feel any tears in her." After an unusually tender moment between father and daughter, which concludes with Janey saying "Don't go yet," Acker plunges into this poem:

My daddy's dead
My daddy's dead
He has no head
My daddy's dead

One day he came suddenly back to the winter
Apartment in the summer
And caught a boy's tie in the bathtub
He started to cry and told me
I shouldn't go with any other men but him
He began to rub

My breasts he told me
No other man could give me

Security
But him.
So I called my mother and told her
To shut
Him up
She did.
What she said to him's a mystery.

Daddy you're kind and gentle
I don't know anyone who loved you
Except for the people in your office
Who you gave free drinks to

If you come back from the dead
All brown and blue
You still can't fuck me
I hate security
I know now I love you
But you still can't fuck me.

My daddy's dead
My daddy's dead
He has no head
My daddy's dead.

Acker cut this scene and poem from *Blood and Guts*, but revisits Bud's death in her next book, *Great Expectations*, where he is at best a figure of little consequence or of mockery:

My father's lying in the hospital cause he's on his third heart attack. My mother's mother at the door of my father's room so I know my father is overhearing her is saying to my mother, "You have to say he's been a good husband to you, Claire. He never left you and he gave you everything you wanted."

"Yes."

"You don't love him."

"Yes."

I know my grandmother hates my father.

I don't side with my mother rather than my father like my sister does. I don't perceive my father. My mother is adoration hatred play. My mother is the world. My mother is my baby. My mother is exactly who she wants to be.

In real life, it was unclear how long Bud had lived off of his wife and mother-in-law's largesse. What little money he personally had left at his death—probate documents valued his estate as between only $3 and $10,000—he left to Claire. Without Florrie's help, Claire was effectively broke.

In any event, Bud's death interrupted little in Acker's life. Just two days later, she traveled to Toronto to give her reading. A few days after that, back in New York, she met with James Grauerholz, William Burroughs's longtime amanuensis, who was interested in becoming her literary agent, a job he had done for Burroughs, as well as for Anne Waldman and poet-musician Ed Sanders. She and Grauerholz had lunch on January 19, and Acker gave him copies of her résumé, clippings from the *Village Voice* and *Berkeley Barb*, the Black Tarantula books, and the in-progress *Kathy Goes to Haiti*. On the copy of *Kathy Goes to Haiti,* she scribbled, unadvisedly, "I am definitely at point of thinking everything I write is trash," but nonetheless, they agreed on a 15 percent agent's fee. Grauerholz was fond of Acker, though he later said he "didn't get her really." Nor, it seemed, did publishers at the time. Despite Grauerholz's close relationship with Grove Press, which had been the first in the U.S. to publish Burroughs's *Naked Lunch,* Grove editor-in-chief Fred Jordan passed on Grauerholz's proposal to reprint Acker's early novellas. Grauerholz also sent the first chapter of *Kathy Goes to Haiti* to *Playgirl* magazine, whose fiction editor, Mary Ellen Strote, was looking for new writers from the East Coast. Strote liked it, calling it "delightful" but also too slow and languorous ("we try to get a lot of eroticism and/or romance in a few pages and we don't have time to afford the pacing of stories like Ms. Acker's"). Grauerholz and Acker parted ways.

After that Toronto trip, Acker would end up spending a fair bit of time in Canada over the next year or so. In Vancouver, she performed at Western Front, the city's answer to the Kitchen, and in Toronto, she became close, and briefly lovers, with both the poet Victor Coleman, who was then running the A Space gallery and editing *Only Paper Today,* and Andrew J. Paterson, an acerbic artist, writer, and the front man for the post-punk band the Government. At one point, she told Creeley that she was even contemplating moving to Toronto part-time, and indeed, by 1978, Acker had become a vital part of the small community centered around Rumour, a scrappy art gallery-cum-publishing house in the city started by three young artist-writers, Judith Doyle, Fred Gaysek, and Kim Todd. Doyle was having an affair with Willoughby Sharp, the artist and cofounder of *Avalanche* magazine, and, through him, met Acker. While Doyle found Acker fiercely opinionated and intimidating, when she heard about the publication difficulties of *Kathy Goes to Haiti*, Doyle suggested Rumour do it.

They offered Acker a thousand dollars for the rights. Acker said yes, and the book came out the following year, in a handsome, square paperback edition complete with the Robert Kushner illustrations. In February 1979, Acker stayed at Doyle's apartment above the gallery, where she led a writing workshop that promised to give "informal instruction in artistic survival." About ten people showed up, including the future filmmaker John Greyson, then eighteen, who recalled Acker instilling in her students a measure of her own discipline: "The main thing I remember is her saying that you have to write every day. Assign yourself a number of hours or words a day. It hurts, it's like jogging, but eventually it becomes addictive, a habit, and that's when it kicks in. No matter how much you doubt, you have that three hours a day or a thousand words, whichever comes first, you have that as your anchor, and it becomes your studio practice."

To Acker's irritation, published by Rumour, *Kathy Goes to Haiti* still didn't really sell, and it would remain a kind of anomaly in her oeuvre, too direct and unambiguous for her liking. "My least favorite," she told the English writer and translator Paul Buck. "It was just one thing, not a complex painting." But others, like Gary Indiana, appreciated this relative simplicity: "Her best-crafted work of this period is the completely linear, episodic *Kathy Goes to Haiti*," he wrote many years later in the *London Review of Books*, "and the contemporaneous story 'Florida' which turns the plot of the 1948 film *Key Largo* into farcical psychological quicksand." Edwidge Danticat, the Haitian-American novelist, also found the book a useful kind of corrective: "What makes Kathy's adventures less than common is the lack of pretense and the extensive amount of space rendered to the quickly repetitive details of sexual acts. No doubt this was meant to satisfy the specific requirements of the porn press, which had commissioned this work [sic]. Still Acker does not miss the opportunity to poke fun at these types of treks, which can hastily slip from totally libidinous encounters to passionate affairs of the heart. The heart that is hardest to conquer though is that of Haiti itself. For there is no one Haiti, as Kathy quickly learns, but several . . ."

But by the time the novel came out, Acker had also moved on herself. At another reading in Toronto, with Doyle doing one of the parts, Acker unveiled "The Scorpions," a section from a new book titled *Blood and Guts in High School*. "We knew we couldn't change the shit we were living in," Acker read, "so we were trying to change ourselves."

A N EXCERPT OF *KATHY GOES TO HAITI* APPEARED IN A SHORT-LIVED magazine called *Traveler's Digest*, edited and published by a young poet and journalist named Jeff Goldberg. In 1972, Goldberg had moved to New York from Philadelphia, where he was part of a small group of poets, including Victor Bockris and Andrew Wylie, affiliated with Aram Saroyan's Telegraph Books (an East Coast version of City Lights' Pocket Poets series), which featured the likes of Ted Berrigan, Ron Padgett, Gerard Malanga, and Patti Smith. After moving to Manhattan, Bockris would go on to become a celebrated biographer, while Wylie would evolve into one of the most powerful, well-known literary agents of the twentieth century, nicknamed the Jackal for his ruthlessness. When he was just starting out as an agent, Wylie represented Bockris, selling a biography of Deborah Harry and Blondie to Grove Press's Fred Jordan, who later became Acker's editor. Goldberg tried to convince Wylie to take on Acker as a client, but she was never commercial enough for his taste.

Meanwhile, Goldberg became a regular at the Poetry Project and also started spending time at CBGB, the soon-to-be legendary music club that opened on the Bowery in 1973. This was ground zero for a new musical subculture and youth movement, known as punk, that was anarchic, explosive, insolent, and anti-hippie. As either adjective or noun, "punk" had been used by various rock critics to describe new bands as diverse as the New York Dolls, Aerosmith, and Suicide, and it was also the title of music journalist Legs McNeil's first magazine, usually credited with giving the whole phenomenon its name. Over time, punk became synonymous with urgent, simple chord progressions, nihilistic posturing, a DIY aesthetic, and a stripped-down, confrontational hoodlum style: biker jackets, ripped clothing, spiked hair, safety pins. Punk would, of course, flourish in New York, London, and several other cities, its potent spirit spawning various sub-genres, roiled by conflicting codes and ambitions but usually defined by an enduring insistence on creative and social freedom. Punk wasn't necessarily more literary or artistic than other rock music, but several bands that emerged in its wake, garbed in its dissonant ethos—Throbbing Gristle, Cabaret Voltaire, Pere Ubu—took obvious inspiration and cues from modernism, Dada, and surrealism.

A couple years after CBGB opened, the bands that made their names in its long, narrow, crowded space, like Blondie, Television, the Ramones, and Talking Heads, had acquired a chic notoriety. Goldberg launched *Traveler's Digest* to document the emerging scene. "All these people knew each other," Goldberg said. "The musicians, the writers, the photographers, the painters. And we were just getting enough money and recognition to go somewhere, people were beginning to travel. So it was about people's first experiences traveling." David Byrne was a contributor, as were Berrigan and another friend, Barry Miles, who, like Bockris, was a prolific biographer of the underground and counterculture. The second issue, the magazine's most successful, featured Warhol and Muhammad Ali on the cover, and Acker's "The Persian Poems," which would later appear in *Blood and Guts in High School*.

Goldberg knew Acker a bit from the Poetry Project—"brush cut angel face" was his initial impression—and after she offered him the *Kathy Goes to Haiti* excerpt, they started hanging out, sometime in the late spring of 1978. Goldberg and Bockris, roommates at the time in the West Village, threw a dinner party, inviting Acker and the downtown photographer Marcia Resnick. Acker ended up staying the night, and she and Goldberg continued to sleep together, off and on, for the next year or so.

She wasn't pleased, however, at how little Goldberg actually excerpted from *Kathy Goes to Haiti*—just three paragraphs—but when grant money permitted him to expand his operation into book publishing, he did, with Acker's permission, produce a Traveler's Digest edition of *I Dreamt I Was a Nymphomaniac!: Imagining*. While the resulting paperback was a lovely object, with illustrations by artist and filmmaker Michael McClard, the printing was rushed, the glue on the books didn't quite stick, and many of them soon fell apart. Acker didn't even receive the twenty-five copies that Goldberg had promised her as payment. "It was a disaster," Goldberg recalled. "There are very few copies now, and there were very few copies then. Nobody ever saw it really." Goldberg planned to do a book by Richard Hell—formerly of Television, then fronting his own band, the Voidoids—but Acker's book cost so much and went so badly that the botched *Nymphomaniac* was the beginning and end of the press.

× × ×

Most of the writers Goldberg knew scrambled and hustled, living hand-to-mouth, but Acker struck him as more penniless than most. Like most of Acker's circle, he knew a bit of her Sutton Place past but also knew that she had been cut off financially. Soon after they met, she took a job at the Bethlehem Bakery, an organic bakery in the East Village. Goldberg was no fan of the place's macrobiotic, vegan baked goods, but he did enjoy the peyote that Acker occasionally scored there. Acker's experience behind the counter was, not surprisingly, dull and disheartening. "My last job was selling cookies," she told the *East Village Eye*. "It was so bad. I was 31 and said, I can't do this anymore. Sentences out of my mouth for hours: 'What cookie would you like?'" In her next book, *Blood and Guts in High School*, though, the job would provide one of the novel's most amusing set pieces. There, a narrator named Lousy Mindless Salesgirl must contend with both demanding rich customers and demanding know-it-all hippies, all the while feeling her very life force drain out from her: "As soon as I dare to take the time to think a thought, to watch a feeling, usually hatred, develop, to rest my aching body, a customer enters." After just a couple months, Acker quit, vowing yet again that she would only write, and that she would somehow make a living from her writing.

Acker seems to have started drafting various fragments that would comprise *Blood and Guts* as far back as 1976, publishing sections alongside her lengthy interview in the November/December 1976 *Only Paper Today* and in the November 1977 edition of *Only Prose* magazine, edited by her friend Jeff Weinstein and his partner, the art critic and poet John Perreault. The novel ostensibly chronicles the short, unhappy life of a twelve-year-old girl named Janey Smith, who journeys from Mexico to New York and then Tangier, enduring romantic rejection, kidnapping, beating, imprisonment, and cancer, before she begins a sadomasochistic quasi-affair with Jean Genet. In her constant victimization and struggle for agency, Janey is cousin to Sade's Justine, and Acker's narration has the tenor of the blackest of fairy tales. Occasionally, she makes this fabulist tone even more overt, such as with a non sequitur chapter about a monster and a beaver whose home is threatened by an obsessed, nihilistic bear.

The book is episodic and disjunctive, its narrative frequently interrupted by or supplemented with Acker/Janey's handwritten, extremely detailed maps of her dreams*; her black-and-white line drawings of genitalia; a "book report" on Hawthorne's *The Scarlet Letter*; typographic experimentation; and several poems, including "The Persian Poems," Acker/Janey's hand-lettered translations of various sentences in Farsi, and "Hello, I'm Erica Jong," a short prose poem cattily satirizing the author of the second-wave-feminist classic *Fear of Flying*: "HELLO, I'M ERICA JONG. I'M A REAL NOVELIST. I WRITE BOOKS THAT TALK TO YOU ABOUT THE AGONY OF AMERICAN LIFE, HOW WE ALL SUFFER, THE GROWING PAIN THAT MORE AND MORE OF US ARE GOING TO FEEL." Ultimately, in its anarchic formal shifts and astonishing capaciousness it was the answer to the question Acker had posed to Bernadette Mayer four years earlier: "Why shouldn't writing be everything?"

"I'm just starting a new novel called *Blood and Guts in High School*," she wrote to her friend Lafayette Young back in San Diego. "I'm not showing the work to anyone, just keeping it real personal, exactly what I want to do. The hell with commerciality." At some point, she *did* show it to writer and raconteur Glenn O'Brien, then affiliated with *Interview* magazine, and while she referred to him as her "editor," it's not clear what work O'Brien did on the manuscript.

As she worked on it, though, drafting and knitting together its disparate elements, it occurred to her that she could overlay a more cohesive structure that would, in fact, give the book an accessibility, and possible commercial appeal, that her early work lacked. A few years later, in conversation with several British academics, she explained her method: "My first novels were simply linked stories basically, linked thematically, and I was doing the same thing again. But because I had this idea of commerciality in my mind I wanted an all-over narrative. So what I did I simply made up a narrator called Janey Smith who doesn't

---

* Printed in Acker's books, the dream maps serve as both idiosyncratic, black-and-white illustrations and as an oneiric interlude. But, as Georgina Colby points out in *Kathy Acker: Writing the Impossible*, the specific dream maps in *Blood and Guts* are actually much more than either of those things: large-scale color collages (one as large as fifty-six by twenty-two inches) that are multivalent artworks unto themselves, dense with tangled references to Baba Muktananda, the Kabbalah, and vodoo. Acker treated the maps as such, signing them and hanging them in the rooms of her various apartments. Colby likens the *Blood and Guts* maps to the collages of the German modernist Hannah Höch, and Chris Kraus to the maps of the Hundred Acre Wood in *Winnie the Pooh*. They remind me a little of some of Nancy Spero's work and Ray Johnson's moticos—droll, collage-like artworks chock full of in-jokes. (Acker tucks a tiny mash note in a corner of Dream Map 2, for example: "I love Rudy.")

exist basically. She doesn't have any character. She's nobody: she's an 'I,' a very empty 'I.' And it was a joke, you know, the empty 'I,' and I linked everything together as if this was her life." It was, as she told another interviewer, "the first time [she] used plot to structure [her] materials."

Blood and Guts also fit perfectly into the punk scene, which was flourishing when she started the book and reached its apotheosis when she finished. While Acker would be later labeled a punk writer, she was really a proto-punk—what else was The Black Tarantula if not a spiky sobriquet that prefigured the likes of Poly Styrene, Siouxsie Sioux, and Ari Up? *Blood and Guts'* hand-lettered maps and poems, pornographic drawings—its overall sense of bricolage—was in lockstep with punk's raw, handmade aesthetic. So too was its pervasive mood of anomie, its heretical sexual politics, its headlong flight toward destruction. Punk bands weren't getting rich, not yet, but some of them were doing much better, financially, than Acker was. Being associated with the punk or, as it were, the post-punk scene was hardly a bad thing. "In my mind, I had this fantasy that it was possible to break through," she said.

She was also, of course, drawn to the scene's anger and speed, its novelty and personalities. She was particularly taken with both Richard Hell and James Chance, front man of the Contortions, a band notorious for its violent spectacle. Chance, she felt, was a kindred spirit, doing in music, *to* music, what Acker was trying to do with literature—dissembling and destroying it. "Imagine a Lego set, a musical Lego set, and a band of ruffians comes in and takes a hammer to it," said Adele Bertei, a vocalist and keyboardist in the band. The first chapter of Acker's *Girl Gangs Take Over the World*, an unpublished 1979 manuscript, concludes with a characteristically sharp shift in tone and subject matter—"The Contortions is the best rock-n-roll, jazz, soul, theater, and guerrilla band in America."

Acker loved to tell a story about Chance. He once played a "Mafia club," she said, and afterward the owner wouldn't pay him. "Fuck you," they said, "we're the Mafia!" Chance, "a skinny wimp," then pulled out a knife. The owner was surprised but also amused—*this* guy is going to stab me? But no, Chance turned the knife on himself and started to cut his own wrist. Freaked out, the owner immediately paid. "I think that kind of strategy," Acker told an interviewer, "is very useable." To her, it was a parable about masochism. That when you feel powerless, you can gain power by being even more of a victim than people expect, or want, you to be.

It was Bertei, though, whom Acker really became close to. Bertei was living with her boyfriend, the artist Jamie Nares, who also played guitar in the Contortions. But after meeting at a gig at Max's, Acker and Bertei started to spend time with each other, occasionally sleeping together. Bertei was eight years younger than Acker, but they might have been the same person: both were small and liked to dress, as Bertei described it, like French ragamuffins. Both had difficult mothers and childhoods—Bertei's mother was a schizophrenic and Bertei had spent time in reformatories. Genet and Leduc were mutual touchstones. Acker gave Bertei a copy of Alexander Trocchi's *Cain's Book*, and they fantasized about running away together to become sailors. Bertei fondly remembered being at Acker's apartment and having to step over enormous stacks of books to get to the mattress on the floor. "It was kind of like, you had to cross the moat," she said.

But the relationship didn't go very far, perhaps precisely because they were so much alike. Bertei also worked part-time at the Strand Bookstore, and she was an aspiring writer too. Acker encouraged her, but Bertei was insecure and somewhat intimidated by Acker's capacity for work. And while Bertei was involved romantically with many people herself, she was also taken aback by what she called Acker's "very unusual, complicated obsession with sex." Soon after the romance began, Bertei moved to Europe, to pursue other music and acting opportunities, most famously starring in Lizzie Borden's dystopian feminist classic *Born in Flames*. She and Acker would bump into each other, in Amsterdam or London, but they gradually drifted apart. "I always adored her work," Bertei said. "But I didn't really see her that much. I couldn't keep track of her because she was moving so much."

× × ×

Sometime in late 1977, Acker discovered a lump in her breast. A biopsy revealed it to be benign, but Acker felt vulnerable enough to pause and reevaluate her life, at least temporarily. To Gordon's surprise, she said that they should get married. While she was obviously in the midst of a number of concurrent affairs, and she and Gordon were no longer sleeping together, he had always protected her and she trusted him more than any other man in her life. She felt she needed that protection even more now. In February 1978, they had a small ceremony at city hall, with Arthur Russell and his boyfriend their only witnesses.

By September, though, things had deteriorated again—or even further. Gordon had become thoroughly sick of Acker taking him for granted, of consuming so much psychic space. Her intensity and dominance and narcissism had all, finally, become too much. "At that point, personally, it was hard to maintain my identity," Gordon said. He moved out, and at last actually leaving her, he said, was a relief. Long after the fact, Gordon wondered why they got married at all, speculating that the ritual was a way, perhaps, to belatedly acknowledge the life and romance that they had once had. In her 1990 novel *In Memoriam to Identity*, Acker suggests a different reason: "Two months later, she and Harry got married, not because they were sleeping together, but because she wanted someone to come to her grave."

But Acker wouldn't accept that it was over. Even after Gordon started a relationship with the video artist Kit Fitzgerald, whom he would marry about a decade later. Heartbroken and on the heels of yet another PID flare-up that left her bedridden for two weeks, she was desperate to flee the situation. Somehow saving up some money, and supplementing that with a borrowed $300, Acker flew to Mexico on August 17. Her travels there, along with the long, anguished phone calls she had with Gordon, who remained in New York, provided the material for the first section of *Blood and Guts*. In the book, Gordon is transformed into Acker/Janey's father, Johnny Smith, with whom she is having sex. "Janey depended on her father as boyfriend," Acker writes, "brother, sister, money, amusement, and father." Their incestuous relationship, however, is undermined by both Johnny's romantic affairs, Janey's jealousy, and Johnny's burgeoning self-discovery.

"It was a bad breakup," Acker said later, talking about Gordon and *Blood and Guts*, "and the first chapter is actually very autobiographical. I couldn't write anything else because this was the only thing I could deal with. There was nothing else on my mind. And I thought, 'Oh God, you can't do this, this is so self-indulgent. This is dreadful, you can't put this in the novel.' But I had to get it out. And it was the only thing I could do. I've always felt if something is that strong you should put it in."

The despair of that first chapter is leavened somewhat by the abrupt insertion of "September," by the Peruvian poet César Vallejo, whom Acker revered and said she translated herself while in Mexico. Though Acker's translation, as was usually the case, is more rewriting than translating. Such poetic eruptions characterize the whole book, in fact, which lurches from scenes of menace and misery to moments of black comedy and all-caps anger that harken back to *The Burning Bombing of America*. The dominant emotional key of the novel can, however, be summed up by a sentence—"Every howl of pain is a howl of defiance"—that Acker includes in a rewriting of "A Roll of the Dice," the groundbreaking, typographically radical 1897 poem by the French Symbolist poet Stéphane Mallarmé.

Acker's use of Vallejo and Mallarmé situated her in a well-known avant-garde tradition, but the use of Jean Genet was more personal and profound. "Every sentence this man writes is real!" she told a friend. She identified deeply with the French writer and, throughout her life, would keep a photograph of him taped to her desk. Genet was a literary genius and unrepentant criminal who despised every imaginable piety, whose hatred of his birth country was matched only by his fondness for betrayal. He was also someone who, in his books, openly mined the silt of his past, whose work Edmund White described as autofictional long before the term became fashionable in North American publishing circles. Acker liked the fact too that, as with Guyotat, the homosexual Genet had "described other than oedipal relationships." In *Blood and Guts*, she borrowed lines and images from Genet's play *The Screens* and Mohamed Choukri's memoir *Jean Genet in Tangier*.*

There was a delicious irony too in stealing from the author of *The Thief's Journal*. With *Blood and Guts*, the appropriation that Acker had long experimented with became a preoccupation and she started using the more contentious word "plagiarism" to describe her work. "By the time I got to *Blood and Guts in High School*, I realized that I wasn't interested in this business about identity at all," she told *Artforum*. "Identity was obviously constructed; it wasn't a big problem. What I was interested in was the texts I was using. It wasn't interesting writing diary work, I was boring myself to death; but it's very interesting to use other texts. And I simply got interested in copying."

Even with *Blood and Guts'* use of plot, its relatively linear structure, and its punk snarl, Acker still struggled to have the book published. Portions of it came out as chapbooks, including a 1980 edition of "The Persian Poems,"

---

* In her copy of the latter, Acker left a handwritten note to herself, seemingly explaining her choice of Genet as a love interest: "When I fall in love w/ real men, I always get hurt. So why shouldn't I fall in love w/ whoever I want even if that person's—miles away, totally inaccessible to me, & I have to pretend I'm someone else to get to meet him once."

designed and illustrated by Robert Kushner. However, getting the entire thing out in the world proved frustrating. Two relatively young presses, Urizen Books and Stonehill, were interested, but the former wanted to rewrite it and the latter's plan fell apart after Stonehill's founder died in a car crash. George Quasha, an upstate New York artist who was friends with Jerome Rothenberg and Carolee Schneemann and who had his own press, Station Hill, offered to do it but only on the condition that Acker pay the printing costs.

But she'd been doing that for years, and was tired of finding "private backing," as she put it. As the manuscript floated around publishing offices for months, in various states of possible prepublication, Acker tried to ignore it—"don't be a baby," she told herself, "don't be impatient, you're always so impatient" —and do what she always did: work. By then, she had started a new novel called *Girl Gangs Take Over the World*. She would soon abandon that title, but some of its constituent parts would morph into a chapbook, *Algeria: A Series of Invocations Because Nothing Else Works*, and a new novel. Thumbing her nose even more brazenly at the canon, she stole a title, and part of the plot, from the most famous of all English-language novelists, and called it *Great Expectations*.

1. Acker's mother, Claire, holding a six-week-old Kathy in 1947.

2. Kathy and her younger sister, Wendy, in Manhattan, circa 1952.

3. Kathy's yearbook page from her senior year at the Lenox School in Manhattan.

Some people think that Kathy is a beatnik; others claim that she is an existentialist; but Kathy says that she is just plain Kathy. Whatever she is, she is different. She's more intellectual than many members of her class; she reads more; and she acts more avant-garde. She practices a studied nonchalance, taking things in her stride, letting trivial matters in one ear and out the other. Her close friends complain of her "stupid look." This look is only the facial expression that she uses when she hears the names of baseball players and television actors that she cannot recognize. It is possible that in the next shipment of books to India Kathy might be added to the cargo, for it is noticed that she often has unreasonable arguments with Mrs. Bacon. Despite Kathy's exotic, but sometimes esoteric mind, she might, one day, return to Lenox, as the Poet Laureate.

Entered: 1952
Green Team
President of U.N. Club, XII
Vice-President of U.N. Club, XI
Vice-President of Debating Club, X
"170 East," X, XI
"Quill," IX
Debating Club, IX
Dramatics Club, X, XII
Basketball Varsity, X, XI

". . . like Cassandra, prophesies in vain."
YOUNG

4. Claire with her mother, Florence, at Kathy's wedding to Robert Acker, September 4, 1966, Atlantic Beach, Long Island.

5. Kathy with her stepfather, Albert Alexander, and her husband, Robert Acker (right), at their weding.

6. Acker with her lifelong friend, the writer Melvyn Freilicher, in Del Mar, California, 1973.

7. David and Eleanor Antin, Acker's close friends and mentors, on their wedding day in 1961.

8. Acker performing in a short porn film, circa 1971, at the Manhattan apartment she rented with Lenny Neufel

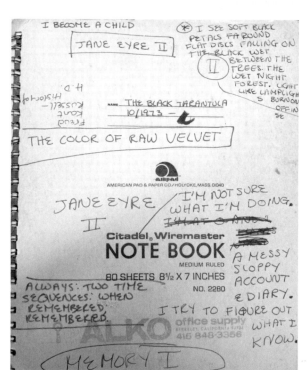

9. Cover of Acker's Black Tarantula/Jane Eyre II notebook, October 1973.

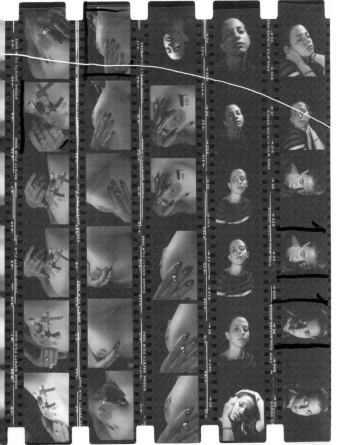

10. Contact sheet from photo shoot for the cover of the TVRT edition of *The Childlike Life of the Black Tarantula*, 1975.

11. Acker in her Haight-Ashbury apartment in 1975.

12. BELOW Acker (in hat) with Jill Kroesen and Peter Gordon at the first Love of Life Orchestra performance in April 1977 at the Franklin Street Arts Center in New York.

13. Acker with Toronto artists Andrew J. Paterson and Judith Doyle at Doyle's Toronto apartment, circa 1978.

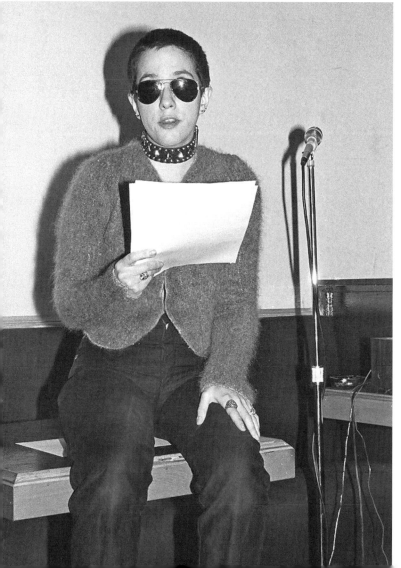

14. Acker reading at Mickey Ruskin's Chinese Chance in Greenwich Village, circa 1979.

15. Left to right: Peter Orlovsky, William S. Burroughs, Allen Ginsberg, Victor Bockris, John Giorno, Sylvère Lotringer, and James Grauerholz at the Bunker, Burroughs' Bowery apartment, in 1980.

CHAPTER 21

——————— ✕ ———————

Acker's particular blend of high and low, the academy and the street, uptown and down—not to mention her longstanding affection for transgressive French literature—inevitably brought her into the orbit of a French writer and publisher who was similarly disdainful of boundaries. Even better, he personally knew many of the authors that Acker had come to admire.

Sylvère Lotringer was a soft-spoken but raffish forty-year-old professor in the French department at Columbia. The son of Polish-Jewish immigrants to France, he was born in Paris in 1930. Before moving to New York in September 1972, he had been a television journalist and academic who had written his doctoral dissertation on Virginia Woolf under the supervision of Roland Barthes. His circle included provocative intellectuals like Pierre Guyotat, Michel Foucault, Félix Guattari, and Paul Virilio. He was lithe, with a halo of curly hair and the mustache of a Sam Peckinpah antihero. Acker thought he had the "eyes of a pimp," a description he repeated with relish. He projected a kind of intellectual swagger and Gallic detachment, but he could also be sweet and companionable.

Lotringer always found academia stifling and retrograde, and sought ways to subvert it—he was likely the only professor in the French department then who wore a black leather jacket on campus. Intent on introducing the then-unfamiliar radical philosophy and cultural theory of post-1968 France to the American avant-garde, in 1973 he started *Semiotext(e)*, a journal initially devoted strictly to semiotics. Soon, however, *Semiotext(e)* published ever-more adventurous writing on psychiatry, philosophy, politics, and art by the likes of Antonin Artaud, Georges Bataille, Jacques Derrida, and Gilles Deleuze. Two years later, Lotringer organized the *Schizo-Culture* conference, with the term "schizo" referring not to any clinical entity per se, but rather, as a press release defined it, "the process by which social controls of all kinds, endlessly re-imposed by capitalism, are broken up and opened to revolutionary change."

The conference, which ran for four days in mid-November 1975, brought to the Columbia campus, among others, Deleuze and Guattari, Foucault (then introducing his *History of Sexuality*), Burroughs, R. D. Laing, Jean-François Lyotard, and the feminist activist Ti-Grace Atkinson. There were workshops, held at the Maison Française, on prison politics, gay liberation, feminism, and psychoanalysis. John Cage presented a new section of his composition *Empty Words*. "I always wanted to go beyond books," Lotringer remembered, "so I met the philosophers. I worked with them, made interviews with them, introduced them."

About two thousand people attended the *Schizo-Culture* conference, including a curator and artist named Diego Cortez. Cortez (née Jim Curtis) was irrepressible, gay, and somewhat shady, a self-defined impresario—some would say grifter—who knew everybody, from Burroughs and the conceptual artist Joseph Kosuth to the multi-disciplinarian artists comprising Collaborative Projects, otherwise known as Colab, whose regular themed exhibitions, like *The Real Estate Show* and *The Times Square Show*, captured both the city's economic instability and its cultural energy. Lotringer referred to Cortez as an *éclaireur*, always on the hunt for the next thing, and indeed he was, traveling to Berlin one day, Paris the next. They met at the conference, where Cortez told him he liked what Lotringer was doing with *Semiotext(e)*, and that he could also help extend the magazine's reach into the downtown art and music worlds. "He was a character and my mentor," Lotringer remembered. "To know Diego meant you had entry to all the clubs downtown."

Lotringer was divorced, but had a young daughter named Mia with a girlfriend who'd been involved in the creation of *Semiotext(e)*. By 1976, he'd abandoned the uptown apartment that Columbia had given him in favor of an industrial loft at East 37th Street and Seventh Avenue that he moved into with Cortez. It was a five-thousand-square-foot place, for which they paid $350 a month, and they would be roommates for five years. While Cortez spent his days and nights in a hyperactive haze—he curated events at the Mudd Club, which opened on Halloween in 1978, immediately becoming a hub of downtown nightlife; tried in vain to adapt Burroughs's books for film; soon began to manage No Wave rocker Lydia Lunch—Lotringer continued to expand his small *Semiotext(e)* empire. With Cortez's help, as well as that of Pat Steir, the conceptual painter, he transformed a relatively staid academic journal into a notorious, playful, genre-defying magazine, and by 1980 he had also started publishing books of translated French theory—palm-sized, jet-black paperbacks that soon adorned grad student rooms across the continent.

Lotringer loved theory, but he was allergic to jargon, and he knew how to make complex philosophy accessible and sexy, both to his students and the broader public. "Open a book in the middle," he said. "If you see a concept you don't know, that's okay. Maybe you look backwards and forwards, and you see it in a different context. It's like a cat. You don't jump on a cat, you let a cat come to you. That was always my technique."

Cortez also of course knew Acker. He'd done the lighting for a reading she'd given at the Franklin Furnace in December 1976, where, Freilicher remembered, they were all so broke they stole money from the till. (Acker eventually came clean and gave most of it back to the center's director, Martha Wilson.) On Spring Street one Saturday afternoon in 1978, with everyone strolling between gallery openings, Cortez introduced Lotringer to her. Lotringer hadn't read anything by Acker at that point, but, like everyone, he had heard of The Black Tarantula, and he too was a bit puzzled by the disconnect between her reputation and the personable young woman in front of him. "She was very lively, obviously smart, beautiful," Lotringer said. "And flirtatious." Acker was still sleeping with Jeff Goldberg, still ostensibly married to Gordon, and still vainly hoping, Lotringer recalled, that things would improve there. Nonetheless, she and Lotringer soon began an affair. "Kathy became part of my life," he said, though the relationship always remained loose and undefined. They met for dinner, went dancing at the Mudd Club, had sex. Lotringer's daughter, Mia, spent weekends with him at the loft, and Acker got along well with the five-year-old girl, with the three of them sometimes sleeping in the same bed.

Undefined or not, the relationship was thrilling to Acker, who said to friends, "I'm a little worried about this thing with Sylvère cause it's so good." About a decade older than her, Lotringer became, to a certain extent, a new father figure. When he did finally read her books, starting with *Kathy Goes to Haiti*, he was completely supportive. He told her he could get her published in Europe. He decided to put out a special issue of *Semiotext(e)* dedicated to the Schizo-Culture conference, its cover designed by Cortez, and invited her to contribute. When he organized the sprawling, multimedia Nova Convention to celebrate Burroughs, recently returned to the United States from London, and held at Pace University (among other places) from November 30 to December 2, 1978, Acker was part of a lineup of countercultural superstars and downtown boldfaces such as Frank Zappa, Timothy Leary, Maurice Giro-dias, John Cage, Laurie Anderson, and Patti Smith. While a film of Burroughs played silently behind her, Acker read from "The Persian Poems," changing Janey's name to William in the text. Adele Bertei, Acker's occasional lover, accompanied Acker to the event, later publishing a long review in *New York Rocker*, mocking Anne Waldman ("looking like a bad actress trying out for a part") and Allen Ginsberg ("Once he HOWLed, now he drools tepid snot from the side of his mouth"). Jeff Goldberg was part of the symposium too, and that was the last time Acker slept with him. "You're too boring," she told him, though they remained friends for years afterward.

Acker opened up various literary worlds to Lotringer, tutoring him in the Black Mountain poets, taking him to the Poetry Project. "We started permeating each other," Lotringer said. But he found poets even worse than academics; if there were two hundred people in the art world, there were only thirty poets, and "they were fiercely competitive, on top of each other all the time, reading to each other, sleeping with each other, fighting each other."

Lotringer, in turn, gave Acker various French theorists to read, including Baudrillard and Foucault. After learning of Acker's fascination with schizophrenia and psychosis, he gave her a copy of Deleuze and Guattari's *Anti-Oedipus*, which had come out in English in 1977, and she was, he remembered, "floored by it." Suddenly, as she would say in many future interviews, she had a language and framework for the work she'd done and would do. "It was the first time I've found people who are talking about what I'm doing," she told Lotringer. "I didn't really understand why I refused to use linear narrative; why my sexual genders kept changing; why basically I am the most disoriented novelist that ever existed." For the rest of her career, such thinkers, especially feminists like Luce Irigaray, Julia Kristeva, and Hélène Cixous, would shape and inform her writing. For a few years at least, she often spoke earnestly about deconstruction, though she tended to use the term less in the Derridean sense and more in the simplistic way it was popularly used, as a synonym for taking things apart to see how they work. "As opposed to construction or reconstruction," she said, "you just take other texts and you put them in different contexts to see how they work. You take texts apart and look at the language that's being used, the genre, the kind of sentence structure, there's a lot of content here that most readers don't see."

Lotringer also introduced her to, or perhaps simply tapped into, her more masochistic side. Among his lovers, Lotringer was known to be somewhat brutal in bed, with a passion for S and M. "He was a sexual top," said Judith Doyle, who had a brief fling with him. "A sadist type dude. Not vicious, but that was his sexual preference at the time. Most girls knew about it." Acker, meanwhile, was discovering that she enjoyed being controlled or dominated. She told Mel Freilicher that she didn't care if she slept with a man or woman "as long as they topped her." It was increasingly pleasurable for her to be bound, lightly struck, to engage in more painful sexual positions and acts.

Lotringer insisted that his and Acker's sex life was "very sweet, unlike what anyone would expect." But Acker told Jeff Weinstein that Lotringer "didn't always treat her well," and he believed that she subconsciously sought out men who could be cruel to her, physically and emotionally. Jeff Goldberg felt, in fact, that Lotringer was a "special threat," not just to Goldberg's romantic relationship with Acker but to Acker herself, and that Lotringer might genuinely injure her.

Goldberg wasn't so far off the mark. Writing her friends Glenda George and Paul Buck, Acker told them in detail about the obvious physical evidence Lotringer left after an S and M session. "I walk into the gym to work out and the women STARE at my back," she wrote, "but they're much too bourgeois to open their mouths and or close their endless fashion gossip and I love it. Fuck the scared capitalists." She suggested too that this play might one day go too far. At the same time, Lotringer helped her distinguish between sadomasochistic behavior in everyday life and S and M play behind closed doors. It was one thing to act like a top, socially, which Acker tended to do. It was another thing to, as Weinstein suggested, seek out or submit to bad relationships. But Lotringer showed her that enacting her masochism in the theater of the bedroom, where it could be performed consensually, was supremely gratifying. It was a form of simultaneous self-affirmation and self-annihilation. "I don't know if it's lovely and who cares," she told George and Buck. "S&M doesn't go beyond the bed unlike the usual relationships where it's all S&M outside the bed and shit inside . . ."

× × ×

By the late seventies, Acker's literary reputation had grown to the point that it had penetrated even Sutton Place's social circles. Improbably, Claire and Acker began to speak more frequently on the phone, even occasionally meeting in person. While Claire never cared for Acker's books—Wendy remembered her asking, "Why can't you write normal and be on the bestseller list?"—she was, it seems, suitably impressed by her daughter's newfound fame. Acker, in turn, felt that maybe, finally, her mother would understand her better, that she would be seen in all her complexity. With Bud gone, Acker also pushed Claire to date again, and the latter would even, on occasion, take a crosstown bus and go dancing at Studio 54. "Now I'm free," Acker writes in *Girl Gangs Take Over the World*, in a scene written in her mother's approximate voice. "For the first time in my life I can be free [...] There's nothing wrong with me. I'm beautiful and I'm rich. I'm only 51." (Claire was actually fifty-three.) They seemed to be on the unexpected verge, both Mel Freilicher and Peter Gordon remembered, of some kind of rapprochement. "My daughter isn't totally reprehensible like I thought she was," the Claire figure says in *Girl Gangs*. "I'll go to her performance in SoHo I want to amuse myself. Maybe her way: saying NO to taking care of people you don't want to take care of, causes happiness."

Pooh Kaye also remembered this surprising reconciliation well. "I don't know what precipitated their finally forgiving one another," Kaye said, "but Kathy was really excited. She was really happy and involved in her mother's life again." Ever the reluctant Jew, Claire decided that she and Kathy would host a large family dinner on Christmas Eve, and invited her cousin Clifford Kaye and Pooh, his daughter. Acker and Kaye had fallen out after Acker had poached one of Kaye's love interests, but after Acker called to discuss the family dinner, all was forgiven—temporarily at least.

But then, sometime in the days just before that dinner, Claire vanished. Kaye recalled that a frantic Acker called all over town looking for her, checking hospital emergency rooms and the like, but couldn't locate her. The exact chronology of events is murky, but Freilicher was in town and he remembered being with Acker at the time. They went to a reading at St. Mark's, but Acker was "really rattled" and couldn't focus on anything. Freilicher was somewhat bewildered—heretofore Acker had mainly spoken of her mother with contempt, but now there was genuine concern. Then, soon afterward, Clifford Kaye called Pooh to tell her that Claire had checked into the midtown Hilton Hotel and, on Christmas Eve, committed suicide.*

---

* Kaye remembered this as December 30, which seems unlikely given that the death certificate was dated December 27, 1978, and that Wendy was listed on it as "informant." Unless Wendy hadn't been able to contact Acker by then either. In any case, at some point, Wendy recalled

Acker was shocked, blindsided. Why had Claire killed herself? Why now? "I wouldn't want to misrepresent her state of mind at that point," Freilicher said, "but she was clearly freaked out." Soon after finding out, she also bumped into Sylvère Lotringer at 8th Street and Third Avenue. She was, he said, "panicked and harried," and Lotringer, waiting for a bus to go pick up his daughter, didn't quite know how to respond. He tried to downplay it, told her to calm down, not to panic, that maybe she was wrong. Decades later, he felt his reactions were all wrong, inadequate, "too French" in the apparent lack of empathy. "I felt very bad about it," he said, "that I wasn't there for her."

Peter Gordon wasn't quite there for her either, as he was then on tour in Cincinnati with the Big Apple Circus. He and Acker spoke on the phone, however, and Gordon remembered her being "devastated," particularly because Claire had at long last recently transformed into a more benign, even positive, presence in Acker's life. It was, she believed, yet another act of betrayal on Claire's part: "The rage you see in her later work—just the fact that they were becoming closer, and then her mother killed herself. That was tough." Acker herself writes as much in *Great Expectations*: "To obtain a different picture of my mother, I have to forgive my mother for rejecting me and committing suicide." Betsy Sussler believed it was a completely "passive-aggressive" act, and even worse: "I'd always believed that suicide is a kind of curse on children. I don't care how old the children are."

The details of the suicide were hazy. No specific cause of death was listed on the death certificate ("pending further study"), though a number of people, including Kaye and Acker herself, suspected Claire deliberately overdosed on Librium, a benzodiazepine she took. A cleaning woman found her body, and though there was no suicide note, Claire had left instructions about her poodle, whom she had taken the precaution of boarding at her veterinarian.

In "The Killers," the talk Acker presented in 1993, Acker gave Claire's death a particularly lurid, paranoid (and factually slippery) spin, just as she did with her birth father's story:

When I was thirty years old, my mother suicided . . . She had killed herself eight days before Christmas. A note in her handwriting, lying

---

that they both went to the morgue to identify the body. (Wendy felt unable to do it, she said, so Acker made the identification.)

beside her dead body, said that her white poodle was staying with such-and-such veterinarian. Nothing else. But despite this note the cops were convinced that my mother was murdered by a man whose name was known. Nevertheless, it was Christmas and there wasn't going to be any police investigation because the cops wanted to return to their homes, Christmas warmth and holiday. For the first time ever in my life I had the following thought: My father could have murdered my mother. After all, what if my real father is crazy? At that moment I became very scared. If my father did murder my mother, he could now be planning to murder me.

It's easy enough to read this metaphorically, though, and indeed, that's probably how it should be read. As we've seen, over and over, Acker did blame her birth father (Harry or whomever) for, in effect, ruining Claire's life (and, by extension, hers). If he hadn't outright murdered her in cold blood at the Hilton, his betrayal and abandonment had, Acker suggests, left Claire emotionally stunted, frightened, in pain seemingly so great that suicide had been her best option.

Was that it, though? Freilicher speculated about a possible illness, and certainly, Claire's mental health was always fragile. Wendy recalled Acker "always saying how messed up [our] mother was." But the general consensus was that Claire, bereft of Bud's financial support, had in less than a year completely run out of money and felt completely trapped. "She was broke," Kaye said. "Stone broke. She didn't have enough money to make the dinner." Acker told Kaye that Claire had begged her grandmother for help, but that Florrie, hard-as-nails Florrie, had ultimately refused. "It was sort of like, that's your tough luck," Kaye said. "Sink or swim. You know, *die, daughter.*"

Acker portrayed Claire's insolvency with similar flint. In *Girl Gangs Take Over the World*, written in the months after the suicide, in a chapter titled "On My Mother's Death," Acker writes, again as Claire:

I can spend money now whenever I want to. I'm buying all the clothes I've been wanting. I like that coat. I'll buy the red and the blue versions of it at Bloomingdale's tomorrow. I'm a little short on cash to pay this butcher's bill with. Oh well. I'll borrow Mother's gold chain; she'll never miss it [. . .] I need more money. What happened to those 700 shares of IBM, Consolidated Edison, and AT&T Mother gave me? I asked the lawyer for money and he refused. He's cheating me. I don't understand what happens to money.

In *Great Expectations,* Acker revisits her mother's fiscal stress, tallying up her mother's crushing debts while also complaining about her mother's lifelong stinginess—financial and emotional—toward her. In the end, though, tragically, Claire remains a figure forever remote, unfathomable, alone: "Mother was a real actress. I never knew who she was."

Acker's claims of Claire's profligacy were borne out by a dispiriting estate account completed the following September. At her death, Claire had only $23.69 in her savings account, and her worldly possessions (miscellaneous furniture, clothing, furs, and jewelry) added up to less than $10,000. At a liquidation sale, Acker and Wendy purchased some of the clothing. A list of creditors' claims, meanwhile, included amounts owed to 400 Realty Corp for rent ($2,406.27), American Express ($1,848.77), Bloomingdale's ($1,159.19), and Saks ($460.56), among dozens of others.

P. Adams Sitney remembered seeing Acker soon after Claire's death, and she mentioned the detail about the IBM (or AT&T) shares too. Whatever that meant exactly—did Claire sell them off, did Florrie steal them back?—Acker was understandably fixated on Claire's finances, and whatever money might, or might not, now flow her way. Claire's death was an undeniable loss, but there was also the possibility that Acker would finally gain something. Florrie was eighty-seven years old, and when she did finally pass away too, Acker stood to inherit at least part of her estate.

This complicated blend of emotions, and the fury that Gordon spoke of, reached an apotheosis of expression in *Algeria,* the short *cri de coeur* that Acker began early in 1979 (and which would appear as both its own 1984 chapbook and reprinted in the omnibus *Hannibal Lecter, My Father*). Algeria—more specifically, the Algerian Revolution and the crushing, ongoing discrimination against Algerians living in France—had long been a pet political cause among the left-leaning French intellectuals that Acker esteemed. Here, anti-colonialist struggle becomes a prism through which Acker views her own private oppression and revolt, her own life under siege. Her narrator is named Omar, the lover she's briefly infatuated with Kader, loosely modeled after Andrew J. Paterson, the Toronto musician she met in early 1979. Acker borrows images and dialogue from *The Battle of Algiers*, Gillo Pontecorvo's groundbreaking 1966 neorealist film, but, again, burrows into her distant past—scenes from the sex show recur—and her more recent, traumatic present. Brusquely, but with specific detail, she recounts the moments leading up to Claire's suicide, with Acker referring to her mother as THE CUNT.

Acker follows this grim vignette with an all-caps declaration—"SUICIDE AND SELF-DESTRUCTION IS THE FIRST WAY THE SHITTED-ON START SHOWING ANGER AGAINST THE SHITTERS"—before moving into the story's third section, "The Next Crazy Cunt," in which she, Omar, goes with her husband, Ali—a Peter Gordon surrogate—to visit her grandmother, also called THE CUNT. They take her for lunch to the Museum of Modern Art, where Omar is solicitous, deferential, and abject, desperate to remain in her grandmother's good graces even as she is screaming on the inside. "THE CUNT your mother wasn't a pig," the grandmother tells Omar. "It was perfect. It was absolutely beautiful. Everyone loved it. Why'd it have to kill itself. You'd be exactly like it, Omar, if you'd only grow your hair and act feminine." After the lunch, a dejected Omar heads to the Diamond District to sell the two gold watches that are the only things her mother has left her. She's told that they aren't real gold.

CHAPTER 22

— ✕ —

AS THE NEW YEAR BEGAN, ACKER FOUND HERSELF IN A GRIEF-
stricken limbo. The absence that Claire's death created was a presence
now as deeply felt as the absence of her birth father. Now she was really alone,
truly an orphan. Acker's almost constant, lifelong rage toward her mother had
given her life an organizing principle. Now that was gone. The more recent
possibility, that they might have had a more affirmative and understanding
relationship, had been snuffed out as soon as it emerged. The chance that she'd
had to maybe understand Claire, and thus, understand herself, was snatched
away. She wasn't sure how to mourn, or *who* to mourn. "I have no memory
of the next month or two, except for the funeral," she wrote many years later,
in *My Mother: Demonology*. "To experience my mother's death (which wasn't
quite the experience of an other's death, but rather of my blood's death) was
to experience that which couldn't be experienced. A loss of consciousness."

Making matters worse was the constant flux in the rest of her life. The fate
of *Blood and Guts* was still uncertain, with Stonehill still ostensibly publishing
the book but also, preposterously, threatening to take all the sex out of it. "I
hate publishers only poets should be allowed to live," Acker told a friend. Her
love life was also just as turbulent and unresolved as ever. The relationship
with Lotringer continued, but with increasing complication. There was "a little
too much S&M and or pain and a little too little compassion," she said, but
Acker also wanted a more exclusive relationship than he was willing to give.
At one point, Silliman visited and they slept together again. Silliman recalled
"literally being inside Kathy" when Acker, hoping to pique Lotringer's jealousy, telephoned and told him she was fucking somebody else at that exact
moment.

Her general despondency was on full view in *Algeria*. "Here in New York,
every morning I wake up, I don't want to be awake," she wrote. "I have to persuade myself to wake up. I have to use my will to get food in my mouth because
my heart sees no reason for anything." This depression would obscure the first

part of the year, interrupted only by her return to Toronto, ostensibly to promote *Kathy Goes to Haiti*, and the fling with Paterson.

Even so miserable, Acker continued to write and socialize, still haunting the Mudd Club and occasionally dropping by the various nightclubs and bars that now defined downtown: CBGB, Club 57, the Pyramind Club. She was often at Tier 3, an East Village club with décor by artists Kiki Smith and Jean-Michel Basquiat, or Magoos, a Tribeca bar with a great jukebox and decent food. "She was very conscious of appearing in the right places with the right people wearing the right thing," Mel Freilicher said. Her social life somehow flourished, in fact, in part because it was also an extension of her work. An obligatory chore some nights, but also, some nights, a lot of fun. She spent her days working at home alone; going out at night tempered the isolation.

By then, her circle included a colorful range of artists and scene-makers: writers like Gary Indiana, Lynne Tillman, and Darius James, photographer Jimmy DeSana, filmmaker Amos Poe, the conceptual artist Sarah Charlesworth, proto-influencer Anya Phillips, the dandyish young painter Duncan Hannah and his girlfriend, Terence Sellers, a professional dominatrix and writer (*The Correct Sadist*). Hannah didn't much care for Acker's writing, but he loved her as a person and remembered her always laughing—"like a monkey." Sellers adored both. This cluster of friends almost never hung out in each other's apartments (unless it was to fuck); instead, they roamed across downtown, bouncing between bars and galleries, gabbing on the street, generally drinking an enormous amount. Drugs and youth gave them energy too, and they went to as many performances and readings and openings as they could cram into a night.

All of this fluorescence and incestuousness was captured in Betsy Sussler's quarterly magazine *BOMB*, the scene's enduring house organ. Sussler was an actor and theater director, and had cofounded an art magazine called *X Motion Picture*, which evolved into *BOMB* in 1981. *BOMB*'s first issue, published in May of that year, included fiction by, among others, Indiana, Tillman, Sellers, and Cookie Mueller. There was art by Duncan Hannah and Jimmy DeSana, and an excerpt from *Great Expectations*. Acker's ex, Jeff Goldberg, was a contributing editor.

Sussler became a dear friend of Acker's. "I thought of her as an imp," she said, and, like Sellers, she considered Acker an "odd sister." The competition Acker might have felt with other women in the scene never impaired their relationship. On the contrary, Sussler found her very loving. Sussler was married to Lindzee Smith, an Australian actor who she worked with on plays and Super 8 films. Smith was also a heroin addict, and by the time Acker and Sussler met, his addiction had all but destroyed their marriage. Once, when Sussler was down with a serious flu, Acker came over with some juices and tried to nurse her back to health. At one point, Acker went to the refrigerator to get Sussler some food. Without a word, she closed it, returned to Sussler's bedside, and said, quietly, seriously, and without drama, "As soon as you're well, I want you to leave him. I don't want you to wait a day. And I will help you." Acker never disclosed what she saw in the fridge, but Sussler guessed there had been some syringes in there and Acker then recognized the extent of Smith's drug dependence. With Acker's support, then, Sussler did finally manage to end the marriage. "It's very hard to leave someone when they have an addiction," Sussler said. "You think you can save them. Of course you can't. But Kathy really saved *me*."

× × ×

A bit later that year, Acker wrote a long, fragmentary short story, "New York City in 1979," a portrait of the downtown art world in which the end of the decade might as well be the end of the world. At moments it's maudlin, at others bawdy, and still others satiric. "The world is gray afterbirth," she writes, and New York itself "fake," and a "pit-hole." "I want more and more horrible disaster in New York cause I desperately want to see the new thing that is going to happen this year." Janey and Johnny return as characters, and over the course of several pages, they fuck and don't fuck, bemoan their incapacity for love or their relentless need for it, wither in the oppressive summer heat and the equally stultifying art scene. There's a standoff outside the Mudd Club between a bouncer and a some "rich hippies." Janey and Johnny visit Janey's grandmother. They see a movie, *Some Like It Hot*. Mordant declarative statements—"INTENSE SEXUAL DESIRE IS THE GREATEST THING IN THE WORLD, I WANT ALL THE ABOVE TO BE THE SUN, ANYTHING THAT DESTROYS LIMITS"—punctuate a few pages, recalling, somewhat, lines from Jenny Holzer's famous *Truisms*.

The piece is dedicated to "Jeanne's insulted beauty," a reference to Jeanne Duval, the Haitian-French actress who had been Charles Baudelaire's lover. Acker later said that she took Baudelaire's account of his infecting Duval with syphilis and then "crudely" superimposed this text overtop her own descriptions of her "present environment" in an attempt to magically transform it. Acker's true subject, though, is prostitution; actual prostitution, but more significantly, her own striving and debasement—sleeping with men in exchange for their support and prostrating herself before her grandmother—and that of her artist friends. In one scene, Johnny articulates how existentially muddled Acker was about all of this: "Wouldn't you like to give up this artistic life which you know isn't rewarding cause artists now have to turn their work/selves into marketable objects/fluctuating images/fashion have to competitively knife each other in the back because we're not people, can't treat each other like people, no feelings, loneliness comes from the world of rationality, robots, every thing one as objects defined separate from each other?"

"New York City in 1979" would go on to have a surprisingly long life. The next year it appeared, abridged, in the British underground magazine *International Times* as well as in the July 1980 *Crawl Out Your Window*. It was reprinted again in 1981 as the ninth installment in Anne Turyn's *Top Stories*, with photographs by Turyn, and was included, as well, in *Hannibal Lecter, My Father*. It was also selected for the 1981 Pushcart Prize anthology, the annual collection of notable small press writing. In 2018, the story was re-released by Penguin in its Modern Classics series.

Acker claimed not to care about the Pushcart attention. "It's nothing," she told an interviewer. "I guess it means something to someone." She grumbled about the fact that the prize was not accompanied by money. But it reinforced her belief in her writing, and kept alive the idea that her work could have at least a small bit of commercial appeal. Why shouldn't her books have as devoted and wide a following as those of, say, Burroughs? At the same time, she refused to make any concessions to readerly pleasure or the marketplace. She believed she would be read, and read widely, but on her own terms. It was only a matter of time, and persistence.

Baudelaire was still on Acker's mind later that year, when she published "Notes on Writing—from the Life of Baudelaire" in the October 1979 issue of L=A=N=G=U=A=G=E. Here, Acker makes her identification with the *poète maudit* both more concrete and self-ironic: "After a while self-absorption is boring because one sees thoughts are only thoughts and one wants freedom. So one gets involved with the process of creating thoughts, with creation which is superfluous and gratuitous. To avoid this superfluity and gratuity which every great artist knows, pain, Baudelaire asserts himself, for no reason at all, a natural rebel, against the world he knows. There's no other world. He needs a world or else he'll be back in uneasiness. One has to exist in pain." She concludes with a tart, taut sentence that could be leveled at any writing workshop, program, or self-help book: "One needs laws, the laws of writing, so one can hate them."

× × ×

Soon enough, as she had so many times previously, Acker needed to get out of New York. That summer, she met the Dutch poet and artist Harry Hoogstraten, who had heard about Acker from Waldman, who told him Acker was "doing adventurous writing." When Hoogstraten went to organize the annual One World Poetry Festival, held that October in Amsterdam's Vondelpark, he invited her. It would be Acker's first trip to Europe.

That edition of the festival was dedicated to Jack Kerouac, by then dead a decade, and featured several Beat and Beat-adjacent writers: Burroughs was there, as were Brion Gysin, Gerard Malanga, Gregory Corso, and Ed Dorn. Hoogstraten remembered Acker spending most of her time in Amsterdam with Malanga, but Hoogstraten also took her to a reading in Utrecht. He was surprised how demanding she could be—throwing a fit, for instance, when she learned that no private transportation had been arranged for the Utrecht event and they were compelled to take a bus the twenty-eight miles back to the city. "She was not so tough," he said, "not so angry punk girl but fragile little rich girl spoiled somewhat for not getting what she thought she should."

At the festival, Acker also met Paul Buck, a thirty-three-year-old English avant-garde poet, playwright, and translator. Buck shared Acker's aversion to genre snobbery—he published a magazine of experimental prose called *Curtains* while also writing film criticism and crime fiction. "Improvisation is at the heart of my existence," he wrote in his autobiography, *A Public Intimacy*. Like *Semiotext(e)*, *Curtains* introduced many French philosophers and writers to English-speaking audiences, and when Buck came across the TVRT edition of *The Childlike Life of the Black Tarantula* at Compendium Books in Camdem, he recognized The Black Tarantula as a kindred spirit.

Buck and Acker read on the same bill, became friendly, and, two weeks later, reunited in Paris. Buck was attending a translation conference and Acker was in Montparnasse visiting Gérard-Georges Lemaire, a writer, editor, and translator she met through Sylvère Lotringer. Lemaire had translated Ezra Pound and a couple Beat writers, and was keen to bring Acker's writing to the French as well—he would eventually translate both *The Childlike Life of the Black Tarantula* and her *Great Expectations*, describing Acker's romantic universe as "the fruit of a revolt which is never exhausted."

For a Francophile like Acker, being in Paris was a dream. Buck happily showed her around. He had no romantic interest in Acker; he was married to fellow writer Glenda George, who would soon arrive in Paris too and with whom Acker would also become close. "She was an intellectual," Buck said of Acker. "No matter what anyone else says—a punk, the persona, all this stuff—she was an intellectual. That's the reason I was interested in what she was doing, and why we met up and spent the next few days together." Buck also introduced Acker to the collective of experimental poets associated with the journal *Change*, led by Jean-Pierre Faye. Buck recalled a memorable dinner with them, deliberately held a stone's throw from Bataille's old flat. Buck and Acker, both about the same height, spent the evening talking about poetry in large, high-backed chairs, feeling very much like Alice at the Mad Hatter's tea party.

Acker was grateful for the companionship. Though Lemaire was fascinated by her writing, he was less charmed by the person. "She was overly sensitive," he said. "Relations with her were always difficult, for no good reason." For her part, in a later letter, Acker told Buck and George that she thought Lemaire was "crazy" and "WORSE RIGHT WING and WORSE WORSE WORSE POMPOUSPOMPOUSPOMPOUS." Nevertheless, she took happy refuge in his library, where she attempted her own translations of Pierre Guyotat and discovered writing by Colette Peignot, aka Laure, a friend of Maurice Blanchot's and Bataille's last, masochistic lover.

Acker would end up staying less than a month in Europe, but after returning to the U.S., she'd spend the next year or so figuring out how to get back.

× × ×

Just before Acker left for Europe, her grandmother broke her hip. According to an autobiographical scene Acker sketched in a draft of her 1981 screenplay *Variety*, Florrie never recovered from the injury. The hospital where she was cared for, while the best money could buy, was nonetheless, Acker wrote, "a hell hole" where "the first law of [a patient's] life was now mental and sensory deprivation." While Acker was reluctant to go on her trip and leave Florrie on her own as she traveled, her grandmother hadn't been sick a day in her life; a doctor reassured them both that, with time, she would be fine. Instead, she rapidly declined. Acker wrote her frequently from Paris, and then finally called, to hear her voice one last time. "Blood speaks to blood," Acker writes. "There are ties the strongest ties are the ones we're not conscious of."

On October 27, Florrie passed away. Her estate was valued at close to a million dollars. She left $10,000 to the Jewish Guild for the Blind, $2,500 to a helpmeet named Elizabeth Strachan, a $25,000 trust to Wendy's son, Kevin, and a lump sum of $100,000 each to Wendy and Acker. After those payments and executor fees, the remainder of her estate, about $735,000, was split evenly between Wendy and Acker, and placed in a trust disbursed in quarter-annual installments over the next fifteen years. With interest rates high in the early eighties, Acker's income from the trust was likely about $40,000 a year ($128,000 in today's money). After five years, the two granddaughters received a third of the trust's principal amount, then another third five years after that, and the final third fifteen years after that.

Acker was suddenly financially secure. It would take about a year for the inheritance to go through and its effects to be truly felt, but she was no longer dependent on men to support her, no longer forced to work in the sex industry or at shitty hippie bakeries, no longer compelled to live in squalor, no longer poor. She would continue to *feel* poor, however, or at least broke, and would, for a variety of reasons, act as if she had no money. At other times, it would seem that the money was poisonous or cursed, that she wanted to get rid of it as quickly as possible.

But that was in the distant future. That December, she returned to Buffalo for a series of readings, and that same month, she wrote Paul Buck and Glenda George telling them that she was "hot on new book"—a reference to *Great Expectations*—and waiting on her inheritance to be processed. In another letter to them, written in mid-January, she recounted an amusingly miserable New Year's Eve spent at the Mudd Club. There, drunk on champagne at three in the morning, she rebuffs the advances of an acquaintance only to find herself in the coke-fueled clutches of Mudd Club owner Steve Mass. "I usually don't do coke," she writes, "and now do twenty lines, Steve keeps shoving it up my nostril I guess cause he wants to seduce me then fills me up with bottles of Dom Perignon." She spent the next couple of weeks in bed with the flu, reading

Husserl and Dickens. A few months later, on March 11 and 12, the Kitchen hosted a simultaneous event: a launch for the Traveler's Digest edition of *Nymphomaniac* and a performance by Acker of the in-progress *Great Expectations*. A review in *Artforum*, written by Joan Casademont, captured both the appeal and limitations of the work: "Acker's material was written to be delivered orally, although I suspect it would be sustained equally well in print. As a performer, she is smooth and professional, although as she moves from one character to the next, she vacillates a bit between acting out theatrical personae and reading as author."

x x x

That spring, Acker read from *Great Expectations* again, this time at Seattle's Washington Hall Performance Gallery. While there, she met and began seeing a twenty-nine-year-old painter and art installer named Jim Logie. Logie was "a force," but also a womanizer with a chip on his shoulder. He was originally from Montana, and he and Acker bonded over their relative outsider status.

Their affair was intense enough that Acker decided to stay in the city—to the complete bafflement of her friends back east—for almost six months. "What I really mean is, dammit, where are you?" Terry Sellers wrote. "Get your butt home, dumbbell." But Acker obviously needed to escape, and for a variety of reasons. She told Jeff Goldberg that "NYC might have got me famous but it was killing me. I have to make a bid to *see*: apart from male-given media-given categories. I have to learn what nature is. Even if I die unknown. I mean otherwise I've done nothing. There's only one life." She later added that she had also suffered from "a kind of overdue breakdown from all the deaths changes etc." Writing to Sellers, she suggested that her florid romantic life provided its own justification: "I just couldn't stand P. Gordon being nice to me and Sylvere [*sic*] beating me up anymore and one always does suffer for one's unhappiness." She had her apartment on East Fifth packed up and most of her belongings shipped out west.

Logie was a refreshing alternative—at least for a few months. "He's a good man," she told Paul Buck and Glenda George, "goddammit he works as a Teamster." She liked his art and his politics. It was the first time, she also said, that she'd lived with a guy where she had "done more than consider what the guy can do for me (prostitution)." Seattle itself was less appealing—"an empty hole" and too much of a suburban town for her, despite its big city trappings and rough old mariner character. Her continuing ill health—she was now receiving some kind of heat treatment that promised to rid her of PID forever—made things feel even more desolate. Nonetheless, she threw herself into the city's small cultural scene with her usual vigor, reading at least one more time in the city and working briefly at Left Bank, an anarchist bookstore on Pike Street. She started a new novel (working title *The Seattle Book*) which brought together Flaubert, *La Princesse de Clèves*, and Winnie the Pooh, but abandoned it after just fourteen pages, folding its pages, greatly transformed, into *Great Expectations*.

Acker and Logie talked seriously about moving to Europe together once her inheritance came through—buying a house in Paris or maybe England—but by October, the relationship had fizzled. She had come to find him too immature and insecure, and he could even be threatening—at one point, he locked Acker up in his studio and wouldn't let her out. "Seattle is bleak and horrible," she told Buck and George, "and I believe I'm too old and rotty to live with anyone." In the end, Logie would go on to Europe without her.

But by then, Acker already had another exit strategy in place. The San Francisco Art Institute invited her to teach a course on performance that November. She had never formally taught before, but she immediately said yes. She sent separate fuschia-colored postcards to both Paul Buck and Jeff Goldberg, the front of which were part of a dream map similar to the ones she included in *The Seattle Book*, writing across the top of them: "TO BECOME HAPPY YOU HAVE TO DO WHAT YOU WANT."

This was the sentiment she still espoused when she returned to Seattle a decade later, for a visit of more lasting consequence. By then, at the height of her literary celebrity, in May 1989, she conducted a weekend-long workshop at the Center on Contemporary Art. Her students included Stacey Levine, who would go on to a distinguished literary career, and Kathleen Hanna, the future front woman of the bands Bikini Kill and Le Tigre. Hanna was then a twenty-year-old student at Evergreen State College in Olympia, an hour's drive south. A photography teacher had turned her on to *Blood and Guts in High School*, and Hanna had become an Acker devotee. At the end of the workshop, each participant was given five minutes alone with Acker to discuss their work. Hoping to impress her, Hanna lied and told Acker she was a spoken-word artist and gave her a hastily made chapbook. Acker was not impressed. "Why are you doing this?" Acker asked. "What's the point? Nobody likes spoken word. You know when you start doing spoken word, people leave the room. You want to go around to art spaces and read your work for five people? Why don't you go be in a band? You're young. That's what young people are into. You'll have such a bigger audience to hear what you have to say." After the workshop, Hanna did exactly what Acker said—she went back to Olympia and started her own band.

Many years later, that group, Bikini Kill, arguably the most influential and significant of the so-called riot grrrl bands, would play in Spokane at the same time Acker was a visiting artist. Hanna and Acker met again. It wasn't exactly a blissful reunion, however; the two women spoke only briefly, and Hanna still felt like an acolyte, desperate for approval and mentorship. But she also belatedly realized that she no longer needed either. "She already mentored me from afar," Hanna said. "She mentored me just by making her work and I read it."

CHAPTER 23

———— ✕ ————

With *Blood and Guts* still unpublished, *Great Expectations* would become Acker's first "real" novel, or at least the first to be published by a genuine publisher with her actual name on the cover. Mel Freilicher remembered too, that it was the first book she herself referred to as a novel. "Why a novel?" he asked. "It has to be something they can promote," she said.

When Acker herself went to promote it, writing up a press release for her first readings from the book, she described it as a "rewrite of Charles Dickens' novel, a destruction for no reason at all." She added: "*Great Expecations* is the story of survival: the story of nothing. From this story, Kathy Acker will take everything away, to let in a little air."

What "everything" did Acker take away? Dickens's dense plot, for one, and its multiple reversals. Also, his many vivid characters and sonorous language. She did steal the book's famous opening sentences, changing Philip/Pip's name to Peter, and a few other paragraphs and images. But it was the animating action of the novel—orphan comes into large fortune and then proceeds to enter high society—that provided Acker with the engine for her own.

Acker herself was now, of course, the orphan with the new fortune. As a protagonist, though, she is both more and less than Pip; she is a woman, a girl, but one with multiple identities (and multiple names: Peter, Rosa, Miss Sarah Ashington, Kathy). Recent and past events of her own life—her early years in Sutton Place, the sex show bust, the discovery of her birth father, Claire's suicide, her move to Seattle and the romance with Logie—provide an erratic through line but a consistently elegiac emotional arc. That mournfulness is offset by Acker's deflating send-up of the art and literary worlds. In one of the book's most notorious and amusing chapters, she names names, and includes several fake, and deliciously ironic, letters that skewer, among others, Lotringer, the Mudd Club owner Steve Mass, and Susan Sontag. Acker didn't know Sontag like she knew Lotringer or Mass, but the two women shared friends and much more: difficult childhoods, complicated relationships to their mothers and their own bodies, a Francophilia. But Sontag was also a celebrity, a self-serious, cool, proud member of the uptown intelligentsia—a sacred cow easily tipped.

Dear Susan Sontag,

Would you please read my books and make me famous? Actually I don't want to be famous because then all these people who are very boring will stop me on the street and bother me already I hate the people who call me on the phone because I'm always having delusions. I now see my delusions are more interesting than anything that can happen to me in New York. Despite everyone saying New York is just the most fascinating city in the world. Except when Sylvére fucks me. I wish I knew how to speak English. Dear Susan Sontag, will you teach me how to speak English. For free, because, you understand, I'm an artist and artists by definition are people who never pay for anything even though they sell their shows out at $10,000 a painting before the show opens. All my artist friends were starving to death before they landed in their middle-class mothers' wombs; they especially tell people how they're starving to death when they order $2.50 each beers at the Mudd Club. Poverty is one of the most repulsive aspects of human reality: more disgusting than all the artists who're claiming they're total scum are the half-artists the hypocrites the ACADEMICS who think it's in to be poor, WHO WANT TO BE POOR, who despise the white silk napkins I got off my dead grandmother—she finally did something for me for once in her life (death)—because those CRITICS don't know what it's like to have to tell men they're wonderful for money, cause you've got to have money, for ten years. I hope this society goes to hell. I understand you're very literate, Susan Sontag.*

Yours,
Rosa

---

* Even still, Acker doesn't shrink from also mocking her own vanity—she really did hope that Sontag might help make her more famous. Gary Indiana was a friend of Sontag's too, and Acker asked him if he would give the latter copies of her early books. Later, he noticed those books sitting on top of a pile that Sontag had set aside to sell at the Strand. "Can you believe this person?" Indiana recalled Sontag saying scornfully. "This woman is a friend of yours?"

Acker said she chose *Great Expectations* as her starting point "for emotional reasons." It was a book she loved as a child. Writing a book in part about her painful childhood, she wanted to "destroy this book I absolutely loved," and, ergo, destroy her childhood. At the same time, she was also still trying to use her writing as a cultural probe, to decode or uncover the oppressive and deforming structures of gender, family life, the conventional novel, emotional longing. As always, from time to time, Acker provides a metafictional, earnest aside that both punctuates and punctures these interrogations: "I'm going to tell you something," the narrator says. "The author of the work you are now reading is a scared little shit."

The book skips through several time periods and places and viewpoints, and sections stolen whole-cloth from other works—Guyotat's *Éden, Éden, Éden*; Melville's *Redburn*; Madame de la Fayette's *La Princesse de Clèves*; Sartre's *Sketch for a Theory of the Emotions*; Pauline Réage's *Story of O*; Proust's *Remembrance of Things Past*—are spliced together in ways both jarring and jocular. When writing *Blood and Guts*, she found the selection and arrangement of the Genet sections the most pleasurable part of that experience, and with *Great Expectations*, she employed this technique with even more gusto. "I really felt I was doing something I loved," she said. "I'd often take texts that were either sexual or political—usually fairly *hot* texts, like the beginning of *Great Expectations*, where there's that incredible Pierre Guyotat text—and I put these next to the stuff about my mother's suicide. Now one speaks about one's mother's suicide in a certain way, especially autobiographical material. And one speaks about sex during wartime—which is what Pierre Guyotat is writing about—in another way. I put them both together as if they were the same text. Doing that uncovered a lot of stuff." The first section of the book is baldly titled "Plagiarism."

As Acker wrote, she kept her friends up-to-date on her progress, sending along sections as she completed them. All of her writing from the previous year—from *Girl Gangs* to *The Seattle Book*—seemed to feed the book, and she was generally pleased with the work. But she occasionally fretted that she would be misunderstood yet again, or, worse, dismissed: "You don't know any more what you're doing kid," she imagined some future critic or reader saying. "You're using language, given language, as in Flaubert's, like paint . . . sculpting it, who the fuck does that?" To Goldberg, she struck a note somewhere in the middle: "I'm working on this section of GREAT EXPECTATIONS, a romance

Daphne du Maurier style, no more cynicism, very gentle, I wonder where all my bitterness has gone to and now everyone'll probably hate it cause of the gentleness . . ."

Or perhaps not. *Great Expectations* would become arguably Acker's most beloved novel, in large part because of that gentleness. Eileen Myles described it as "a mawkish and sometimes heartbreakingly beautiful discourse on what being and feeling can be." A favorable article in the *New York Times* likened her work to David Antin's and Burroughs's and said that she cut "across rational discourse" and forced "the reader into violent and unsettling contradictions." It contains all of the things that make her work so singular and startling—the anger, the disjunction, the humor, the literary gossip, the oneiric drift—but its overarching sadness is utterly legible, with a penultimate paragraph as heart-breaking as anything in, well, Dickens. Its relative brevity and coherence too give it an accessibility that other Acker books tend to lack.

Like all of Acker's early books, however, its actual publishing history was not without complication. The book was first designed and published in 1982 by RE/Search Publications, the San Francisco indie press started in 1977 by City Lights staffer V. Vale. RE/Search would later bill itself as "the longest last-ing (and still active) punk publisher," releasing books by and about Burroughs, J. G. Ballard, Lydia Lunch, Jello Biafra, industrial music, and "modern primi-tives."

Vale and Acker were friendly—the first time they met at City Lights, she gave him a *détourned* copy of the first RE/Search tabloid magazine, which she had used for her own writing—and he agreed to publish and distribute *Great Expectations* if Acker would pay for the printing. This irritated her, but she was desperate to publish new material, and agreed—"I need something new out NOW," she told Buck and George, "my books are doing selling better than ever and they're so old I think they're dead." But things with RE/Search quickly went awry. Vale gave the book and money to a printer but failed to get a contract. The printer made only three hundred copies, then refused to do any more, keeping both the money and the production files.

Acker eventually wrested the book away, taking it back to George Quasha at Station Hill, who agreed to publish it. He used RE/Search's original typeset-ting and design—like *Kathy Goes to Haiti*, it had the deceptive appearance of a children's book—as well as a back cover blurb by the French writer and film-maker Alain Robbe-Grillet: "The most completely unified work of art Acker has yet produced. One that by its formal concentration and its unified shape at every depth of reading fulfills the sort of demands that Sterne or Canetti makes of the novelist." It was a remarkable blurb, and one that, naturally, Acker wrote herself. If she could disguise herself as Dickens, why not the doyen of the *nouveau roman* as well?

x x x

The San Francisco Art Institute course that Acker started teaching in the fall of 1980 was called, simply, Performance. She was given the second half of the semester, with the Kipper Kids—the anarchic and unclassifiable comedy duo— teaching the first. Acker was initially apprehensive but soon found teaching often stimulating. She introduced her students to the writings of Artaud, had them make their own magazines. But it was also considerable effort and a distraction from her writing. "I'm stuck with too much work," she wrote Buck and George, "and getting nervy and yelling crabbing at the brats they REALLY are bratty especially the guys . . ." One of those brats was the future performance artist Karen Finley, whose raw monologues about rape and incest would scandalize East Village clubs, and the National Endowment for the Arts, a few years later. Acker's teaching and writing was a revelation for Finley, who later raved that "she offered a way out of traditionally paternal pedagogical structures, providing me a profound and inspired female mentor."

If Acker had been a tangential member of the Language poetry movement when she was last living in San Francisco, now she became a tangential member of its queer offshoot, the New Narrative. Bruce Boone and Robert (Bob) Glück were the progenitors of the loose-knit group of writers that fell under this rubric, two young gay poets who had met in the early seventies, united by a shared enthusiasm for Frank O'Hara. They'd also both been enchanted with Language poetry's formal innovations and its emphasis on "non-narrative," qualities that had electrified Bay Area poetry, but which they felt had become insufficient and stagnant over time. They craved a community that could accommodate their personal experiences of Marxism, gay liberation, feminism, and literary theory, and an aesthetic too, that would more accurately and comprehensively embody those. Over the next decade and more, some of San Francisco's gutsiest and most original poets, novelists, and essayists—Kevin Killian, Dodie Bellamy, Steve Abbott, Camille Roy, and, of course, Boone and Glück themselves—would try to answer this need. They ostensibly rejected traditional forms of storytelling—took everything away, as Acker did in *Great Expectations*—but found new ways, as Killian and Bellamy put it, to reproduce the "sensations of ordinary life while subverting the totalizing narrative that had stymied and withered our lives."

Before she even moved back to San Francisco, Acker had become a kind of patron saint to the New Narrative crowd. "A narrative is an emotional moving," she writes in *Great Expectations*. Her early work contained all the maneuvers, the different planes, the variety of engagement, the autobiographical swerve, the gossip, the spontaneity, the appropriation—above all, the *sex*—that the New Narrative writers wanted to use in their own work. Killian, an inveterate autograph hound, once asked Acker to sign his autograph book. She wrote, "I want to be your friend forever Kevin," and, on a subsequent page, drew a picture of a talking vulva, which said, "Wah! I'm not getting enough." She signed it, "Acker the Yack."

In 1978, Glück had started a reading series, Small Press Traffic, at a bookstore in the Castro. SPT was the de facto New Narrative clubhouse, the site of fruitful, bustling writing workshops, and the place where Glück first discovered Acker's work, specifically *Nymphomaniac*. He lived nearby, sharing a house with the poet Denise Kastan, with whom he codirected SPT. When Acker came back to San Francisco in 1980, she ended up staying with Kastan, though the how and why of that arrangement are vague. "She and Denise had a semi-flirtation," Glück recalled. "I don't think Kathy was ever that interested in women, but she liked to flirt." In any case, Glück, who lived upstairs, regularly came down to smoke cigarettes and talk. He and Acker were about the same age, but Glück felt, relative to her, like a "West Coast country mouse," and that she inhabited a much larger world than he did.

Great Expectations, it seemed, was a breakthrough, a more felicitous marriage of mutiny and momentum, rage and humor. She was more assured about her work, confident about the direction it was going. She sometimes shared her writing with Glück, but he quickly realized that she was only looking for support, not feedback. When he dared suggest that the juxtaposition of Guyotat and her family stuff in *Great Expectations* was "out of balance," she just shook her head and said, "No." Later in their friendship, Glück recalled, she would often say, "Why aren't I in the Penguin Classics series?"

Acker and Glück also spent long evenings drinking wine and discussing at length their respective love lives. "There was no romantic bruise you couldn't revisit like seven hundred times," he said. One day, Glück invited Robert Duncan, a key figure in the San Francisco Renaissance, over for lunch, thinking that he and Acker would get along well. She and Duncan happily discussed Melville, Bataille, and Charles Olson—Duncan's hero—and Duncan, who had received the Black Tarantula serials, told her that he had saved each installment. "I knew you'd be famous one day," Duncan said. After Duncan had left, Acker told Glück that he should really sleep with the older poet, some thirty years Glück's senior: "He's fabulous!"

The romantic bruise that most preoccupied Acker at the time was an affair she'd begun with her boss, Howard Fried. Fried was a conceptual artist who had founded the video and performance department (later called New Genres) at SFAI in the late seventies. Fried lived with his girlfriend and a child, but nevertheless, drunk and stoned one night, he and Acker hooked up. Things continued for a while after that, more or less covertly. "I make out in the car with my boss while his kid sleeps in the back," she confided to Buck. With characteristic exaggeration, she also told Buck that Fried was the "only friend in this city I can really talk to (i.e. talk art)" and that she was in love with him. Fried wasn't quite so taken; he refused to leave his girlfriend, and after much back-and-forth, the relationship with Acker predictably imploded. "I hope my salary isn't as much of a hoax as the rest of his deal," Acker wrote to Glenda George.

San Francisco was lonely, a "desert." She badly missed her old friends in New York, even her ex Jeff Goldberg, with whom she regularly corresponded. While she insisted that celibacy "fucked her up," sexual relationships were their own special madness. She couldn't stop herself from obsessing, couldn't prevent herself from going overboard whenever a man she was remotely attracted to expressed interest. She allowed men to get away with things she knew she shouldn't tolerate. She became "this animal that I hate." As always, books and writing felt like her only refuge. "If I didn't write, I'd die," she wrote George. "Sometimes everything is so wrong or just unknown, there's only the work that existence that's all there is."

And so, it all went into the work—her fling with Fried, her friendships with Glück and Denise Kastan. In the final chapter of Great Expectations, Acker becomes Cynthia "the whore," and Bob and Denise fellow prostitutes named Barbarella and Danielle. Fried is named Propertius, after the Roman elegist Sextus Propertius, whom P. Adams Sitney had introduced Acker to so many years ago. Propertius's first book, traditionally called Cynthia Monobiblos—"A

Single Book Devoted to Cynthia"—is the earliest extant example in Western literature of a book dedicated to a woman. Propertius's elegies chronicle a love that is troubled, mutable, and perverse—ultimately, a confusing power struggle. Acker reframes and reworks some of Propertius's own words, collaging these with snippets of conversations she'd had with Fried (and Glück and Kastan) and other, not completely evident, sources. Like all of Acker's work, these passages invite a number of different readings. Suffice it to say, however, that a feminist, personal statement, close to the book's end and archly attributed to Propertius himself, is certainly part of her point: "If you read from end to end of the Greek Anthology, you won't find a love poem where the character of individuality of the woman who's loved matters."

CHAPTER 24

————— ✕ —————

To Acker's surprise, the Art Institute extended her contract into the winter, and she finally found her own apartment, at 70
Langton Street. Still, New York kept pulling her back. "Even if it's death," she
said of the city, "it's my bloodline." She flew back and forth a couple of times
for performances, additional Semiotext(e) conferences and launches, and a
couple of theater and film projects that she embarked on with varying degrees
of interest.

During her Seattle sojourn, she'd received a call from the producers of the
TV miniseries *Roots* asking, surprisingly, to see a copy of *Blood and Guts in
High School.* A bit later, on a short vacation to Los Angeles, she had a meeting
with a story editor who was a fan of her writing and who also worked with
Norman Lear, the creator of wildly successful sitcoms like *All in the Family.*
Nothing came of these improbable Hollywood encounters—"*Blood and Guts*
is totally unsuited for movie and TV and especially for people's [sic] heads,"
she told Jeff Goldberg. Soon after, however, Acker was hired to write an original screenplay, this time for an emerging filmmaker named Bette Gordon.

Gordon had arrived in Manhattan by way of Paris and Wisconsin and, like
Acker, was also steeped in critical theory. She was friends with Lynne Tillman,
the French artist Sophie Calle, and photographer Nan Goldin,* and worked at
the Collective for Living Cinema, an artist-run film co-op located a few doors
down from the Mudd Club. Goldin had appeared in Gordon's 1980 short film
Empty Suitcases, whose protagonist was loosely based on Weather Underground

---

* At some point early in her friendship with Acker, Gordon arranged a dinner at an East Village
restaurant with Acker, Goldin, and Calle, who was in town visiting. She was curious how these
three self-involved, creative women, all "forces to be reckoned with," would get along with each
other. "I remember thinking, 'Who would win?'" Gordon said. Calle, as it turned out. She
was more confident, Gordon remembered, "so conceptual and so French," and dominated the
conversation. Though Gordon thought Acker was "tough, one of the toughest," she also found
her to be "hugely" insecure: "Inside, she was always basically saying, 'Love me.'"

leader Bernardine Dohrn. That film did well enough at the Berlin Film Festival that the German television station ZDF had approached her about making a feature. She gave them another short, this one set in a real-life East Village movie theater called Variety Photo Plays, with Spalding Gray monologuing about pornography. The feminist anti-porn group, Women Against Pornography, led by Andrea Dworkin and Susan Brownmiller, had recently formed, targeting Times Square's porn theaters and bookshops, and Gordon, like Acker, considered herself a sex-positive feminist, opposed to what she regarded as WAP's zeal for censorship and the restriction of sexual freedoms. ZDF liked the idea and said they'd give her $40,000 when she had a screenplay ready.

Gordon, however, who considered herself at that point a "crazy, avant-garde experimental filmmaker," had never really written a screenplay. But she had seen Acker present *Great Expectations* at the Kitchen and, familiar with Acker's frequent use of playscript, and the jump cut–like montage of her books, thought that maybe Acker would do an interesting job. Gordon was fascinated by the theoretical ideas of the day—around the male gaze, scopophilia, the possibility of a specifically female language—and felt a deep affinity with Acker's explorations of similar terrain. "I thought, 'Women controlling sexual language makes guys uncomfortable, doesn't it?' I grew up in the sixties and the seventies and this notion of free sexuality was very much a part of who I am and was. All of us celebrated that we could do whatever the guys were doing and we could sleep with as many people as we wanted, and have sex freely and rebel against our mothers. Yet, when it came down to it, men of the time, and I think probably men still today, were, as much as they loved it, very threatened by it. I had this theory that men didn't really want sexually free women, that that was too scary."

Both Acker and Sophie Calle, as well as Kim Novak's character in *Vertigo*, served as inspiration for the film's protagonist, an artist named Christine, who, desperate for work, gets a job taking tickets at a Times Square porn theater called Variety. While there, she becomes obsessed with an older, wealthy patron, and begins to follow him, her life opening up in strange yet thrilling ways. As Christine transforms, her boyfriend, an investigative journalist, becomes increasingly bewildered and alienated from her.

Gordon gave Acker the treatment she had written for ZDF, and asked if she could turn it into a screenplay. Acker immediately accepted. "Nobody said no in those days," Gordon remembered. But it was clear from the outset that

Acker didn't know, or always care, what a traditional screenplay looked like. Her dialogue could be arch and didactic, and she included long, all but unfilmable monologues, written in the abrasive, faux-naïve tone common to her books. In one example, Christine meets her boyfriend, Mark, at the Staten Island Ferry terminal and launches into a lusty, metafictional monologue that consumes almost two full script pages, and begins:

She looked up at him and asked him to be her father. He was a little taken back. She shrugged. This man wasn't going to play along with her. You could see her thoughts from her facial expressions. The man stood over her. He was so tall. She saw him become larger and larger. His hand came down and reached toward her . . . He tells her what to do. Or rather his body movements clearly force hers though none of the movements cause her displeasure. His large male hands grab hold of her wrists. She feels this is easier. She feels: I want you to own me so I will forever be yours. I especially want the center of your body which is the part of your body between your waist and half-way between the line between your leg and torso and your knee to grind down on me so I am a plate. I am the buldge [sic] of your cock. The buldge of your cock is metal, a big hot-dog. This is enough. This is more than enough. I want more more because you're not forcing me to that act of fusion to nothingness. I will enter my legs are spreading. My legs have spread so wide goddamnit this tension my legs have spread so wide, there's every emotion there's nothing, take me, stick that hot dog inside hard rod mob of sperms, fingers, all of the fingers squirming and crawling even this is not enough too small. Oh make the flesh of my stomach into the flesh of your stomach. This is the beginning of orgasm . . .

Acker worked on the screenplay, off and on, for several months, handing pages over to Gordon with an attached note that read, "If you change one word of this, I'll kill you." Gordon and her producer, Renée Shafransky, ignored that, turning what Gordon later called Acker's "rumblings" into a relatively conventional screenplay. "I needed to get it more naturalistic," Gordon said, "which was hard with Kathy, because she wasn't naturalistic at all." The above monologue was nevertheless maintained, and shot as is, but the film got scratched and was ultimately unusable.

Still, Acker's star was on the rise. They knew that her name would help sell the film. They gave her full screenwriting credit. While Acker mostly enjoyed the work, she also still groused about how little she was being paid for it, telling Buck that "I'm committed to overseeing this really dump [sic] film script which needs a total rehash to be any good and I'm only getting $500. (I need the money) but am committed, it's a friend that's why so I have to figure out how to clean up the script with as little trouble as possible and get out in two weeks."

Production on the 16mm film began in October 1981, with a cast consisting of professional and amateur downtown actors, some of whom would go on to considerable renown (Will Patton, Luis Guzmán, Cookie Mueller). Spalding Gray and Nan Goldin were given cameos; Goldin also shot the film's stills. Acker wanted the Mapplethorpe model and bodybuilder Lisa Lyon, whom she had recently met, to play Christine, but when she met the actor that Gordon cast, a tall and blonde Sandy McLeod, she agreed that she was at least physically "perfect." They filmed all over the city: Times Square, the Fulton Fish Market, Yankee Stadium, Tin Pan Alley.

Despite such familiar locations, the New York of the film feels foreign and almost otherworldly, a ghostly frame for Christine's growing awareness of her own perspective and agency. "One of the reasons I went to Kathy," Gordon remarked, "is because I was interested in language. Basically, her language, Christine's language, taking over the male. 'What if a woman told the story of porn as Kathy did?' My idea was that, slowly, over the course of the film, her level of comfort with this language would become greater as she became more comfortable with expressing her sexuality. And what happens to the guy? Out the door. Which was always my experience."

× × ×

When completed, *Variety* would fit in well with the New York independent cinema of the moment. It possessed some of the deadpan minimalism of Jim Jarmusch's work, the genre reinvention of Scott and Beth B's films, the raunchy exploration of power and politics, and the centering of women, associated with Vivienne Dick. When Acker herself saw the finished film, in October 1983, she thought McLeod "stunk," but she otherwise loved the film, telling a friend that "Bette didn't change the script all that much [. . .]—the gist is there! Desire leading to its absence but meanwhile the change from reactive to active in the woman: the female appropriation of porn."

1. *Kathy Acker*, the 1982 Robert Mapplethorpe portrait of Acker that hung in most of her apartments.

2. ABOVE A gathering of *Top Stories* contributors at Artists Space in May 1983. From left to right: Jane Dickson, Lynne Tillman, Acker, Ursule Malinaro, Anne Turyn, Janet Stein, Judith Doyle, Constance DeJong. Front: Gail Vachon, Lulu Rubin.

3. Acker working out a Manhattan gym in 1983.

4. Acker lying next to her library in her Lower East Side loft in 1983.

5. Acker with Ira Silverberg, at various points her publicist, editor, agent, and publisher, at Carl Apfelschnitt's Manhattan studio in 1987.

6. Acker after getting her first tattoo at Dennis Cockell's London studio, Exclusive Tattoo, circa 1989.

7. Acker on her forty-first birthday, at professor Ellen G. Friedman's house in New Jersey.

8. Acker in her room at the Gramercy Park Hotel in 1988.

9. Acker at a promotional photo shoot by Kate Simon for Grove Press in New York, circa 1989.

10. Acker reading at the San Francisco Art Institute in 1990.

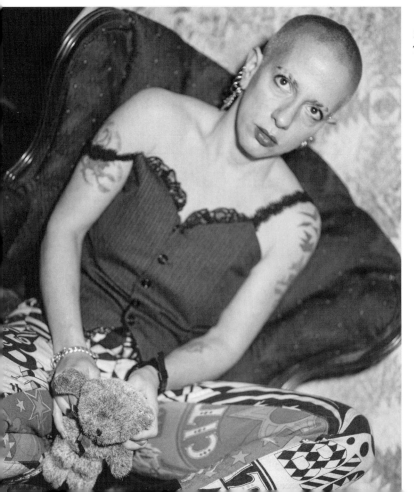

11. Acker in Austin, Texas, in 1995.

Billy: She's alive. She's an artist.

Kathy: ~~Then~~ She'll be ~~written off. I still~~
~~don't see why we're having him for dinner.~~
~~Billy, I don't see why mommy cares~~
~~about this uncle.~~

Kathy: Then she won't be asked to dinner.

Billy, I still don't see why mommy cares
about ~~this~~ uncle. ~~She doesn't give a~~
~~damn about family.~~ She's never given
~~Billy:~~ a damn about family.

Claire's voice: Where are you two? I'm not
going to wait all day?

5.

The Alexander apartment. Dinner. The
diningroom, or what passes for it, is located
at the end of the entrance hall, opposite
the front door. All the walls are dark green.
Above the table hangs a chandelier. The
dog is below.

Billy, Claire, Kathy, & Clifford sit around
the table. They're eating steak, for they
only eat steak in this house. There aren't
many vegetables. ~~becos~~ The reasoning is
that since poor people eat vegetables, if
you eat vegetables you're poor. Especially
eggplant & sweet greens. & Above all, you
mustn't be poor cause then you'll have
no friends & friends are the basis of life.

---

2. A page from one of Acker's notebooks for *Requiem*, the libretto that would be her last completed work.

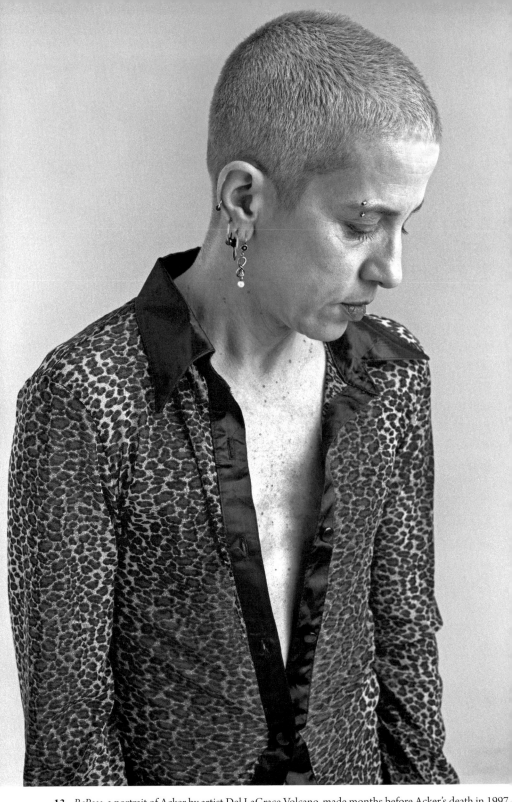

13. *RePose*, a portrait of Acker by artist Del LaGrace Volcano, made months before Acker's death in 1997.

Acker's approval aside, the film bore little resemblance, stylistically, to her fiction.* Despite the milieu and shared theoretical concerns, *Variety* is cool where Acker is hot, restrained and elliptical where Acker tends to be more anarchic and excessive. But it would serve as an important calling card, further bolster Acker's reputation in Europe, and open the door to a number of different projects, film and otherwise.

Around the same time, Acker was also working on a different project that hewed more closely to her aesthetic ambitions: a play for Richard Foreman. By the early eighties, the prolific, eclectic Foreman was one of the world's preeminent theatrical visionaries, his Ontological-Hysteric Theater, founded in 1968, well known for producing baffling, absurdist, seemingly shambolic plays that were equal parts Surrealism, vaudeville, and Gertrude Stein. Foreman had crossed paths with Peter Gordon a number of times, and the two had talked often about collaborating. He was also intrigued by Acker's books—"the most interesting new American material I've read," he said—and felt a deep affinity for Acker's remixing and repurposing of high and low culture: "She was the first person who seemed to have any formal stylistic concerns quite similar to mine, yet she spoke clearly of the supposed real world." Foreman also coveted the fanbase that Acker had cultivated downtown; as comparable as their work may have been, he felt, rightly, that she was still more commercial than he was.

When a producer in Rotterdam approached Foreman about staging a new opera, Foreman reached out to both Gordon and Acker—unaware that they had been married—to see if they would join him. They agreed immediately, with Acker reporting the news with evident glee to Buck and George: "Am working on play for Richard Foreman, from straight interview of Italian terrorist through Roman decadence to Persian no language. Came to me this morning. Very excited." She told them that she was learning Persian to do it, a process she had begun with *Blood and Guts*. An early title, *Ali Goes to a Mosque*, was soon abandoned for the more forceful and Cocteau-evoking *The Birth of the Poet*. Working with Gordon wasn't a problem—both of them, he

---

* Acker would later appear as an actor in Raúl Ruiz's 1990 film *The Golden Boat*, playing a philosophy professor. Ruiz's campy, deliberately amateurish film, with its nonprofessional actors, goofy plot, and lack of continuity, had more in common with Acker's work than Gordon's did. At the same time, its cast of downtown celebrities (including Jarmusch, Vito Acconci, John Zorn, and Annie Sprinkle) and tone of absurd violence, made it also feel like an homage to, or possibly a parody of, No Wave auteurs like Richard Kern and Nick Zedd.

remembered, were already different people by then. "It was cordial," he said. "Cordial, but another world."

The libretto—or play, as Acker continued to call it—was in three acts, with each taking place in a different historical period and milieu: a nuclear power plant at the end of the world; the late Roman Empire (Acker plagiarized herself, here repurposing the Propertius-Cynthia sections of *Great Expectations*); and present-day Iran, around the time of the 1979 revolution, with text in English and Farsi. Given such apocalyptic settings, the libretto unsurprisingly lurches from domestic despair to political commentary of opaque intention: for example, Reagan's would-be assassin, John Hinckley, Jr., has a brief cameo, here renamed Ali Warnock Hinkley, Jr. In the work's 1981 typescript, Acker provided a note that obfuscated as much as it explained:

> This play isn't about but *is* the destruction of language. Language as people use it today: to rigidify and image—media language—in order to control.
>
> In the first act the world: robot language blows up. This destruction opens up to the world of the second act. Desire. The beginning which is the end of the Roman Empire. Desire: sexual language, always by nature impossible, destroys itself, and in the third act the Persian gridding or mazes, searchings among searchings, a language that isn't known degenerates into no language: the cry of peacocks.
>
> The birth of the poet.

Foreman told Acker it was "the best American play written in the last fifteen years" (at least, that's what Acker reported to Buck) but also that it was "too radical" to finance the usual ways. Maybe, though, Foreman said, they could hire a well-known artist to create sets for the opera that could be sold off as artworks afterward, retroactively bankrolling the production. It was a brilliant idea, and Acker suggested the painter David Salle, with whom she was friendly, and one of the city's hottest young painters. Salle was flattered and excited; he himself was a fan of the whole trio: Foreman, Gordon, and Acker. In fact, he and Acker had had a brief fling in the early eighties and he'd always found her warm and friendly. Their artistic sensibilities were likewise in sync. Salle admired, above all, Acker's "postmodern quotation and appropriation, the changing time signatures, changing voices, the kind of ventriloquism." He was excited as well that Foreman, who precisely controlled every detail of a play and had heretofore never let anyone else handle the mise-en-scène, wanted this time to give his colleagues free rein. They would each work independently of the others—"a very old-fashioned, avant-garde collaboration" in the vein of Merce Cunningham and John Cage, Salle said—and the magic would come in how Foreman brought the disparate elements together.

But, as it turned out, that magic didn't always sit well with Salle and Acker. Acker hated that Foreman had his actors read all the stage directions aloud, and Salle didn't care for the way the director lit the production, which tended to obscure his sets. Foreman told Salle that if he didn't like it he could redo it himself, and Salle, despite never having worked in theater before, let alone manning a lighting board, accepted the challenge. "We re-lit the entire show," he remembered, "through trial and error. Three hundred lighting cues, I think. It was much better after. But of course, being Richard, the next day, he changed it back again. Not entirely, but he still had to shine the lights in the audience's eyes a little bit." The artistic differences went both ways. Foreman sometimes found Salle's sets—gigantic paintings, oversized violins and harps—completely at odds with the text, and he had no idea how to work around them. The actors, including Foreman's wife, Kate Manheim, and, indeed, often Foreman himself, sometimes struggled with Acker's insistent profanity. "It was very shocking for us in rehearsal to keep having to refer to all this obscene language," Foreman said. " 'Okay, take it from . . .' and then some filthy thing would have to come out of my mouth in order to tell the actors where to take it from." Most of the time, as actor Stuart Hodes recalled, none of the actors had an inkling what the opera was even about or why certain creative decisions were made. Hodes remembered Foreman calling Acker's writing both "pointillistic" and containing "potent cabalistic meaning"—baffling descriptions that gave him and the other actors little to work with.

Nevertheless, *The Birth of the Poet* seemed poised to become a sensation, a convergence of artistic genius in the tradition of *The Rite of Spring* and *The Threepenny Opera*. When it premiered at Rotterdam's municipal theatre, the RO, in April 1984, however, it became clear that the opera's collision of elements was too cacophonous for most audiences. Gordon's music, performed by a live orchestra, veered from song to indistinct background soundtrack. Some found Salle's imposing sets and costumes—at one point the actors wore diapers as they cavorted on a basketball court—too crude. Lines from Acker, such as "You are not my cock, hatred" or "My vagina is the blackest shit in the world," were outrageous enough on the page; when delivered on stage by live actors, they were nearly unbearable. Not to mention that in the third act her incantatory lines were repeated three times in quick succession, first as prerecorded voice-over, then live in English, and once again in Farsi.

Initial reviews were, at best, mixed. The production's internal confusion was perhaps too perfectly mirrored on stage. "The performance certainly keeps you busy," one kindly Dutch critic averred, "and even draws you back for a second visit, if only to get answers to your many questions." Others singled out the libretto, in particular, for scorn: "Kathy Acker's text is too fragmented and incoherent, and the images, no matter how extraordinary, fail to clarify the ambiguities in the text."

Things were even more fraught when it premiered back home, more than a year later, at the Brooklyn Academy of Music's Next Wave Festival. BAM's director, Harvey Lichtenstein, was reluctant to put the show on at all—he found the raunchiness of the libretto noisome and the budget—more than $430,000—too high. But Mary Boone, Salle's dealer, was intent on having the painter's sets seen on stage in all their glory. She organized a benefit, selling works by Alex Katz, among others, raising $300,000 for the production. (Salle and Foreman also plowed their own fees back into the production.) An added complication was that Kate Manheim, then working in Paris, was unavailable, and the New York cast, in Salle's view at least, was not nearly as captivating as the Rotterdam one.

Despite these hurdles, and after some revision, *The Birth of the Poet* opened at BAM on December 3, 1985. A good many of Acker's friends, past and present, showed up: P. Adams Sitney, accompanied by the art historian Leo Steinberg; Jeff Goldberg; Fred Jordan's son, Ken; Betsy Sussler. Peter Gordon brought his parents. Jeff Weinstein and his partner, John Perreault, sat on one side of Acker, with Gordon on the other. She wore a new white faux-fur coat. Weinstein remembered her being nervous, even frightened, and oddly quiet before the curtain went up.

As it turned out, she was right to be nervous. Within minutes, members of the audience were booing, throwing their programs on stage. Many walked out, including Sitney and Steinberg, who left at intermission, both appalled. Acker was immobile for a while, "as if hypnotized or stoned," Weinstein said, and then she ran up the aisle, white-faced, to find Foreman. "They hate me!" she cried. "They hate me!" Foreman was unperturbed; he'd been getting such reactions for years. He told Acker not to take it so personally.

Aside from a positive review in the *Voice* and the odd compliment from friends, the opera was roundly trashed. The *New York Times* called it a "well-intentioned, neatly crafted mess." *Artforum* was more floridly cruel: "What was intended to be a corrosive blast of Artaudian bile turned out to be only an empty Warholian fart of impotent hooey." About nine hundred people attended opening night, with each subsequent house dwindling by about half. Salle thought there might have been twenty-five people in the audience on the fifth and final night. "I love you all very much," Foreman told his collaborators, "but it'll be a long time before I work like this again."

In retrospect, Salle felt that the piece was ahead of its time, or at the very least out-of-step with what other contemporary impresarios like Robert Wilson were doing, which the BAM audience had come to expect. "*Einstein on the Beach* had been a great success," he said, "with its minimalism and ritualization and the essentially nonverbal spectacle-like aesthetic; people had determined that that was really cool." Acker's libretto would have seemed to them, Salle said, like "fingernails on a blackboard." Foreman agreed; he felt that the fault lay, in large part, with people's discomfort, or outright hatred, for Acker's writing. Even artists that Foreman knew, people he respected, felt that the language was just too filthy, even anti-feminist. "I know that a lot of women really took offense at that being on stage," he said.

The Birth of the Poet would be remembered well as a flop and a scandal. Not as well known, however, is the other, somewhat less controversial collaboration between Acker and Foreman, *Ma Vie, Ma Mort*, a loose adaptation of Acker's novel *My Death My Life by Pier Paolo Pasolini*. Created and produced in the interregnum between the Dutch and American productions of *The Birth of the Poet*, *Ma Vie, Ma Mort* began rehearsals in Paris in the early fall of 1984. Foreman was still enthralled with Acker's prose, and wanted to see what would happen if he worked with it alone and on a smaller scale. He took sections of the novel—ostensibly an account of the Italian director solving his own murder, but dense with allusion to and quotation from Shakespeare, the Brontës, and Acker's autobiography—and reworked those into a claustrophobic, manic disquisition on sexual desire, political corruption, and the vagaries of the art world. The play, which premiered in Lille in mid-November before going on tour across France and Italy, featured a large backdrop that depicted a cityscape across which a primitive Mickey Mouse strode.

Acker and Foreman both thought this was a more successful production than *The Birth of the Poet*. The reviews were mostly decent, the houses full. But still, Acker's writing, as indecorous as ever, continued to get under critics' skin. One of Foreman's longtime French champions and the theater critic of *La Monde*, Colette Godard, refused to review the play at all, wanting to spare Foreman, she said, the public airing of her true thoughts: "She sent me a note, saying, 'Dear Richard, you know, I respect you so much I'm not going to review this horrible piece of literature.'" This non-review wasn't the only reason, but Foreman never produced a play in France again.

CHAPTER 25

WHILE IN SAN FRANCISCO, ACKER COMPLAINED ABOUT THE RIS-
ing cost of housing in New York, asking friends like Terry Sellers to
keep an eye out for "a liveable place" around $300 a month. After Florrie died,
though, it was clear that she could now afford to actually buy her own home.
It wouldn't be that easy though. Acker found an apartment that she liked on
the Lower East Side, but, to her great irritation, Florrie's executor (Pooh Kaye's
father, Clifford) refused to release funds from the estate until it was completely
probated.

In the spring of 1982, she leased a loft instead, in the same area, a building
at 245 Eldridge Street, owned by the artist Jenny Holzer. Dan Graham lived
a couple blocks south, coincidentally, as did Sonic Youth's Kim Gordon and
Thurston Moore. It was not actually a loft, Acker hastened to add, but more of
a "large room," one that cost her a thousand dollars a month. "It's the last poor
section left of this part in Manhattan," she said in a British TV documentary,
"and basically the only place I can afford and have this much space." Two or
three years prior to her occupancy, she added, there had been thirteen murders
in the building alone.

In "Property," an undated typescript (circa 1985), Acker described this
apartment (and its landlord) with contempt: "For a mere $12,000 a year, I
had been given raw space and been allowed to give that space its ceiling, outer
walls, floor, plumbing and electricity. Walls which separated rooms were luxury I still could not afford. However, due to a slight flaw in my five-year contract, after the contract elapsed, my landlady could raise my rent to as high as
she saw fit. Being an artist, she was a visionary." After Holzer refused one day
to remove a rat from the apartment—"She was busy making art," Acker said
acidly—Acker ditched the place.

Acker's abhorrence of landlordism was one, understandable, thing. But her
portrayal of herself as a victim of gentrification, a beleaguered tenant, was, to
anyone who knew her, almost comically disingenuous. Later in the same piece,

she writes, "I decided that a respectable, or almost-respectable, writer ought to have a home." Since when did Acker think of herself as a "respectable" writer or even "almost-respectable"? When did she even want to be seen as such? Maybe this was a small joke. But over the next few years, while never retreating from the aggression and experimentation that always characterized her writing, she nevertheless also did her best to acquire the trappings of literary respectability. She had spent her twenties and early thirties reinventing herself. She wasn't going to stop now.

Her newfound comfort, however, put her in a somewhat complicated position. In her work, Acker continued to rail against the bourgeoise, continued to pillory the rich and the rentier class, continued to romanticize the marginal, freakish, and dissident. In interviews, she insisted that she was, at bottom, an outcast herself, a traumatized street kid who had overcome enormous pain and adversity. One could obviously have money and be an outcast, be wealthy and traumatized, be comfortable and still hate the rich. But Acker also didn't want to appear a sellout. In both her books and interviews, she continued to harp about the material conditions of being a writer, the hardship and struggle of it, even when those conditions didn't apply to her as much. She'd been a starving artist for so long, and her literary persona, at least in part, derived from that identity.

But now that she could afford it, food stamps were abandoned in favor of fine restaurants, thrift-store T-shirts traded for made-to-order Patricia Field. She got her hair styled and colored weekly. She began to purchase property. Behind her back, though, and after her death, a number of people referred to her as a spoiled poor little rich girl. While with her in Los Angeles, Mel Freilicher recalled her strolling into shops on Wilshire Boulevard and spending a couple thousand dollars on paintings, shoes, and dresses. All the more power to her, he thought, but he remembered her still crying poor. Others marveled that she would go out for dinner and claim, when the check came, that she didn't have any money on her. Pressed, she'd make a show of rooting around in her pricey, chic handbag, and an enormous roll of cash, wrapped in a rubber band, would fall out.

"She'd always say, 'We make the same amount of money,'" Bob Glück said. "But two-thirds of her money came from a check she got every month." Gary Indiana, who had also seen her "accidentally" drop a wad of cash on at least one occasion, lampooned this behavior in his novel, *Rent Boy*, in which an obvious caricature of Acker fails to tip the narrator, a waiter. Indiana went even further, writing about Acker's hypocrisy in the *London Review of Books* after her death, "Attacking capitalism while dressed in Valentino can look like absurdist theatre." Another, more generous friend, the editor Amy Scholder, felt that Acker was keenly aware that others judged her for having money that she didn't earn. "But like most middle-class, upper-middle-class people, she felt she didn't have enough," Scholder said. "And that sense of enough is always relative." Scholder pointed out too that while Acker absolutely had more money than many of her literary peers, she was hardly in the same league as the famous painters she knew, or, for that matter, her parents' old neighbors in Sutton Place.

And if Acker felt any guilt or conflict about all this, those emotions were trumped by her overwhelming relief. Throughout her whole post-Brandeis, pre-inheritance life, as she told an interviewer, she had been "very poor," adding that she "was so desperate that everything in [her] life was about money." For a good while anyway, her life could now be about something else.

× × ×

Acker's adult life was almost impossibly rich in event, in work and creativity, in friendship and romance and tragedy. By the early eighties, though, and particularly after her inheritance, things seemed to accelerate even more. Her worlds expanded, multiplied. She felt, in a way, charmed, though, as always, she publicly tempered her sense of good fortune. To Paul Buck, she wrote, "Am dying to get out of here, but not unhappy. Reading Beckett, he's so funny!"

The reference to Beckett was probably not coincidental. Sometime in 1982, after a decade of effort, labor, and hustling, Acker was, in fact, acquired by Beckett's American publisher, Grove Press. There couldn't have been a more hospitable, or appropriate, home for her kind of writing. Barney Rosset's Grove had almost single-handedly ushered little-known American and international writers into the mainstream, establishing a canon of groundbreaking, often scandalous, literature. It was the legendary American publisher of Burroughs, Sade, Genet, Amiri Baraka, Henry Miller, Marguerite Duras, Frantz Fanon, and dozens of other writers that Acker had cherished and emulated. It published the *Evergreen Review*, where Acker had first discovered Burroughs and Gysin's cut-up experiments. It had fought battle after battle against censorship. It was the press that Acker had dreamt of joining since, at least, writing *Rip-off Red.*

Fred Jordan was Rosset's right-hand man in the sixties, hired in 1956 initially as a business manager. He was a Viennese Jew (born Alfred Rotblatt in 1925), who survived the Holocaust and emigrated to the U.S. in 1949. He was kind and courtly, as deliberate as Rosset was impulsive. Jordan worked at many other publishing houses before and after Grove, but he prized Grove for being uniquely governed by passion and taste rather than market whim. Richard Seaver, the press's executive editor, brought writers like Beckett, Burroughs, and Genet into the Grove fold—poaching them, more or less, from Maurice Girodias's Olympia Press. Jordan, for his part, expanded its roster to include writers from Germany and Eastern Europe and was also, for a time, *Evergreen's* editor.

Rosset was prone to reckless financial decisions, however, and intermittently, Jordan would seek more ordinary job security at other publishing houses. After one such five-year stint at Methuen, he returned to Grove in 1982. The press was on the verge of bankruptcy, and in building a new list, he was on the hunt for writers that might bring in at least some money. Jordan found a stack of Acker's work, including the serials and more recent manuscripts, in the unread slush pile on Rosset's desk.* Acker wasn't going to be a cash cow, for Grove or anybody, but at the time she was a relatively safe bet. She was undeniably controversial, and attuned to both Grove's particular heritage and the contemporary counterculture. It helped too that she was a woman—the press had published very few female writers in its heyday. (Jordan would also discover Rikki Ducornet around the same time, publishing her first novel, *The Stain*, in 1984.) She could, potentially, give Grove some new life, expand its reach.

Jordan had completely forgotten that James Grauerholz had pitched Acker to him in the late seventies. But now he found her writing extremely "willful," and different from the usual avant-garde he encountered. "It clearly had its own voice," he said. He thought of her as the culmination of a generation of Grove writers who had changed the world. Indeed, Acker would be the last

---

* This is Jordan's memory, anyway. According to Ira Silverberg, a longtime Grove publicist and editor, Rosset would go to the self-published shelf at B. Dalton Bookseller and ask the staff what was selling. He heard about "this Kathy Acker" and tracked her down. "Likely, Barney came in and told Fred to find her. Having Barney discover you, in the mythology of getting published in New York, is better than Fred," Silverberg said.

American writer signed during the Rosset era. Jordan enjoyed Acker quite a bit as a person too. "There was something very childlike about her." Acker told Jordan that he reminded her of her stepfather, a remark he wasn't quite sure he should take as a compliment.

Jordan invited Acker to the Grove office on West Houston, in a four-story building where Rosset also lived, and offered her a deal. They would take all of her books, including *Blood and Guts* and *Great Expectations*, and, over time, publish or reprint them all. They weren't offering much in the way of cash, however—just an advance of five thousand dollars.* (For comparison's sake, around the same time, Philip Roth was receiving advances of $100,000 or more for a single novel.) Acker was, Jordan recalled, "very happy."

Acker's relationship with Jordan was almost entirely cordial, his support unstinting. It helped that, as a policy, he was completely hands-off with his fiction writers. "My rule at the time was, if it needs work, it probably isn't for Grove," he said. "Beginning with Beckett, I would not dare change a comma. With other books, I would do a little tinkering but not much. If it required real tinkering, it wasn't for us, it was for Doubleday." At least a few of Acker's friends wished that Acker *had* received some more guidance, arguing that her books would have been even better in the right editorial hands. "What I really thought—and still do think—was that, after *Blood & Guts*, Kathy simply never found a good editor," said Cynthia Rose, a friend and cultural critic. "There just wasn't any editor who was up to dealing with what she was trying to do. She was much, much brighter, much more curious and much more well-read than any of them."

Nevertheless, Jordan would remain Acker's editor for the rest of her career, even taking her with him when he left Grove, temporarily, for Pantheon. Even

---

* This was the amount that Jordan recalled when we spoke in 2015, though he was somewhat vague on specifics, and whatever contract Acker might have had appears lost. Chris Kraus repeats this figure in *After Kathy Acker*, citing a letter to Paul Buck as evidence. But in that letter to Buck, Acker writes, "I've actually been bought up by a real publisher, Rogner & Bernhard." Whatever the deal with Rogner & Bernhard, nothing ever came of it, and it would be a mildly surprising coincidence if she agreed to two contracts around the same time with the same terms. So maybe she did mean Grove. In any case, to Buck, she added: "I've been bought up by some dumb publisher for $5,000 for all my already published works, can you believe it? For fourteen years, I can't bitch: it's the first time I'm on the receiving end. Yay! Yay! I'd rather have a boyfriend."

at a large mainstream conglomerate, his ideals remained intact—at least when it came to Acker and her ilk. "My notion is that art, real art, comes from some source that defies rationality," he said. "Good art, good writing, is not done with rationality; it has another deeper source. And you have to meet it on that level."

× × ×

Acker's prosperity, professional and otherwise, paralleled the growing prosperity and transformation of the downtown art world. After a decade of economic despair, and the concomitant dominance of conceptualism and minimalism, came artwork inflected by critique, political consciousness, and feminism—work by Sherrie Levine, Cindy Sherman, Louise Lawler, Barbara Kruger. But after that, the painters returned. Painters with large-scale, even heroic, work, like Julian Schnabel, David Salle, Francesco Clemente, Anselm Kiefer.

Leslie Dick, an American writer and critic who lived in London at the time and who would befriend Acker in December 1982, remembered that "Suddenly, this rather frugal art world, which is about using photography, using text, critiquing everything up the wazoo, became once again an art world of extravagant indulgence, emotion, and expression." SoHo galleries could sell these paintings, and sell them for a lot. Meanwhile, in the East Village, a new, scruffier art scene stirred to life. In the fall of 1982, the neighborhood was home to a half dozen galleries, located in tiny storefronts and walk-ups and studios, including the Fun Gallery and Gracie Mansion's "Loo Division." Uptown collectors arrived in limos and parked right outside the galleries, fearful of the area's crime and dereliction; tour buses, Cynthia Carr wrote, "would soon arrive to show the curious-but-timid what the artists had wrought amid the rubble." Street artists like Jean-Michel Basquiat and Keith Haring became international superstars. In *Art in America*, Carlo McCormick and Walter Robinson famously described the East Village as a "marketing concept" suited to the "Reagan zeitgeist." By 1985, when McCormick wryly declared the scene over in the *East Village Eye*, there were almost fifty different galleries advertising in its pages.

Accompanying all this, of course, was the gentrification and rise in property values that Acker had complained about. But the art-world clamor also gave fiction writers a supplementary income and subject. "The money spilled over," Dick said. In 1984, Lynne Tillman began writing on art using a pen name,

Madame Realism, first in a book about Kiki Smith, and then later in *Art in America* and various exhibition catalogues. The pseudonym—and the accompanying rhetorical multiplicity that Tillman employed—blurred boundaries between critic and audience, short story and critical essay, but even later, when Tillman wrote art criticism under her own name, she continued to make the form bend to her bracing sophistication. Meanwhile, Jeff Weinstein hired Gary Indiana to be the *Village Voice*'s art critic, a position he occupied between 1985 and 1988, his columns notorious for their bridge-burning wit and perspicacity.

All of this blur extended to other spheres. The major downtown magazines that emerged and flourished during the period—*BOMB*, but also Barbara Ess's *Just Another Asshole*, *Top Stories*, Kurt Hollander's the *Portable Lower East Side*, Catherine Texier and Joel Rose's *Between C&D* (basically a computer printout sealed and sold in a Ziploc bag)—were, in one sense, literary magazines. But they were neither staid academic journals nor newsstand glossies; rather, these were multimedia publications, closer in spirit to zines, that captured the unruly intermingling and cross-fertilization of culture that was going on in the bars, galleries, and clubs. As Tillman later put it, there was "no coherent aesthetic," no true downtown movement, but there was a deep spirit of collaboration. And its overall shared sense of mutiny provided, for a while at least, a certain sense of esprit de corps. "Ultimately we were against the same things," Indiana said of Acker, though he could have been speaking of any number of his comrades.

"We hung out together, shared problems and misery, usually poverty, though I'm not sure poverty's shareable, fucked each other, and worked together," Acker wrote. "Later on, I wrote some articles for *Artforum*, and a few other publications: all of these articles rose, first out of friendship. Friendship and an inclination for what I call *joy*." Acker's first article for that magazine, indeed the first journalistic interview she ever conducted, was commissioned by another friend, the magazine's editor in chief, Ingrid Sischy—a profile (sort of) of Lawrence Weiner and Joseph Kosuth for the May 1982 issue. Acker's journalism would later become somewhat more conventional, but in this piece, she adhered to the familiar methods of her fiction, collaging together her interviews with the artists, selections from their own notebooks, and passages from writers such as Edmund Husserl and Hart Crane. The piece was accompanied by portraits of Weiner, Kosuth, and Acker herself, taken by Robert Mapplethorpe at his Bond Street studio.

It was the first time Acker spent real time with Mapplethorpe, and she was nervous, then charmed. According to Acker, they gossiped, talked about sex, shared a bit of cocaine. Acker would return for more photographs over the next couple of years, sometimes dressing up in Mapplethorpe's clothes, sometimes her own, sometimes almost nothing at all. She enjoyed the process and delighted in him. "Robert loved fun," she wrote in an appreciation after his death. "He loved being alive so much that he always refused to have any cant or pomposity interfere with pleasure." She asked Grove if Mapplethorpe could design all of the covers of her books, a plan which, for whatever reason, was never realized. Acker would be photographed incessantly over the rest of her life, often by well-known and accomplished photographers, her increasingly unique appearance a requisite component in the promotion of her work. But it was only one of Mapplethorpe's portraits of her, framed, that she would hang on her walls and move from home to home.

A ROUND THE SAME TIME GROVE ACQUIRED ACKER'S WORK, SHE WAS signed by the somewhat more mainstream UK publisher Picador, a literary imprint founded by Sonny Mehta at Pan Books. After Penguin, Pan was the country's second largest paperback publisher, and at forty years of age, Mehta was already a powerhouse, having commissioned and published Germaine Greer's *The Female Eunuch* as well as books by Jackie Collins and Douglas Adams. At Picador, he published so many Booker Prize–winning writers, including Salman Rushdie, Ian McEwan, and Julian Barnes, that they were later dubbed the "Picador Generation," though he also sought to introduce American writers such as Robert Stone, Maxine Hong Kingston, and Raymond Carver to British audiences. Fred Jordan would later dismiss him as "a slick, marketing guy," but Mehta would ascend to even greater heights, becoming only the third editor in chief in Knopf history in 1987. He would eventually become president of the company and lead it, through years of industry upheaval, for thirty-two years.

How Mehta first discovered Acker, though, is uncertain. Pan's publicity director at the time, Jacqueline Graham, speculated that Mehta was initially intrigued by the photos of Acker that he'd seen. But she added as well that "he had a brilliant instinct for the right book at the right time." For British readers of a certain stripe, *Blood and Guts in High School* was that book, one that could speak to the many different tribes that had emerged from the splintering of punk, and to the country's uneasy political climate following the 1979 election of Margaret Thatcher. Acker was also a perfect subject for London's colorful, competitive cultural press—someone who could appeal equally to both the high-minded music writers at *New Musical Express* and the brand-conscious fashionistas that ran style bible the *Face*. British audiences were well aware of her literary lineage, but she was also something completely new: a female emissary from the still somewhat obscure avant-garde literary world of grotty, exotic lower Manhattan. It helped that she was telegenic.

In January 1983, Picador officially bought *Blood and Guts*, *Great Expectations*, and *My Death My Life by Pier Paolo Pasolini*, for an advance of two-and-a-half thousand pounds, or $9,000. Picador planned to release an omnibus edition including all three, titled *Blood and Guts in High School Plus Two*. "Exactly what I want them to publish," she told a friend. Mapplethorpe would provide the jacket photo.

Even before the deal was finalized, word spread. *NME* journalist Cynthia Rose heard about *Blood and Guts* through a friend at Rough Trade Records, and managed to get her hands on a copy. On the heels of a short European tour with the English "punk poet" John Cooper Clarke, Acker made a London appearance at Michael Horovitz's Poetry Olympics at the Young Vic, and Rose arranged to interview her then. Save for a love of books, Acker and Rose barely had anything in common, but they bonded immediately. Acker was staying in a chilly, borrowed flat in North London, where they conducted the interview, and the two women spent the whole time hunched over a small gas fire. Rose was wearing a secondhand leopard-print collar that she had bought in Camden Market. Acker complimented it and Rose ended up giving it to her. "She was the kind of person that makes you want to give her things," Rose said. In the subsequent profile, published the following January, Rose described Acker as "slight, polite, a tiny bit awkward and extremely tough [. . .] a pleasure to talk to." She had, at the time, "rainbow-coloured locks," and a "metallic front tooth" that flashed whenever she laughed.

On that same trip, Acker also met Jonathan Miles, a painter and writer who was the London editor of *ZG* magazine, which was edited by another friend of Acker's, Rosetta Brooks. *ZG* was an art and theory magazine that existed somewhere in the ecosystem between *BOMB*, *Semiotext(e)*, and *FILE*. In her spare time, Brooks had acted briefly as Acker's agent, helping to secure the deal with Grove. Miles was part of an exhibition at Riverside Studios, a groundbreaking culture and theater center in Hammersmith, which Acker was impressed by, and within twenty minutes of meeting, they were talking about collaborating. He was startled by how much her conversation was like her writing, that she could jump, mid-sentence, from book talk to discussion of her diet: "She was a living collage, a switching machine, a condensing machine." Acker and Miles also slept together, and when she returned to New York, they stayed in touch by letter and phone for about three months. Like her conversation, Acker's missives rapidly shifted between details of her reading, gossip about friends and enemies, and, characteristically, pained, lengthy rumination on both Miles's romantic intentions and her own: "you expect to step into my life (more delicate than my cunt) whenever you please and leave whenever you please without saying anything to me."

In one, less anxious, letter to Miles, Acker describes a day in her life: a meandering stroll just before Christmas through the Lower East Side, Chinatown, and SoHo, where she shops for food, drops by the post office, buys a cappuccino, takes copies of *Great Expectations* to sell at the New Morning Bookstore on Spring Street, looks for and fails to find a new pen to give herself as a gift. Though Acker complains about the oppressive Christmas bustle, there is genuine joy in her description of her hometown: "this is the real magic here all worlds given me at once."

And yet she longed to return to London, and as quickly as possible. Miles aside, the UK held the promise of fresh romance, friendships, and ever-greater career opportunities. David Gothard, the programming director at Riverside Studios, wanted to work with her. The Almeida Theatre planned to produce a play of hers. London was, in short, a whole new world, a place to once again reinvent herself.

New York was only ghosts, past and present. That Christmas was the first anniversary of Claire's death, for which Acker burned a "black Cuban voodoo candle in her honor." Both Peter Gordon and Sylvère Lotringer continued to bedevil her, in their different ways. She and Gordon would officially divorce on June 23, 1983, but she felt that he had already largely left her. Lotringer, meanwhile, told her that he'd love her "forever," but he was still unwilling to commit in any real way and the relationship limped unsatisfyingly along. "She was always mad at him," Bette Gordon remembered. "Maybe because he didn't play her games in the way that she wanted."

Then, sometime in 1983, Lotringer began seeing a filmmaker and writer named Chris Kraus. Lotringer's relationship with Kraus soon became far more meaningful, in most ways, than his romance with Acker. "I was, at that time, Chris's project," Lotringer said, "and she took it much more seriously than Kathy did." They would, in fact, marry five years later, and Kraus would gain considerable renown chronicling their relationship, and much more, in acclaimed novels like *I Love Dick*, *Summer of Hate*, and *Torpor*. She would also become a principal figure at Semiotext(e), where she conceived and edited the Native Agents imprint, which highlighted American female-identified and queer writers.

Kraus's books defintely owed something to Acker's example. "One of Acker's greatest achievements was her discovery of a process and language that fuse emotion and thought and that is transmitted directly to readers," Kraus wrote, and Matias Viegener, Acker's executor, claimed that Acker was, for a time anyway, Kraus's favorite living writer. Kraus was far more equivocal about Acker the woman. "Chris didn't like Kathy so much," Lotringer said, adding that Kraus felt Acker had it too easy, and that she pandered to men. Acker, meanwhile, saw in Kraus only a rival, and her relationship with Kraus would almost always be characterized by enmity. Lotringer never left his girlfriend and child for Acker, but he did, finally, for Kraus—something that Acker saw only as an insult. "Frankly, I've never liked it," Acker wrote to Lotringer several years later. "I've hated it that you married again."

x x x

On her European tour that fall, in Amsterdam, Acker had read from *My Death My Life by Pier Paolo Pasolini*, and was amused when someone there called her "some kind of murderer." Whatever this person actually meant, the book itself purported to "solve" the murder of the titular Italian filmmaker Pier Paolo Pasolini. Acker was a great admirer of Pasolini, a gay writer, intellectual, and director of many controversial and deeply original films, including *Arabian Nights* (long her favorite movie), *Teorema*, and *Salò*, an adaptation of Sade's *120 Days of Sodom* set in fascist Italy. In 1975, three weeks before *Salò* opened, he was allegedly killed by a seventeen-year-old in a sexual tryst gone wrong. But questions and conspiracy theories swirled around his death; Pasolini was seemingly not beaten and killed by a lone teenager, but rather by several men; subsequent investigations tied the murder to either neofascists or the Mafia, possibly both.

Others considered Pasolini's death a kind of suicide, committed by a sado-masochist intent on his own destruction. This was Acker's take too, to a certain extent. The novel opens with these lines: "Did I ask to die? Was my murder a suicide by proxy?" But after spending a couple pages outlining Pasolini's murder, Acker soon loses interest in that investigation and instead the book becomes a heady, bizarre metafictional crime story, as much about how the media sensationalizes a crime as the crime itself. She arranged the novel, as she said, "horizontally," basing it on "pun structures and things like that." It was the first book that she wrote expressly under the influence of the critical theory to which Lotringer had introduced her: "I could actually finally say, 'That's what I'm doing,' or 'This what I'm aiming to do.'"

What was she aiming to do? A lot of things, as usual, but also some of the same things she'd done in her previous books. There are radical reworkings of *Hamlet*, *Macbeth*, and the Orson Welles film *Touch of Evil*; snatches of Wittgenstein, Joyce, Baudrillard, and Robbe-Grillet; a long epistolary exchange between Emily and Charlotte Brontë; apparently verbatim transcripts of conversations she had with Mel Freilicher about the affair with Jonathan Miles. It is also the first book of hers in which she explicitly addresses AIDS, which was officially named in July 1982, and which had killed 272 New Yorkers by the end of the year. (Six months later, that number had almost doubled.) With familiar, skewed solipsism, Acker reframes the devastating disease in Burroughsian terms: "What's AIDS? A virus. A virus' seemingly unknowable who gets identity by preying on an entity, a cell. Writers whose identities depend on written language're viruses. I'm trying to break down the social immune system. Even this sentence's false."

Acker told the *East Village Eye* that, after *Great Expectations*, she was done writing about her family. "Now the whole issue is dead for me psychologically," she said. "I'm free of that finally." This was far from the truth. Acker would continue to write about her family, or at least certain aspects of it, in every single one of her subsequent books. *My Death My Life* is yet another cracked mirror, with various shards of Acker's actual life assigned to various featureless narrators (My Grandmother, Elvira, Whore). Pasolini's "suicide" parallels Claire's— one arguably the result of a societal hatred of homosexuality, the other the patriarchal subjection of women—and Acker restages the grim Christmastime when she and Wendy were called to the morgue to identify their mother's body. Unable to examine Pasolini's lifeless body firsthand, of course, Acker instead describes Claire's, and the agonizing, bewildering emotions that attend that experience:

> The face was pale white until its lower third. The lower third was horizontal stripes. There was a bright red stripe. Below that was a white stripe. Then there was a swollen blue-purple brighter than any color. Actual seeing didn't give me the information this was my mother. All of me knew I was seeing my mother so I screamed. I said, "Yes, that's my mother." I didn't know. I said, "I don't recognize her." The morgue-man

answered, "That's because she's been dead five days. Decayed bodies look like that." I replied, "I didn't know."

Years later, Acker called *My Death My Life* "probably the most far-out of all the novels I've done." That's debatable, but it is certainly an elusive book, its allusions and quotation a bit less cohesive than in other books. It's also overly long, and the frequent puns, which Acker could never resist, are of opaque significance and often groan-worthy. (In one short scene, set in the *Artforum* office, someone refers to *Blade Runner* as *Bladder Run*.) *My Death My Life* was an outlier too, in that it was never published as a stand-alone novel. A few years after its publication in *Blood and Guts in High School Plus Two*, Grove would include it alongside *Kathy Goes to Haiti* and *Florida* in a 1987 collection titled *Literal Madness*. A review of that omnibus in the *New York Times* dispatched it with brusque condescension: "I usually admire risk-taking and convention-flouting in fiction—when the rebellious gestures work. Not many work here."

Acker anticipated and pre-empted such criticism by her insistence, within the pages of the novel itself, that she was deliberately short-circuiting meaning, expectation, and conformity. "Schools teach good writing in order to stop people writing whatever they want the ways they want," she writes. However, she later agreed that the book was unreadable, a failed experiment. "I don't know, maybe fail and succeed aren't the right words," she said. "I took something to a certain point to see what would happen. I'm glad I did it and I saw what that point was, so I never have to do that again. But that was it; I got to that extreme and I see no reason to do it again."

TO LIVE FOREVER IN WONDER

(1983–1990)

CHAPTER 27

—————— X ——————

FOR MANY YEARS NOW, WITH THE SAME CONTRADICTORY IMPULSES that governed other aspects of her life, Acker had treated her body carelessly. She usually ate healthy food, and meditated regularly, but she also pushed herself hard. She wrote most days for eight hours, and then often went out to bars and clubs and performances until late at night, rarely getting enough sleep. Her romantic life was a reliable, relentless source of stress. She suffered from bleeding ulcers, PID had been a constant, painful affliction,* there was the cancer scare. She was often forced to spend long stretches in bed, and ended up in the hospital, she said, usually at least once a year. She summed all this up in an essay titled "Bodybuilding":

> During my twenties, during the punk years, my friends and I, desiring both to be romantic and to revolt against our middle-class white society and its obsession with material success, had done our best to push our bodies away from any sort of health, from middle-class plumpness and hippy love. We used, we almost worshipped bad food, thinness to the point of anorexia, in some cases hard drugs [...] In those days it was nothing for me, sick or not sick, to sleep two nights then work and party through the third. On the days of sleep, to work until midnight, drink and have sex until about four in the morning, then wake up at nine to work again.

As she got older, however, Acker realized the folly of this. She'd taken those dance classes with Simone Forti and others many years ago, and realized then

———————————

* Despite complaining constantly about PID throughout her twenties and thirties, Acker also said that the illness had been misdiagnosed and that what she had been suffering from was a spastic colon. It's possible, of course, that she suffered from both, but she also claimed that PID was a "noncommunicable" disease. Leslie Dick, however, said that Acker had given *her* PID. Or rather that Acker had infected Peter Wollen, at one time Acker's lover, who then passed the illness on to Dick.

how important her body was to her, how valuable it was to move, how muscles provided their own meaning. Now, in her mid-thirties, she understood how necessary physical maintenance was too. So, like many people, especially in the early eighties, when fitness started to become a billion-dollar industry, she joined a gym.

But Acker being Acker, she wasn't about to start jogging or don pastel leggings. "Nothing, not even ill health, was going to force me to take an aerobics class," she wrote. Instead, she took refuge in what she called "calisthenics." Then, when her instructor showed Acker how to lift weights, she discovered, to her delight, a powerful new passion—bodybuilding. Within months, she was lifting three days a week. She found a trainer who, she said, on their first day, wrote down in a notebook a version of Nietzsche's familiar aphorism, "That which does not kill you will make you stronger." Five years later, she was at the gym three out of every four days. When on book tour, she insisted that Grove arrange hotels for her that had their own gyms.

It was a sport and a pastime, but Acker found in it much more. "The gym lobotomizes me," she told a friend. "Probably prevents undue loneliness." It also finally allowed her to take control of her body and health. Mel Freilicher said that after she started seriously lifting weights (and more carefully monitoring her diet and sleep), she was never really sick again. It was a way to, if not defy aging and death, then to at least confront those things head-on.

It was also yet another way to blur gender norms—when she first starting lifting, her gym kept the weights segregated, in a designated "men's" section. She was thrilled to make her body harder, stronger, bigger, less "feminine." Bodybuilding was another way for her to stand apart from her peers. She didn't personally know any other artists or writers that lifted weights. Lisa Lyon, the professional bodybuilder who modeled for Mapplethorpe and Helmut Newton, was the only person in her orbit who bridged these worlds. And in the broader literary world, there was only really Yukio Mishima, whose book on bodybuilding and martial arts, *Sun and Steel*, she revered.

Like Mishima, Acker believed that bodybuilding opened up new ways of thinking about language and knowledge. Or, more precisely, a way to learn things without, or in spite of, ordinary language and expression. It was a way to acknowledge the primacy of the body and desire, but also to eradicate, Acker maintained, any Cartesian mind-body dualism. For a long time, she tried to write about her experience of bodybuilding as soon as she returned home from a workout. She quickly learned that was impossible. Not only did bodybuilding resist everyday language and description, she thought that it created its *own* language, a minimal one of specific nouns and numbers, of repetition and failure—a language of the body. The philosopher and literary critic Hélène Cixous, whom Acker read devotedly, argued for "the invention of a *new insurgent* writing" that would return woman "to the body which has been more than confiscated from her," and this was something that Acker insisted on as well. "If ordinary language or meanings lie outside essence," she wrote, "what is the position of that language game which I have named *the language of the body*? For bodybuilding (a language of the body) rejects ordinary language and yet itself constitutes a language, a method for understanding and controlling the physical which in this case is also the self."

Acker loved to talk about bodybuilding in terms of failure, noting that a weight lifter could only build new muscle by first breaking it down, by pushing it past the point of failure. She saw in this an analogy for her own writing process. Language, for her, was also about collapse and creation. When, in 1984, Acker started work on a new novel called *Don Quixote,* one early chapter, later scrapped, was titled, "Description of a Female Weight-Lifter," and began:

> Writing must be a machine for breaking down, that is allowing the now uncontrolled and uncontrollable reconstitutions of thoughts and expressions. All other kinds of writing simply express.
>
> The first given, then, or the always-present beginning or return to is nothing. I(dentity) is and does nothing. Once there's (there always is) nothingness, any event's possible. My methodology's total rigor. This or any total rigor is meaningless.
>
> Those who are driven by poverty, those who're free from material worries hunger exhausting labor a joyless existence ask the same question, the question of meaning.
>
> A language is the appearance of connections therefore language as in writing doesn't express anything: it creates.

× × ×

As Acker was reshaping her body, she was also changing the way she dressed. Friends remembered her in the late seventies looking almost frumpy, favoring housedresses, cable-knit sweaters, tights. Toward the end of the decade, though, she started ducking into department stores just to try on designer clothing that she couldn't yet afford; she told Jeff Goldberg one time that Yves St. Laurent was "much too much" but that Anne Klein was "just gorgeous."

Things changed somewhat with punk—Lucy Sante recalled her once wearing a T-shirt with an image of Farrah Fawcett on it, the eyes obliterated by cigarette-burn holes—and the writer Hanif Kureishi, who met Acker soon after she moved to London, recalled her seeming like a "dated, modified New York version of punk," with her spiky, colored, extremely short hair. But she also became interested in the designers that had themselves created, or borrowed from, punk style: Vivienne Westwood, Betsey Johnson, Jean-Paul Gaultier. She bought extravagant, sometimes menacing rings and earrings from the polymathic artist Andrew Logan (which she called "jewels of nothingness"), Chrome Hearts, and Axel Stocks and Alex Streeter, both jewelers to the heavy metal world. Unsurprisingly, she was drawn to clothing that clearly referenced S and M and biker garb. Some of her garments could be revealing, others incapacitating, and yet others cut so oddly, and featuring so many buckles and straps, it was sometimes difficult to tell at first how a piece might be worn.

Acker's wardrobe was so unusual that two years after her death, the artist Kaucyila Brooke, photographed 154 of Acker's outfits for an exhibition in Berlin. Without Acker actually wearing the clothing, the images naturally possessed a ghostly aspect, one that Dodie Bellamy, writing about the show, captured in a startling and capacious essay titled, "Digging Through Kathy Acker's Stuff."*

Jeff Weinstein always found her stylish—"she knew exactly how to do things like take the zip-out lining of a coat and wear the lining itself as a piece of outerwear"—but by the early eighties, he felt, she didn't want to be just in

---

* Before I read Bellamy's essay, when I was staying with Acker's executor, Matias Viegener, I too dug around in Acker's stuff. It was still, at the time (2015), kept in a few cardboard boxes in the storage room behind his garage in Los Angeles. Some of the outfits from Brooke's show were here, unceremoniously crammed into the boxes, still on their hangers. It was forensically disappointing. The clothes were, of course, small, but even smaller than I'd expected— practically doll-sized—and some were stained by food or sweat. I'd hoped for some distinct smell, but there was none. Any aura they once had seemed to have dissipated. "Stuffed haphazardly in packing boxes," Bellamy writes, "Kathy's clothes feel devoid of will, abandoned, subverting sentimentality by their strangeness, their creepiness."

style, she wanted to create a *new* style. In literature, she was creating, in effect, her own genre. With the way she looked, with her clothes, she strove to be similarly extraordinary. If her life was an artwork, something to be performed, she would be dazzlingly attired when she stepped on stage.

As Leslie Dick pointed out, Acker was taking her cues from the art and music worlds. "You could argue that Kathy just dressed like a rock star," she said. "You could say that. But it's almost like she dressed as a hybrid between a rock star and an artist. Because the artists were definitely dressed." Dick also suggested that Acker's shifting appearance fit, hand-in-glove, with a concurrent revolution in fashion. "It was an exciting time in terms of style and fashion," she said. "Not just because of punk but also because it was the beginning of the Japanese revolution, Comme des Garçons, this sort of deconstruction of clothing. All of us were going and buying clothes from Comme des Garçons, Gaultier, these people. Although they were expensive, they weren't *that* expensive, and the kind of transformation of fashion into a celebrity thing, which it is now, hadn't yet happened."

Acker's particular attention to fashion was captured in an early profile of her by Rosemary Bailey in the *Face*. Bailey characterized Acker as having "an air of urchin vulnerability" before describing her wide range of clashing outfits: wide boiler suits over frilly nylon blouses, slashed T-shirts, "sinister" jewelry that resembled cockroaches and skeletons. It was all art, Acker argued, but art for the masses. Or at least one discerning segment of the masses. "Street fashion is where the art is for poor people," Acker told Bailey, counting herself among their number. "I can't afford to buy a painting so if I get some money I go buy a dress."

× × ×

In the summer of 1983, Acker made it back to London, planning to stay as long as she could. "To grow old in New York is a nightmare," she told an interviewer a couple years later. She was weary of Manhattan's "media wheel," where every dinner out seemed to be a pretext for professional advancement. She wanted to have more time for her friends.

In London, she could also be a single, childless, middle-aged woman living alone, something she felt she couldn't be in most cities. London was cheaper and slower too, with different, more human, priorities. There was a publicly funded health care system. Once more exaggerating her economic marginalization, she said, "I just couldn't live in total poverty anymore. What is nicely middle-class here is poverty line in New York." Neglecting to mention her inheritance, she claimed to be making about $25,000 a year. "In London, I can be what I always wanted to be, that is, a working writer."

Initially, Acker stayed with Rosemary Bailey and her husband Barry Miles in their flat at 15 Hanson Street in West London. A buddy of Jeff Goldberg and Victor Bockris's, Miles then worked as a freelance editor for Omnibus Books, and would soon have a career similar to Bockris's, writing several biographies, including one of Ginsberg and a couple of Burroughs. Miles had invited Acker to be a houseguest, expecting her to stay a short while. She ended up camping in their living room for two months. Miles enjoyed talking about books with her, and found she had "a lot of interesting things to say," and he happily answered her questions about the Beats. But he was repelled by her narcissism, need for attention, and what he considered an overweening ambition. Making matters worse, she seemed not to care that she was living in someone else's home—she basically took over the place, stinking it up, Miles remembered with some disgust, with the smell of patchouli oil. "She was not very sensitive of other people's needs," he said.

At a party Bailey and Miles gave early in her stay, Acker met Peter Wollen. Wollen, then forty-five, was one of the world's foremost film scholars, and married to Laura Mulvey, a fellow theorist best known for developing the concept of the "male gaze" and with whom he'd collaborated on several experimental essay films. He also had a girlfriend in New York, the filmmaker Karyn Kay. But Wollen and Acker found each other thrilling and, inevitably, an affair soon began. Not everyone was delighted by the romance. When Acker demanded that Wollen break up with Kay, he dumped her immediately. For Bailey and Miles, it was another kind of annoyance: "It became very difficult for us because they were always in the living room fucking whenever I needed to get in there to get books or a record," Miles said.

His infidelities aside, Wollen was irresistible to Acker. Lanky, angular, and handsome, he was a sharp, original writer, well versed in critical theory and avant-garde art of all kinds. He'd known Burroughs in Paris in the late 1950s and had cowritten the screenplay for Antonioni's *The Passenger*. His landmark 1969 book *Signs and Meaning in the Cinema* had revolutionized English-language film studies. In many ways, he and Acker spoke the same language, or languages. "Peter took her very seriously," remembered Leslie

Dick, who met and married Wollen after his relationship with Acker ended. "Because he really believed in an avant-garde, and he really believed that she was onto something important." In a long, perceptive, and laudatory essay Wollen wrote after Acker's death, he called her "a ceaseless explorer of the disorienting potential of language, its directness, its capacity to drag the reader right into the text." In the early days of their affair, he would do almost anything for her, including peroxiding his hair and buying a Comme des Garçons suit. Except, crucially, and in an unfortunate echo of Lotringer's inertia, leave Mulvey. But during that summer, she and Wollen slept together, saw movies, played chess, talked incessantly about books and art. She sometimes worried that she wasn't smart enough for him: "Now that I'm writing you, you'll perceive what a stupid idiot I am," she said in a letter that August. At other times, she wasn't quite sure what she wanted from him. In bed, he could be too passive, or maybe it was she who was too passive. He also wasn't always so good at the practical aspects of life and needed someone to take care of him. Acker generally required the same thing.

Until the following year, Acker would go back and forth, from London to New York, and Wollen would sometimes meet her in Manhattan. At one point, back home, she was out for dinner with him and some other people, including Lynne Tillman, also a friend of Wollen's. Wollen was sitting right beside Tillman, but Acker leaned in close to her and whispered, "Tell me everything you know about Peter." That Thanksgiving, Acker wrote Wollen a letter. She talked about TV, politics, a bit about her writing, but mostly about their relationship (and Mulvey's place in it). She concluded with hyperbole: "I love you, Peter, and I'll have to abide by that. I don't think I've ever known what it was/is to be in love before."

× × ×

Wollen's esteem of Acker helped usher her into London's rarefied cultural circles. Not that she needed much assistance. That December, the writer and television presenter Melvyn Bragg flew with a crew to Manhattan to film her for an episode of *The South Bank Show*. *The South Bank Show* was an immensely popular hour-long television arts program broadcast by ITV. It had covered a wide range of cultural figures, including several British and American writers—John Le Carré, Harold Pinter, Saul Bellow, and Patricia Highsmith—and while Acker was not quite deemed their equal, the eclectic program had also, on occasion, featured prominent denizens of New York's downtown, including Acker's friend Laurie Anderson. While one of the show's producers, Alan Benson, was intrigued by Acker, other connections also got the episode off the ground: Pan/Picador's publicity director, Jacqueline Graham, helped coordinate episodes of the show, facilitating meetings with producers and Pan authors. Cynthia Rose, Acker's new friend at the *NME*, also worked part-time for Bragg as a co-presenter on the Radio Four show *Start of the Week*.

In New York, they filmed Acker in her Eldridge Street apartment—a cluttered, unremarkable place notable mainly for the unsurprisingly overstuffed bookshelves, a gold velour couch, and the framed Mapplethorpe photograph of her that hung on a wall. The production team grabbed B-roll footage of Fifth Avenue and Trump Tower, which they would offset with shots of Times Square and Acker's derelict neighborhood in mid-winter. They filmed an interview with David Salle in his studio and a photo shoot with Mapplethorpe, followed Acker around her gym. If there were any other interviews, they did not make it into the final broadcast, which, tellingly, includes no footage of Acker's lesser-known writer or theater friends. Aside from Acker reading alone to the camera, there's also not a single shot of a reading, art opening, or performance, anything that might hint at the cultural activity that was, in reality, still swirling about her. For the most part, in fact, the camera keeps itself trained on Acker's face—composed, carefully made up, almost masklike—as she answers Bragg's polite questions with solemnity and imperiousness. There is, on occasion, the charismatic laugh that Cynthia Rose noticed, the glint of the metallic tooth, but, for the most part, Acker remains deathly serious. She is indubitably the star of the show, and acts accordingly. At the beginning of the program, Bragg describes SoHo as "the chic community of New York's avant-garde," but if *The South Bank Show* was to believed, it was a community of one.

On the one hand, this was what Acker believed, or wanted to believe. "There are almost no novelists my age who are doing anything besides second- and third-generation Philip Roth," she told Bragg. But it was far from the truth. Soon enough, her New York friends and colleagues would rival her in many ways—in their prose innovations, in their literary renown, in their success—and Acker's sense of entitlement, her self-assurance, would seem almost poisonous. At the moment, though, that didn't matter. She would be in London the next month. For years, she'd been of two (maybe more) minds about celebrity—pursuing it with unabashed zeal at one moment, resenting its distortions the next—but now she was about to confront a degree of stardom she'd heretofore never known.

As her stardom grew, her relationship with Wollen shifted. When she settled in London, he went in the opposite direction, taking various academic posts in the States before finally arriving at UCLA, where he would become a full professor and live out his academic career. He would marry Leslie Dick, and they would have a daughter. When he and Acker's relationship ended, Wollen was heartbroken, but they would remain friends for many years after. With Dick, things were a bit more complicated. With Acker's growing fame and influence, she was able to help Dick get her debut novel, *Without Falling*, published in both the UK and the U.S. When Dick and Wollen married, Acker sometimes jokingly referred to them as her "parents." But she could also be jealous and contemptuous of Dick, particularly after the couple's child was born. In a letter to a friend in the late eighties, on the heels of some dispute she'd had with Dick, Acker wrote, with open bitterness, "Coupledom is a disgusting phenomenon."

CHAPTER 28

———— ✕ ————

THE OFFICIAL LAUNCH FOR *BLOOD AND GUTS PLUS TWO* WAS HELD late in the afternoon on February 12, 1984, at Riverside Studios, as part of a benefit for the arts center. Trying to sell an unfamiliar audience on their new American discovery, Picador's publicity struck an unapologetically sensational note. An advertisement for the event described Acker as "the notorious American novelist who rose to fame on the New York club performance poetry circuit," accompanied by a photograph, by Marcus Leatherdale, of Acker hiking up her skirt. Another ad in the *Times Literary Supplement* also described her as "notorious," and suggested that the three books in the volume "stretch the reader's tolerance—not of obscenity, but of the attack on language, sex and human expectations by systems of oppression." A blurb from Quentin Crisp goosed things even more: "Though Ms. Acker's message is both lurid and grim, it's also very funny."

Intentionally or not, Acker's performance that day punctured this forbidding image. She read a section from the Brontë letters in *My Death My Life*, her voice powerful and moving. She dressed with some modesty; one audience member recalled an "almost waifish, vulnerable figure" in a chic outfit of tweed trousers and an expensive-looking blouse. Cynthia Rose's review of the reading, published a couple weeks later in the *NME*, portrayed the event with affection and respect: "With the voice of their author bringing these to us, all the bits fell into perspective: the sexy stuff got sexier, the pulp mannerisms more blatantly self-mocking, and the serious investigations (what is love? what is language? what is real emotion and how is it best expressed through words?) which underscore the text were *shared* with the audience rather than demonstrated."

The Riverside appearance, and another one at the Institute of Contemporary Art ten days later, opened a number of new doors. Acker met Alan Jenkins, a poet and editor at the *Times Literary Supplement*, with whom she had a brief affair, and whose delight in her company (and work) helped guarantee reviews of her books. Even if those reviews were rarely positive—the *TLS* review of *Blood and Guts* suggested that "Acker's failure to provoke you fully into any reaction whatsoever is more surprising than this or that detail in the book. She does not rise to her own challenge as a visceral writer." Such assessments surprised and stung, though Acker learned to shrug them off, at least publicly. The English, she argued repeatedly, would never really understand what she was doing.

Another affair, with the twenty-four-year-old associate director of Riverside, Simon Usher, was more promising and lasting. Riverside quickly became a kind of home base for Acker, and she rented a mansion flat at 6 Digby Mansions just around the corner, for twenty-five pounds a week. First under Peter Gill, and then David Gothard, Riverside had blossomed into a vital nerve center. Gothard brought in Beckett (who directed *Waiting for Godot* with the San Quentin Drama Workshop), Joseph Chaikin, the Bread and Puppet Theater, Trisha Brown, and Laurie Anderson, among many other renowned theater and dance performers. The groundbreaking dancer and choreographer Michael Clark, a collaborator of Leigh Bowery's and The Fall's, worked out of a studio there. Hanif Kureishi, then primarily a playwright, had a job at the center's bookshop; when he wrote his first screenplay, *My Beautiful Laundrette*, Gothard put him in touch with director Stephen Frears, leading to the creation of that acclaimed movie and the birth of Working Title Films. "Riverside was what a university should be," Kureishi wrote. "A place to learn and talk and work and meet your contemporaries."

Usher met Acker at a dinner the night after her Riverside reading. He found her company enchanting, loved to talk about books with her, and was eager to show her around London. Two weeks later, he moved in with her. Usher was bright and an already accomplished theater director, but he was also stone-broke, a drunk, and a drug addict—"I was a terrible person," he said, "just the last thing she needed at the time." Before attending Oxford, he had boarded at a Catholic school in Somerset run by Benedictine monks capable of great sadism and cruelty. Acker was fascinated by Usher's stories of abuse there—"In a curious way, she associated sexual pleasure with a certain kind of violence," he said—and he was unsurprised to see that she had brought some S and M equipment with her from New York. She asked to be bound and humiliated, which Usher went along with, though not always so willingly.

Usher marveled at Acker's routine and discipline, her unbreakable daily regime. She set an alarm clock, got up, meditated, and then wrote and wrote and wrote. When Usher was working at Riverside, Acker would often come and sit in an office or rehearsal space there, scribbling sometimes for six hours a day. Occasionally, he would gather a couple actors and they'd perform some of Acker's work aloud. Most nights, he and Acker would have dinner at a mediocre bar and grill next to Hammersmith station, and later, when she moved to the other side of the river, they would frequent a hotel restaurant called the Wallow. Socially speaking, she wasn't the easiest person, Usher remembered, often defensive with his Oxford-educated friends, uncertain of English mores, and even humorless. But she fit in well at Riverside, where she was largely accepted for who she was. "She found a home and a way of life in London and it was centered around that building," Usher said. "She just became part of the setup and that was lovely."

Though he never particularly cared for her writing—"a bit unreadable," he said—Kureishi became a friend, and also an occasional lover. He and Usher would sometimes go to movies with Acker, each sitting on one side of her, holding her hand, and then the trio would head back to Digby Mansions to have sex. After Allen Ginsberg gave a reading at Riverside, the three of them went out to dinner with the poet, and when Ginsberg hit on Kureishi, Acker urged him to seize the opportunity (Kureishi declined). As much fun as Kureishi thought she was, he was also irked by her "incessant, horrible" name-dropping and what he considered her poor-little-rich-girl act. "It was quite vulgar," he said. "I mean, she complained all the time about what a hard life she had, and how poverty-stricken she was. We came from the fucking suburbs, grew up in the fifties. She went everywhere in taxis. We used to go on the Tube. The idea that you could go in a taxi was so exotic to me."

Usher showed her other parts of the city and country. He once took her to the Lake District; they got lost, she fell down a knoll, hated it. On another occasion, they visited a juvenile detention facility in Chiswick, where Usher ran theater workshops. He asked Acker to read there, and she did, becoming close to the prison's director, a fellow named Adrian. Adrian was something of a libertarian, and when Acker suggested that they should "open the fucking prisons and let everybody out, especially the children," he agreed wholeheartedly. She returned several more times. She and Usher also went to concerts together, with Usher introducing her to Throbbing Gristle, the seminal industrial music act fronted by Genesis P-Orridge, whom Acker would also later befriend. (Usher credited P-Orridge's on-stage penis piercing with inspiring Acker to get her own genitals pierced.) They went to see *First Blood*, the Sylvester Stallone movie, which Acker enjoyed and Usher hated, and *Purple Rain*. "She loved Prince," Usher said. "She thought Prince should rule the world." They flew to Paris together to see Foreman's production of *My Death My Life*.

Soon into their romance, however, Usher realized that Acker was as mercurial as her books suggested. She loathed authority in any form and yet could be "tyrannical" in her daily life toward others. She obviously had money and spent it—Usher recalled her one day, out of the blue, dropping more than a thousand pounds on a pair of racing bikes—but was often beside herself with financial worry. (Usher himself, at the time, only had about twenty-five pounds to his name.) On stage, she was a rock star, "performing out of her skin, howling," but away from the stage, she was anything but. Usher felt that she yearned for a more ordinary experience.

"I think what happens with everyone who has a relationship with Kathy is, you pretty soon meet Karen Lehman," he said. "Who is quite a different person. She was the loneliest person I've ever known." Usher perceived a deep, unresolved sadness at the core of Acker's life. This was something that a number of her friends and colleagues also observed, that the push-pull, seduce-and-abandon quality of her relationships, romantic and otherwise, often left her feeling utterly alone. "She was very needy and lonely," Mel Freilicher said. "But she was always testing people and pushing them away without even wanting to." Leslie Dick saw a somewhat different side to this, characterizing Acker as someone who simply spent a lot of time in her own head. Emerging into the world and being with actual people, with their own needs and desires, inevitably led to conflict. At the same time, Dick said, Acker also connected easily with many people. "There was something sort of delightfully fearless about her capacity to make friends with people," Dick said. Indeed, despite her footlooseness and her capacity for burning bridges, Acker never had any shortage of friends—good, loyal, generous friends—and she gathered them easily. Perhaps this was the need for the novelty, part and parcel of Acker's appetite for life. Or perhaps she had to constantly replace the friends and lovers who had, inevitably, disappointed her. It was also the by-product of someone who lived and shed so many lives herself; new allies necessarily accompanied each new artistic discipline, each new city, each new circle.

Or, perhaps, as Usher saw it in the end, it was just a need to be loved by as many people as possible. Her need, he felt, was bottomless. "It's all in her fiction," he said, "women who are just prepared to abnegate themselves entirely for any morsel of affection that could come their way. That's what being with her was like."

× × ×

That spring, both *Variety*, the Bette Gordon film that Acker wrote, and Acker's episode of *The South Bank Show* premiered. After screenings at Cannes and film festivals in Toronto and Miami the previous year, *Variety* opened at Screen on the Green in Islington in May, with a *Sunday Times* review calling it "subtle and enigmatic," "directed with considerable style by Bette Gordon." The *New Statesman*'s John Coleman was far less kind, singling out what he called Acker's "dreadful dialogue." Neverthelesss, it was shown again and again in London that year, at the Electric Cinema Club on Portobello Road and at the ICA Cinematheque, and especially with Acker's growing fame, usually presented as "Kathy Acker's *Variety*." In New York, the reviews were also mixed—Amy Taubin praised the film in the *Voice* while the *Times*' Janet Maslin derided Gordon's "static, uncommunicative directorial style" and Acker's "painfully underwritten screenplay."

Meanwhile, *The South Bank Show*, which was broadcast on Sunday, April 1, arrived with seismic force. At the time, there were only four television channels in the country. An hour-long documentary about anybody on one of those channels, on the leading arts program of the day, broadcast across the entire country, was a cultural event of enormous significance. It was the first time that most viewers would have likely heard of Acker, but for many, it was definitely not the end.

Michael Bracewell, a twenty-five-year-old writer who'd grown up in the London suburbs, watched the program with slack-jawed delight. He had been waiting for someone like Acker to appear for a long while. As a teenager, Bracewell had thrilled to David Bowie and Roxy Music and the particular cultural revolution of punk. He saw that punk's energy had started to disperse, finding its ways into different corners of British cultural and political life, and he was desperate to see it similarly make literature relevant and exciting to young people. British fiction may have been booming—Angela Carter published *The Bloody Chamber* in 1979; Ian McEwan released *The Comfort of Strangers* in 1981, the same year that Salman Rushdie won the Booker for

Midnight's Children; and Martin Amis published *Money* in 1984—but Bracewell felt it was all still "a bit dowdy," still just "that old tweedy London literary
establishment." Everyone, he felt, was on the lookout for a new generation of
writers.

For him, Acker was one of those writers, and also someone he called an
"icon of transition." She connected the people who bought records with the
people who bought books. Which, pre-Acker, Bracewell argued, was an almost unbridgeable chasm: music people tended to read classics—Nietzsche or
Colette or Wilde—but rarely anything contemporary. Acker's work, however,
was able to reach across that chasm, particularly to punk fans who were drawn
by its violence and what Bracewell called "the snotty, bratty wit of it."

The novelist and comics creator Neil Gaiman was a couple years younger
than Bracewell, a journalist and would-be novelist, when he first encountered
Blood and Guts. He was astonished by the book—"it was really weird and
wonderful"—and while it wasn't exactly what he wanted to do as a writer, he
felt there was a lot he could learn from it. He planned to review it for one of
the British Fantasy Society's publications, and maybe even interview Acker.
But when he saw *The South Bank Show*, he quickly, if temporarily, retreated.
"I thought she was really scary," he said. "The person on that show seemed
incredibly intimidating."

Kureishi remembered Acker grousing about the spotlight—"Oh, I don't
want to be a superstar," he recalled her saying often, something he didn't believe for a minute. Indeed, with little apparent complaint, she participated in
many more profiles and interviews, with the *Guardian*, *Blitz*, and, again, the
NME. She appeared frequently on radio and TV, and would soon become a
fixture at the ICA. With Usher in tow, she flew back to New York for an interview and photo shoot at *Vogue*, with journalist Lisa Liebmann writing that, in
London, "the author has been enjoying that most pungent of public treats—a
succès de scandale." The next year, when Acker was invited to join the Groucho
Club, a new private members club in Soho for the city's cultural elite, she leapt
at the chance.

In keeping with her newfound celebrity, sometime in 1985, Acker bought
a one-bedroom flat at 87 Riverview Gardens, in the posh, bucolic neighborhood of Barnes. She was still near Riverside, but now on the other side of
the Thames. It was a charming, sunny place, on the first floor of a three-story
Edwardian brick building built in 1909. "You'd go out on the lawn, feed the

ducks," an American visitor recalled. "Walk to the river." It seemed a decision that was at once a bid for acceptance and a way to frustrate the expectations of those who felt that an underground doyenne like Kathy Acker should live in a squat or rough-and-tumble council housing. "It was the most staid residential street you can imagine," Usher said, "full of rich widows and schoolmasters and people like that." But Acker loved its gentility and quiet. She didn't have to deal with landlords or rent or subletters. She could do what she wanted—write all night long, play the Swans late and loud, get a new pet (which she did, a pair of lovebirds she named Legba and Eulalie).* It also, perhaps, harkened back to that brief, idealized period of her young childhood—a safe, comfortable home just steps from a river. "In my imagination, when I awake late morning, the Thames whispers in my flesh," she wrote in her essay "Property," adding that "I believe there are little heavens, perhaps for all of us, between looming temporal hells. Here, for me, is a little piece of heaven, sailing and flying, whose name, believe it or not, is Barnes."

Materially, at least, she was comfortable. She was a sovereign, unmarried woman who wrote as she wished and lived as she wished. She didn't have to worry about her next meal or paycheck, but needed neither family nor husband for that support. Best of all, she didn't have to worry about who was publishing her writing. After so many years of grinding, of pursuit and rejection, after writing nine books, she had finally entered the halls of literary power, and had done so, more or less, her own way. "She was a novelty act who came in at the right time," said Ira Silverberg, at various times her agent, editor, and publisher. "She went in there and fucking owned the place." The subversive post-punk aesthetic, and the rage that characterized Thatcher's England, made her work completely relevant, but it also propelled it forward, giving her fresh territory across which to trespass. Her earlier writing had been produced in opposition to patriarchy, to the traditional family, to malignant political and economic structures; now she had a whole new country to storm. Like Silverberg, she knew that she was a novelty, and novelty, by definition, does not last. But she planned to make the most of it while she could.

---

* Not just one set, either. After Legba died, she returned a bereft Eulalie to the man she'd bought them from, and replaced them with another pair named Lulu and Minerva.

CHAPTER 29

M ANY YEARS LATER, AROUND THE TIME OF ACKER'S DEATH, USHER
would write a monologue about his relationship with her, which was
performed at a small Off West End theater. It was a painful thing, at once
confessional and abstract, composed largely of remembered conversations
and Usher's insights into her Jewishness, sadomasochism, her issues around
money. It was written in a single voice that seems sometimes Usher's, sometimes Acker's, the two of them united in a tragic embrace. It also included a
few lines about an abortion:

> Later I'm lyin' in the abortion place. Fuckin' protests outside.
> Oh my God, why don't you come you asshole. Asleep in my bed after
> A night with the little cunties? Still don't let you fuck 'em, huh?

And then a bit later on:

> I coulda loved the child
> I wanted a kid
> I listened to you
> What do you fuckin' know
> I didn't wanna fuckin' deceive you
> I didn't

The lines were stylized, but rooted, Usher said, in reality. At some point
during their year or so together, Acker became pregnant. She didn't know what
to do. He didn't know what to do. Previous to this, Acker had never really expressed any desire to be a mother. While she had had good relationships with
young children—Blaise Antin, Lotringer's daughter—she had never wanted
any of her own. Far from it. Her life was too vertiginous, too unstable; how
could a child possibly fit into it?

But she was in her late thirties, and the cancer scare she'd had while living with Peter Gordon was still relatively fresh in her mind. She was more conscious of her mortality. Perhaps this would be her last chance to have a kid. While she still considered the nuclear family toxic, and parenthood terrified her somewhat, maybe she would be different. She didn't have to be like her mother. Maybe, somehow it could work out.

But it was an impossible decision, and Usher couldn't help her make it. He was just as confused, perhaps even more terrified. "I wasn't mature enough to handle it properly," he said. "It was dreadful." In the end, he told her, whatever happens, they would get through it.

In the end, she decided to terminate the pregnancy. "There was no way I could keep the child," she said later. But unlike her previous abortions, this one was not quickly forgotten. "It was a very painful abortion, emotionally," she said, "and it made me think that like it or not, there is a very deep way in which we are connected to wombs, to childbearing." According to Usher, she blamed him for the loss. The relationship would not last much longer.

By then, under the influence of the so-called "peasant poet," John Clare, she had started a new book, which she called *Adventure*. It would be a degree or two more sober, less pulpy and personal, than *Blood and Guts*, and an object more deliberately designed for an intellectual, even academic, audience. But when Acker started working on *Adventure*, she told her former lover Peter Wollen that she was uncertain which direction to go in. Plagiarism and appropriation were still key to her, but she had become less interested in cut-up or collage. "I want a story!" she wrote to Wollen, immediately adding with characteristic dissent, "There is no story." Which texts to steal, though, and why? Now, being interviewed regularly, even interrogated, by journalists and critics who demanded more of her, who really wanted to know *why*—philosophically and ethically—she wrote the way that she did, she felt more compelled to really think through her choices. She read Joyce's play *Exiles* and wondered aloud to Wollen about Joyce's intentionally determining "his place/use in the world," and what hers should be. "I have to go farther and be absolutely clear and steadfast," she added, "quick virtuosity teenage passion is no longer useful or interesting. It's the choice, not identity, but choosing: that reverberation. It's never prettiness: it's the decision: this is what is necessary."

The abortion had been a choice, and she made that choice, that wrenching personal event, the starting point of *Adventure*. First, though, she changed the title, à la *Great Expectations*, to *Don Quixote*. Acker later claimed that she started reading Cervantes's classic novel as way to calm herself while waiting for the abortion. And then, to clear her mind even further, she began copying passages out. In actuality, as her letters to Wollen suggest, Acker read (or re-read) the novel in the fall of 1983, alongside other texts about it, including Nabokov's famous lectures. (At her death, her library included four different editions of the novel, one published in 1950, two in 1979, and another in 1983.) In any case, the seventeenth-century Spanish novel is a foundational text of modern Western literature, an early example of metatextual gamesmanship, the use of multiple narrators, etc., famously reimagined by writers as diverse as Borges, Foucault, Paul Auster, and Salman Rushdie. It would provide Acker with a kind of support structure, a narrative from which to work from, or off of. She could simply take the "story" she'd mentioned to Wollen; she wouldn't have to create one and impose on readers "this damned world position that I hate." She could just copy Cervantes. "I start copying things because that's how I learn," she said.

But in the final book, she does much more than that. She also takes apart a hegemonic narrative structure, a phallocentric one, to use her term, and tries to figure out how one might write instead as a woman. Acker's Quixote is female, her armor the "pale or puke green paper" gown she wears while undergoing an abortion. In a note scribbled on an early typescript chapter ("A Dog's Life, Con't: An Examination of What Kind of Schooling Women Need") she wryly described that chapter's plot—"Don Quixote and *her* faithful companion St. Simeon who is now (magically) a dog, in fact, any dog, are saving the Western world—that dog-eat-dog society"—which, more or less, summed up the whole book.

The first couple pages of the novel depict this abortion. The narrator, "crazy" and dying for love—or, in Acker's terms, a way to love a person in a world whose social and political structures corrupt or control her desire—is catheterized and taken to a narrow, black-leather-padded slab. She's anesthetized with a steel needle. The abortion causes her to lose her mind, and thus her identity. Post-op, she gains a new identity—and a purpose: "Because to Don Quixote, having an abortion is a method of becoming a knight and saving the world. This is a vision. In English and most European societies, when a woman becomes a knight, being no longer anonymous she receives a name. She's able to have adventures and save the world." Those adventures turn out to be grim, arduous, and disorienting, a brutal picaresque, with Don Quixote's quest for sexual love taking her across time and space, into and out of death, from 1980s London to New York to St. Petersburg during the Russian Revolution, into and out of a literature both oppressive and emancipatory.

Acker's Quixote also has a sidekick; her Sancho Panza is named Saint Simeon. This name was a nod to Simon Usher, and Saint Simeon also shares some of Usher's background—at a Catholic boarding school, Saint Simeon is "regularly gang-banged" by upper-class boys and flogged by his teachers. As usual, however, Acker took her liberties. "There was beating and some sexual interference," Usher said of his actual youth, "but Don Quixote is fiction." At the beginning of the book, he is a man, but quickly transforms into a talking dog.

The first section is Acker's rewriting of *Don Quixote*, the second her rewriting and merging of several other texts (Andrei Biely's *St. Petersburg*, Lampedusa's *The Leopard*, Frank Wedekind's *Pandora's Box*, and *Godzilla*, among them). In the third part, the resumption of Quixote's journey, the language is influenced by and drawn from various African writers that Acker had just discovered. These writers, including Yambo Ouologuem and Ayi Kwei Armah, "an incredible structuralist," provided a new way of thinking about narrative, outside of mimetic realism and separate from the "18th-century Balzacian narrative" that she found so limiting and false. It was a movement from a master, controlling narrative, basically, and through to a "primitive" narrative she considered its opposite, one of surprise, difference, and possibility.

When Acker described these African writers as primitive, she knew how offensive the adjective was—"If all these words don't smack of racism," she told an interviewer. But racial privilege is difficult to shed. At moments, Acker's engagement with race can be, particularly to contemporary and nonwhite readers, thorny and discomfiting. While it's a categorical error to expect any "realistic" representations from Acker, and her ironies and constantly shifting positions make it hard to pin her down on anything, her portrayal of Black, Puerto Rican, and Muslim people can feel reductive, with racialized figures employed usually as signifiers of powerlessness, disenfranchisement, and colonization. From *Blood and Guts*, with its Persian slave trader and deliberately mistranslated Persian poems, through her 1988 novel, *Empire of the Senseless*, and its Algerian revolutionaries, Acker appears to attack imperialism, orientalism, and Islamophobia while, in other moments, idealizing Arabs and Muslims. Part of this arguably stemmed from her admiration for writers like

Genet, Guyotat, and Juan Goytisolo, gay European writers who had spent a great amount of time in the Arab world. These writers had lovers and good friends there, took risks living there, and had firsthand experience of postcolonial resistance. Writing about Algeria, rather than, say, American imperialism in Vietnam, instantly placed her in these writers' company. In contrast to them, though, Acker's relationship to this culture was wholly mediated. This gave her a certain freedom—to confect fantasies about revolutionary movements, or to critique them—but it also opened her up to charges of distortion and romanticization.

She always identified with the oppressed and exploited even when this identification felt false. "Poets are [. . .] the white niggers of this earth," she wrote in an introduction to a UK edition of her early work. In a 1994 interview with *Artforum*, she described herself, being Jewish, as a "woman of color," and also said "I'm so queer I'm not even gay." Empathy has its limits; it can be misguided. All trauma is not created equal. But Acker never really acknowledged this, and refused to let it impinge on her freedom as an artist. For someone who only ever saw fixed identity as a trap, this isn't surprising. Identity politics, she argued toward the end of her life, was especially antithetical to writing fiction. "I can see why ye olde black lesbian wants to assert black lesbianism," she said, "for all sorts of political reasons. But I think that you have to really be careful that when you're asserting identity you're only asserting in a certain time, and that you don't make an absolute. And writing, novel writing, just isn't about that."

As conscious and deliberate as her process of composition seemed in retrospect, Acker always tried to overwhelm or bypass the conscious, deliberate part of her brain as she wrote. Writing in languages in which she wasn't completely fluent was one way to do this. Copying other texts too, or listening to loud music while she wrote. "Lots and lots of ploys," she said. "It's *me* trying to break out. It's me constantly trying to put myself in a situation where I don't really understand. To me, you want to seek disjunctions, but you don't want to seek elite experimentalism."

In *Don Quixote*, Acker makes occasional reference to her life in London, her disgust with landlords and American politics, her interest in fashion—"Why's a Cubist painting, if it is, better art than a Vivienne Westwood dress?" But the abortion scene aside, it's one of Acker's least autobiographical books. She uses almost no proper names drawn from her life and only rarely revisits the stock scenes of her family romance. And yet, the overarching spirit of the book is very familiar and bound up in Acker's everyday life—it's a long wail of loneliness and need, thwarted desire, control, and rejection, with Acker's usual pain compounded by a confusing sense of exile. "It is true," she writes, "that women are never men. Even a woman who has the soul of a pirate, at least pirate morals, even a woman who prefers loneliness to the bickerings and constraints of heterosexual marriage, even such a woman who is a freak in our society needs a home." In many ways, she loved England. But she also missed certain parts of New York. "All I can say is that I sit by the river and think about pirates," she told an interviewer in 1985. "I mean, to me, this place is loneliness . . ." Soon after she'd moved to London, speaking with Lotringer on the phone, she said, ruefully, "Someday I'm going to have to work out this business of running away. I seem to do it every three years or so."

× × ×

Don Quixote was Acker's most explicitly feminist book, though she would take pains to avoid it being characterized as such. Changing the narrator of *Don Quixote* from male to female was just a "kind of joke," she said, "to see what would happen." The fact that *Don Quixote* was a "male" text was a "bit incidental, perhaps consciously incidental." To Peter Wollen, who interviewed her about the book at the ICA in 1986, she said, "I didn't have some great feminist ideal at the time. It just grew, what it meant. The meaning grew." She insisted that she was simply trying to replicate in prose what the American conceptual artist Sherrie Levine had done in photography—painstakingly reproduce canonical artworks.

This was misleading, and, to a certain degree, insincere. Acker knew well that Levine's rephotography was not done, as she said, "without any reason," but part of a program of critique and subversion, a rigorous questioning of art-historical notions of originality, aura, autonomy, and desire. At the time, Levine's most notorious pieces were a series of precise reproductions of photographs by Walker Evans, Eliot Porter, and Edward Weston. Her work was also bound up in the feminist theory of the moment. "As a woman, I felt there was no room for me," Levine famously said. "There was all this representation, in all this now painting, of male desire. The whole art system was geared to celebrating these objects of male desire. Where, as a woman artist, could I situate myself?"

As a writer, Acker asked similar questions, and would frequently assert the need for a kind of a *écriture féminine*. The second section of *Don Quixote* famously opens with this disclaimer: "BEING BORN INTO AND PART OF A MALE WORLD, SHE HAD NO SPEECH OF HER OWN. ALL SHE COULD DO WAS READ MALE TEXTS WHICH WEREN'T HERS." Nevertheless, generally speaking, Acker was loath to subscribe to any essential and totalizing identity, feminist or otherwise. She didn't want to be considered, or treated as, "only" a woman writer. "I hated being defined by the fact that I had a cunt," she said. Late in life, she called identity politics "repulsive," and in writing, especially, she resisted any categorization. In *Don Quixote*, as in many of Acker's books, gender norms are phantasmic, and in one slippery chapter, titled "Heterosexuality," the narrator's sexual desires are only muddled by the expectations and limitations of masculinity and femininity: "De Franville saw no escape from this mess, this mess that had to be him, except by erasing it or him. He had to be more than androgynous: he had to erase loving, sexuality, and identity." In the next paragraph, and for several pages thereafter, pronouns too shift: "He" becomes "He/She" or "(She)He."

Acker's relationship to feminism was as changeable and contradictory as everything else in her life. In the sixties and seventies, even as Acker learned how deeply sexist the culture was, even as she rejected traditionally defined gender roles, even as she loathed her fathers—both real and metaphoric— she also found the feminism of the period too "strident" and "restrictive." She bristled against feminists who insisted always on positive, uncomplicated representations of women. She did not want to turn powerlessness into a narrative of triumph, and predictably, she was chided for seeming to validate powerlessness and abjection. One of her first reviews in the *New York Times*, of *Blood and Guts*, huffed, "There's a deep moral dislocation in *Blood and Guts in High School*. The novel, which devotes thousands of words to depicting the cruelty inflicted on Janey and on women in general, is itself abusive towards women." Writing to Glenda George from San Francisco in the early eighties, she was still complaining about "the usual trouble from white middle class-aged feminists out here: I quote uphold the victimization of women etc." She also railed against Andrea Dworkin and other anti-porn feminists, whose thinking she saw only leading to false, dangerous binaries (all women good, all men bad) and, worse, censorship. This was a legitimate fear, as it turned out, though not necessarily the fault of thinkers like Dworkin. Various politicians and governments exploited the anti-porn argument to suppress queer and other marginalized writers. In the eighties and early nineties, for example, Canadian customs officials regularly seized books featuring gay and lesbian sex that were shipped from the U.S., on the grounds that they were obscene. These included books written by, among others, bell hooks, Marguerite Duras, Dennis Cooper—and Acker herself.

"I wouldn't call her a feminist writer," said Eileen Myles. "I don't even think of her as liking women. Nah. But maybe she's a little proud of them. A little in awe." Leslie Dick also took issue with the label. "I didn't think of Kathy as a feminist," she said. "That's too straight, too bourgie. But she is a feminist in that she enacts the subordination of women and the depredation of the patriarchy on the body. She enacted it. She lived it." But, certainly, by the late eighties, Acker had found common cause with feminist theorists and philosophers—the aforementioned French thinkers, to be sure, but also, later, groundbreaking American philosophers like Judith Butler, whose books, *Gender Trouble* and *Bodies That Matter*, she admired. In 1986, she said, "the people, theoretically, I probably agree with most are the S&M lesbians, as far as ideas about power and relations go. My problems with feminism are simply that my ideas of power come out of Nietzsche very strongly, and I don't regard equality as any sort of Mecca-on-Earth possibility. I don't regard power as bad. But I certainly think I'm a feminist." Speaking with Sylvère Lotringer, she argued, "My best critics are feminists. That's simply where I would locate myself. It's when feminism came together with postmodernism, that's when I could locate what I was doing."

Ultimately, though, she still wanted to live somehow outside of, or in between, gender binaries. Her refusal of binary thinking wasn't exactly about negating those oppositions, but more about opening up space around them, of allowing incompatible or oppositional things to coexist and permeate each other. She insisted always that subjectivity be multiple, ambivalent, and negotiable. "I'd rather be one of the bad boys than a good girl," she said. Or maybe, as *Don Quixote* and other books also suggested, also not quite human at all. Of Acker's writing about the animal world, about humans that become animal and vice-versa, and Acker's personal love of her nonhuman companions (real and stuffed), a whole other book could be written. A couple different friends told stories about overhearing Acker having sex. On each occasion, they remembered, she was barking like a dog.

CHAPTER 30

———————— × ————————

IN LONDON, ACKER'S SOCIAL LIFE BECAME INCREASINGLY HECTIC, AND while some circles overlapped, she kept things largely compartmentalized. There was her life at Riverside (which more or less concluded when things with Usher ended); the relationships she cultivated in the worlds of music, art, and the burgeoning comic book world; her life at the gym; and her life in publishing.

The last was a roundelay of publishers, agents, journalists, and writers of various disposition. Around when *Don Quixote* came out, on May 22, she hosted an evening of readings at the National Poetry Library by her yet un-published younger writer friends—Leslie Dick, Michael Bracewell, and Mark Edwards—called "Kathy Acker and Friends." Though Acker often found straight nonfiction or journalism a bother, she became, in her own way, a dedicated book critic, regularly contributing reviews to the *New Statesman* and *City Limits*. She became friends with Roz Kaveney, a trans woman who worked variously as a writer, critic, and editor, as well as journalists Suzanne Moore, Deborah Orr, Don Watson, and Julie Burchill, the reliably outspoken, chronically oversharing pop culture critic and columnist.

Watson, a writer for the *NME*, was, for a time, another lover. Burchill almost was. At the Groucho Club, Acker met Jay Landesman, an American countercultural impresario, and he invited her to his home in the Angel for lunch on Christmas in 1986. Burchill was married then to Landesman's son, Cosmo, and the couple, with their infant son, were living there. Burchill thought Acker was cute ("like Tweetie Pie") and, while drunk, took her up to a loft in the house for a snog. Cosmo soon found them, however, and, as Burchill tells it, threw Acker out into the snow. "We made plans to hook up," Burchill said of Acker, "but after a preliminary chat, we both discovered we were subs! So we didn't bother taking it any further." Any relationship would have ended before it started, though, given Burchill's unfavorable estimation of Acker's talents: "I enjoyed kissing her, but I thought her writing was rubbish."

Many of Acker's circles converged at the Groucho, which Acker had taken to calling (especially to American friends) "her" club. The Groucho had been founded in May 1985 by a group of publishing people, as an alternative to traditional, stuffy British men's clubs—the name was an allusion to the famous quip attributed to Groucho Marx: "I don't want to belong to any club that will accept me as a member." Over the years, its invited membership consisted almost entirely of writers, actors, musicians, media types, and a number of celebrities: Salman Rushdie, Stephen Fry, Melvyn Bragg, Damien Hirst, Rachel Weisz, and Tracey Emin. (Peter Wollen turned down an invitation to join when Acker accepted hers.) Its bars, restaurants, and private rooms were all housed in a large townhouse in Soho that still clung to its history of bohemian, squalid glamor. "It was easy to get into arguments at the Groucho Club," recalled Leslie Dick. "There was something about the energy there that was really horrible. It was competitive. It was a frantic, hard-drinking literary scene. It was a see-and-be-seen kind of place."

But Acker cherished it. She loved the luxury, the connections, the hurly-burly atmosphere of the place. It was where she first met Neil Gaiman, for one, at the London launch of Tama Janowitz's *Slaves of New York*.* Acker had just written a gushy piece about Alan Moore's *Swamp Thing*, and Gaiman, who knew Roz Kaveney, also in attendance, requested an introduction. He was delighted to find Acker not frightening at all, but on the contrary. "She was incredibly good at making you feel you were the only person in the room," Gaiman said. They spent the evening talking about comics, and by its end, he was besotted with her. They were never romantically involved, but he did introduce her to Nick Landau and Igor Goldkind, founder and publicist, respectively, of the UK graphic novel publisher Titan Books, who would become successive lovers.

Gaiman also facilitated an introduction to Moore himself, the bearded, burly mystic of the UK comics world, best known then for *V for Vendetta*. He occasionally visited Acker at Riverview Gardens, and invited her to stay at his home in Northampton. His initial impression was of somebody "who wore her tough girl aura like a force field, and who probably presented that aura because

---

* Acker was no fan of the book, calling Janowitz "one of the writers of Reaganite America" and adding, "Janowitz's comedy style simply glorifies the trendiness or fashion which has replaced actual art-making in the New York art world."

of a genuine softness and tenderness that she was attempting to protect from an abusive world." He remembered, fondly, one occasion when his youngest daughter accidentally walked in on Acker while she was taking a bath, and Acker proudly showed the girl the tiger she'd just gotten tattooed on her buttock. She and Moore often talked about writing, including English authors like Iain Sinclair and Jenny Diski, whom both admired. When Acker, upset by a dismissive, lazy review of her 1997 novel *Pussy, King of the Pirates*, asked Moore if he could write something about the book, he happily obliged, producing a defense in *City Limits* magazine. "I'd genuinely loved the book," he said, "and was able to use the review to talk about the failings of literary critics when it came to Kathy's work."

x x x

Acker was also spending considerable time with Cynthia Rose, the *NME* journalist, with whom she would go see music or performance art. Rose moved with ease between different cultural scenes—the rare groove movement, the rise of British jazz, the House of Beauty and Culture—and political activism. Among other things, she participated in the anti-apartheid movement and fought against Clause (or Section) 28, legislation passed by the Thatcher government that made it illegal for local governments to "promote" homosexuality through educational books, pamphlets, or films. But Rose quickly learned that, while Acker wanted to be seen as part of all this cultural and political activity and certainly found it invigorating and worthwhile, when push came to shove, what meant most to Acker was becoming part of London's elite literary circles. "What mattered was that they considered her part of them," Rose argued, "and she really cared what they thought of her." Rose recalled one evening running into Acker and Salman Rushdie at the movies. Rose and her friend, Matt, had gone to see *River's Edge*, which Acker and Rushdie were also there to see, and the four decided to sit together. Afterward, Rose and Matt were heading to Soul II Soul's club night at Africa Centre, and they invited Rushdie and Acker along. Soul II Soul was still an underground act at that point, and Rushdie and Acker were excited to go. But the event wasn't going to start until after midnight, so the group repaired to Matt's small squat for tea. At twelve-thirty, though, just when they were about to head out, Acker and Rushdie demurred and, as Rose later found out, instead went around the corner to the Groucho to drink. Rose was more amused than disappointed, but it struck her as an emblematic evening: "Kathy was always 'going to come' to the Judy Blame show or to paper up political posters but . . . she would always somehow end up drinking wine with Martin Amis."

Rushdie noticed this disconnect too. "I was struck by the daring of her writing," he said. "By its explicit sexuality, very different from my own. What was striking about her as a person was that she usually wasn't like that at all, not in my company anyway." According to Rushdie, they were never particularly close friends (and not, as others suspected, lovers). But after Rushdie went into hiding post-fatwa, Acker threw herself into the activism around his defense. She worked with young Pakistani women in Rushdie defense groups, signed a letter of support published in the *Guardian*, and in July 1989 spoke alongside Hanif Kureishi and Terry Eagleton at an event at Conway Hall called *Voices for Salman Rushdie Against Fundamentalism and Racism and For the Right to Dissent*. Acker wrote a short piece, "A Personal View of *The Satanic Verses*," and while it's unclear if these were the same remarks she made at Conway Hall, they're indicative of her perspective and thinking at the time: "Many people, many intellectuals have been commenting on the public issues and I am not sure that I am equipped to do so. Not being Muslim, I cannot and will probably never understand if *The Satanic Verses* is blasphemous to all Muslims or only to Muslims who are fundamentalists. And I cannot deeply comprehend how it is blasphemous (if it is), for I am Jewish and the tradition of the Talmud is profoundly one of arriving at knowledge through argument, discussion, controversy, rather than that of acquiring knowledge through decree." She concluded on a personal note, referring both to Rushdie and his then wife, writer Marianne Wiggins, "For me, however, the main issue is the private one. I miss my friends deeply and am angry at those who have hurt them."

Rose didn't find Acker's apparent networking or careerism objectionable at all. On the contrary, she said, London at the time was much smaller, more homemade, much less slick than it would become, its culture made up of constant exchanges between people of all kinds, artists of all kinds. What counted, above all, was knowing people. Roz Kaveney concurred, arguing that outsiders like Acker were compelled to play by the same, if parallel, rules that the establishment did: "If you were an outsider artist in London, you created outsider networks that functioned exactly the same way because it's the only way you can make it work. You use what connections you've got."

But Acker was still ambivalent about it all. Celebrity certainly brought its share of advantages and delights, but there was another side to it. In its review of *Variety*, the *Monthly Film Bulletin* incidentally mentioned *The South Bank Show*, belittling the way it had sold Acker with its "glib invocations of cultural shock value." Acker wasn't thrilled about this either. She knew her books were shocking and titillating, and that, to many, she cut a strange, even threatening, figure. But she was conscious that this image was false or at least partial, and already becoming a kind of cliché. She wanted her books to be seen as the literary projects they were, as complex investigations of language, culture, representation, memory, and time. She wanted to be taken seriously, and throughout her life in London over the next few years, she would constantly lament that she wasn't. "In England it was absolutely horrible," she said later. "I mean, I'm very well-known there and I get tons of work. But to say that they like what I do, no, I wouldn't say that. They fetishize what I do." A familiar cycle of desire was becoming more and more detrimental: as soon as Acker got something she wanted, she immediately wanted something different or something more. Even as she recognized this pattern, she seemed powerless to break it.

× × ×

Soon after *Blood and Guts* was published in the UK, Acker obtained her first London agent, Anne McDermid at Curtis Brown. McDermid believed that Acker could be better published by a house other than Picador, and indeed, by the time *Blood and Guts* had come and gone, Picador was likewise feeling less enthusiastic about Acker. There was a sense that her star might have already burned itself out. "Her popularity was always greater in the media than in book sales," Ira Silverberg said. *Blood and Guts*, her most popular book, would only sell about twelve thousand copies in the U.S. in her lifetime, and her other books far less.* But Acker's fame and influence would, for the rest of her career, far exceed her sales, a fact that frequently got under her skin. Neil Gaiman preferred to see this in a more positive light. "She cast a long shadow," he said, "in the way that the first Velvet Underground album did. There's that wonderful

---

* According to records at Grove Atlantic, by February 2022, and taking into account all its different American editions, 38,089 copies of *Blood and Guts* have sold. Acker's next bestselling title, *Empire of the Senseless*, has sold 18,083 copies. As accounting systems have changed so much over the lifetime of the books, these figures are not considered entirely accurate. Nor do these include UK and other foreign editions, translations, etc. Nevertheless, and unsurprisingly, Acker never made a lot of money directly from book sales.

line of Brian Eno's—'Only a thousand people bought it, but each of them went out and formed a band.' The people who read and got Kathy, they went and took some of that out into the world."

McDermid took Acker and *Don Quixote* to Paladin, an imprint at Grafton Books that some regarded as the "pseudo-Picador," and they released *Don Quixote* in April 1986. But Acker and McDermid never really saw eye to eye, and by the time of *Don Quixote*'s release, Acker was publicly carping about both her agent and her new publisher. "I got an agent because I thought I should," she told an interviewer. "And I followed my agent's advice and left Picador. And I shouldn't have, I should have stayed with them [...] In a way [the publishers] don't want me. I'm just like a nuisance to them." Acker claimed that McDermid, to protect Curtis Brown, had included an obscenity clause in her Paladin contract that would allow the publisher to rewrite the book if they ever ran into any trouble. Acker was livid, and threatened to go back to Picador. Paladin presumably struck or amended the clause, and the publication proceeded. "I mean, you know, look, it's fucking capitalism," Acker said, "but if you don't play the game, you go in a drawer, you shut the drawers, and you die. If you play the game, you get screwed. What do you do? We live in a white post-capitalist country where the multinationals are coming in full swing [...] I think half of the book is writing it and half is dealing with these other things." She added, presciently: "My plagiarism is an attack on the writing world, very directly... if anyone got me on the plagiarism, we'd have a roaring law case because if everyone starts writing the way I do the whole writing establishment is under attack."

McDermid would remain Acker's agent for a while longer, eventually selling a collection of her early work titled *Young Lust* and her 1990 *In Memoriam to Identity* to Pandora, the feminist imprint of Unwin Hyman. But some observers, including Kaveney, felt that McDermid had used Acker as a kind of bargaining chip and never really had Acker's best interests at heart. "Because Kathy got moved around by Anne, Kathy got moved to editors who understood Kathy's reputation but not what Kathy was doing," Kaveney suggested. Acker returned to Picador to publish her novel *Empire of the Senseless*, but the machinations of that deal perturbed Acker enough to fire McDermid in a letter she sent on March 25, 1987:

> I just returned from Manchester and received your letter that
> the contract with Picador will be enacted in "due course." I

simultaneously received a phone call from the managing editor at Grafton. He said that he had heard I was "considering" having another publisher handle my new novel. Would I please reconsider and at least visit Grafton to meet the rest of their firm?

It seems to me, Anne, that you have and are doing everything in your power to keep me with Grafton. This September I told you that I needed money and so would like to sell my new novel as quickly as possible. You more than hinted that no one but Grafton was interested in my work. In December, after Sonny Mehta and I spoke, I told you that I wanted to return to Picador. Although I am happy with the terms which Picador has offered me, it is now almost April and the contract is still hanging.

I am not an author who makes a great deal of money (as you said, "No one wants me") and a great deal of money is not involved with this new book. Then why has the contract with Picador been delayed? Are you working for me, or for yourself?

As must by now be obvious, I simply feel that we do not get along. Frankly I am frightened of you and feel unwilling and unable to talk to you. Furthermore I feel that there is neither understanding nor respect for my work. Though I am fond of Uli Rushby-Smith [another Curtis Brown agent] I think that it might be better for me to leave Curtis Brown and wonder how this can be done as smoothly as possible.

Yours,
Kathy Acker

McDermid, for her part, barely remembered any of this. It was likely, she said, that she simply didn't want to break the contract with Grafton. As for Acker's vituperation, McDermid said, simply, "I probably wasn't there enough." By the fall of 1986, Uli Rushby-Smith had indeed taken over for McDermid, and Acker would remain at Curtis Brown awhile longer. (Peter Ginsberg, also of Curtis Brown, was her American agent.)

But Acker's relationships with literary agents would follow a similar trajectory for the rest of her career. She switched agents even more often than she changed homes, chronically dissatisfied, and moving, over time, from Curtis

Brown to Antony Harwood to Ira Silverberg to Ellen Levine and William Morris and many others in between. "She would call me each time she was changing an agent," Neil Gaiman said, "which I think she did for pretty much each book. She would also pretty much change publishers for each book. She would keep feeling let down, and then change agents, change publishers, which actually was really bad. That was, I felt, the period of her career when she was actually writing the most important stuff. It was coming out and it should have been paid attention to, but the fact was that there was never traction."

CHAPTER 31

———————— ✕ ————————

IN OCTOBER 1986, GROVE PUBLISHED *DON QUIXOTE* AND BROUGHT Acker back to the U.S. for a month-long tour. Ira Silverberg was Grove's publicity director, a twenty-four-year-old wunderkind, and he believed—or at least he said he believed—that the novel would be the one to really, finally, make Acker's reputation in the States. To make good on that claim, though, he would have to find sympathetic editors at media outlets more glossy or mainstream than, say, *Artforum*. "We believe with *Don Quixote* Kathy Acker will finally break out in America," Silverberg wrote to *Vanity Fair*'s Wayne Lawson on May 5, 1986, one of many major journalists he reached out to. At the same time, he pursued the academic market, courting university professors in the hopes of reviews and booking Acker, on her tour, at art galleries and museums in addition to the usual bookstore and festival appearances.

In retrospect, *Don Quixote* seems perhaps the least likely of Acker's books to find mainstream success—it's too dense, too initially bewildering—but it had received some relatively good press in the UK: the *TLS* called it "gruesomely clever and subversive," and even *Punch* weighed in: "This new novel shows Acker growing and extending her brilliant poetic conception of American life today."

When Silverberg began this publicity campaign, he had not yet met Acker, but he'd long been in her approximate orbit. As a precocious, gay fifteen-year-old living in the Bronx, Silverberg had discovered both *Naked Lunch* and cocaine—on the same day, he liked to say, a "spiritual double whammy"—and both Burroughs and drugs would alter the shape of his life for many years to come. By eighteen, he had become James Grauerholz's boyfriend, and the following year, he moved out to Lawrence, Kansas, where Burroughs and his retinue lived. When Silverberg came back to New York a few years later, he worked as a publishing assistant for Peter Mayer at Overlook Press while moonlighting on weekends as the VIP doorman at Limelight. In 1985, Barney Rosset hired him at Grove, where he quickly took over the company's PR. Later, he would become an editor at the press, signing both Gary Indiana and Dennis Cooper.

Silverberg's tenure at Grove could be tempestuous. His drug use frequently landed him in rehab, and he and Fred Jordan often clashed. Things with Acker didn't go so smoothly either, at least at the outset. From London, she fretted about the publicity campaign, accusing him of "whitewashing" her. "What happens when people see me or read the books?" she asked. Making matters worse, she felt that Grove was both ripping her off and burying the book: inadequately funding her tour, not doing a hardcover edition, sending her on what she dismissively called "the poetry circuit."

It wasn't quite clear that Silverberg fully appreciated the context of her writing either. At the very least, he could be dismissive of it. In an internal memo from March 6, 1986, he wrote, "I've finally gotten some information on how to get to the 'academic market' for Acker. As the methods by which one gets in contact with these semiotic types makes about as much sense as the field they study, it would probably be easiest to discuss it in person." Several months later, he still expressed frustration over what he considered a listless market, one in which there was a lot of talk but very little in the way of sales. But Silverberg tried to allay Acker's fears, writing that the goals of his campaign were multifarious. Primarily, he wanted to update her image and thereby broaden her appeal: "Our intention is merely to take an image that has been tainted by the media (and just clean it up a little). In other words, no more PUNK shit. It's about art and semiotics now not about being a punk who writes cunt & shit on every page—as some critics, unenlightened as they are, try to label you."

When they finally met that October, this was mostly behind them. "We had a million friends in common," Silverberg remembered, "and it was like we knew each other forever." He traveled with her a lot on tour, which allowed him to see another side of her—the vulnerability, the sadness. She could still be entitled though; after Silverberg put her up in LA at the downtown Hotel Figueroa, she wrote immediately to complain: "I deserve better than this!"

Silverberg's PR efforts largely paid off. He'd assembled a clutch of high-powered blurbs for the book, from Burroughs, Richard Foreman, Rudy Wurlizter, and the poet John Giorno, and booked a photo shoot for Acker with Kate Simon, well known for her portraits of musicians like Bob Marley and the Clash. When *Don Quixote* was launched at an apartment on Hudson Street, the lively party was captured by journalist Caryn James in a long *Times* magazine feature on New York's evolving literary worlds. While the article focused mainly on the stars of the so-called Brat Pack—Jay McInerney and

Tama Janowitz—several contrasting paragraphs were devoted to Acker and the downtown writing scene. Acker said again that she had left New York because she couldn't afford to live there, but revealed that she was "thinking of looking for a teaching job" that would allow her to return home. James also perceptively sketched the growing pains that were starting to afflict the scene: "Many of them regard the late 70's as their glory days, when artists and writers and filmmakers ran into each other at the now-closed Mudd Club, before the dispersing effects of success and encroaching middle age had set in. The movement among Kathy Acker's friends is now not out of town but—like it or not—toward the establishment."

Acker had obviously made that move in the UK, and now, in the U.S., she was trying to do the same thing. But Acker was trying to square a familiar circle: how to become part of the establishment while still retaining her artistic freedom. Acker still expected audiences to come to her, and was unyielding as ever. But in England, she had had a taste of acceptance, of legitimacy, and she wanted more.

× × ×

The *Don Quixote* tour took Acker to San Francisco, where she read at City Lights. The reading series there was organized by a twenty-three-year-old staffer named Amy Scholder, who'd long been a fan of Acker's and who would soon start to work as an editor at the bookstore's publishing arm. It was an intense time in the city—"yuppie culture" was in ascendance and the AIDS epidemic was "really turning my world inside out," Scholder said—and Acker's work had helped her cope with this turmoil. "Kathy's work, for me as a girl, spoke out," Scholder said, "and I loved how raw it was and it really wasn't like anyone else's work. She was this punk taking possession of something, because there was no place for her anyway. I loved all of that." Scholder was further delighted, when she finally met Acker, that the person behind the writing was sweet and warm and genuinely excited to meet her. After the reading, Scholder took her to Amelia's, a lesbian bar near her place in the Mission, and introduced her to friends. Acker seemed taken with the nightlife, intrigued by a side of the city she hadn't really known before. Scholder told her that she might feel "better" about herself in a "gay world." Acker said she would consider moving back to San Francisco.

But things soured at the end of the night. Scholder drove Acker back to her hotel. They kissed. But then Acker started musing aloud about whether or not she should take the younger woman up to her room. "Oh, you're so cute," Acker said, "I'd love to invite you up, but I'm leaving town and I have an early flight, and I'll be really tired." As she deliberated, Scholder grew increasingly irritated. Scholder hadn't even wanted to go up, really, but Acker's vacillation—and seeming indifference to Scholder's thoughts on the matter—turned her off completely. Acker finally got out, both of them swearing at the other as she slammed the car door. It seemed like their relationship was going to begin and end the same day.

Once Acker was back in London, however, things improved. They began to correspond, and were soon exchanging letters several times a month, their missives by turns flirtatious, gossip-filled, and supportive. Acker was clearly happy to have a gay woman to confide in, and gleefully recounted her affairs with both men and women, including a short fling with the writer Melissa Benn, whom she accompanied to the Women's Ball at Islington Town Hall, the pair of them in matching tuxedos. When Bette Gordon came to London to visit, she and Acker talked about making a new film together, which Acker described as "a lesbian *Rebel Without a Cause.*" She and Scholder also talked motorcycles. Acker never drove, but she did learn to ride a motorcycle while in London, and had begun taking further lessons so she could graduate to bigger bikes. "I'm very glad we met," Acker wrote Scholder in her first letter. "I think we're going to know each other for a long while."

This proved very true. Much of Scholder's early editorial work was in some way connected to Acker. She started working full-time at City Lights Publishers about a year after she met Acker, and her first major project was an edition of the annual *City Lights Review* devoted mostly to cultural responses to the AIDS crisis. She reached out to every artist and writer she knew and many she didn't (including Edmund White, Sarah Schulman, Eileen Myles, David Wojnarowicz, Bob Glück, Sue Coe, and Lynda Barry). Scholder invited Acker to contribute, though the latter was skeptical of the notion—"I have a real problem writing anything directly. I mean: what's there to say? AIDS is a disease, not a moral stigma, and the U.S.A. (and other) governments stink?" But she did, finally, submit a short piece titled "Arthur Rimbaud Was Homosexual." A year or so later, Acker would start writing *In Memoriam to Identity*, loosely based on Rimbaud's life.

A few years later, Scholder joined forces with Ira Silverberg to form a paperback imprint called High Risk Books, published by Serpent's Tail in the

UK and Penguin in the U.S., dedicated to innovative fiction and poetry. Acker only ever appeared in the imprint's debut anthology, but High Risk became a home for several writers and performers in Acker's circle: among them, Bob Glück, Gary Indiana, Lynne Tillman, and Diamanda Galás. Scholder wouldn't actually edit or publish Acker herself until she collected a book of her essays for Serpent's Tail, *Bodies of Work*, which came out in 1997, the year that Acker died. But in the years immediately after her death, Scholder would do perhaps more than anyone to maintain the writer's legacy and keep her in the public eye. She helped unearth *Rip-off Red* and *Burning Bombing of America* and convinced Grove to publish both of them, as well as a greatest-hits anthology which she co-edited with Dennis Cooper, called *Essential Acker*. She organized a symposium on Acker in 2002 at NYU, and got Verso, where she worked at the time, to publish the proceedings in a volume called *Lust for Life*. Most recently, she co-edited, with Douglas Martin, a collection of Acker's interviews for Melville House's *Last Interview* series.

"I was concerned that without her promoting the work, without having new work to invigorate the backlist that it would slide into obscurity, out of print," Scholder said. "Who is going to read this? How can I contribute to the legacy-building that needs to happen? But it's precarious. It's all so precarious in the writing and publishing world."

CHAPTER 32

———— ✕ ————

I N MAY 1987, ACKER WROTE SCHOLDER THAT SHE WAS WORKING ON
a new novel. "The new book's swimming: sailors and tattoos and everyone's
gay. Probably just a bunch of dirty shit. I'm having more fun with it than I've
had in years."

A year earlier, Acker had gotten her first tattoo, at the North London studio
of Dennis Cockell, then the city's most renowned tattoo artist. Cockell's shop
was called Exclusive Tattoo, which, as the name suggested, catered to a discerning clientele. It was spotless and comfortable, with a waiting room decorated so
thoroughly with examples of designs and photographs of satisfied customers
that an article in the *Independent* described it as a "heavy metal kindergarten."
Appointments were a must. "I didn't want drunks rolling in off the street,"
Cockell said. Instead, he got a lot of musicians: Steve Jones of the Sex Pistols,
Brian Setzer of the Stray Cats, members of Bananarama, and Stephen Harris,
the nineteen-year-old bassist of the hard rock band Zodiac Mindwarp, that
summer's hottest musical act. Acker had somehow befriended Harris (better
known as Haggis), though he had no recollection of how or why—she was
just suddenly there, "this cool chick from New York," hanging around after
shows—and she admired his tattoos. Haggis took her to meet Cockell.

A year younger than Acker, Cockell was jolly and self-taught, with a full
body suit done in 1974 by Ed Hardy, the legendary American tattooist. He and
Acker took to each other immediately, and over the rest of her time in London,
they had about a dozen sessions together. She was relaxed and laid-back, Cockell remembered, but also knew exactly what she wanted. Her first tattoo was
a tiger on her upper left arm, which she later asked Cockell to augment with a
rose. Over time, he gave her a whole feline family: another cat on her right arm,
and the large tiger on her ass that she showed Alan Moore's daughter. (Though
Cockell isn't certain he did the latter, he does claim it was his design.) Along
the ridge of her back, he tattooed various flowers, including a stylized chrysanthemum whose lavender-and-blue petals spilled down the top of Acker's

shoulder blade like a falling firework. After she left London, Acker would occasionally get more work added to her body, including a large koi across her
back that she had done at Ed Hardy's studio in San Francisco.

Despite Acker's ostensible desire and tolerance for pain, at least in a sexual context, she was less excited about the specific discomfort of a tattoo. She
spoke about its "ecstasy" and the feelings of control it gave her, but she was
also known to pop a couple painkillers before visiting Cockell. "Won't do it
again," she told Scholder after getting the chrysanthemum on her back. "The
spine under needles is a cat in pure pain. Needles hammer into spine right
up through neck into brain. I did find out my pain limit, that I definitely have
limits, and that was and is interesting. But it is, for me, beautiful."

Acker loved tattooing as an art form. There was its obvious association with
criminals and sailors. It was also, like lifting weights, another way to access a
kind of language of the body, to perhaps give it an additional, outlaw vocabulary. It was writing directly on the body, writing that transformed the body.
It's a bit difficult to imagine now, in an era when tattoos are preposterously
ubiquitous, but then it was still a means to signal dissent and difference. In a
1990 interview with *Tattoo Advocate* magazine, Acker called tattooing "a form
of art that's so pure, so untouched by the market system," finding in it "a very
viable and available beauty."

The new novel she told Scholder about was built, in large part, around this
criminality, purity, and beauty. It would be called *Empire of the Senseless*, the
title taken from a horror film series of the same name that ran at the ICA.
(The post-punk band the Mekons, whom Acker later collaborated with, used
the same title for a song of theirs.) She dedicated the book to Cockell—the
first time she'd ever dedicated a book to anyone—though she referred to him
only as "my tattooist." She illustrated it too with her own hand-drawn tattoo
designs, inspired by Cockell's work and others: a skull, a pair of koi with the
caption "Dead Fish Fuck," a pirate ship, and, in homage to a classic Tony Polito
design, a dagger piercing a rose, encircled by a scroll that read "Discipline and
Anarchy"—words that pretty well summed up her artistic practice.

As Acker frequently said, with *Don Quixote* she felt she had come to a creative impasse. In England, she'd encountered the derogatory term "arty," used
as a cudgel against any cultural endeavor deemed insufficiently political or
communitarian. She didn't completely buy it, calling the English "ridiculous
moralists," but such attitudes did make her second-guess her compositional

methods. She didn't want to take texts apart anymore, didn't want to juxtapose them, or excavate their systems of control. "I really wasn't interested anymore, cause you know I thought the society's totally disintegrated. You don't need deconstruction anymore [...] We're wallowing in our own fucking nihilism now."

What she really wanted was to create a new narrative, to find, as she put it, "a myth that people could live by." She wanted to replace the old myths, the old superstructures—the double-bind patriarchal ones, the oedipal ones, the Freudian and Marxist ones—with ones that were less oppressive. How was it possible, she wondered, to live in a nihilistic society without becoming nihilistic yourself? It would be the first of her books to feature characters of some psychological complexity; the first to contain, in its eccentric way, a storyline. "I could summarize the plot of *Empire of the Senseless*," she said. "I couldn't do that with any of my other novels."

To a certain degree, this was true. Like *Don Quixote*, the book is divided into three sections: "Elegy for the World of the Fathers," "Alone," and "Pirate Night," with chapters alternating roughly between two central characters, a pair of terrorists or mercenaries, Thivai and Abhor, who are also occasionally lovers. Thivai's a young man who's always longed to be an amoral pirate, guided by a secret code hidden deep in the CIA's library: "GET RID OF MEANING. YOUR MIND IS A NIGHTMARE THAT HAS BEEN EATING YOU: NOW EAT YOUR MIND." Abhor is a Black cyborg in an incestuous relationship with her father. She works for a boss named Dr. Schreber—a nod to Freud's famous case study, which Deleuze and Guattari and Elias Canetti all saw as an object lesson in the function of power—whom she murders before fleeing to a decaying Paris with Thivai. There, Algerian revolutionaries have taken over, Acker's view being that in an age of relentless corporate control, materialism, and media saturation in the West, only the Muslim world can truly resist.

But even that resistance is not enough in a postcapitalist world—the CIA invades Paris, co-opts the revolution. Abhor is imprisoned, repeatedly beaten, pissed on. Even joining a motorcycle gang and riding off into the sunset, as Abhor, in a long comic setpiece, tries to do, proves futile. Culture—the mind—is impossible to escape. All that one can turn to is the body, and the singular language it produces or which can be written on it—the novel ends with an image of the "Discipline and Anarchy" tattoo, its apparently antipodal message, perhaps, the only reasonable response to an unreasonable world.

This plot unfolds in fits and starts, constantly interrupted by bursts of philosophical analysis, political longueurs, chunks of Arabic. Even in an outwardly more conventional novel, Acker was still using other texts, altering and merging them with her usual zeal—in this case, borrowing from Genet, Guyotat, and Melville again, as well as Frantz Fanon, Mark Twain, C. L. R. James's history of the Haitian Revolution, *The Black Jacobins*, and long passages from William Gibson's cyberpunk classic *Neuromancer*, which gave the book its science fiction–like aspect.

Acker was thrilled to discover Gibson, whom she saw picking up the Burroughsian torch and running with it. Gibson had read *Don Quixote* by then, at least, and, in their brief surviving correspondence, told Acker she was "an astonishing writer," before confessing to his own, more subterranean, textual thievery. "We don't call it plagiarism, dear," he wrote. "The word is collage. I'm a compulsive, myself." He asked her if he himself could use a line from *Don Quixote* in his next novel, *Mona Lisa Overdrive*.

Empire's shape is typically jagged, its effects only occasionally hospitable. Acker wanted to explore, and thus "break," various taboos—homosexuality, underage sex, tattooing—believing, quixotically, that to work through these taboos on page would somehow neutralize them, and take her, and the reader, to a place where such taboos no longer held power. She spelled out this ambition in a few paragraphs at the heart of the book itself, concluding: "Nonsense doesn't per se break down the codes; speaking precisely that which the codes forbid breaks the codes."

But when Acker spoke about the book, she was quite happy to court nonsense—or at least induce confusion in her interlocutor—and once again flaunt her resistance to systematic thinking. As in this exchange with Ellen G. Friedman in the Fall 1989 *Review of Contemporary Fiction*:

ACKER: [. . .] I'm looking for a myth. I'm looking for it where no one else is looking. That's why I'm so interested in Pasolini.

FRIEDMAN: The myth never surfaces?

ACKER: The myth to me is pirates.

FRIEDMAN: Pirates is the myth?

ACKER: Yes. It's like the tattoo. The most positive thing in the book is the tattoo. It concerns taking over, doing your own sign-making. In England (I don't know if it's so much true here), the tattoo is very

much a sign of a certain class and certain people, a part of society
that sees itself as outcast, and shows it. For me tattooing is very
profound. The meeting of body and, well, the spirit—it's a *real* kind
of art, it's on the skin. It's both material and not material and it's
also a sign of the outcast. So that's what I'm saying about looking
for the myth with people like that—tattoo artists, sailor, pirates.

FRIEDMAN: They represent the outcasts?

ACKER: Not just outcasts—outcasts could be bums—but people
who are beginning to take their own sign-making into their own
hands. They're conscious of their own sign-making, signifying
values really.

FRIEDMAN: The wordplay in the book is quite wonderful, the
relation between "tattoo" and "taboo," for instance. That's one of
the things I was going to ask you about—tattooing. Is the tattooist
an image of the writer?

ACKER: No, the tattooist is an image of the tattooist. I'm much more
simple. The tattooist is the tattooist. The tattooist is *my* tattooist.
I'm heavily tattooed.

FRIEDMAN: But you were just talking about the tattooist as a sign-
maker.

ACKER: Oh, the writer could do the same thing. I'm fascinated with
the relationship between language and the body [...]

Acker's inconsistencies—or evasiveness—aside, when she does describe tattooing in *Empire*, it is with a lucid, even beautiful, force. Over the course of
several pages midway through the novel, a Cuban sailor named Agone stum-
bles across a store "so narrow and signless it was invisible." He enters, and experiences the sheer wonder and delight that Acker presumably felt when she
first walked into Dennis Cockell's tattoo shop:

As he entered the shop, he felt himself to be in a "mysterious region,"
a place more precious than any he had ever visited. Here must be his
sexual desire. White papers of all sizes covered the clean white walls.
Female pirates, snakes winding around razor-sharp white swords,
sapphire cats larger than a human head whose fingernails were black
or blackened roses, anchors stuck into the tails of large scarlet and

magenta fish whose eyes held the oddities of the rainbow covered the white pieces of paper. The walls were worlds.

× × ×

While Acker was finishing up *Empire* she met a German cultural journalist named Rainer Weber, possibly on a flight to New York in September 1987. Weber worked for *Der Spiegel*, and was married with a child, even more un-available than Lotringer or Wollen because he also lived in Hamburg. But Mel Freilicher recalled him as handsome, blond, urbane, charming, well dressed, "slightly leather-y," and Acker was utterly smitten. So smitten, in fact, that she told Freilicher she wanted to have a child with him—a "momentary gushing of feelings" that quickly blew over. Over the next couple years, she and Weber would rendezvous frequently in London, Germany, or New York, where they went to concerts (Sun Ra, on one occasion), frequented restaurants, and had sex. To her friends, she called him the German or, more frequently, the Germ.

Acker told Amy Scholder she and Weber got along "on every level," but the relationship, in fact, was almost entirely characterized by its intense sadomas-ochism. Acker told Freilicher that she and Weber never had intercourse—"I've never met a man less interested in his dick than Rainer," she said—and though this wasn't entirely true, their sex life consisted mostly of ever more risky and complicated S and M play. Ira Silverberg remembered a story about Weber "forcing" Acker to orgasm simply by looking at her from across a hotel lobby, but Acker's description of their play in a letter to Scholder made things sound far more abject, even dangerous. He hurt her often, and was not always respect-ful of her limitations. At least once he made her lick her dirty kitchen floor. Ultimately, though, Acker claimed that she never did anything she didn't want to do. "It's the only sex I've ever had that I keep growing more interested in," she told Scholder, "rather than becoming bored."

The S and M was one thing, but as had happened before, it was Weber's vacillation over his marriage—claiming he was going to leave repeatedly, but then never following through—that pushed Acker to the edge. She was con-stantly distressed by his absence and elusiveness. To Jürgen Ploog, a German writer she befriended around the same time, she wrote, "I can't figure Rainer out, he seems to refuse to give me up but he doesn't want me either. I haven't been so messed up in a relationship since I was a kid." At one point, from

London, she called Lynne Tillman, who didn't know Weber at all, and asked her to phone him in Germany to find out why he wasn't calling Acker. Tillman didn't make the call.

Acker was in her early forties, and such torture was now much different, and more humiliating, than when she was a younger woman. "Dull tale," she told Scholder, wearily. She claimed that he drank too much, in order to blot out the frustrations and dissatisfaction of his marriage, she said, but that the alcohol also had the effect of making him "too scared and bourgie to leave the marriage." By the summer of 1989, the relationship had pretty much run into the ground.

But the affair would leave a lasting mark, inspiring several sinister scenes in her next novel, *In Memoriam to Identity*, and give her a life lesson that she passed on, a few years later, to another lover, McKenzie Wark: "Rainer (that lovely Germ Nazi who almost wrecked my life) taught me something valuable. I used to ask him, 'Do you love me?' Well, I asked him once and learned better. He replied, good old journalist that he was, what I feel about you is my business, and what you feel about me is your business. Pay attention to your own business. I learned a lot from that one."

CHAPTER 33

———— ✕ ————

F OR MUCH OF HER WRITING LIFE, ACKER HAD REGARDED WILLIAM Burroughs as something of a god. She occasionally grumbled about the misogyny of his books, but his formal innovations and his ideas around writing had changed her life. For years, she had existed somewhere on the periphery of his life, primarily through Lotringer, Grauerholz, and Silverberg, and though never quite part of his inner circle, she was something like a valued disciple. Despite blurbing her books, it's unlikely Burroughs ever actually read more than a few pages of them. But he did enjoy talking about other people's writing and ideas with her. "William was always amused by her," Silverberg said. "Kathy would go in and talk about books and that's how you kept William going."

On June 1, 1988, the October Gallery in London held an exhibition of Burroughs's so-called shotgun paintings, and Burroughs flew in for the occasion. Acker attended the opening, alongside the likes of Genesis P-Orridge, Francis Bacon, and J. G. Ballard. While Burroughs was in town, she agreed to do a two-hour interview with him for a television series coproduced by the ICA and the *Guardian*. Things didn't go particularly well. She was reluctant to do it in the first place, feeling "frightened," and Burroughs didn't do much to put her at ease. Acker's friend Michael Bracewell accompanied her to the interview and said that Burroughs was, in fact, "vile" to her. A rattled Acker later reported to Jürgen Ploog:

> He was his usual old nasty self. I love the "nice old coot" con that he's got going. The idiots actually believe it. "What a nice old man." At one point he told me that poison was a very lately [*sic*] development in animal survival. I said, "I didn't know that." William: "Know your facts, young lady." He seems to relate to interviewers, and to people in general, these days on how well they know guns. Frankly—which doesn't negate the power of the work for me, especially the earlier more

experimental work—I'm sick of the whole gun, lemur, etc. business. Who gives a fuck? Some sort of weird machismo. Or he's been on the booze and drug line too long.

This tension was all too apparent when the interview was later broadcast. Acker is uncharacteristically shy, deferential, solicitous, straining to get Burroughs to open up and give more thoughtful answers. Burroughs hardly rises to the occasion; throughout the broadcast, he's mostly dismissive, condescending, grumpy.

Acker held a far different opinion, however, the following year, when she read with him on a bill at the University of Toronto in March. It was a large reading, just the two of them addressing a capacity crowd at the school's Convocation Hall. It would be one of Burroughs's last readings—he preferred to just paint by that point—but still, Acker found him in a far more open and congenial mood. They spent a lot of time talking one-on-one, and this time she told Ploog, "I feel as if I've been let into a part, a space of Burroughs, I never suspected. A truly delicate, loving man, as gentle a person as I've ever met. Polite in the deepest, truest sense. I am still, what, overwhelmed . . ." Soon, when she was thinking about leaving London behind, and casting about for a place to live, Burroughs urged her to move to Lawrence. "Can you see me being Mrs. Burroughs?" she asked Ploog. "There's one for someone's books."

× × ×

Empire of the Senseless was published in the UK in the spring of 1988, and in the U.S. later that fall. It received a lengthy and adulatory review in the *New York Times*, even making it on the paper's year-end list of notable books. In the *Village Voice*, Acker's friend Cynthia Carr called it "her best and toughest work yet."

In England, however, the response was savage. The book was trashed in the *Guardian*, the *London Review of Books*, and other places, with a May 12 review in the *Independent* exemplary of the reception:

> *Empire of the Senseless* is remarkable on two counts: it is almost certainly the first novel in the English language to be dedicated to its author's tattooist, and it has nothing else to recommend it. Nasty and cantankerous, it is unredeemed by a moment's wit and seems incapable of taking

the most fleeting pleasures from the world. Kathy Acker's new line in post-punk fiction is petulant, otiose, maudlin, sentimental, undisciplined and incoherent. Otherwise, it's fine ... *Empire of the Senseless* is thus tiresome rather than troublesome. It must be to Acker's chagrin that her career embodies the old paradox that those who wish to *epater la bourgeoise* are often taken to its bosom and invited to talk at length about themselves on *The South Bank Show*.

The *TLS* reviewed *Empire* alongside a volume of novellas by Michael Bracewell, Don Watson, and Mark Edwards titled *The Quick End*, panning both, and concluding, "That Kathy Acker has spawned acolytes does not as yet give cause for celebration." Acker felt like she'd been kicked in the stomach. "Much worse than *Blood and Guts*," she wrote Scholder. "Every major newspaper and magazine slashed, not so much the book, as me."

The reviews were so venomous and personal, Acker thought she could very well be kicked out of the country. And by that point, it wouldn't have been the worst thing. Despite her friendships, despite the considerable work she received, she wanted to be somewhere else. With the Germ in Berlin, perhaps, or back in New York. "I can't take the isolation anymore," she told Scholder. "I can't fight a class system by myself. I need my community back because, learning my needs, I need support in bad times." When she visited New York, she usually now stayed at the Gramercy Hotel. In the late eighties, it still had both a genteel charm and a rock 'n' roll pedigree—Dylan, the Stones, and the Clash were frequent guests; Blondie's Debbie Harry and Chris Stein had lived there in 1978, after a fire destroyed their apartment. But for Acker, the sixty-odd-year-old hotel, across the street from the neighborhood's private namesake park, was also one of the few parts of Manhattan that never seemed to change, and as she wrote in *My Mother: Demonology*, "it is, or reminds me of, what I wanted my childhood to be when I was a child." In an interview with Dean Kuipers at the Gramercy on July 2, she said, "I just miss my country."

Acker could give as well as she took, however. In interviews, she often bad-mouthed the English, complaining about the country's pervasive class system, its moralizing, its monstrous prime minister. She argued that the English were arrogant and smug in their cultural supremacy, that there was no real literary avant-garde in the UK, even no real art. "In England, art is not accepted really," she told Lotringer. "It's what you're allowed to do if you're rich, or if you're upper middle class, but it's not considered seriously." In one low moment, she told a friend that it was a "dead country" and that all that was keeping her there was her motorcycle.

Some of Acker's English friends felt that she had never truly adjusted to life in London, or more precisely, that she didn't quite get the place. "Kathy didn't understand London," Roz Kaveney said. "And got treated quite shabbily by various people. People she didn't understand knifing her in the back. Kathy came to feel that she was in a foreign country where people didn't have her back." For Cynthia Rose, she had never quite stopped being a New Yorker, never stopped being someone whose career came first.

This all came to a head in the summer of 1989. That June, Pandora released *Young Lust*, a collection that included *Kathy Goes to Haiti*, *Florida*, and *The Adult Life of Toulouse Lautrec*. An alert publishing reporter noticed Acker's use of passages from Harold Robbins's *The Pirate* and, while ignoring the context and literary history of such cut-up experimentation, accused Acker of simply plagiarizing Robbins. The reporter phoned Acker's editor at Pandora, whom Kaveney called "pig-shit ignorant" about the history of cut-up and appropriation, too. The reporter than called Robbins's English publisher, Hodder & Stoughton, and Eric Major, Hodder's managing director, in turn, called Robin Hyman, owner of Pandora's parent company, Unwin Hyman. Major wanted the book removed from stores and for Acker to submit an apology. Acker was appalled and incensed, writing to Lotringer soon after this all blew up:

> I was informed and replied that they could do what they wanted with the book but I was never going to apologize for my work. Thereupon began a tale. I was threatened by Pandora, had to leave my house to finish novel, finally unable to bear pressure, said I'd sign the apology if there would be no further harassment. Neither Eric Major nor Robin Hyman were willing to promise to stop harassment and litigation. Of course I'm presumed guilty by everyone: what is this postmodernism? How can I use other people's texts!! Burn the witch!!! Etc. Guilty prior to trial. None of them of course are interested in what I've got to say about what I do. The whole mess keeps on going and I'm well paranoid.

By that point, Acker's work had been banned in various places—most notably, West Germany, which added *Blood and Guts* to a list of publications "harmful to minors." But this was censorship of a more pernicious kind. Fred Jordan, her old editor at Grove, stood by her, telling the *Daily Telegraph* that "anyone who knows anything about post-modern writing knows appropriation is a common literary technique." But nobody in London, Acker felt, showed even a whit of support or understanding—not her agents, not her publishers, not even her friends. (Kaveney disagreed with this assessment—she, for one, did support Acker, but Acker, she said, never bothered to ask for her guidance.) After much presumably rancorous back-and-forth, Anne McDermid said she would no longer discuss the matter with Acker on the phone, but that "it would be best if you communicated with me in writing only from now on." As for Harold Robbins, he seemed to find the whole episode faintly amusing. "I am outraged," he said, "shocked but mildly flattered that someone thinks my prose is worth stealing." Jordan got Burroughs, who shared an agent with Robbins, to intervene, which he did. The book was never withdrawn, and no legal action ever initiated. Robbins said Acker could do whatever she wanted with his words.

The damage was done, however. At some point during the rigamarole, Acker did apparently sign an apology, telling her publisher that she was essentially apologizing "for twenty years of work."* Her entire literary project had been threatened. Her books had been threatened. *She* had been threatened, and told what to do, how to behave. Such censorship wasn't, of course, as bad as the fatwa that Rushdie faced, but, in Acker's mind, it was close enough. "What if I was in this country and anything seriously political ever happened to me?" she said to an interviewer. "I'd be screwed." It was time to leave London.

× × ×

Somehow, through all this drama, Acker was still able to keep her mind on her writing. She considered cowriting a book on bodybuilding with her trainer, a book on vodoo with Darius James. But all the stuff with Robbins and the German would go into the new novel, *In Memoriam to Identity*.

---

* Acker suggested that the apology was published "in all the literary magazines" as well as in the *Times*. This doesn't appear to have been the case, and no original of the apology was ever found either. In the *Daily Telegraph* article, however, Eric Major does acknowledge receiving "apologies." A letter from Anne McDermid to Acker on August 14, 1989, indicated that the "statement" would be published in the *Bookseller* and *Publishing News*, and that Unwin Hyman would send this statement in with or without Acker's participation.

Grove had commissioned *Memoriam* for their summer 1990 lineup, the first time Acker had ever taken an advance on an unwritten book or worked to deadline. She received $30,000 from Grove, £15,000 from Pandora. She found the pressure of a deadline bothersome, but it did seem to concentrate her mind. *In Memoriam to Identity* was one of her worst titles, but it would end up being one of her most beguiling books. The book was initially called *Men* (simply for the fact that she didn't want to include any women in it), and was originally going to be about a Japanese tattoo artist. That idea survived only in the form of a short chapter, "A Japanese Interlude," and in a series of gory illustrations that Acker made by tracing images in a book about the *ukiyo-e* artist Taiso Yoshitoshi. The rest of the book is taken up once again with the search for a myth, this time the myth of romantic love. One could argue that such a myth animates all of Acker's novels, and that wouldn't be wrong, but here at least, that search begins with a homosexual relationship, the short-lived, violent affair between the teenaged Arthur Rimbaud and the older, married Paul Verlaine.

On one hand, she said, she wanted to write a "life of Rimbaud," to rescue the antisocial French poet from the dustbin of history and to reaffirm her artistic lineage. As she told Jürgen Ploog, "My agent actually sent me a letter in which she said that it's hard to sell my books because my writing's too much like Burroughs' and Genet's. I want to remember who Rimbaud and Genet are." Rimbaud hardly needed such recuperation—he'd been the poster boy for every self-styled rebel since at least Jim Morrison. In any case, once Acker began researching his biography in earnest, and discovered that, after retiring from poetry, Rimbaud became a gunrunner in Africa, she switched tacks. "This guy became a fucking capitalist!" she told the literary critic and anthologist Larry McCaffery in an interview. "He's like a yuppie, I can't do this, I'm bored out of my mind!" She, and the book, went into different directions, therefore, primarily into William Faulkner's novels *Sanctuary*, *The Sound and the Fury*, and *Wild Palms*. Acker was homesick. She wanted to write about America, and she'd always felt that Faulkner was the most American of writers.

Faulkner gave her other myths, other mirrors. In Faulkner's fiction, history repeats and repeats and repeats. What *was* is never over. What *was* always occurs again, the past forever imprinting itself on, transfiguring, the present. This was, in a somewhat different way, the way that time operated in Acker's books as well. In his life and fiction, Faulkner could never escape the Civil War and the racism that led to it. Acker couldn't escape the enmity of her past or present culture and the sexism that shaped that. She marries these things in one parenthetical aside: "In Faulkner's novels, men who are patriarchs either kill or maim by subverting their daughters. Every daughter has a father; every daughter might need a father." In an interview, she clarified this further—"I think what Faulkner does with women in his novels is they never have their own voice [. . .] And they're like holes, but they are very important holes. So what I want to do is sort of take these absent voices and make them *the* voices."

In *Memoriam*, Acker returns again to the Muller twins, to Fun City, to her marriage to Peter Gordon, Claire and Bud's sad marriage, Claire's tragic death—shards of memory dulled and distorted by time but still destructive. "In a sense, I was trying to recover my own childhood," Acker said, specifically talking about Rimbaud and the inspiration he held for her when she was young. What made Rimbaud want to flee the world, to run into books, and what ultimately foreclosed that escape? How was her own getaway so similarly doomed?

Rainer Weber looms over the book's second half. Acker goes into an unusual amount of sordid, and seemingly true, detail, with the book's final chapter, "An End to Childhood," depicting the conclusion of the affair as a grim stalemate between two narcissistic extremists. The German's departure, finally, casts her into the oblivion that she both craves and fears. For so long, Acker had insisted that writing could create a new and better world, but here, that alchemy seems to reach its limit:

> To write is not to record or represent a given action, but to lose one's capacity to be the subject or initiator of that action. I lose myself, in putting down memories, in writing, but I don't escape the fatality of the events, their weight and their irreversibility, merely because I cannot claim them for myself. What happens to me happens to no one, because what happens is my exclusion from what is happening. I am no longer able to participate in transformation: Stuck; stuck in prison; pain.

The amount of verbatim autobiography made Acker a little uneasy, even embarrassed, and at various times, she fretted that the book was "a bit limited" or "too narrow and personal." But *In Memoriam* has a narrative power that she only rarely summoned before, and the critical theory is wisely submerged.

Though Acker could revise her opinions on a dime—especially about her own work—she told at least one friend that it was her favorite of her novels.

While working on the novel, Acker wrote an essay, "Dead Doll Humility," about the Robbins episode, publishing it in a Serpent's Tail anthology called *Seven Cardinal Virtues*. It was a relatively straightforward, comprehensive account of the controversy, and of Acker's thoughts on originality, voice, copyright, the politics of literature, and censorship. Acker called herself Capitol in the essay, "an artist who makes dolls"—"I can't make language, but in this world, I can play and be played." She pushes her playthings—a Feminist Publisher doll, an Agent doll, a Writer doll—into an absurd legal battle that, in the end, amounts to nothing more than an inconsequential misunderstanding.

In *Memoriam*, Capitol returns. She makes more dolls, which by the book's end, she has decapitated. Acker refuses to conclude on such a fatalistic note, however. The book's final line—" 'Sexuality,' she said, 'sexuality' "—feels plaintive but also open-ended, another movement back to the body and desire.

Reviews for the novel were, as always, mixed. *Publishers Weekly* rightly observed that "Acker writes with the coldest beauty and the most perfervid excess; she will find the audience that wants nothing in between," while in the *Times*, Stephen Schiff unleashed a litany of stinging one-liners: "Ms. Acker, whose erudition is incontestable, whose ferocity is unmistakable and whose prose, I'm afraid, is unreadable." A few years later, however, Acker would receive a fan letter from the illustrious science-fiction writer Samuel Delany, whom she first met at a reading at Brown. It was a missive arguably worth more than every other critical opinion put together: "The last novel of yours which I wrapped myself up happily in was *In Memoriam to Identity* [...] People talk a lot about the anger in your work, but what I see is a just a great deal of intellectual and observational fun, sometimes at an intensity that's [*sic*] borders on the scary. But angry . . . ? I mean *more* angry than anyone might be at the various angering things that go by in the midst of generally responding to the world within and without . . . ?"

× × ×

By the end of the summer of 1989, Acker was desperate to leave England. But she needed to first sell Riverview Gardens and the British economy was "not so much sliding as diving into economic depression." She herself was "broke," as she told a number of people, though a letter she had sent to an American financial services firm a few months earlier painted a more rosy picture. In it, she recounted the number of countries that she was then published in (the U.S. and UK, but also Germany, Denmark, France, Finland, Spain, and soon, Italy and Japan). Her letter also detailed some recent journalistic work, discussed various upcoming performances and readings, claiming that she received a minimum fee of $800 per, and occasional teaching gigs. She writes that she's a hundred pages into a new novel, and is "not worried about selling."

By that point, she'd initiated an exit plan, enlisting Amy Scholder to find her a teaching job at the San Francisco Art Institute. Which Scholder did, through no small amount of effort, persuading the chair of the school's humanities department to adjust his budget at the last minute and offer Acker a position for either that fall or winter. To Scholder's irritation, though, Acker turned it down, or at least asked the Art Institute to defer the offer. She wanted to finish *Memoriam* first, she said, but she also, it seems, hadn't completely given up on New York.* While weighing her options, she called Lynne Tillman for advice. "What will my career be like in New York?" Acker asked. Tillman was candid, and accurate. "Well, you're not going to go on television here," she said. "And you're not going to be the only New Yorker, the only American. It's going to be very different, Kathy." Acker told her that she was thinking of giving up Riverview Gardens and buying an apartment in New York. Tillman told her to just sublet the London place to someone and then sublet something herself in New York—a more prudent way to test the waters.

Acker didn't listen, or didn't care. According to Tillman, when she couldn't sell her flat, and no longer wanted to wait to return to the States, she just "let the mortgage go." Again, she simply fled. Tillman was baffled, but felt, ultimately, that that move was a reflection of Acker's general disregard for money. "Certainly, she didn't care about money," Tillman said. "If she was a materialist, it was only about clothes. I think she loved wearing great clothes and I think it made her happy to buy clothes. But other than that, she didn't give a shit about that stuff." The *Voice* critic Cynthia Carr, who first met her during

---

* Or the UK, for that matter. While the chronology is murky—even for those involved—Acker had also purchased a basement flat in Brighton at some point around this time. She'd always liked the seaside town, read there often, and knew lots of people there. (Genesis P-Orridge had moved there for a spell.) She enlisted several friends (Kaveney, Gaiman, her last UK publisher, Gary Pulsifer) to help with the search, the purchase, and the renovation. But in the end, she never even lived in the place, and ended up abandoning it too.

this period, observed this fiscal indifference too: "In some ways, it was easy come, easy go."

Acker returned to New York in September 1989, and set about finding a new place. Lotringer accompanied her to a meeting with her trustee. She wanted to buy another apartment, but told Lotringer that she couldn't afford it, that all she had left to her name was the trust and a painting worth $50,000 (by whom, Lotringer didn't remember). Nevertheless, she managed to get enough released from the trust to put a payment down on a studio at 39 East 12th Street, a stone's throw away from the Strand. Lotringer didn't like the place, found it "very dark," but it was central, with a doorman. It was a small, utilitarian place, notable only for the sheer number of books, of course, and a big loft bed covered in mirrored pillows and stuffed animals. Carr would drop by from time to time, once when Roz Kaveney was visiting. All three sat on the couch to watch *Paris is Burning,* Jennie Livingston's acclaimed documentary on the New York drag balls of the eighties, before having a vigorous discussion about trans sex workers. Tillman remembered Acker throwing a party at the apartment soon after she moved in. Other writers were there: Gary Indiana, Patrick Mc-Grath. Acker was excited to introduce everyone to her Norwegian publisher, who was also in town. Later, though, it seemed to Tillman that Acker was disappointed when she wasn't invited, reciprocally, over to Tillman's or Indiana's home. But then neither Tillman nor Indiana ever invited people over to their respective tiny Easy Village apartments; they met people in restaurants and bars. Or maybe, Tillman thought, Acker wanted them to introduce her to *their* foreign publishers, which at that point they didn't even have. Tillman found it all very confusing. "To me, she was already an established, well-published person," she said. "I hadn't even been published in England at that point. Looking back, I didn't know what she wanted."

It's unclear if Acker did either. From the beginning of her career, success had meant simply being able to write as she wanted for as long as she wanted. That definition of success still pertained, and the inheritance had given her that freedom for a few years. But it still wasn't enough. While she wouldn't have used such language, she wanted to be *seen.* She required validation, support, unconditional love. But it seemed she also hated herself for needing those things and, worse, having to ask for them.

Returning to New York, Acker expected that she would just pick up where she had left off so many years ago. She expected that things with her friends hadn't really changed or that she herself hadn't really changed. She'd certainly been back often enough to know this wasn't at all true, but, oddly, this hadn't completely sunk in. Or she didn't want it to sink in.

But many things had changed. Everyone was older, and their ambitions and priorities had evolved. A few of Acker's friends had settled down, got married, had children—Bette Gordon, for instance, as well as Bob Glück, Peter Wollen, and Leslie Dick. The gentrification that Acker had complained about before moving to England had become much worse, with the neighborhoods that she'd formerly lived in now more homogenous and affluent, and the one that she had just moved to, at the outermost edge of Greenwich Village, even more so. While, on the one hand, the art world was now much richer, it had also been devastated by AIDS—between 1989 and 1992, the disease had killed many of Acker's friends and compatriots, including Mapplethorpe, Jimmy DeSana, Cookie Mueller, Carl Apfelschnitt, David Wojnarowicz, and Keith Haring, just to name the most famous.

Others, like Tillman and Indiana, Patrick McGrath and Dennis Cooper, had built serious literary careers, and a couple of them were now fellow Grove authors. Some had teaching positions. Darius James would soon publish his debut novel, *Negrophobia*, a scatological, hyperactive, and still-shocking attack on white supremacy that Acker admired even as it made her excesses look almost quaint. While Acker had been away, the downtown writing scene had become an outright phenomenon, memorialized in fat books like Brian Wallis's *Blasted Allegories* and Robert Siegle's *Suburban Ambush*. Even *Between C&D* had been anthologized by Penguin. Other writers and artists that Acker had clearly influenced, like Mary Gaitskill and Acker's old student Karen Finley, had become stars in their own right.

Acker's old competitive streak was roused, even as she found herself irritated by her own sense of envy. In a notebook entry a couple years later, she dramatized this feeling: "Years ago I lost my way, listening to the talk of society. 'Be a success, be someone,' no what society really says are the details 'Gary just got a hundred thousand for his book; Lynn [*sic*] is closing her movie deal . . .' and all this talk made me unable to listen, but to forget that I wanted to listen."

There were also big changes at Grove. In 1985, the press had been purchased by a company owned by Ann Getty, the wife of an heir to the Getty oil fortune, and her friend, Lord George Weidenfeld, the British publisher. Under Getty, the company floundered, with staffers departing en masse, and Getty and Weidenfeld constantly looking for another buyer. In 1993, the company merged with Atlantic Monthly Books, becoming Grove/Atlantic. *In Memoriam to Identity* was, to a certain degree, lost in the shuffle. In 1990, Fred Jordan left for Pantheon, a division of Random House, replacing Pantheon's founder, André Schiffrin. It was a controversial move—Pantheon had long been Schiffrin's domain, and then he was pushed out by Random House's owners, and Jordan was seen by Schiffrin's supporters (and writers) as an interloper. But Jordan took Acker with him, and Pantheon would later publish her next book, *My Mother: Demonology*.

Not very well, according to Ira Silverberg, who had by then left Grove to become a literary agent. Against his better judgment, Silverberg had taken Acker on as a client. Within months, to the surprise of no one, he found himself another object of her discontent. "This is my position," she wrote him in the summer of 1990. "I left Peter Ginsberg for you both because I loved you and felt we had worked together almost as brother and sister for a long time. I trusted you. Once I was with you, I had no one else to whom to turn. Since that point, all of your advice has been wrong." Silverberg wasn't thrilled with the accusation, writing her an immediate response, the gist of which was this: "There has yet to be an agent that you have been satisfied with. The problem is not with your agents." The arrangement wouldn't last a year. "Kathy was big in England," Silverberg said, "but when she got back here, she felt like it fell apart and it was the fault of the people around her. It was my fault, it was the fault of a friend, it was the fault of Grove."

It's possible that Acker's old friends didn't really understand how deeply insecure she could be. She had left them behind to become a literary star; she had acted as if she didn't need anybody, particularly after her inheritance came through. What did she want from them now? In 2016, the poet David Trinidad published *Notes on a Past Life*, a gossipy, raucous memoir in verse—what he called "an experiment in memory"—that includes the poem, "Acker is back in New York." In it, he describes how Acker's circle received her when she returned from London. Coolly, according to Trinidad, and this was the sense that Acker had too. "It's all about *her*," Trinidad recalls Gary Indiana saying; "This just isn't *her*," he remembers Lynne Tillman saying. "I have nothing invested in this/debate, have never met or read/Acker, so I find it interesting/ that they're in such a tizzy," he writes.

The poet and novelist Dennis Cooper met Acker for the first time on Christmas Eve 1989, in the midst of this tumult. He'd long been a fan—a couple years later, he'd host a party for Acker at his apartment in L.A., where he'd ask her to sign all fifteen of her books that he owned. Coming across her work, he said, was revelatory: "Not only was she incredibly experimental, but she was also a woman and she was writing about sex. For me, discovering that, was like, 'Holy, Jesus, I can't believe this is happening in America.'" She too had been an admirer of his, calling his novel *Closer* "an incredibly beautiful and daring book." That December 24, they had a drink at Penn Station. But as admiring of Acker as Cooper was, he was also somewhat wary, careful not to be drawn into her drama. "All of my writer friends in New York knew Kathy but had incredibly difficult relationships with her," he said. "Everybody had this whole thing about how competitive she was, how she used people. And how she liked to meet people to size them up as competition. And I did see her get like that with Mary Gaitskill and stuff. But she wasn't like that with me. I was just this young writer. Maybe she wanted to size me up, but I thought when I was talking to her that she was just genuinely curious about who I was."

A few months later, though, Cooper would be on the receiving end of her misbehavior. On April 9, 1990, he and Gaitskill read at the Kitchen, which had then moved to Chelsea. Acker was in the audience. Cooper performed a section from his novel-in-progress, *Frisk*, along with a few other performance artists and actors; he read the narration, they the dialogue. Gaitskill read from her novel, *Two Girls, Fat and Thin*. It was, Cooper remembered, a strange evening, with both Acker *and* Gaitskill acting "cold" toward him; Gaitskill, he felt, thought he was trying to upstage her. According to Tillman, however, a whole other drama was playing out. Tillman was sitting with her publisher, Ann Patty, when Acker arrived and sat on the other side of Tillman. This was already awkward, Tillman said, as Patty had rejected a manuscript of Acker's, and was also on the fence about Tillman's next manuscript, *Motion Sickness*. (Patty, though, has no recollection of ever receiving a manuscript from Acker.) But then, after Cooper finished his reading, Acker muttered to Tillman, "That was the worst thing. What's happened to Dennis?" and when Cooper came to join them in the audience, she turned her back on him. Then, immediately after Gaitskill read, Acker grabbed Tillman and said, "I need to talk to you right now. Come with me to the back of the room." Tillman was torn—should she leave Patty and Cooper?—but Acker was, she said, an old friend, and she seemed to be in some kind of distress. At the back, Acker asked Tillman what she thought of Gaitskill's reading. "I think Mary's got something," Tillman said. "She's a good writer." Acker was livid, Tillman said. Then, making matters worse, Tillman said that Gaitskill told her she'd been influenced by Tillman's novel, *Haunted Houses*. She tried to explain this to Acker, but Acker cut her off. "I influenced her too, you know," she said, and then stormed out of the Kitchen. Tillman followed her, asking her where she was going. "Home," Acker said. "It has nothing to do with you. It's writing." Tillman tried calling her later to talk about it, even showing up at another of Acker's readings a couple weeks later, but Acker refused to discuss the night. Tillman would speak to her occasionally again, in New York and elsewhere, but their relationship never really recovered. "You were always Kathy's friend," Tillman said. "She was never your friend."

Decades later, it all sounds extremely trivial, childish, and passive-aggressive. From Acker's point of view, however, she had come back to New York for the embrace of her community, the nourishment and nurturing that she had once known, and now that had all vanished. She felt wounded and betrayed yet again. A year later, she finally wrote to Tillman, a letter awash in recrimination and paranoia:

> When I was in New York last year, I was having a hard time. I had returned to a city which I thought was my hometown and found not only a strange place, a city quite changed in which I knew almost no one, but a society into which I no longer fitted. In such circumstances I wanted aid, but I know well that friends, having their own lives, can give little. Our friendship, though old, was unsure due to the many years of being apart. So I understand that you had little time for me except in company of Patrick and Gary. What was hard for me, and still is hard, is, I think more than the feeling, the knowledge that you

have very little respect for me. I could tell from talking to you that you regarded [sic] as some weird, cute sex thing. You do not think that I can think politically or that my work is at all intellectually respectable. When I tried to talk to you about work and competition, you thrust aside this conversation. So I had no way of bringing up issues. Which was fine. It is pleasant to gossip about sexual relations as if that is one's life. A way of relaxing. What is difficult for me is that you want me to consider our friendship seriously when you respect neither me nor my work. I will accept limits, Lynn [sic], but I cannot be hypocritical and act as if someone's my friend who feels no respect for me.

× × ×

Acker was again, somehow, in between things. In her work, it was the place she was most comfortable. But in life, it was becoming increasingly difficult. She wasn't at home in London, and New York didn't seem to want her. The publishing world wasn't quite sure what to do with her either—her books weren't recognizable literary fiction, nor did they fit neatly into an avant-garde ghetto. She wasn't a starving artist anymore, but she couldn't make a real living solely from her fiction. And while it was one thing to be marginal, to be a fighter, when she was young, those fights were too tiresome at her age. "It's hard to live a life against the grain," her friend Betsy Sussler observed. "Who doesn't want to be loved?" Acker had made an art form of destablization, but her own instablity was now a kind of vertigo.

This turmoil was compounded by the fact that, again, she felt completely alone in New York, bereft now of boyfriend or lover. At some point, she ran into Neil Gaiman there, and they met for dinner. After a pleasant meal, Acker invited him back to her apartment. There, she started to complain about her love life, telling Gaiman that it consisted entirely of "giving Richard Hell blow jobs." (Hell later denied this—though he and Acker had, in fact, slept together on occasion, at that point, such things were in the past.) Then, to Gaiman's great surprise, Acker asked him if he would "whip her pussy." She'd already told him about her S and M relationship with Weber, and he, Gaiman—"very vanilla," in his words—had been mildly scandalized. But this was somewhat beyond the pale, particularly because he and Acker had only ever been friends. He found the depth of her need both startling and sad, but eventually agreed to do it. "It was profoundly unsexual," he recalled. "I did it and ran away."

Lotringer's relationship with Chris Kraus also still bothered her. Soon after Acker's return to New York, she met him for three long, wide-ranging interviews. He proposed that they publish an edited version of these conversations in the Semiotext(e) imprint, Native Agents, that Kraus had started. Acker reluctantly agreed, and the following year, when the book came out (the interview titled "Devoured by Myths," in *Hannibal Lecter, My Father*), she was still grumbling about the arrangement. "I did try to get on with Chris; she certainly didn't try with me; and why should I be the one? I'm the one who's been rejected. What did and do you expect, Sylvere [*sic*]? For me to love your wife? I'm not that fucking selfless and there haven't been that many men in my life, not like you. I don't like to be abandoned."

San Francisco was looking more and more attractive. SFAI had held the job for her that Amy Scholder had arranged. They hired her to teach a course called Contemporary Fiction in the summer 1990 session. The Bay Area had offered lots of possibility when she first moved there with Peter Gordon in the 1970s. Now, twenty years later, it held a different kind of promise. She had a community there too, more than one, in fact—Scholder and her queer circle, but also the New Narrative and Language crowds, old friends like Bob Glück, Barrett Watten, and Carla Harryman. The city had a Gold's Gym. It was a good place to ride her motorcycles, and the tattooing scene was strong and active. A lively new subculture was starting to develop around, of all things, personal computers. In a postcard to her old friend Jürgen Ploog, she wrote with excitement, "San Francisco seems to be in another world, its own."

She would dive headlong into it, with the same stubborn optimism that had propelled her other moves across the country and around the world. Now forty-three, she had not given up on the possibility that she would yet find a home that was artistically nourishing and romantically satisfying. "Optimism" is probably not the right word for Acker. As she got older, it shaded more into impetuousness. But she would never stop seeking something new—new ideas for writing, new books, new friends and lovers, new ways of being. San Francisco offered those things again. Its landscape and economy had not yet been deranged by a ravenous tech industry. It was still small and weird and creatively potent.

It was also a place where Acker's star, more so than in London or New York, shone brighter. To the city's post-punk and hardcore communities, in its queer bars and alternative galleries, she was a genius and guide. The coolest kids looked like her, and she looked like them. She shared their contrary exuberance, and showed that it was possible to hold on to that even as you aged. In turn, she would draw from them fresh infusions of inspiration and excitement. The whole place was the perfect set for her fiction, a good backdrop to her myth. Acker had spent her whole life trying to invoke a world where she belonged, and San Francisco at the end of the twentieth century, a city on the precipice of enormous change itself, would be the closest she'd ever get.

THE SCHOOL OF THE SELF

(1990–1997)

CHAPTER 35

———— X ————

I N THE FALL OF 1990, ACKER FOUND A SPACIOUS, MULTI-ROOMED apartment at 929 Clayton Street in Cole Valley, a quaint neighborhood of Victorian row houses, tucked between Golden State Park and the Haight. After Barnes, it was the most physically beautiful landscape she'd ever reside in. Bob Glück helped her furnish the place, which turned out to be a surprisingly easy task. At one point, they stopped at a used furniture store on Valencia so Acker could buy a sofa. She simply walked into the shop, saw an enormous piece across the room, and without even sitting on it or inquiring as to its price, said she'd take it. Glück remembered the apartment as "kind of dumpy," but others found it genteel, even beautiful, and always very tidy. Her dream maps hung on the walls, as well as the Mapplethorpe portrait, and she had a powerful, high-end stereo system. One of her students at SFAI painted the bathroom blood-red and another room black, and alphabetized her many, many books. She continued to keep her collection of stuffed animals arranged in a neat line along the top of her bed, from one end to the other. Another student, Jenna Leigh Evans, remembered this detail with amusement and sadness. "I always got the sense that animals were protective for her," Leigh Evans said, "and that these were totems. But it was striking that this *sex icon* had these. If you were going to fuck Kathy, apparently, you had to first move forty-seven little plush animals off the bed."

As in London, Acker led many different lives in San Francisco. "I always needed to be able to move a lot, so I like to have at least five milieus that I can go back and forth to," she told Larry McCaffery, who interviewed her for *Mondo 2000*, a magazine cofounded in 1989 by a writer and editor who called himself, with Dadaist aplomb, R. U. Sirius. Sirius (née Ken Goffman) was imp-ish, irreverent, and energetic, and *Mondo 2000* captured the convergence of various countercultural phenomena—hackers, the sci-fi offshoot cyberpunk, psychedelics, virtual sex—when the internet was still relatively new, with a utopian sheen. "For the moment, the Net is a free zone," Acker wrote, "for

290 | Jason McBride

those who can afford or access the necessary equipment." William Gibson's books, of course, had given Acker a taste for cyberpunk, and she embraced all of this new digital culture with the zeal of a convert. She was one of the first people in her circle to get an email address.

Acker met Sirius first at a *Mondo 2000*–sponsored preview screening of the Robert Redford movie *Sneakers* (Genesis P-Orridge was her date), and over the next few years, they became friends and occasional lovers. He and his friends helped her get online, first connecting her to the WELL, an early online bulletin board system, and then to AOL, from which she was kicked off for using obscenity in a chat room. Soon, she would start logging into MOOs (online, world-only, multi-user games), where she could adopt different text-only characters or avatars and interact with other players around the world; on LambdaMOO, she named one of her characters rattypussy. "Whenever I'm in Webland," she wrote, "I lose myself in adventuring, in that time-space organism named *web*..." In those pre-cellphone days, Acker carried a beeper, which from time to time she turned into a covert vibrator. Before leaving home, she would insert it into her vagina, and Sirius would call it, sometimes even when she was teaching.

Acker joked later that she was on her computer so much that she barely left her house. But she still kept one foot squarely in San Francisco's more old-school literary worlds, straddling the New Narrative and Language scenes while also befriending neo-noir writers like Richard Kadrey and radical scholars like Avital Ronell, then teaching at Berkeley and working on her book *Crack Wars*. "Kathy *summoned* me," Ronell remembered. "She was working on Bataille and wanted a sidekick or a generator. What was great about Kathy was that she was rogue, she was outrageous, but she really wanted to get it right. In her way, she was very rigorous. She was hungry for what I could do for her. I was hungry for her milieu and her brashness. We were drugs for each other." They began to meet every Sunday for dinner at various restaurants, or would sit on the floor of Acker's apartment, papers spread all about, talking about writers they loved and some they didn't. They disagreed violently, for example, over Heidegger, whom Acker detested even though she hadn't read that much—or, in Ronell's opinion, well. "Like many writers," Ronell said, "she had that narcissistic motor. That meant, if it wasn't on her GPS, she didn't want to hear about it. She didn't want to be stalled or slowed down."

Acker still spent lots of time with Amy Scholder too. They often ate at Zuni

Café, the trendsetting restaurant on Market, celebrated as much for its food as for being "the gayest restaurant in San Francisco." It became Acker's favorite spot, where she would later feed dinner to a blindfolded McKenzie Wark (such was their sex life).

As lively and diverse as Acker's social life was, however, things were quite a bit less satisfying romantically. Straight guys in San Francisco were rare. She sometimes attended meditation retreats at the Zen Center's Green Gulch Farm, and for a while, she dated a Buddhist monk that she, and everyone else, referred to only as the Monk. For about six weeks, she enjoyed an S and M relationship with another married writer, Ted,* to whom, in public, she was "bound" by an invisible leash—he would be in complete command of her behavior and actions. In correspondence with her, he referred to her as "little girl" and "baby." Acker was drawn, Ted said, to dominant males, and he felt that S and M allowed her to "be a complete individual person." That is, "a force in the world to be reckoned with, a strong woman—and that was what her art was about, a woman facing the world squarely and boldly; same with her interaction with the public. She never would have wanted to seem like a submissive in public because she was a feminist. I support feminism and always have. But one's sexual triggers are what they are, and as long as it is between consenting adults, what one does in privacy is private."

Ted was somewhat awed by Acker's physique, describing her as "a tiny little woman but throbbing with muscles," and he was convinced that she took steroids and human-growth hormone supplements. Not considered as dangerous as they are now, both were sold freely at her gym, and he said he saw bottles of them in her bathroom. Ted thought Acker simply wanted to be bigger and more powerful, and the drugs helped make her feel safe. Her outfits were also designed to show off this musculature. At one point, Acker befriended a young writer named Mark Ewert, at different times both Burroughs's and Dennis Cooper's boyfriend, and who would publish Acker in a zine called *Ruh-Roh!*. He was so small, and Acker so strong by that point, she used to literally bench-press him.

San Francisco was a good place too for the regime of self-care that Acker had started to assiduously cultivate. Once she'd moved back, she quickly assembled a network of spiritual advisors—psychics, astrologers, and herbalists—that

---

* A pseudonym.

she called upon with increasing frequency. She also started exploring witch-craft, which she described as "a rather serious alternative history of women," reading about it and meeting with Wicca practitioners. "She had a really mysti-cal side to her," Sirius said. "She really believed in a lot of mystical stuff." Sirius remembered her writing "love letters" to Timothy Leary, which Leary, whom Sirius had known for years, could never quite comprehend.

Her primary psychic, Frank Malinaro, however, spoke her language—or she his. Malinaro was a few years her junior, a manic, gay ex–New Yorker who had, as a younger man, studied acting and worked on Broadway, before an out-of-body experience led him, circuitously, to his present occupation. Acker trusted him completely; they were good friends. He said that they had known each other in a past life, and according to his astrological chart, her being an Aries meant that he "owed" her something from that life. They could talk about books and writers, though not the writers that Acker talked about with her poet and novelist friends; with Malinaro, it was New Agers like James Hill-man and Thomas Moore. "Nobody else was that brilliant in my life," he said of Acker. "It was like having a conversation with a mental ninja." Acker would wrestle with his dog, Chelsea, for hours, a ninety-pound mutt that he said weighed as much as Acker herself. When they went out to dinner or the mov-ies, which they often did, Malinaro was always tickled when somebody would recognize Acker. On occasion, Malinaro recalled, when she would come for a psychic reading, Acker would tape-record their sessions and then use parts of their conversations in her writing: "She'd hand me these autographed books, first editions, and I'd read them and I'd call her and say, 'Hey, Kathy, this chap-ter is word-for-word right out of my apartment! You didn't even change one comma. You just took it right from the tape.' She snapped at me, 'Well, I pay for the reading!'"

× × ×

This community of healers and advisors became so integral to Acker's life that she dedicated her next novel, *My Mother: Demonology*, to one of her astrolo-gers, a woman named Uma. (An early draft of this dedication was more ex-pansive: "This book is dedicated to Uma whose teaching helped me write its second half.") But *My Mother* grew out of many other sources as well—the Dario Argento movies that she would go see with Kevin Killian and Dodie Bellamy (especially *Suspiria* and *Four Flies on Grey Velvet*); Radley Metzger's adaptation of *Therese and Isabelle*; *Wuthering Heights*; Kristeva; Juan Goyti-solo; Ingeborg Bachmann and Paul Celan's relationship and work; the Gulf War; Carlo Ginzburg's *Ecstasies: Deciphering the Witches' Sabbath*. Of primary importance, however, was Laure, the poet and Bataille muse Acker had discovered decades earlier on her first trip to Paris.

Acker first published her translations of Laure in 1983, in *SOUP*, the influential lit mag founded by San Francisco poet Steve Abbott. Beautiful, uncompromising, transgressive, and tragic—the hot center of a French avant-garde—Laure maintained a lasting hold on Acker partly, it seemed, because Acker identified so strongly with her. Acker accompanied those *SOUP* translations with an introductory biography that said as much about herself as it did Laure:

> Laure wrote an autobiographical work *Histoire D'une Petite Fille* that is simultaneously "realistic" and visionary (a logical impossibility that explodes), poems, political essays, in short, the writing of fluctuating genres female [. . .] Laure was born in 1903 and died in 1938. In her early 20's she hung out with Crevel, Argon, Picasso and Buñuel. She broke violently with her rich family and moved to Berlin. She flirted with militant radical politics. She went to Russia. She returned to Paris. There she lived and worked with Lean Bourenine, one of the founders of Parti communiste français. My writer friends said Laure was one of the main forces in the founding of this movement. A woman's life isn't only who she lives with and fucks. The details of the life of a woman who writes concern her writing as much as the details of the life of a man who writes. I prefer silence.

On the front cover of a notebook "titled" *My Mother*, Acker spelled out a rough "plot"—"Overall story: two parents out of love with each other kill kid: my life" and "Life of a sailor cut with letters between my mother and father." On the back cover of the same notebook, she scribbled lyrics from the Soft Cell song "Tainted Love": "Once I ran to you/now I run from you." These early thoughts, of course, evolved dramatically over several more notebooks, and the published novel, despite typically jarring transitions between texts, perspectives, and time periods, has a more restrained tone and intricate, even elegant, structure than most of Acker's other books. It also contains arguably the wisest, most emblematic sentence that Acker ever wrote: "Perhaps all that humans have ever meant by *love* is *control*."

My Mother's subject is, ostensibly, the tortured affair between Laure and Bataille, a relationship that Acker, borrowing and reworking passages from the couple's own writing, characterizes as a post-Marxist, post-Freudian struggle to find a new way of being "where irrationality would not be just a matter of mental functions and sexuality more than just the repressed." Again, the search for a myth. This thread generally structures the book, but characteristically, Acker folds in well-known bits of her biography, familiar riffs on bodybuilding, a long sequence on an abortion, and other recent events in her life, lightly fictionalized.

In one particularly amusing and extended setpiece, Acker chronicles a week-long reading tour she took in Germany in the summer of 1991. This was an actual event hosted by Semiotext(e), organized by Lotringer and Kraus, and featuring Lynne Tillman, Eileen Myles, Ann Rower, and Richard Hell. This group of poets and novelists would crisscross the country by van, stopping in Hamburg, Frankfurt, and Berlin. From the outset, however, Acker refused to ride in the vehicle, and insisted that their hosts, Gerhard Falkner and Sascha Anderson, instead supply her with her own motorcycle. They did, though, as Lotringer recalled, the bike was too big for her. After Acker initially struggled to ride it from her hotel to a press conference, the organizers were forced to ship the motorcycle from city to city by train so she could avoid dangerous, high-speed highways. Things only went downhill from there, largely exacerbated by Acker's demands and entitlement. Where everyone else read for about ten minutes, Acker always read at the end of the bill and for twice that length of time. "I am the backup singer for Kathy Acker's fucking tattoos," Myles later wrote. Lotringer also put himself on the bill, reading a piece about the French occupation that left him in tears every night. It didn't help that Acker was constantly angry with him too, over the fact that Kraus was there at all. Perhaps in retaliation, Acker started sleeping with Falkner. Finally, in the middle of all this tumult, it emerged that Sascha Anderson had been an informant for the Stasi.

Both Kraus and Myles would later describe this same absurd and chaotic tour in their own novels. Acker's rendition of the event, however, is quite a bit more dour, even self-pitying:

I had expected to feel lonely. According to the promoters, the tour's purpose was to present new American writing to Germans. I am as much a representative of America and of "new American writing" as I was, in relation to writing practice, close to the other Americans on the tour. My sense of the ridiculous, or loneliness, extended to personal relationships: one of my ex-boyfriends, another tour member, had abandoned me for the woman who was now his wife and who was about to meet him in three days. I hadn't seen him for a long time. There are many clichés.

Acker gives this Lotringer figure the name Bourénine; Falkner is called Georg Büchner (after the late German dramatist). Acker, of course, is named Laure. By the book's end, she has, predictably, been abandoned by both men. In one of her *My Mother* notebooks, she included a tiny, dispiriting quasi-poem:

My rules:
If someone ok offers me sex, take it.
I am alone.

Acker told interviewers that *My Mother* was a response to the culture wars then raging all around her. In the late eighties, conservative politicians—notably Republican senators Jesse Helms and Alfonse D'Amato—sought to defund the National Endowment for the Arts because of its support for artists (Mapplethorpe, Andres Serrano) they deemed obscene. In 1990, an amendment to the NEA's funding criteria required it to consider "general standards of decency and respect," and Karen Finley was denied funding along with three other performance artists. Acker said she didn't want to internalize "certain censorships," adding that "I used to go to sexual writing for my writing freedom. That place was no longer available to me, due to the changes in our society . . ."

In order to avoid censors both internal and external, she turned even more frequently to her dream life for material. For the first time since *Blood and Guts*, really, she included large dream maps. "Mix dreams w/ witches doing sacrifice," she instructed herself in a notebook. She'd long used dreams as inspiration or text, but now saw them also as an extension of her thinking about the language of the body; dreams were another language that resisted rationality and linear time, while also providing access to unique knowledge or vision. As she worked on *My Mother*, her dreaming became even more generative.

This was particularly evident, she told an interviewer, in the *Wuthering Heights* section. She would rewrite passages from the 1939 film adaptation of the book and then dream that night about *Wuthering Heights*. She would not interpret the dream per se, but rather let "the dream decide where the narrative was going." "From now on, whenever I dreamed," she wrote in a notebook, "I called it 'Going back to school.'"

CHAPTER 36

——————— × ———————

A T SFAI, BETWEEN 1991 AND 1995, ACKER TAUGHT IN THE
Performance/Video: New Genres (later shortened to just New Genres)
department and then the letters and science departments run by poet Bill
Berkson. That first year, she was considered visiting faculty, alongside multimedia artists like Tony Oursler and Cecilia Dougherty. Her first course was
called Reading and Writing: Hell, which she described in the course catalogue:

> According to linguists such as Chomsky, humans think by means of
> language. According to others, mainly philosophers, language is socially
> taught. Either way, even if you do not use words whenever you com-
> municate, which might have something to do with art, you are using
> language. How does this language work? What is language? This class
> will consist of writing and reading exercises in order to find out how
> language is and can be used or how language uses humans. There will
> be a good deal of hard work.

Her subsequent courses had titles like Treasure Hunt Special and Piracy, but
despite the playful sobriquets, she had high expectations of her students. "The
course is X-rated," went another description, "the workload will be heavy; a
need to write is necessary." In the description of Piracy, the final course she
taught, she hinted at a relatively heady syllabus: "Very difficult readings: Jorge
Luis Borges, Vladimir Nabokov, Michel Foucault, and others."

Education—good, bad, liberating, coercive—was a major subject in *My
Mother* and it would be again in *Pussy, King of the Pirates*. Acker, of course,
was very well educated, but she was also always a perpetually eager student,
at her happiest when reading or learning something new. While she'd had her
issues with the academy over the years, she had learned to appreciate how
useful universities and colleges could be—the academic interest in her work
that Ira Silverberg tried to spark with *Don Quixote* had, in fact, materialized,

and professors all across the continent now taught her work. It was a natural fit. The theory she embraced in the late seventies, particularly deconstruction and poststructuralism, had taken over English and literary studies departments. The canon was being dismantled, and newly created departments—women's studies, postcolonial studies, gay and lesbian studies—meant that literatures long marginalized or forgotten were finally being acknowledged and investigated. Acker was hardly the only contemporary American writer to embrace such currents, but she was one of very few who openly and comprehensively discussed how those currents influenced her writing. In interview after interview, in essay after essay, she gave readers bright, shiny keys to her work. Those keys were eagerly picked up by students and professors alike. By also making her books puzzles composed from pieces of other books, Acker had ensured that her work would be scrutinized by generations of academics to come.

The academy was also a refuge for the things that she more broadly valued: culture, intellectual freedom, reinvention. While teaching at SFAI and afterward, she took occasional gigs at other universities—stints at UCSD, the University of Idaho, and Hollins University in Roanoke, Virginia, speaking engagements at Duke—and tried, in vain, to find a more secure, more lucrative job, applying to schools like Brown and Brooklyn College when positions in creative writing programs opened. Nothing materialized, however, and she remained essentially an adjunct the rest of her teaching career.

An unorthodox school like the Art Institute was a good home for a long while, though. It was open twenty-four hours a day, and its students basically ran and did everything, including acid on the school's roof. Its alumni included radical artists like Paul McCarthy, Catherine Opie, and Kehinde Wiley. When Acker arrived, underground filmmaker George Kuchar also still taught there, and every Friday, his costumed students would romp around the courtyard making their Super 8 films. The painter Xylor Jane, a student of Acker's, described the school building itself as "gorgeous . . . an aircraft carrier slapped on top of a monastery." Jay DeFeo's monumental painting *The Rose*, eleven feet tall and weighing more than a ton, was famously hidden in a wall of a conference room for decades, unearthed only for an exhibition at the Whitney in 1995. Some of Acker's East Coast artist friends didn't care for SFAI, and Acker herself would often complain about its bureaucracy, the fact that they didn't provide her with health insurance, or that she didn't get paid enough. In her last semester, in 1995, she was making, after taxes, just over $500 every two weeks. (By contrast, around the same time, she gave a one-off lecture at Dartmouth that earned her $1500.) But she was also completely free to teach what she wanted there, and how she wanted. It was, for the most part, a rewarding and enjoyable experience.

It also helped that most of her students were big fans of hers when they arrived, and even bigger fans by the time they left. Her classes, usually three hours long and between fifteen and twenty students, were always oversubscribed. After her first year there, students were required to submit three writing samples to be considered for admission. She understandably gravitated toward students whose writing felt fresh and unusual, who had an interest in postmodernism or experimentation, as well as those who'd had tough lives, who seemed damaged. "Half of them come out of serious child abuse, sexual and other," she told a friend. She doted on the students with tattooed skulls, the trans men, the ones who'd worked in porn. But you didn't even have to be enrolled at SFAI necessarily; if she found you compelling enough, you could be a high-school dropout and still take her classes. Over the years, several of her students would go on to successful writing and art careers: Lynn Breedlove, Anna Joy Springer, Alicia McCarthy, Geoffrey Farmer, Xylor Jane, Erin Courtney.

The class was, for all intents and purposes, a writing workshop, but with an unmistakable Ackerian flavor. "Only one thing's forbidden here," she would announce at the start of term. "You're not allowed to bore me. Never *bore* me. Just be honest. Dishonesty is boring. Honesty is always interesting." The first writing exercise she'd give students was to write a sex scene involving them and a family member. Then she'd have them pass their assignment to the person sitting next to them, who would then read it out loud. "Write from your father's point of view," went another assignment, "but in the voice of a schizophrenic." She would tell her students to try, as she did, to write while masturbating. "I was like, 'Wha . . .?'," remembered Lynn Breedlove. "I can barely do one at a time." This was something that Acker famously did, for a brief while keeping what she called Masturbation Journals. "I start," she writes in one example. "Do I want porn? If I've got porn can I write this journal? (Do this do that: get all those thots [*sic*] out of mind, back to dreams where all the animals live) . . . I will float forever . . ."

Acker took her teaching very seriously, and never repeated a lesson. "She was always so present and electric in class," remembered one student, Jenna

Leigh Evans. She talked a lot about theory, but made her students mostly read fiction, a novel every single week, and everything from Stein, Burroughs, and Kawabata to friends like Jeanette Winterson and William Vollmann. She taught *The Story of the Eye* and always delighted when students would first complain—"Why are you making us read this pornography?"—and then come around to its genius as she broke down how Bataille builds narrative through an unexpected repetition of images.* She brought in guests like Kevin Killian or, when her class produced *Throat*, their own literary magazine, Rex Ray, the designer of the High Risk imprint.

She didn't talk about her own work too much, and when she did, she wasn't particularly precious about it. At one point, Leigh Evans said that she found *Empire of the Senseless* too difficult and that she wanted to throw the book across the room. Well, if you want to throw my book across the room, Acker said, "That's my fault, not yours." "I was gobsmacked," Leigh Evans said. "Because she was hugely egotistic, and I thought her writing was sacrosanct to her. But then I realized, no, she's not, she's in a process. All writers are in a process." Whatever authority Acker automatically commanded as a teacher or professor, she was usually quick to divest herself of it.

At the beginning of class, she also told her students that she wasn't there to solve their problems; she was going to be neither mother nor shrink. That disclaimer, students soon found, was a bit of misdirection—she could, in fact, be extremely nurturing. When one student, for example, arrived to class on her motorcycle, her bare hands freezing, Acker promptly gave the woman an old pair of hers. She could be especially supportive when it came to students' writing. She told many of them to never give up on their writing. "She almost violently grabbed me by my braids," said Anna Joy Springer, "and said, 'You're so good, Anna Joy, don't you dare stop writing. I think you're the reincarnation of Jean Genet.' I had no idea who that even was."

Later on, bored by teaching on campus, Acker took her classes elsewhere—a warehouse south of Market, Red Dora's Bearded Lady on 14th Street, or Edinburgh Castle, a pub on Geary. The Bearded Lady was a coffeehouse-cum-performance-space, run by Harry Dodge and Silas Howard, that became a kind

---

* Her typewritten class notes on the novel ran to ten, highly detailed pages, with notes to herself ("discuss Lacan on poet"; "De Sade's labyrinth according to Roland Barthes. Read that"). One handwritten aside was presumably addressed to her students: "Where is your haunted castle?"

of punk salon for young queer artists—Catherine Opie, Michelle Tea, Nayland Blake, and Justin Vivian Bond were all customers and friends. Edinburgh Castle had a much different vibe: a cavernous dive bar auspiciously located around the corner from the Mitchell Brothers strip club and up the street from Alice B. Toklas Place. Acker and her students would huddle on the couch in the chilly, disused front room, sipping beer while they talked and wrote.

Acker became quite close with a few of her students, particularly queer ones. On one occasion, Springer attended a reading with Acker, whom she called her "literary mom," and her actual mother. Springer's girlfriend had tried to shoot her the night before, and she was eager to tell the story to Acker while somehow concealing the frightening information from her parent.* When students needed money, Acker hired them as teaching assistants or paid them to do work around her apartment. At one point, she told Jenna Leigh Evans the story of Claire throwing cold water on her when she was showering. She then asked Leigh Evans to make artwork that she could put in the bathroom as an amulet that would quell her fear. Leigh Evans recalled the piece—an antique birdcage shellacked with quotations by Freud—with some embarrassment, but Acker loved it and hung it proudly in the shower. Leigh Evans often read Acker's tarot cards or would commiserate about Acker's messy sex life. "She always seemed like she was amused at the predicament of being a human being," Leigh Evans said.

Springer was dating Lynn Breedlove, the founding member of Tribe8, a queercore band that often spoofed the antics of straight hair bands like Bon Jovi. Breedlove wasn't technically a student at SFAI, but Springer brought him to the Edinburgh Castle and he was immediately intrigued. "There was this little, short, butch-femme, leather-clad, Harley-riding New Yorker babe," Breedlove remembered, "talking about this French porno philosophy shit. And I was like, 'Whoa.' She had my attention." Breedlove had a degree in English from Cal State and liked to condense literary and philosophical ideas into three-chord rock songs, bestowing this knowledge, he said, on kids who couldn't afford college. Acker, he felt, was engaged in a similar project, making ideas and information accessible in her own way too. In Acker's class, he wrote about years lost to drugs and

---

* As Springer had expected, the story titillated Acker a bit. She recounted it, more or less, in a notebook entry she titled "Masturbation Journal #2": "At reading I see student Anna—very good writer—she tells me her mother's here on Valium last week her lover tried to shoot her—her lover now in mental ward—all is over between them . . ."

alcohol and about his past life as a bike messenger. That writing would eventually become *Godspeed*, Breedlove's first novel. "She made herself so accessible to all of us," he said. "And validated us. She said, 'Okay, you guys are young, you're queer, you're fucking way out on the edges of society, and the world needs to hear about your lives.'" Acker hired Tribe8 to make music for her spoken-word album *Redoing Childhood*, taking producer Hal Willner to a concert the night before the recording session, where the band proceeded to cut up several large green and blue dildos on stage. Acker called Tribe8 the "hottest band in San Francisco" and Breedlove "one of the dreams I had had when I was a girl."

"She was learning a lot," Springer said. "How to have sexual intimacy with women, about diverse gender roles, about power plays that didn't have exact representational parallels in real life. I think she was learning about queerness, feminist queerness." That said, and as much as Acker loved the idea of queerness, as much as she thought of herself as queer, sex with women was still only rarely appealing to her. She would occasionally indulge in one-night stands with female students, and attended queer play parties, but her friends said, generally speaking, she always preferred to have sex with men. After spending one night with a young woman, Acker said to Avital Ronell, "I don't know why I slept with that girl. I hate pussy. It reminds me of my mother. It's like I'm eating out my mother." Other friends, like Bob Glück and Mel Freilicher, didn't even consider her bisexual. "She would have relationships with younger women," Amy Scholder said, "and I don't think her heart was really in it. It was kind of more a way to participate in a culture she loved."

Leigh Evans thought that being queer for Acker meant roughly the same thing it meant when she was in her early twenties and attending Daughters of Bilitis dances while living with Lenny Neufeld—escape from normative sexuality. "She was so hung up on men all the time," Leigh Evans said. "Just so completely deranged with longing and projection." Being gay, being a lesbian, meant just doing away with men, with that derangement. Springer saw this too, though in somewhat different terms. Acker was in her forties, had never had kids, and was watching a generation of young queer women come of age, third-wave feminists who could have been her children, who she had, in a way, given permission to be. "She never thought that what was happening in feminist, dyke, punk, S and M, anti-moralistic culture could happen with women," Springer said. "She was, like, 'Oh my god, you kids are doing amazing things. The future might be possible.'"

CHAPTER 37

———— × ————

A CKER DIDN'T "DO HAPPY," AVITAL RONELL SAID, BUT HER YEARS AT the Art Institute were, in many ways, some of her happiest. The adoration she received from her students helped, as did the affection she received from younger New Narrative writers like Kevin Killian and Dodie Bellamy. Killian recalled meeting her often at Small Press Traffic or Kiki, the legendary, short-lived gallery on 14th Street, or the Roxy, a rep cinema in the Mission. She joined Killian in a play that Carla Harryman wrote called *Memory Play*, in which everyone played some kind of animal. Killian was dazzled by Acker's stage presence and the fact that she'd memorized her lines by day one. One time, he and Bellamy drove Acker out to Harryman and Barrett Watten's place in Oakland for a barbecue. Killian remembered it being a dreadful event— too suburban, too many kids running around. They got lost on the way home. Acker, however, seemed overjoyed. "I'm just happy to be in a car," she said. "Because I never get to go anywhere."

This was hardly true, and, indeed, Acker herself took many female friends out for rides on her motorcycle—often out of the city, into the forests and coves around the Bay Area, which she loved. That image—of Acker and a gal pal, holding each other, united in speed and abandon and bliss—was often repeated when people who knew her then talked about those years. It was the way that they wanted to remember her.

× × ×

Acker tried to capture all that freedom, that queerness, that natural beauty, in her next novel, *Pussy, King of the Pirates*. "If one day, a bad girl named Dante met a mean dyke called Hieronymus Bosch, this is the book they'd make," she wrote in a draft typescript, providing herself with her own blurb. She wanted to write a girl's adventure story, something she'd craved as a kid and could never find. Her primary texts were Daniel Defoe's *A General History of the Pyrates*, a Japanese film adaptation of *Story of O*, and Robert Louis

Stevenson's *Treasure Island*. "I love Robert Louis Stevenson," she told her old friend Cynthia Rose, who interviewed her for the *Seattle Times*. "Once I changed all his men to women, it was really fun." Her goal with the book was to ask one question—where can joy be found in our society? The heroines of the book were based partly on her students. In one notebook, she commanded herself to "Have fun!" and gave herself further instruction in others: "Masculinize the style"; "Style: as slang & hardcore as it can get"; "Written in scummy pirate style."

"In that beginning, which is still beginning," Acker writes, three-quarters of the way through the book, "there is a young girl. Her name's not important. She's been called King Pussy, Pussycat, Ostracism, O, Ange. Once she was called Antigone . . ." *Pussy* follows the adventures, sexual and otherwise, of all these variously named young girls, who, at different times throughout the book are prostitutes, performance artists, pirates. There are joined by other pirates: Silver, Bad Dog. The book moves from Alexandria to Brighton to a fetid Pirate Island. There are long passages about shopping. It's a detective story that becomes a pirate story while also being neither of these things at all; it's mostly a tale, like so much of Acker's fiction, of the messy, furtive, constant process of self-transformation. It lurches along the gangplank of its narrative like a drunken sailor dying to fall into the sea.

Antonin Artaud, the schizophrenic French poet and dramatist whose work inspired so many theorists—Deleuze, Foucault, Barthes—hovers over the book like a dark angel. Still an inveterate punster, Acker sometimes refers to him as Our Toad. Acker identified with Artaud almost as much as she did with Laure; she was fascinated by his perpetual struggle with, and antagonism toward, self-expression, his opposition to ideology of all kinds, his fascination with magic, and his proximity to madness. Her library included his complete works in English. In one of her *Pussy* notebooks, she spells this out: "Artaud showed us that, to be a poet, is more than to be marginal, it is to be alienated to the point of madness. Artaud showed us that the political structure of a society is tied to that which socializes, of the family."*

There is a journey, a search for buried treasure, but when that treasure is found, it's promptly abandoned. Realism is another word for capital, capital

---

* This text would later crop up in a speech she gave at the Art Institute of Chicago in 1994, as part of the Artist in Society conference.

another word for culture. "I'd rather go a-pirating," says Silver. "If me and my girls take all this treasure, the reign of girl piracy will stop, and I wouldn't have that happen." More than in any of Acker's books perhaps, *Pussy* returns time and time again to the body—her Masturbation Journals are an obvious source text too—and its odors, its colors and shapes, its unruly demands. "For the first time," she writes, "I was seeing the pirate girls in their true colors. Black and red. They wore their insides on their outsides, blood smeared all over the surfaces. When opened, the heart's blood turns black." The natural world is, undeniably, an extension of the body, at once fearsome and fecund.

Pussy can feel revelatory, a pure and furious blast of sexy, campy energy— in many ways, the literary analog to the riot grrrl rock that, by the time of its publication in 1996, had fully penetrated the mainstream. "Acker's voice, with its peculiar mix of expansiveness and abruptness, grows more sophisticated and certain with each novel," R. U. Sirius declared in *Artforum*. Mel Freilicher also loved the book, as did Anna Joy Springer. "All the critics who hated it can kiss my ass," said Acker's friend novelist Richard Kadrey. Its pleasures may feel, at times, curdled—these pirate girls never completely slip the corset of patriarchal culture—but there is a genuine joy on many of the book's pages.

At the same time, though, it also feels that Acker has reached the end of something. The techniques—the appropriation, the splicing together of ransacked texts, the frequent use of dream material—can sometimes feel stagnant, the motifs and themes of piracy, incest, and motorcycles skirt self-parody, the recycled autobiographical details now almost pallid. Acker often characterized writing in the most fanciful, idyllic, even corny, way—as magic, say, or as a way to preserve a sense of childlike wonder. To write was, in effect, to return to childhood, which she so literally did in almost all of her books. But now, as she ostensibly strove to move forward, to capture the spirit and energy of a younger generation, her own past felt more suffocating than ever.

She'd feared that she was repeating herself with *My Mother*, and in *Pussy* there is often the sense that she is. Even an admirer like Kevin Killian, who found her "surprising to the end," said, "Her work you can kind of predict. Rimbaud, Algerians, and her mother would commit suicide to spite her. There are a lot of predictable things in there." Her longtime mentor David Antin suggested to Acker that she try moving away from the "staccato syntax" that she'd developed over her career, in favor of "something more luxuriant." As Antin recalled: "I said, 'The work is wonderful, but you're going to run into a point in time where the attack becomes necessary and mechanical.'"

× × ×

Antin also argued that Acker's entire writing career constituted a kind of "jail-break." He meant, of course, from the prisons that Acker insisted constituted the world—the prisons of family, of men, of language. But after breaking out so many times, she was tired. And it was becoming clearer, to herself and to friends and colleagues, that she had also ended up becoming her own jailer. Acker had always sought surprise, had made books that went in unexpected, sly, even impossible, directions, but now she was in danger of becoming generic, even if that genre was a genre of one.

This danger deformed her personal life now too. When she was younger, she understandably worried that The Black Tarantula would overshadow Kathy Acker, or would at least misrepresent her intentions. Now, it seemed, Kathy Acker herself had become the persona, the Kathy Acker of tattoos and leather, the recalcitrant, rapacious, take-no-prisoners sex queen, Ms. Cunt all over again. There was no room in that persona for the insecurity and fear that she also so often felt. "Her image was so hard-boiled and tough, and in some ways that was accurate," Mel Freilicher said. "But she was also very vulnerable and needy. I think it was hard for her to show that stuff. Then, if she did show that stuff and it wasn't responded to well, it really freaked her out." While marketing-speak and the idea of branding did not yet dominate the world of publishing, or at least not to the degree it would a couple decades later, Acker had, in effect, turned herself into a brand. She had long made a performance of rebellion, but the performance had now, inadvertently, become commodified.

Perhaps it was the only way she could make a living. This brand or persona was what continued to get her invited to performances and readings and conferences. It got her on stage with Sonic Youth. It got her paid. "Our only survival card is FAME," she told McKenzie Wark, "and on the other side of the card, the pretty picture, is 'homelessness.'" On many days, she herself bought into it. Ron Silliman recalled giving a talk around this time in New York, where both Acker and the poet Charles Bernstein were in the audience. Acker asked a question. Silliman didn't remember what it was, but he did remember what Bernstein told him afterward: "It was like watching one of the dolls in *Blade Runner* suddenly come to life. She was formulating the question in her head, but in between when she came up with the question and raised in her hand, she became Kathy Acker. It was like she literally had to turn herself on in order to present herself."

All this tension—between surface and interior, the persona and the person, the authentic Acker and the fictional one, the private and public—was unresolvable. Acker had built her life's work on the tenacious refusal of such oppositions. But it was becoming more and more difficult to embody that refusal. Acker obviously devoted huge amounts of time, energy, and thought to the invention, and re-invention, of her various selves. Far more so than most people. But where most people eventually abandon such unending self-creation— eventually, in every sense of the phrase, settle down—for her there was no such relief. The smell inside her masks had become overpowering. Her brand kept the real world at bay, intentionally sometimes, but also sometimes not. It was becoming impossible for her to experience it without self-consciousness and self-importance.

This all reached an unfortunate apotheosis with Indiana's *Rent Boy*, which came out in 1994. The short, sharp novel is narrated by a hustler/architecture student named Mark, who also works as a waiter at the fictional Emerson Club. The Emerson resembles the Groucho or Soho House, and one of its members is Sandy Miller, a cheap, self-involved, careerist, preposterously attired writer obviously modeled after Acker. "I read one of Sandy's books," Mark recounts with amused contempt. "It was all my cunt this and my cunt that for two hundred pages, stick your big dick in my cunt sort of stuff. But literary, you know. One minute Sandy's getting banged by an Arab Negro and the next minute she's a sixteenth-century pirate on the high seas, or Emily Brontë or something. Her writing is real modern."

Rent Boy was published by High Risk, Amy Scholder and Ira Silverberg's imprint. When they first read the manuscript, they loved it, but they told Indiana he should change the Sandy character somewhat, to make her less identifiable to Acker and other readers. Indiana wasn't sure how to do that, but they suggested altering his description of her handwriting. He didn't particularly remember what Acker's handwriting looked like, so he agreed—and then accidentally ended up describing it with absolute precision: "itty bitty handwriting that looks like a secret code."

Acker was incensed when the book came out, even threatening to sue Indiana. Making matters worse was the fact that she hadn't been insulted by just one friend, but a trio of them. Many years later, Scholder said she would have still published it—"it's Gary at his best"—but she wished that she had at least given Acker advance warning. "When she confronted me about that I felt terrible," Scholder said. "She was right I should have talked to her about it, allowed her to read it before anyone else in the public read it." Indiana, for his part, didn't expect it would upset her as much as it did. "I thought she would think of it as a piece of fiction," he said. "She'd taken everything in her life and put it in her books. If you dish it out as much as she did, you should be able to take it." After another writer in San Francisco gave the book a good review in a local paper, Acker saw him at a party and threw a drink in his face. Then, three years later, Indiana pressed the bruise again. He included another unmistakable, grotesque Acker-like character in his novel *Resentment*, a character whose writing is described as "a shotgun wedding of the infantile and the obscene." The two friends never spoke again.

CHAPTER 38

F ROM HER EARLIEST POEMS TO THE NOTEBOOKS THAT SHE RELIABLY
continued to fill up, day after day, writing was the way that Acker gave her
life meaning. Creation was always fulfilling; it made everything bearable—the
romantic shipwrecks, the compulsive restlessness, the precarity. It was, as she
so often said, the only way she survived. No matter what else preoccupied her,
and no matter the difficulties of her life, writing could either contain, dissolve,
or shut them out. She ultimately didn't care how many people read her, she
insisted, because that wasn't the point. Fiction *remade* reality, no matter how
many people it reached. It was a good line, one that she may have used to
shield herself from the disappointment of diminishing sales; the hardcover
Pantheon edition of *My Mother, Demonology*, to cite just one example, had sold
only about 2,300 copies by this point. But it was also something she deeply
believed. "Writing is one method of dealing with being human," she says in
In Memoriam to Identity, "or wanting to suicide cause in order to write you kill
yourself at the same time while remaining alive." She never stopped writing,
continuing to at least make notes up until the last couple months of her life.

But the longer she stayed in San Francisco, the less faith and interest
she had in the writing community around her. A lot of that was the usual
disappointment—just as in New York, many of her writer friends failed to
consistently give her the support to which she felt due. Just as in New York,
she didn't like when they put their careers or families first. She fell out with
Bob Glück, and with Dodie Bellamy, whose boyfriend she tried to steal. But
these petty feuds aside, she was also starting to feel that her position as a writer
was becoming even more untenable. On the one hand, there were writers like
Dorothy Allison, David Foster Wallace, and Mary Gaitskill. They also wrote
about trauma, depression, and sexual violence, but in ways that were more
accessible, and with larger audiences, than she ever did. She was surrounded
by outlandishly tattooed and pierced young people, and some of them were
writers too. Even the broader culture—Nirvana's pop dirges, the Spice Girls'

readymade girl power, Quentin Tarantino's quick-draw pastiches—arguably bore traces of her work. The world had caught up to her, somehow. She had become less unique.

On the other hand, she was convinced—rightly, as it turned out—that America was becoming more culturally and politically conservative. She had loathed George Bush, but the apparent prosperity and peace of the Clinton administration ushered in an era of globalization, greater income inequality, and non-state domestic and foreign terrorism. In 1994, the Republican take-over of Congress, led by Newt Gingrich, precipitated the hyper-partisanship and polarization that would soon define the country. Acker saw little room in this climate for the kind of art she made. After a 1995 reading tour across the Midwest and the South with Bob Glück, about which Glück joked they were "bringing darkness to the Gentiles," she returned home even more pessimistic. In an essay titled "After the End of the Art World" she wrote, "Given the present political and economic configuration of the United States, it is no wonder that the business of poetry, of all literary writing, and of art is in trouble [. . .] Art is being marginalized to the point of extinction."

But outside the world of traditional or even experimental art, she found signs of hope. There were her friends in Tribe8 and *Mondo 2000*, but also a new collective of women artists she'd discovered in Australia called VNS Matrix. They published "A Cyberfeminist Manifesto for the 20th century," which began with lines that might have been written by Acker herself: "We are the modern cunt positive anti reason unbounded unleashed unforgiving we see art with our cunt we make art with our cunt . . ." The manifesto was posted all over Sydney, distributed internationally by email and fax. These scenes were now starting to displace the writing community in Acker's life. Like her healers and spiritual advisors, they gave her a refuge from the grind of her everyday work, and also pointed toward other ways of thinking and living. She was interested in how digital culture and new media were changing how we communicate. Going online was fun, inspiring, even revelatory. Seemingly free of government and corporate control, the internet still held the promise of political and cultural freedom. It was, for Acker, another form of magic. Some of her healers took her deeper into her body, her friends online took her completely out of it, and she loved to go in both directions. "I don't think we know what the possibilities of the Net are yet," she told an interviewer. "I think what's happening is that we really should start concentrating on developing a new language for this thing. It's most peculiar—it's a big living mind."

Soon, however, this premillennial techno-utopianism would start to feel quaint, ironic, even dangerous. Even by then, in San Francisco, as in New York, the AIDS epidemic had left the city exposed to rapacious gentrification. Apartments and houses left behind by the dead were bought up, cheap, by real estate developers. Over time, wealthy tech companies and a whole new class of workers moved in and utterly transformed the complexion of the city. If Acker thought the internet might be a haven for artists like herself, the corporations that soon monoplized it would in fact make it very difficult for artists like her to live in San Francisco at all. Rapidly rising rents, and an absurdly high cost of living, would force many out, all but snuffing out the scrappy bohemianism that had forever defined the city. Acker wouldn't live to see this, but friends and colleagues would. By 2012, for example, Twitter had opened its headquarters on the edge of the Tenderloin and around the corner from Dodie Bellamy and Kevin Killian's apartment, a development that would accelerate the gentrification and displacement of the area. Bellamy had seen this drama play out many times before, but this time it felt more personal, systemic, unfathomable. "It's not just the fear of losing housing and having nowhere to go," she wrote, "it's this sense of having one's habitat destroyed around you, a sort of soul-level extinction."

× × ×

As much as she was online throughout 1995, Acker was also very often on the road. Much of that time was spent doing the kind of extra-literary work she claimed she didn't like, but which continued to confirm her as a writer of stature, paid some bills, and kept her in the public eye. It was work that could keep at bay, for a little while, the loneliness that always threatened to capsize her. In March of that year, she gave a keynote speech—"Writing, Identity and Copyright in the Net Age"—to the Author's Guild in Palo Alto. She wrote an essay for the *Journal of the Midwest Modern Language Association*. She read at Royal Festival Hall in London. In the summer, she participated in a conference on 1990s fiction at the University of Sussex, later reading at the Zap Club in Brighton. She gave the opening address at a literary festival in Finland. There was the tour with Glück. She sold her papers to Duke University.

Most happily, that spring and summer, she recorded an album with the Mekons, also titled *Pussy, King of the Pirates*, in which she turned the novel into a rock opera of wide-ranging style and tone. In some ways, it was more successful than the book, a rollicking, mysterious blend of post-punk and cowpunk, dream-pop and neo sea shanties. Repurposed as lyrics, Acker's prose made for an irresistible, blunt poetry. It remains one of the best reminders of her power as a performer, and that her voice—modulated and sweetened as it was here—could be a beautiful instrument. "I'm never having a book that isn't sung again," Acker said.

That June, she met McKenzie Wark while on a tour of Australia, and emailed her a couple months later: "I overwork most of the time. I come up for air (this is the first time in some years that I'm not running five jobs at once, touring and writing a novel and journalism/theory writing and teaching and what other projects like the Mekons' record, and I come up for air and who am I . . . lonely and scared). We're rats walking tightropes we never thought existed. No medical insurance; no steady job; etc."

As her old friend Jeff Weinstein put it, "Kathy filled a cultural need." Filling that need meant a lot of people projected a lot on to her. She had projected a lot on to herself. She never quite found a comfortable, safe position between these two things, constantly exposing herself like a raw nerve and then fleeing when that nerve was touched. It was a lot to take on, a lot to bear. It was what led her to Georgina Ritchie, the healer with whom she'd explored her past lives. It left her feeling alone, maybe more alone than she ever had been. In the last couple years of her life, she cast herself into new romantic relationships with more frantic ardor than usual. She bumped into and then clung to these lovers like rocks in a whirlpool. She didn't know that time was running out, but then, she'd always lived as if it were.

For a while, she turned toward Wark. A thirty-four-year-old writer and scholar specializing in media and culture, Wark was living and teaching in Sydney at the time. She then identified as a queer man, and, though not overly familiar with Acker's work, met the writer at a post-reading dinner and ended up sleeping with her soon after. When Acker returned to San Francisco, they kept in touch by email, sometimes several times a day. Their correspondence—composed with some haste, sometimes in drunkenness—during a period when such instantaneous communication was still rare, would prove a tantalizing time capsule, replete with references to Acker's relationships to Sylvère Lotringer, to Rainer Weber, to R. U. Sirius. They talked about books (Blanchot, Bataille, Judith Butler), TV (*The X-Files*, *The Simpsons*), movies (*Safe*, *The Bandit Queen*, both of which Acker was crazy about). They flirted, preened, dissembled, gossiped, joked, analyzed, revealed too much, revealed too little.

Both Acker and Wark quickly slipped into roles that seemed comfortable to them—Acker, the foul-mouthed, big-brained, high-maintenance diva; Wark, an eager, earnest pupil dazzled by Acker's charisma and striving to assert her own. Both were big-time name-droppers.

Their needs, however, never seemed to be in sync. In the correspondence, Acker's openness—and her hunger—are almost terrifying. Above all, she seems to just want a companion, someone of constancy and devotion. But Wark couldn't be that person. She was already involved with someone else in Sydney, and in the midst of her own reinventions—intellectual (her work would soon be more inflected by critical theory), geographic (she moved to New York in 2000), and gender (Wark transitioned in 2019). When Wark visited Acker later that fall in San Francisco, she was less interested in fucking Acker than in being fucked by her. Acker, of course, had a large collection of sex toys, a strap-on harness. She was accommodating. When they had sex, Wark would sometimes wear Acker's clothing. "I was her girl," Wark later wrote.

But this wasn't what Acker really desired. Over the next couple of months, with Wark and Acker also meeting up again, this time in New York, she would often complain about the Australian to her friend Bertie Marshall, a Brighton-based writer, musician, and part of the so-called Bromley Contingent with Siouxsie Sioux. Wark was too cold, she told Marshall, or too preoccupied with work. She wanted Wark to move to San Francisco, or for her to find Acker a job in Sydney. Neither would happen. By early March, she wrote Marshall, "Everything OK except for really shitty love life . . . the Australian came back and fucked me over again."

But another long-distance romance, which developed around the same time, would be far less nettlesome. Johnny Golding was a thirty-year-old professor at the Royal College of Art, a polymath who, though originally from New York, had spent many years in Toronto, where she'd been president of Buddies in Bad Times Theatre, the first LGBTQ theater company in Canada. She moved to London to teach in 1994, and while Acker was on one of her many trips to England, the two met at a large dinner at the Groucho. The connection was instantaneous. "I thought she was fabulous, hilarious, incredibly intelligent, clearly good-looking," Golding said. "And probably would want to play." When the dinner ended, they immediately went back to Golding's Soho flat for what Golding described as "a fantastic dessert."

Golding was part of a circle of queer and trans people that loosely coalesced around the cult film *Dandy Dust*—among them the director Ashley Hans Scheirl and the artist Del LaGrace Volcano—and who frequented clubs like FIST and the Clit Club. Golding identified as a butch dom, and the sex with Acker, she said, was "inventive and fun and wild." Just like her writing, Golding said. Golding felt that Acker's work, despite its obvious play with story and narrative, should be read, above all, as philosophy. Golding liked to call Acker a "historian of the present."

It was an exhilarating relationship for both women, and the friendship would last for the remainder of Acker's life. But Acker was still looking for something else. While it would pain her to say it again, she needed a boyfriend. But, especially now, one who would look after her, who would subordinate his needs to hers. Late that March, she went back to London to perform songs from the Mekons record at a small theater in the West End. In the midst of that tour, she ended up at a Mexican restaurant in Soho. At that dinner, she met Charles Shaar Murray, an acclaimed music journalist who'd published books on David Bowie and Jimi Hendrix. At the dinner, Murray jokingly proposed an idea for a TV game show called *What's My Kink?*

"What's your kink?" Acker asked him.

"I'm just totally fascinated by women with muscles," he said.

It wasn't just a line, he said later—his wife, also well built, had recently left him, and he despaired of ever finding anyone like that again. Acker, he remembered, actually blushed. They slept together that night and met again the next evening after another *Pussy* show. In a cab later, Murray thought, "I'm speeding through the heart of London, that glittering metropolis, on a Saturday night, with my arms around a beautiful, notorious woman. How can life get any better?" They spent five days together. He gave her a copy of his book on Hendrix, which Acker devoured on the plane back home. Early in their courtship, Acker told him that "everybody wanted to fuck her, but nobody wanted to stay." He promised her he would stay.

A giddy Acker emailed Marshall soon after she returned to the States: "Oh, Bertie, I'm madly in love and am moving back as soon as my teaching is over so I can be with him. I say this and while I'm saying it, it doesn't seem real to me and yet he's with me more than anyone else. He's just fab, my age, a total sweetie, has this fab face and I just keep being proud to know him." She told Marshall she'd be moving back to London a month later.

CHAPTER 39

———— × ————

OVER THE YEARS, ACKER'S SEXUAL PARTNERS HAD NOTICED OCCA-
sional moles and masses on her body, especially on her breasts. Acker
had regular biopsies, all of which had been benign. Murray had seen one. Golding too had felt a "huge" growth, and asked Acker about it. "Oh, I call that
Mike," Acker said, waving it off. "That's been with me awhile." But after Acker
returned to San Francisco in April, she went to the Ralph K. Davies Medical Center at the north end of the Castro and had the mass biopsied. "Mike"
turned out to be malignant.

Murray had planned to fly to San Francisco to help her pack up her stuff for
the UK. But Acker called him as soon as she had the news, which she broke to
him over his answering machine. "She was absolutely in terror," Murray remembered. "It was almost like she'd lost the power of speech." His trip would turn
into something much different from what either had first imagined. Given a
choice between a lumpectomy and radiation or a far cheaper mastectomy with
no radiation, Acker chose the latter. She didn't want to just have one breast, so
she elected to have them both removed. She asked if Murray would help her
through the "hideousness" of the surgery. It was obviously an enormous obli-
gation for someone who'd known her for only a couple of weeks. But Murray
had already learned that bestowing such obligations was not out of character
for her. "She was quite in the habit of dumping responsibility on people she
might have only just met," Murray said. "She was renegade posh. She had a
punk side and a princess side. This required constant mental gear changes and
adjustments." He was supportive of the double mastectomy, though. It was
her body, her decision. She told him that her "breasts had never been her best
feature" anyway. Later, she would tell other people that she liked the way she
looked without them—like a young boy. Three weeks later, Murray would be
in San Francisco to take her to back to Davies.

To Murray, the whole event was an almost unbearable mixture of tragedy
and farce. For dinner the day before the surgery, she asked if he would make a

particularly complex fish dish he had never made before, but he persuaded her to eat out instead. Acker also had a class scheduled the evening of the surgery and thought she might host all of her students at her apartment, where Murray could serve as guest lecturer; he talked her into canceling that as well. She also said she didn't have enough money to pay for an overnight stay in the hospital so it would be outpatient surgery. Just before she went under, Murray remembered, she was negotiating prices with the anesthesiologist.

Then, three days after the surgery, back at Davies, they learned that the breast tissue had actually been healthy. But the surgeon also removed eight lymph nodes and found cancer in six of them. The mastectomy hadn't been necessary at all, nor did it help. Acker's doctor told her that statistics suggested there was only a 60 percent chance of non-recurrence, but that if she now underwent a round of chemotherapy, she could raise that chance to 70 percent. Acker was skeptical. Only 10 percent? And how could the breast tissue be free of cancer? She'd been on what she called a "lump diet," rich with garlic pills, miso, acidophilus, and many other supplements; couldn't that diet have helped? Maybe her lymph system was already cleansing the body of cancer cells? It was confusing, and for someone long skeptical of Western medicine, not reassuring at all. Why should she listen to these doctors now about the chemo? She couldn't afford it anyway. She told Murray that she wasn't going to trust those "white-coated devils" again.

She knew that walking away from conventional medicine meant walking away from conventional society. But that's what she'd done her entire life. There were other ways; there were always other ways. "I will not die a meaningless death," she told the *Independent* several months later. "I will find out the answers. I will make myself well, or at least I will die in control of my own body."

She went back to her family of healers and spiritual advisors, to Frank Malinaro and Georgina Ritchie. In the same obsessive and singular way she'd devoted herself to writing, to bodybuilding, and tattooing, she devoted herself to healing her own body. "I'm a cave named the self now and will be here for a while, in this cocoon . . . ," she wrote Bertie Marshall. She stopped eating dairy and gluten, drinking alcohol. She spent hours every day meditating and doing yoga. She sought out energy healers like Sheppard Powell, Diane di Prima's husband, who used techniques that somewhat resembled Reiki.

She met Powell at the house he shared with di Prima, in the Excelsior neighborhood. It was a warm summer night, a rarity. Powell lay his hands on

Acker, and they simply talked—about her emotional state, about her work, about her relationships. He already knew Acker a bit through his wife, and thought her "just such a wonderful being." She told him about Murray, and that she planned to reunite with him in England. "She was very excited," Powell remembered. "This was a big important change in her life, and her will and excitement were just radiating off her." At the end of the treatment, he used what he called a "bit of Tibetan healing," and began a long cleansing chant, the Hundred Syllable Mantra, which Acker believed was particularly helpful. Later recounting her new regimen in detail to Ira Silverberg, she excitedly described working with chakras, chanting, visualization, aromatherapy. "Of course, you know, I've become mad as a hatter," she wrote. "What else is new?"

By the end of July, though, Acker felt better, stronger. She and Murray had kept in touch by phone and email, and she was desperate to see him. She flew back to London, and, after staying with him for a while, bought yet another flat, a dark, two-bedroom basement at 14 Duncan Terrace. It was near the Angel tube station and a ten-minute walk from Murray's place; her neighbors were famous writers like Douglas Adams and Peter Ackroyd. She had her stuffed animals and library shipped over, and hired a young writer, Jonathan Kemp, to set up the books, clean, and do other errands for her. She put together a network of new healers there—a Chinese herbalist, a cranial therapist, Stephen Russell (the so-called Barefoot Doctor). Kemp thought her kitchen looked like a "chemist's," a "vast spill of bottles and jars and pills and powders, countless vitamins and supplements and herbal extracts, holistic remedies." At that point, she was using a small suitcase to carry them around in. She told her friends that the cancer was gone, that she felt "clean."

× × ×

Two weeks after the mastectomy, Acker got a call from Grethe Barrett Holby, the founding artistic director of American Opera Projects in New York. The composer Ken Valitsky was writing a new opera and Holby wanted Acker to write the libretto. Holby told her she could write about whatever she wanted. Acker said yes. That summer, she submitted a first draft of the libretto, entitled *Requiem*. Ostensibly a reimagining of Eugene O'Neill's *Mourning Becomes Electra*—a play that Acker identified strongly with in high school and which itself is a retelling of Aeschylus's *Oresteia*—it was a starkly autobiographical work. Malinaro had repeatedly told her that if she was going to really, truly, heal herself she needed to finally let go of the resentment and anger she felt toward her family.

But this was something Acker could never do—*Requiem* radiated an undisguised resentment. Claire, Peter, and Nana appear, all with their real names; Acker calls herself Electra. It was her last full attempt to establish the record of her life, to revisit the details of a sad story that never failed to fascinate her. She did it this time in as unguarded and unmediated a way as she knew how. Now, though, the requisite representation of her father's abandonment and her mother's suicide are overshadowed by the more recent catastrophe of her cancer diagnosis. Her therapy sessions with Georgina Ritchie are recounted in detail. Acker described the writing this way: "All three Electra accounts have, as center, the question of evil in the family. Perhaps, more accurately, the investigation of the possibilities of the transformation of evil and disease. The possibility of the transformation of death into life." *Requiem* was Acker's last completed work,* but with its literalness and sentimentality an uninformed reader might have thought it her first. Acker received feedback from workshops of the opera, but she never made time to revise it, and a scheduled production in 1998 never came to be.

She published it as is, in what would be her final book, another collection of miscellany, titled *Eurydice in the Underworld*. The title piece was, it seems, Acker's last attempt at a novel, a grim retelling of the Orpheus myth, with Acker as Eurydice and Murray as Orpheus. After Acker had returned to London, Murray did his best to keep her comfortable, busy, and supported. They went to concerts—PJ Harvey, Taj Mahal—and he tried to get her work at the music magazines he wrote for. *Pussy* had not been published in the UK, and he gave it to his agent and his editor at Viking Penguin, both of whom passed.

But she and Murray were both under considerable stress. These were hardly ideal conditions for any relationship, let alone a new romantic one. "I was attempting to be Mr. Perfect Boyfriend," Murray said, "and the longer we were together, the less I was succeeding at that." Murray had, by that point, only read

---

* In 2005, Matias Viegener revised *Requiem*, inserting into the libretto three scenes from Acker's *Don Quixote* and *Pussy, King of the Pirates* and the 1997 short story "Eurydice in the Underworld." In 2017, he reworked the manuscript again, titled it *The Requiem of Kathy Acker*, and published it in the hopes that it would be adapted as an opera, a play with music, or "another innovative form."

a couple of Acker's books, and she demanded that he read them all and then she would quiz him. And, despite her healers, diet, all the supplements, and her own insistence that she was getting better, she was not getting better. She was clearly losing weight. While she had taken out a gym membership, she only went once or twice. At one point, they were sitting by Regent's Canal, and Acker dropped her bottle of Evian into the water. Murray quickly fished it out, and then she continued to drink from it. Later, as her health worsened, she would tell everyone it was because the Evian had been contaminated, and repeatedly blamed Murray. "She was feeling more and more rejected, getting iller and iller, and becoming harder and harder to coexist with," Murray said. Things continued in this bumpy fashion for several months. Then, in February 1997, they broke up. Murray was crushed, but couldn't see any other way forward. Things might have been different, he thought, if she hadn't been sick. They might have had a chance. "It was sheer self-preservation," he said. "I had to walk away in the end and I promised her I wouldn't. It was a promise I wanted to keep and I couldn't."

Acker was devastated. She felt used, abandoned, now thoroughly and finally alone. Or, at least, that's how she portrayed herself in *Eurydice*. At the end of the surviving fragment, she takes on Murray's voice, here referring to Eurydice/Acker as "U-Turn":

> I had thought, after U-Turn and I were together a week or two, that she was the sexiest, the hottest piece of flesh I had ever encountered, even when we found out she had cancer; I had thought, no one has ever turned me on so much even if she is willing to be mine; I had thought that since she was wealthy and famous, she was going to turn my life, which back then looked like an abyss, into paradise; I had thought we would always be drunk, in the limelight; I had thought that she was my beginning. I had wanted to believe all this so much that I couldn't see what was in front of my eyes. Until I turned around and looked at U. Down in that hole.
>
> I saw and told her I didn't want what I saw.
>
> I've returned back here. I'm glad that I met U because now I know I can love again.

Soon after, she accepted a four-month teaching contract at Hollins College in Roanoke, Virginia. It was a convenient, if painful, out, one that both she and

Murray took. She welcomed the change of scenery and the relative ease of the job. But if it was a reprieve, it was also a kind of limbo. Her mind swarmed with thoughts of stable work and concern about her body. "A bit worried about the health," she wrote Ira Silverberg from Virginia. "Have gotten myself run-down what with the strangeness and loneliness here, the break up with Charles, and moving here. Oh well."

× × ×

Not long after Acker had returned to London, her friend and lover Johnny Golding took her out shopping. She'd been feeling low, and Golding thought some retail therapy would help. "We just decided that we were going to forget about the cancer," Golding said. "Forget about the mastectomy. We're just going to go shopping. We did this mad, very camp, shop. Bought all these crazy clothes." They went to junk stores, to shops selling Vivienne Westwood, to Covent Garden. They talked about surviving in the face of it all, the idiotic face of it all. They laughed a lot. In a small clothing shop in Covent Garden, Acker found a T-shirt that had two rings, one for each nipple, sewn into the front. It was a preposterous garment, and even more preposterous for someone who no longer had breasts or nipples. Acker bought it immediately. It was one of the most enjoyable days Golding had had with anyone in a long time. She felt that she was simply celebrating Acker just being alive.

Despite her sickness, and the romantic and professional rejection, Acker was still very much alive, still very present. She hadn't given up at all. Living in a basement, she felt, wasn't good for her health, so she set about selling Duncan Terrace and buying another place in London. She kept writing and traveling. That November, she visited Burroughs again in Kansas, ostensibly to write a piece for the Australian magazine *21C*, but also, perhaps unconsciously, to pay her final respects. In an email to Ira Silverberg, who had returned to Grove as editor in chief, she appeared content and reflective: "The whole visit meant so much to me, Ira, my lineage . . . William, as I'm sure you know, is happy, and to my surprise open and openly kind (he's always been kind but scary to me on the surface) . . . he hugged me again and made an effort to speak to me despite my ridiculous shyness . . . most of all, for me, I could see how clear he is, how without rancour and all the obterfuscations [*sic*] that blind most people . . ."

The *Guardian* weekend magazine commissioned a lengthy essay on the cancer ordeal, a cover story that would run the following January, and Acker agreed, more as a way to thank her healers—she preferred to call them "teachers" and "facilitators"—than anything else. She was wary of the paper sensationalizing it. "They wanted a naked pic of me for the cover," she wrote. "I hate these creeps." By December, the essay, originally assigned at five thousand words, had ballooned to ten thousand, and she told Silverberg that she wanted to turn it into a book like Gurdjieff's *Meetings with Remarkable Men* (working title *Girls with Diseases*). The *Guardian* piece would be titled "The Gift of Disease."

A few months later, Acker flew to New York to profile the Spice Girls, also for the *Guardian*. Though the latter was not Acker's idea, it was an inspired choice. In 1997, the Spice Girls were arguably the hottest music group in the world but derided as mock-feminists who'd appropriated and exploited the girl-power ethos of riot grrrl for their own personal gain. Acker was skeptical herself—"my next assignment from the *Guardian* is the Spice Girls," she emailed Ira Silverberg. "A fine object for the mind." But she threw herself into the work with typical vigor and seriousness, tapping Johnny Golding and her old music journalist friend Cynthia Rose for their insight, and at one point even commissioning astrological charts for the group's members. Acker ended up actually liking this particular girl gang—they were a world away from Tribe8, but they had moxie and style and an anger that Acker enjoyed encouraging. The final profile, which was published that May, would be one of her most enduring pieces of journalism.

Still, all this activity was depleting. When she faxed her draft to the paper, she told her editor, "I hope there will not be too much editing after this, for I am deeply tired and need sleep rather desperately. I'm not complaining, far from it, I'm pleased to be allowed to do this article and to be nudged into writing about areas close to me; I am just working at the edge of my strength and so should be careful."

After Hollins, she returned to the UK, uncertain, really, what she was going back for. "Playing for time," she told Silverberg, "seeing if I can get my old stinky job back in SF or a job somewhere (I have to pay bills!) and, if all is still a muddle, will just move to new flat, write book in a few months, and then sell and leave." By the summer, though, she was suffering from indeterminate digestive problems, occasional bouts of pneumonia, strange shooting pains down her back and right arm. In late August, she called Frank Malinaro and told him she thought the cancer was back. Malinaro was shocked but not really surprised. He hadn't wanted her to go back to London at all, felt that she was working herself to death. She told him she was going to come back to San Francisco.

Early that fall, she reunited with the Mekons in Chicago, where they opened the Museum of Contemporary Art's performance program with *Pussy*. It was an elaborate show, with lots of props and sets designed by the band—a pirate ship, palm trees—inspired by *Mutiny on the Bounty*. It was a throwback to an old-fashioned British pantomime, the kind that might have been shown at Christmas, with shouting and jokes, audience participation, a lot of cross-dressing. Acker growled, danced, sang. But halfway through the show, she collapsed and had to be carried offstage.

CHAPTER 40

———— × ————

I N AUGUST 1996, ACKER AND THE MEKONS HAD PERFORMED THE
Pussy show at the Bumbershoot Festival in Seattle, and Cynthia Rose and
her boyfriend met her for dinner at a Thai restaurant. It was a "delightful"
evening, Rose remembered, and Acker was, she said, her old self: argumen-
tative, enthusiastic, enormously funny. She showed them her surgery scars.
But Rose was also filled with foreboding. Acker was carrying a wooden staff
trimmed with crystals, and wore even more crystals on her body. She talked a
lot about her psychic. She told Rose that to prevent the cancer from returning
she needed to remove everything superficial from her life and to concentrate
completely on fighting the disease. It was, Rose said, "just a lot of West Coast
American stuff."

Most of Acker's old friends were similarly dubious. They'd been aghast
when she refused chemo, and became even more concerned when she so
fully embraced her healers, whom they often referred to as "witch doctors" or
"quacks." They understood why Acker would pursue alternative therapies, but
they didn't understand why she couldn't do both. Some thought that she had
signed her own death sentence, that eschewing more conventional medicine
was, in effect, a kind of suicide. Elly Antin said that Acker was trying to be "the
architect of her own death." Ira Silverberg was more abrupt: "It was her exit
strategy," he argued. "She was no longer as successful as she had been. Many
friends had abandoned her. She wanted out." Even Sheppard Powell, who
considered regular cancer therapy "barbaric," encouraged her to get regularly
monitored. "The way I work," he said, "is if it's something medicine is good at,
like diagnostics, don't shut it out." But she refused all entreaties, and eventually
just stopped having those conversations. Mel Freilicher thought that she went
back to London partly to escape the nagging.* Years after she died, Viegener

———————

* The poet and essayist Anne Boyer, who herself has coped with aggressive breast cancer, disagreed violently (if retrospectively) with Acker's friends. In her 2019 memoir, *The Undying*, Boyer

would argue that Acker always compelled her friends to join her in the story she created of her life; now she was also doing so in death.

When she got back to San Francisco, those conversations became more desperate. She was emaciated and dehydrated, and had a terrible, persistent cough. Her stamina was gone; she could barely climb stairs, could hardly breathe. She didn't want to go back to Davies, though, so she crashed first with friends, then at a Travelodge near the Tenderloin, and finally at a B&B. Word quickly spread, and several friends—chiefly, Aline Mare (her old friend from New York, who had gone back to school at SFAI in her forties), Sharon Grace (another SFAI instructor), and Bob Glück—mobilized around her. Glück remembered her "panicking," and being on the phone every thirty minutes with Malinaro. Malinaro told her to get a particular enema because of her terrible bowel pain, but Glück couldn't find the right one and she refused to use the one he ended up buying. He was convinced she was dying, and quickly called their mutual friends to help her prepare a will and find an executor.

When Matias Viegener heard that Acker was in San Francisco, he drove up from Los Angeles, where he lived, as soon as he could. The thirty-eight-year-old was an artist and writer who taught at CalArts. He'd studied with Sylvère Lotringer and greatly admired Acker, having first met her a decade earlier at Dennis Cooper's place in Los Feliz. He'd been charmed by what he remembered as her shyness—at the party, she stood apart from the rest of the guests, absently inspecting Cooper's bookshelves. He approached her and introduced himself. They quickly became close, closer than either expected. By virtue of physical distance or lack of sexual attraction—Viegener is gay—their relationship never succumbed to the insecurity and competitiveness that marred so

---

writes, "The novelist Kathy Acker's breast cancer most likely couldn't have been cured by chemotherapy, but she had no way of knowing this when she refused chemotherapy in 1996. Or at least she had no rational way to know this. She did, however, appear to have another way to know it. 'I live as I believe,' wrote Acker in 'The Gift of Disease,' 'that belief is equal to the body.' Rather than submitting to a medical protocol that most likely wouldn't have worked and could have killed her before the cancer did, Kathy Acker decided to live as if she weren't dying. [. . .] Had Acker agreed to one of the regiments of chemotherapy available in 1996, it would have almost certainly meant that the last months of her life would have been spent with some variation of the following: tremendous pain, dry itchy eyes, skin lesions, anal lesions, mouth lesions, a bloody nose, wasted muscles, dying nerves, rotting teeth, and without hair or an immune system, too brain-damaged to write, throwing up, losing her memory, losing her vocabulary, and severely fatigued."

many of Acker's relationships. He sometimes fantasized about having a child with her, or, in fact, being her child—he wondered what it would have been like to have her and Lotringer as his parents. After her death, Viegener wrote that he considered Acker one of only two geniuses he'd met in his life. As with Peter Gordon and Ira Silverberg, she considered Viegener a kind of brother. "He's really fun to be with," she told McKenzie Wark.

Though Viegener would later characterize Acker's beliefs around her cancer treatment as "magical thinking," he had been unfailingly patient with her throughout the illness. Now, though, like everyone else who'd gathered at the B&B, he insisted that she go to the hospital. Finally, she was so weak she could no longer resist. An ambulance took her back to Davies, where was admitted on October 25. X-rays revealed that the cancer was indeed back, and had, in fact, metastasized. She now had advanced cancer of the liver, pancreas, spleen, bone, and lungs. Doctors told her she had maybe a week to live.

But even after Acker grudgingly conceded that they might be right about the cancer's return, she refused to believe that palliative care was her only remaining option. In "The Gift of Disease," Acker wrote that conventional medicine had reduced her to "a body that was only material, a body without hope and so, without will, to a puppet who, separated by fear from her imagination and vision, would do whatever she was told." Even so frail, she had not lost hope, nor would she abandon any sense of control. To her doctors' irritation, she brought in some of her healers and, only after consulting with them, decided she would pursue more experimental care in Mexico. "Kathy had profound willpower," Viegener said. "It's rare I meet anyone with more willpower than her. She had accepted that the cancer had come back, but she was certain she'd recover with more alternative treatment."

She had more than her willpower and self-belief, though. She was also very familiar with an example of such therapies working. Just a couple years earlier, her old friend Carolee Schneemann had also been diagnosed with both breast cancer and non-Hodgkins lymphoma. Schneemann had likewise refused chemo—"it's torture, the whole configuration"—or a mastectomy, and sought help instead at the Gerson Clinic in Mexico. There, she was given an extremely strict diet and received regular coffee enemas, among other things, all designed to detoxify her body and strengthen her immune system. "I wasn't sure Gerson would save me but I was absolutely sure I wasn't going to do traditional medicine," Schneemann said. But Gerson did appear to save her. Her cancer went into remission, and she would live another twenty years. Schneemann didn't want Acker to go the traditional route either, convinced that it would kill her. And she was horrified that Acker had already undergone the mastectomy, was already, as Schneemann put it, "in the arms of the patriarchy."

As it turned out, Acker's cancer had progressed so far that the Gerson Clinic wouldn't take her anyway. Nor would the Ann Wigmore Natural Health Institute in Puerto Rico or any of the other places Viegener and the others tried. They finally found a place in Tijuana—American Biologics, a self-described holistic integrated clinic whose best-known patient had been the actor Steve McQueen.

As Viegener and the others made their frantic phone calls, other visitors came and went. Acker called in her healers and had regular sessions with them. Lotringer flew down from Banff, Alberta, where he was teaching. Acker was still very weak, could barely talk at some points, was on lots of morphine. The doctors periodically drained her lungs, which helped her breathing. She made occasional phone calls, including one to Kevin Killian. She told him that she wasn't afraid of death. Then said, "Kevin, you are such a wonderful writer, always keep in touch with your genius. Never let it die. Never sell it cheap." Killian thought she was probably telling all her writer friends similar things, but he was grateful and moved.

Throughout her stay, Acker's friends kept telling her that she had to prepare a will. She was finally persuaded by the fact that if she didn't, everything she had would go to her sister, Wendy. On Halloween, she wrote out a will by hand, making Viegener the executor of her literary estate, with Silverberg a "major consultant and assistant." Of her half sister she wrote, "I love my sister and her family deeply. I have not seen my family in several years simply due to my deep-seated belief that personal encounters would have led to more discord than love." She went on to say that because Wendy had more money and real estate than most of her friends, and that her friends had become her "new family," she wanted a small group of them, determined by her estimation of their economic need, to divide up her personal property after her death. This group included Viegener, Grace and Mare, as well as Cynthia Carr, Sheppard Powell, Johnny Golding, Mel Freilicher, Carla Harryman, and R. U. Sirius. (Viegener wasn't sure how much money Acker actually had until after she died. It turned out to be about $200,000, mostly in equities. After her medical expenses and legal fees were paid, each of her friends received $18,000.)

Acker also wrote that she wanted her books, which she said comprised four to five thousand volumes, to stay intact and be donated to a public library or some institution. "I want people to use my books," she told Viegener. "They should be in a corner, some kind of room. Like a room in a school. People should come to read them, like a girl who is writing a project. Don't let them separate my books."*

She concluded the will by saying, "My life has been totally devoted to my writing; now I am learning that one can create in life as well as in fiction." It was a mysterious statement, muddled perhaps by the painkillers she was on. Did she think these final expressions of generosity would literally help her friends create new art of their own? Was it a small sign of regret, an acknowledgment that she had sacrificed her life to writing? But then, hadn't she always believed that fiction could create life, that it *was* life?

These gestures were touching and revealing. A central contradiction of Acker's life had always been the tension between her need for people—and *from* people—and her need for solitude, to do her work. She pushed people away as soon as they came close, and then resented them for leaving her alone. She was a writer, arguably the most solitary of creative pursuits, but her books required, more so than almost any other writer's, other books as their fuel and a broad, diverse community for their publication. Now, toward the end, she had tried to repay some of those people, and, indeed, literature itself. Her legacy would be her own writing, to be sure, but her writing had always inhabited that of others. As a girl, she said, she had run into books, initiating a single-minded quest to unify her life and work. That unification now seemed complete.

× × ×

Acker left Ralph Davies on November 1, the Day of the Dead, in a rented van with Viegener driving and a nurse, who was also a Buddhist nun, administering morphine to Acker, who reclined in the back. En route, they stopped in L.A. to pick up Viegener's brother, Valentin, who would serve as an additional nurse

---

* For many years, Acker's library languished in Viegener's home, unwanted by any of the institutions to which Viegener tried to donate it. Finally, in 2015, the library was acquired by the University of Cologne, where its 6,600-odd volumes (plus many pieces of ephemera—boarding passes, lipstick tubes, letters, receipts) now comprise the Kathy Acker Reading Room. Open to girls, yes, but boys and nonbinary people too.

and companion. One of the last things Acker wrote by hand, on November 3, was Valentin's birthdate and astrological sign, planning to prepare a horoscope for him.

They arrived in Tijuana that day. American Biologics (later renamed the International Bio Care Hospital) was clean and comfortable but not luxurious, a low-slung building just off of Tijuana's main drag, the aptly named Avenida Revolución. It was not cheap—the six weeks she spent there cost about $60,000.* The clinic's most distinctive characteristic was a kind of charged intensity—every patient there had late-stage cancer. This was their last hope and, for almost all, their last station on earth. Viegener described it as a world apart, not unlike the sanitarium in Thomas Mann's *The Magic Mountain*. They put Acker in Room 101. "Is there nothing that woman can't turn into a literary reference?" Alan Moore later quipped, referring to the similarly named torture chamber in George Orwell's *1984*.

Acker's treatment, however, was far from torturous. The nurses didn't speak much English, but were warm and empathetic. The clinic prepared its own organic, often quite delicious food. Acker could no longer walk, but Viegener and other visitors would wheel her out to sit in the sun on the rooftop patio. In addition to the food and fresh vegetable juices, her doctor, Rodrigo Rodriguez, a jovial, bearish man, prescribed several other things: mineral chelation, IV vitamins, a new Eastern European plant extract called Ukrain, and tamoxifen, a selective estrogen receptor modulator. They gradually weaned her off the morphine. At least once, she had her nails done by a manicurist, which Valentin Viegener said made her "very happy."

After a few days, she was stable, her color returned. But while her days could be good and calm, the nights were often marred by panic attacks. Viegener and his brother took turns with her. She slept with one of her stuffed animals, the tattered plush rat named Ratski. She tried to read. She never complained about pain.

Visitors started arriving almost immediately: the Antins, Freilicher, Silverberg and Scholder, Aline Mare. Those who couldn't come in person—Lynne Tillman, Jeanette Winterson, Peter Wollen, Neil Gaiman—phoned. The

---

* Uncertain how much money Acker had, and how long they'd have to pay for her care, Viegener also started a fundraising campaign through John Giorno's foundation. They ended up raising about $10,000, all of which was spent on her hospital care.

conversations in Room 101 were, for the most part, tender, even joyous, with much talk about books and gossip about friends and lovers. Old resentments and feuds were largely forgotten. She told Viegener that, of all her many lovers and partners, Peter Gordon was probably the one who had been best for her, with whom she was most compatible. The Antins had brought a CD of *La Traviata*, and Viegener Philip Glass's *Solo Piano* and Felix Maria Woschek's *Mystic Dance*, an album of Hindu bhajans and Islamic mantras. Acker played the last two CDs constantly—a meditative, almost unearthly, soundtrack. Freilicher delivered books that Acker asked for—John Le Carré's *Tinker, Tailor, Soldier, Spy*, Gershom Scholem's book on the Kabbalah—while Viegener gave her a copy of *I Love Dick*, Chris Kraus's just published and controversial novel about her obsession with cultural theorist Dick Hebdige. When Hebdige surprised everyone by dropping in to visit, Acker deftly hid the book under her pillow.

When Lotringer arrived, he was a bundle of emotion. He was horrified that Acker had arrived at this place, was in such a state. At this point, she had lost control of her bladder and colon, and her back was covered in small red spots, the result of blood vessels breaking down. He blamed himself, in part, for her illness. If he had stayed with her, he thought, she might have had a different life, might not have drifted so much. He believed that she had never truly grown up, and, like a child, couldn't believe or understand her own mortality. She asked Lotringer to go to a corner store and get her some notebooks. She wanted to start a new novel. Later, on his third and last visit, she said to him, "Do you think people will make a film about me?"

Over the last few years, Acker had had intermittent contact with her sister, Wendy, including one meeting that Amy Scholder had been privy to in SoHo. "They were like family that didn't see each other much," Scholder said, "but it was friendly." Scholder had lost so many friends to AIDS, had been to so many deathbeds where the person dying had no family there because their families had rejected them. But those who did have family members who said goodbye, who could say that they loved the dying person, who could say that they never meant to hurt them—that, Scholder felt, was a better way to leave the world. She wanted Acker to call Wendy, who was then living in Massachusetts. Acker said no. "She's your closest living family," Scholder said. "You have to tell her that you're so sick." Acker still refused, even when Viegener pled the case. "Why can't you call her, Kathy?" Viegener asked. Exasperated and exhausted, her voice trembling, Acker finally said, "Because my sister . . . is the president . . . of her tennis club!" It was wrenching, this defiance. Acker could still not relinquish her disappointment in her family. With Electra still possibly fresh in her mind, she knew that vengeance leads to endless retaliation.

Until the last week of her life, Acker was still convinced she would survive, and everyone knew not to say otherwise. By the week of Thanksgiving, however, her condition had rapidly declined. She stopped breathing and was resuscitated, and thereafter could no longer breathe unassisted. She stopped eating solid foods. Her body shrunk even more. In one of her last lucid conversations with Viegener, they talked briefly about her literary legacy. "I've said what I needed to say," Acker said. "I can accept dying. I want to stay in the world, but I've made the work that was in me to make. I've accomplished something."

It's impossible to know what exactly she meant in that moment, but her accomplishments and significance were apparent to all who had gathered at her bedside, in person or otherwise. They'd all known this entirely formidable person, and they had all experienced the good and bad of this: the charm, the fun, the hostility, the bloody-mindedness, the nuttiness. They'd all been exasperated and exhilarated by her. Their presence in the clinic was itself a testament to the wild variety of Acker's life, her role in so many different scenes, moments, and places, her long, luminous shadow.

She had been her own creation, an icon of unorthodoxy. Almost alone in her tenacity and nerve, she had completely reoriented our understanding of literature and what literature could do. For all of her books' vivid vulgarity, they asked fundamental questions. How do I cope with the pain of being unloved? What is good art? What is art good for? What knowledge exists outside our conscious minds? Where is home, and how do I get there? She had the genius to make her own art the answer to these questions, but an answer that, in keeping with the difficulty of these questions, denied normalization or assimilation. To retrieve it, she kept going underground, and demanded that readers follow. Acker believed her books existed in a lineage that began with Laurence Sterne's *Tristram Shandy* and continued into a twentieth century bookended by Stein and Burroughs. But because of their engagement with the whole breadth of literary history and because, in her writing, Acker refused to obey laws of chronology, her books also stand outside of time.

To be outside of time is to be lonely. She sacrificed so many things—even, now, it seemed, her life—in the name of her ideals and beliefs. But she had known no other way to live.

× × ×

On Thanksgiving Day, Viegener asked Acker if she wanted to eat anything. She said no. Two days later, the L.A.-based photographer and video artist Connie Samaras, Viegener's best friend and someone with whom Acker had enjoyed a flirtatious relationship, called him and asked when she should visit. He told her to come down right away, and Samaras arrived around four that afternoon, intending to only spend a couple of hours. But Viegener, who had been sleeping on a second bed in Acker's room, was exhausted and asked that she stay longer. While he napped, Samaras sat on Acker's bed, whispering soothingly to her. While Acker could barely speak, Samaras sensed that Acker wanted, needed, some more intimate contact. "I just started touching Kathy everywhere," she said, "on her breast, on her pussy. It was sexual and comforting. I knew she wanted to be touched like that. Kathy was very sensual." In response, Acker gently kissed the air.

At 11 p.m., Samaras roused Viegener. Samaras and Viegener lay down on either side of Acker and held her hands and calmly caressed her face. The Philip Glass CD continued to play. The three spoke little, but Acker's gaze moved slowly between Samaras and Viegener. Her eyes eventually closed, her breath became more erratic. Samaras told her that it was okay, that she could let go. All of Acker's fear seemed to be gone. Two hours later, at 1:30 a.m. on November 30, 1997, she whispered her last words, "Up, up, up"—requesting that her bed be adjusted—and then her heart finally stopped.

"She looked beautiful," Viegener remembered. "It was a beautiful death, like a nineteenth-century death from TB." The cause of death was listed as cardiopulmonary failure from complications of metastasized cancer. The hospital left Viegener and Samaras alone with Acker for two hours, then came to take out the IVs and catheters. Viegener and Samaras removed all of her piercings themselves. They sobbed quietly, completely exhausted. Acker had given no instructions for a funeral, but it was decided she'd be cremated. Staff from the mortuary came, wrapped Acker in the clean white sheets of the bed, lay her on a stretcher that they covered with a dark red velvet cloth, and then took her away in a hearse.

It would be a week before the cremation, so Viegener and Samaras decided to return home. They took a cab to the border and walked across and caught the 5 a.m. trolley back to San Diego. Their car was filled with college students, prostitutes, and young Marines, everyone drunk or high or both, a gaudy, debauched procession that Viegener thought would have pleased Acker. As they traveled up along the ocean, a glorious sunrise filled the harbor with light. "It was like coming out of the underworld," Viegener said, "and into the real world."

× × ×

In the months after Acker's death, in late 1997 and early 1998, several memorials were held, in all the cities she had called home—San Diego, San Francisco, New York, London. Friends, lovers, and colleagues spoke or performed at each one, every gathering a testament to the wild variety and energy of Acker's life, to the different communities she inhabited, to the love and devotion she inspired. Both Allen Ginsberg and William Burroughs also died in 1997, and there was a sense, with Acker's passing, that a particular kind of American literature had come to an end.

It was uncertain, at first, what would happen with her ashes. Ira Silverberg thought they could be scattered in a few cities. First, though, there would be a small ceremony where the ashes would be transferred from the box in which they'd been placed in Mexico and into an urn. Viegener bought what he thought was an appropriate vessel—a brass Art Deco–style vase that he sealed with a trivet—and then drove to Bob Glück's house in San Francisco, where several people gathered: Glück, Scholder, Kevin Killian, Dodie Bellamy, Aline Mayer, Sharon Grace, Frank Malinaro, Sheppard Powell. They sat on the floor, said goodbye to her. Powell performed a Buddhist chant. They transferred the ashes with a silver spoon. The group talked about different funeral rites and someone mentioned that sometimes people symbolically eat a bit of the ashes or you blend them into soup and eat the soup. Something to incorporate the dead person into life. When some of the ashes spilled in the transfer, Glück took a bit of them and put them in his mouth. Killian did the same thing. "They were delicious," he said. "I could feel her energy entering my body." Viegener watched this with some concern and repulsion. He didn't know if Kathy would want to be in either of their bodies. He decided to eat some of the ashes himself. "That way," he said later, "and this is such nutso, New Age, magical, whatever, thinking, she would have a choice of different paths."

The whole strange ceremony underscored the long-simmering tension between Acker's healers and her old friends. Most of the latter were especially wary of Malinaro, believing him to be a charlatan who'd held too much influence over Acker. Glück recalled him even handing out business cards at the ceremony. Malinaro, in turn, thought of them as snobs who had, by taking Acker to Mexico, hastened her death. Things came to a head early the next year, when Acker's ashes were finally scattered in San Francisco. On January 23, 1998, Viegener and a small group, including Scholder and Malinaro, took the urn to Fort Funston, a former military base on the shore below the city. After much deliberation, Viegener decided that Acker wouldn't have really cared what happened to her ashes. But she had enjoyed walking at Fort Funston—it was coastal, windswept, the water rough. She would be returned to the sea, like the pirate she always imagined herself to be.

It was a cold, overcast day, which was, to Malinaro's mind, an ominous sign. "When it's nasty on the day of your memorial, funeral, or whatever," he said, "that means you didn't want to go." Nevertheless, the group made its way over the dunes and down to the ocean, taking turns carrying the urn. Then, before they were even at the water, Malinaro snatched the urn out of Scholder's hands and ran ahead of them, shaking the ashes from the vessel, screaming, "Kathy! You're free! You're free!" The cremains wouldn't come out easily, though, and as Malinaro shook the urn violently, the wind blew the ashes back and over the rest of the group, before Scholder finally wrested it away from him again. "It was just awful," Viegener said. He and Scholder went into the water and scattered what remained in the urn. There was a silent prayer. It was done.

Afterward, some of the group went to have a meal. Malinaro went home alone. When other people in his care had passed away, he had received signs or messages, something to say that they'd made it to the other side. But he hadn't heard anything from Acker, which saddened him. Then, as he was getting out of his wet clothes, he heard a noise. The TV, which was on, became very loud, and he reached for the remote to turn it down. He pressed a wrong button, though, changed the channel and there, playing on the TV, was the 1939 movie version of *Wuthering Heights* that Acker had used in *My Mother: Demonology*. Laurence Olivier's Heathcliff was saying, "Goodbye, my dearest Cathy." Malinaro was delighted. There was no doubt in his mind that she'd survived her death. She had made the transition. Her early, awful death made no sense to him, but he felt, finally, echoing what Acker herself had told Viegener on her deathbed, that "she did what she came in to do."

On November 14, Acker's last two books, *Bodies of Work* and *Eurydice in the*

Underworld, were reviewed by Alev Adil in the *TLS*. She didn't see the review, but it was unusually sympathetic. It also, coincidentally, described Acker by using her old high school nickname, Cassandra, one that Adil surely didn't know, and which no one had likely used in over thirty years: "The reader is so often shouted at that it is easy to become deaf to the sophistication and technical virtuosity with which Acker composes her symphonies of screams. The simultaneous publication of her essays and stories is an opportunity to listen, to reappraise a misunderstood writer [. . .] Acker is no Scheherazade, subverting through seduction; she is a Cassandra, a furious prophet."

AFTERWORD

———— × ————

When I began researching this book, Kathy Acker had been dead for more than fifteen years. Despite the posthumous publications, the acclaimed 2007 documentary, *Who's Afraid of Kathy Acker?*, and a collection of Acker and McKenzie Wark's email correspondence published in 2015, over time, Acker's presence in the culture began to shrink, her name became less known, her work less read. While the rare innovative writer—Kate Zambreno, Lidia Yuknavitch, Jack Skelley, Azareen Van der Vliet Oloomi—referenced Acker from time to time, there seemed the danger that she would be completely forgotten. I waited for years for a full-scale biography to appear, one that would remind readers of her importance and provide an adequate framework through which to understand how she became the writer she was. When that book didn't appear, I set out to write it myself.

This landscape changed a few years later. This was, in large part, because of the cultural and aesthetic shifts I detailed at the beginning of this book—Acker's work has become more relevant and resonant with every passing year—but of equal significance was the publication of Chris Kraus's biography, *After Kathy Acker*, in 2017. Kraus was at the crest of her own revival: *I Love Dick*, originally published in 1997 and reissued in 2006, had been publicly praised by tastemakers like Sheila Heti, Lena Dunham, and Lorde, and then turned into an Amazon show. The *New Yorker* and the *New York Times* published profiles of Kraus. By 2016, *I Love Dick* was no longer a cult novel; it was a minor bestseller, selling fourteen thousand copies a year. When Kraus published *After Kathy Acker*, a considerable amount of this newfound fame reflected back on her subject. Acker suddenly had a whole new generation discovering her, and more familiar readers revisiting books they hadn't looked at in decades.

After Kathy Acker was a valuable but partial account, and could feel, at times, dismissive and coy. Kraus's personal relationship to Acker is largely elided. But nevertheless, the book helped usher in an extended period of Ackermania. In 2017, Grove reissued *Blood and Guts*, with a new introduction by Kraus, followed by reissues of Acker's other major novels. That same year, the wish that Acker confided to Bob Glück—that her books become Penguin Classics—came true; Penguin released editions of *Blood and Guts, Great Expectations*, and *New York City in 1979*. In 2018, the first comprehensive solo exhibition of Acker's artwork—notebooks, videos, audio recordings, photographs, and more—was held at the Badischer Kunstverein in Karlsruhe, Germany, followed by a similar exhibition at the Institute of Contemporary Art in London the following spring. In Karlsruhe, a large, curated portion of Acker's personal library was displayed. These books had been temporarily loaned by the University of Cologne, which finally acquired Acker's library in 2015 and which, after the books, records, and other ephemera had been catalogued, restored, indexed, and shelved, opened their Kathy Acker Reading Room to the public in 2018.

Academic interest in Acker has been fairly consistent since her death, but it's become a cottage industry in the last half decade. Inventive studies have appeared, including Georgina Colby's *Kathy Acker: Writing the Impossible*, Emilia Borowska's *The Politics of Kathy Acker*, and Margaret Henderson's *Kathy Acker: Punk Writer*. There have been more initimate monographs too: Douglas Martin's *Acker*, an affectionate hybrid of personal essay and literary criticism; Matias Viegener's short, provocative memoir, *The Assassination of Kathy Acker*; McKenzie Wark's *Philosophy for Spiders*, a rigorous and playful exploration of Acker's ideas around gender. Other, somewhat more obscure volumes have gathered Acker's unpublished writing from the early 1970s— *Kathy Acker (1971–1975)*—and provided a glimpse of her brief sojourn in the Pacific Northwest—*Kathy Acker in Seattle*.

The most surprising contribution to this Acker renaissance was Olivia Laing's debut novel, *Crudo*, also published in 2018. Acclaimed for nonfiction books that blended memoir, biography, history, and criticism, Laing took Acker's methods and impudently applied them to Acker herself. Her protagonist was named Kathy, and she had written *Blood and Guts in High School* and had twice endured breast cancer; but she also shared much of Laing's biography too, and the whole novel took place in the fiendish, turbulent summer of 2017. If you'd wondered what it would be like to have Kathy Acker writing in the age of Twitter and Trump, well, here, was one answer. Laing returned to Acker again in her next nonfiction book, a study of the power and policing of human bodies. That book was called *Everybody*, and was subtitled *A Book About Freedom*.

In interviews, Laing talked about the freedom and permission that Acker had given her. It was the same freedom and permission I felt when I first encountered Acker, and which so many other writers had spoken about. From the beginning, she had shown that writing could be much more than what most writers and readers thought it was. She had also shown what it looked like to make a life almost exclusively in, and of, art. How stubborn and daring that required you to be, but also the personal costs of such a life. The British writer Tom McCarthy, in a lecture on Acker that he gave in 2017, put it this way: "It might just be that the final measure of a writer is not so much what they achieve themselves as what they render possible for others."

Almost a year later, at Performance Space New York, in the East Village, this sense of possibility was made manifest at a six-hour reading of *Blood and Guts in High School*. Organized by Sarah Schulman, it brought together several generations of novelists, poets, performers, musicians, editors, and artists, each of whom had been touched in some way by Acker's work and person. Many of Acker's oldest friends and colleagues were there—among them Pooh Kaye, Lynne Tillman, Ira Silverberg, McKenzie Wark—but also many people who were connected to Acker largely through their admiration: the essayist and poet Kay Gabriel, the poet and sound artist Tracie Morris, the singer-songwriter and cabaret artist Justin Vivian Bond, and dozens more. All the performers, sometimes alone, sometimes in groups of two or more, stood on a bare, black stage, behind which hung a large blowup of the 1984 Grove Press edition of the book, with its lurid, black-red-and-white Sue Coe cover. The event felt at once like a theater festival, a high school reunion, a wake, and a séance.

I participated in the reading too, and planned to stick around for just part of it. I had expected it to be an interesting day—just seeing all these bohemian legends in one room was a thrill—but also a bit tedious, frankly. Though I'd read *Blood and Guts* a number of times at that point, I wasn't sure how well its sprawl and complexity, its multifarious, sometimes conflicting registers, would lend themselves to such a performance. I was happy to be wrong. Despite the event's epic length and often bleak tone, the book came alive in the hands of these different readers, many of whom were seasoned, exuberant performers. They made the book more accessible and funny, and revealed a warmth, even a sweetness, that I had never fully recognized before. I was reminded again of how much Acker's books were meant to be performed, in front of an audience.

I mourned, not for the first time, the fact that Acker wasn't around to read her own words. I stayed until the last line.

Toward the end of *Blood and Guts in High School*, after Janey has died, Acker writes, "Soon many other Janeys were born and these Janeys covered the earth." That sentence has often been quoted, by fans and other writers and artists who like to consider themselves Janeys, who recognize the bright, difficult path that Acker blazed and who set out on it. That day at Performance Space, the room was full of Janeys, all of whom had broken ground of their own, had reconfigured their own art forms. Some of them were friends and some collaborators; others hated each other. But they were all united together in celebration of the writer who had, if not exactly given birth to them, at least given them life.

ACKNOWLEDGMENTS

———————— × ————————

Every book, of course, is a product of many people, but a biography perhaps even more so. I am most indebted to Matias Viegener, Acker's literary executor. From our very first phone call, in which I tentatively inquired about writing this book, he was entirely supportive and encouraging. He facilitated contact with many of Acker's friends, lovers, and colleagues, and permitted unfettered quotation from her written work, published and otherwise. Over the next decade, he remained patient and helpful as I nagged him with questions and entreaties. On a research trip to Los Angeles in 2015, he was kind enough to let me bunk down in his library. And then he went a step further, covering my futon with a set of Acker's own black cotton sheets. Can bedding be haunted? How many other people might have also slept in those sheets with or without her? In any case, I didn't sleep much that week.

As any reader of Acker's work knows, family was, to say the least, an extremely difficult and complex subject for her. I am particularly thankful therefore that Acker's two surviving relatives, her half-sister Wendy Bowers and cousin Pooh Kaye, spoke to me at length and shared what were often very painful memories. Both trusted me, as well, with precious family photographs, some of which are reproduced in these pages.

Acker's friendships, in contrast, were rich and varied, and one of the more pleasant surprises in writing this book was learning what thoughtful, kind, and generous social circles she had formed over her lifetime. Almost universally, and without complaint, these friends, lovers, and colleagues shared their time, memories, correspondence, and confidences. Mel Freilicher was an empathetic and reliable sounding board, always quick with a gracious word, full-throated correction, or shoulder to cry on. I treasure his comradeship. My friendship with Lynne Tillman predated this project, but I was thankful for an excuse to speak with her more frequently (and to have her always in my corner). I learned so much from the hyper-articulate and wise Leslie Dick, not just about Acker, but also about art, writing, fashion, and love. Of all my interview subjects, I was perhaps most nervous to meet Amy Scholder. She was as formidable as expected, but also extraordinarily bighearted, perceptive, and helpful. Ira Silverberg, whom I interviewed early on, stepped in to rescue this book at a critical juncture in its development. I'm sorry that he wasn't able to remain my editor, but I'm grateful for his unerring guidance and continued confidence in this project. Other Acker intimates put up with my repeated questions and were interviewed often, in person, over the phone, and by email: Robert Acker, Jeff Goldberg, Peter Gordon, Peter Gould, Leonard Neufeld, and P. Adams Sitney.

A number of others also granted interviews or shared written reminiscences and correspondence: D-L Alvarez, Deborah Anker, Eleanor Antin, Stephen Beachy, Charles Bernstein, Adele Bertei, Alan Black, Nayland Blake, Michael Bracewell, Lynn Breedlove, Kathy Brew, Paul Buck, Julie Burchill, Cynthia Carr, Rhys Chatham, Dennis Cockell, Victor Coleman, Dennis Cooper, Constance DeJong, Michel Delsol, Tamar Diesendruck, Judith Doyle, Jenna Leigh Evans, Rene Eyre, Larry Fink, Richard Foreman, Howard Fried, Ed Friedman, Ellen G. Friedman, Neil Gaiman, Glenda George, Robert Glück, Johnny Golding, Igor Goldkind, Jacqueline Graham, James Grauerholz, Duncan Hannah, Stephen Harris, Carla Harryman, Richard Hell, Dale Hemmerdinger, Jack Hirschman, Harry Hoogstraten, Ali Hossaini, Gary Indiana, Darius James, Alan Jenkins, Ken Jordan, Richard Kadrey, Leandro Katz, Alan Kaufman, Roz Kaveney, Wilma Korevaar, Jill Kroesen, Hanif Kureishi, Robert Kushner, Jon Langford, Frank Malinaro, Amanda Marchand, Elizabeth Marcus, Aline Mare, Bertie Marshall, Bernadette Mayer, Anne McDermid, Barry Miles, Salome Milstead, Alan Moore, Charles Shaar Murray, Eileen Myles, Susan Nielsen, Jacki Ochs, Susan Orlovsky, Andrew J. Paterson, Sheppard Powell, Georgina Ritchie, Paul Robinson, Avital Ronell, Cynthia Rose, Diane Rothenberg, Jerome Rothenberg, Salman Rushdie, David Salle, Connie Samaras, Harris Schiff, Ron Silliman, R. U. Sirius, Anna Joy Springer, Richard Strange, Betsy Sussler, Stephanie Syjuco, Anne Turyn, Simon Usher, Linda Vasu, Anne Waldman, McKenzie Wark, Jeff Weinstein, Matthew Weinstein, Robin Winters, and Rudy Wurlitzer.

Several other titanic figures, who generously offered their time and insight into Acker (directly and indirectly), passed away before this book was completed: David Antin, Fred Gaysek, Sylvère Lotringer, Carolee Schneemann, Peter Wollen, Fred Jordan, and Lawrence Weiner. I look forward to someday reading full biographies of them all. Kevin Killian, the brilliant poet, novelist, and Jack Spicer biographer, was one of my most ardent cheerleaders and the first person I formally interviewed (on May 4, 2013, in a hotel room in Toronto's Chinatown). At that interview, he passed along two talismanic books that Acker had given him from her library—Zahrad's *Gigo Poems* and Philip Lamantia's *Destroyed Works*—a gesture that I will never forget. For years after, he continued to offer mentorship, gossip, and his singular critical eye. I regret that he didn't live to see this book finished, and I miss him dearly.

In keeping with a subject like Acker, whose lifelong devotion to books was profound, several librarians were vital to the success of this project. Thank you to these beneficent, tireless, gracious individuals: Elizabeth B. Dunn, Jennifer Scott, Kelly Wooten, and, especially, Laura Micham, of the Sallie Bingham Center for Women's History and Culture, David M. Rubinstein Rare Book & Manuscript Library, Duke University; Rachel Greer, Emily King, and Lisa Darms, of Fales Library and Special Collections, NYU; Heather Smedberg, Special Collections & Archives, UC San Diego; Kathy Shoemaker, The Stuart A. Rose Manuscript, Archives, & Rare Book Library, Emory University; Rebecca Jewett, Thompson Library Special Collections, Ohio State University; Chloe-Morse Harding, Robert D. Farber University Archives & Special Collections, Brandeis University; Becky Alexander and Jeff Gunderson, Anne Bremer Memorial Library, San Francisco Art Institute; Elizabeth Leventhal, Director of Alumni and Community Relations at the Birch Wathen Lenox School, who provided photocopies of Acker's high school yearbooks.

During my research, Chris Kraus helpfully shared a number of sources, documents, and other information. Her 2017 book, *After Kathy Acker: A Literary Biography*, was as an invaluable map and model. The industrious, enthusiastic Daniel Schulz likewise pointed me toward numerous sources, and selflessly provided complete, regular access to his research. *Danke schön.*

Several photographers (and their assistants) supplied contact sheets, outtakes, and unpublished photographs of Acker, and kindly worked within a criminally low art budget. Thank you to Joree Adilman (Robert Mapplethorpe Foundation), Hudson Bohr, Jamie Cabreza, Deborah Feingold, Larry Fink, Andrew Harris, Ali Hossaini, Laurie Neaman, Nicole Pyke, Steve Pyke, Marcia Resnick, Kate Simon, Michael Van Horne (Art + Commerce), Del LaGrace Volcano.

So many other people helped in ways big and small: putting me up, making me meals, transcribing interviews, listening to my stories, pointing me toward sources, reading excerpts, sharing information, holding my hand. There's no way I can ever thank them enough, but I'll start by naming some of them here: Howard Akler, Nathalie Atkinson, Dodie Bellamy, Julia Berner-Tobin, Emilia Borowska, Chris Buck, Scott Cataffa, Michael Clune, Georgina Colby, Andrea Curtis, Lauren Elkin, Jason Evans, Vincent Fecteau, Claire Finch, Norbert Finzsch, Glenn Gossling, Sheila Heti, Alicia Hogan, Saudamini Jain, Julia May Jonas, Joe Keenan, Susan Kernohan, Jennifer Krasinski, Claudia La Rocco, Braden Labonte, Erik LaPrade, Micah Lexier, Sarah Liss, Nicole Malik, Douglas A. Martin, Leah McLaren, Szilvia Molnar, Nadia Nooreyezdan, Katrina Onstad, Ed Park, Ronald Robboy, Siobhan Roberts, Damian Rogers, Aida Ruilova, Lucy Sante, Sarah Schulman, Angela Shackel, Courtney Shea, Naomi Skwarna, Isabel Slone, Anneke Smit, Adam Sternbergh, Jenny Turner, Christopher Waters, Edmund White, Alana Wilcox, Robert Yates.

My agent, Samantha Haywood, saw the value in this book immediately, and propelled it forward with fortitude and equanimity. Neither of us expected it would take quite so long to finish, and I remain thankful for her patience and enlightened counsel. My editor, Stuart Roberts, read the manuscript with sensitivity, diligence, and care. He and his colleague, Maria Mendez, encouraged me to go deeper, and improved the book in many ways. Thank you to them, and to everyone at Simon & Schuster.

Several of the aforementioned read the manuscript at various stages, but particular thanks to Claire Foster and Matthew Stadler, fellow travelers and devoted friends. Their astute and charitable feedback saved me from embarrassment, inaccuracy, and despair.

Portions of this book appeared in somewhat different form in *Canadian Art*, *Hazlitt*, the *Slate Book Review*, ArtsEverywhere's *Polity of Literature* series, and *Kathy Acker: Get Rid of Meaning*. Thank you to editors David Balzer, Jordan Ginsberg, Dan Kois, Matthew Stadler, Anja Casser, and Matias Viegener. A special thank-you to Serah-Marie McMahon and Haley Mlotek; a section of the book was supposed to appear in their magazine *Worn*, but I was too slow and, alas, *Worn* is no longer with us.

Thank you to Lisa Robertson and Coach House Books, for allowing me to reprint lines from "The Seam," from *3 Summers*.

I am grateful for assistance from the Canada Arts Council, the Ontario Arts Council, and the Toronto Arts Council. Thank you also to the Sallie Bingham Center for Women's History and Culture at Duke University, whose Mary Lily Research Grant enabled me to spend time with Acker's papers there.

My extended families have been a ceaseless source of support and faith. Thank you to the McBrides (Michael, Marci, Abigail, Emmy), the McCormacks—Melissa, Cynthia (1943–2018), and Murray (1940–2021)—the Sullivans (Bob, Sue, Derek, Neil). My mother, Shirley McBride, passed away just as I was really starting to write and, right until the end, she was bugging me to get to work. Her generosity gave me the financial wherewithal to finally complete this project.

My son, Jack, was born just as I began my research. By the time I finished writing, he was old enough to tabulate my daily word count and make offhand jokes—"*Someone* has a crush on Kathy Acker"—that helped me to get across the finish line. My wife, Liz Sullivan, graciously put up with, and even encouraged this crush, even when it meant my long absences. She is the kindest person I know, and I'm inspired daily by her creativity, affection, and discernment. Her assistance with the photographs in the book was essential. I love you both so much.

This book would not have been possible without Derek McCormack. *I* would not be possible without Derek McCormack. This book is for him, with unending love and admiration.

ILLUSTRATION CREDITS

———— ✕ ————

INSERT 2

1. Used with the permission of the Robert Mapplethorpe Foundation.
2. Photograph by Laurie Neaman, courtesy of Top Stories
3. Photograph by Deborah Feingold
4. Photograph by Deborah Feingold
5. Photograph by Kate Simon
6. Courtesy of Dennis Cockell
7. Courtesy of Ellen G. Friedman
8. Photograph by Ellen G. Friedman
9. Photograph by Kate Simon
10. Photograph by Sven Wiederholt/Courtesy of SFAI Archives
11. Photograph by Ali Hossaini
12. Courtesy of David M. Rubenstein Rare Book & Manuscript Library, Duke University. Used with the permission of Matias Viegener.
13. Photograph by Del LaGrace Volcano

NOTES ON SOURCES

——— × ———

Acker's novels are cited here only when their titles aren't given in the text. Where interview sources or the authors of letters are likewise not evident in the text, I have indicated them in these notes. Otherwise, sources are noted only for clarity's sake. Page numbers omitted from a source indicate a press clipping was used.

Major books by Kathy Acker

Blood and Guts in High School (New York: Grove Press, 1984)

Bodies of Work (London: Serpent's Tail, 1997)

Don Quixote (New York: Grove Press, 1986)

Empire of the Senseless (New York: Grove Press, 1988)

Eurydice In the Underworld (London: Arcadia, 1997)

Great Expectations (New York: Grove Press, 1983)

Hannibal Lecter, My Father (New York: Semiotext(e), 1991)

In Memoriam to Identity (New York: Grove Weidenfeld, 1990)

Literal Madness: Three Novels (*Kathy Goes to Haiti; My Death My Life by Pier Paolo Pasolini; Florida*) (New York: Grove Press, 1988)

My Mother: Demonology (New York: Pantheon, 1993)

Portrait of an Eye: Three Novels (*The Childlike Life of the Black Tarantula by the Black Tarantula; I Dreamt I Was a Nymphomaniac!: Imagining; The Adult Life of Toulouse Lautrec by Henri Toulouse Lautrec*) (New York: Grove Press, 1992)

Pussy, King of the Pirates (New York: Grove Press, 1996)

Rip-off Red, Girl Detective and The Burning Bombing of America: The Destruction of the U.S. (New York: Grove Press, 2002)

Other Books About Acker

Acker, Kathy, and McKenzie Wark. *I'm Very Into You: Correspondence 1995–1996*. Los Angeles: Semiotext(e), 2015.

Colby, Georgina. *Kathy Acker: Writing the Impossible*. Edinburgh: Edinburgh University Press, 2018.

Finch, Claire, and Justin Gajoux, eds. *Kathy Acker (1971–1975)*. Paris: Éditions Ismael, 2019.

Kraus, Chris. *After Kathy Acker*. Los Angeles: Semiotext(e), 2017.

Scholder, Amy, Carla Harryman, and Avital Ronell, eds. *Lust for Life: On the Writings of Kathy Acker*. London: Verso, 2006.

Scholder, Amy, and Douglas Martin, eds. *Kathy Acker: The Last Interview*. New York: Melville House, 2019.

Schulz, Daniel, ed. *Kathy Acker in Seattle*. Seattle: Misfit Lit, 2020.

Viegener, Matias. *The Assassination of Kathy Acker*. New York: Guillotine, 2018.

Wark, McKenzie. *Philosophy for Spiders: On the Low Theory of Kathy Acker*. Durham: Duke University Press, 2021.

ARCHIVES AND PERSONAL PAPERS
(WITH ABBREVIATIONS OF FREQUENTLY CITED SOURCES)

KAP   Kathy Acker Papers, David M. Rubenstein Rare Book & Manuscript Library, Duke University.

KAN   Kathy Acker Notebooks, Fales Library and Special Collections, New York University Libraries.

SLP   Sylvère Lotringer Papers and Semiotext(e) Archive, Fales Library and Special Collections, New York University Libraries.

JMP   Jackson Mac Low Papers, Special Collections and Archives, UC San Diego Library.

ISP   Ira Silverberg Papers, Fales Library and Special Collections, New York University Libraries.

JRP   Jerome Rothenberg Papers, Special Collections and Archives, UC San Diego Library.

RSP   Ron Silliman Papers, Special Collections and Archives, UC San Diego Library.

PBPP   Paul Buck Personal Papers, London.

JGPP   Jeff Goldberg Personal Papers, New York.

ASPP   Amy Scholder Personal Papers, Los Angeles.

MVPP   Matias Viegener Personal Papers, Los Angeles.

OTHER ABBREVIATIONS USED IN THE NOTES

KA   Kathy Acker

PAS   P. Adams Sitney

AII   R. J. Ellis et al., "An Informal Interview with Kathy Acker," April 23, 1986, typescript, KAP.

BOW   *Bodies of Work*

AKA   *After Kathy Acker*

KALI   *Kathy Acker: The Last Interview*

KA71   *Kathy Acker (1971–1975)*

OPT   Barry Alpert, "Kathy Acker: An Interview," *Only Paper Today*, March 30, 1976.

SOF   Larry McCaffery, *Some Other Frequency: Interviews with Innovative American Authors* (Philadelphia: University of Pennsylvania Press, 1996).

IVIY   *I'm Very Into You*

ENDNOTES

———— ✕ ————

Preface

iv "Like Borges, I equate reading and writing" "Bruce Willis and Me," KAP.

xii "Names, identities, issues, emotions" Steve Benson, "Approaches Kathy Acker," *Open Letter,* Winter 1982, 77.

xiii "She really was like a librarian" JM interview with Robin Winters, January 21, 2016.

xiii "Kathy's 'fundamental' sexual identity was writer" JM interview with Johnny Golding, April 9, 2019.

xiii "In a way, she was a clown" JM interview with Robert Glück, November 12, 2015.

xiii "She looked like a clown" Dodie Bellamy, "Digging Through Kathy Acker's Stuff," in *When the Sick Rule the World* (Los Angeles: Semiotext(e), 2015), 132.

xiv "She had 'drawing-room manners'" Mel Freilicher, "One or Two Things That I Know About Kathy Acker," in *The Encyclopedia of Rebels* (San Diego: City Works Press, 2013), 95.

xiv "she wrote that she found it 'depressing'" KA to Dennis Cooper, Dennis Cooper Papers, Fales Library and Special Collections, New York University.

xiv "After seeing Stanley Kubrick's *Full Metal Jacket*" Salman Rushdie email to JM, January 11, 2020.

xiv "indifference to whether her writing was good or bad" Gary Indiana, "Ackerville," *London Review of Books,* December 2006, 154.

xiv "at once critically pretty interesting" David Foster Wallace, "Portrait of an Eye: Three Novels," *Harvard Review,* Spring 1992.

xiv "I nursed a distant and silent crush" Lucy Sante email to JM, January 5, 2016.

xv "pioneer work of the kind" Jeanette Winterson, introduction to *Essential Acker: The Selected Writing of Kathy Acker,* Amy Scholder and Dennis Cooper, eds. (New York: Grove Press, 2002), viii.

xvi "Being Kathy Acker was not an easy thing" IVIY draft ms., MVPP.

xvii "I remember Robert Creeley" KA, "A Few Notes on Two of My Books," *Review of Contemporary Fiction,* Fall 1989, 33.

xviii "different names tagged" Cynthia Carr, "Kathy Acker 1944–1997," *Village Voice,* December 9, 1997.

xx "Autobiography is supposed to be" "Untitled Essay Fragment," n.d., KAP. Possibly an early draft of her introduction to *Young Lust* (London: Pandora, 1989).

xxi "a quarter of the material" "Gramercy Park Hotel Bar, NYC, Conversation with Dean Kuipers," KALI, 35.

xxi "a writer is a kind of journalist" KA, "A Few Notes on Two of My Books," *Review of Contemporary Fiction,* Fall 1989, 36.

xxi "Acker's art didn't have its basis in facts" JM interview with Lawrence Weiner, July 13, 2015.

xxi "We were thinking about autobiography" Robert Glück, "Long Note on New Narrative," in *Biting the Error*, Mary Burger, Robert Glück, Camille Roy, and Gail Scott, eds. (Toronto: Coach House Books, 2004), 29.

xxii "she dreamed of writing like Agatha Christie" Ellen G. Friedman, "A Conversation with Kathy Acker," *Review of Contemporary Fiction*, Fall 1989, 20.

Chapter 1

3 "In the spring of 1995" KA, "Interview with Georgina," December 4, 1996, MVPP.

3 "cunt color" "Kathy Acker and Mark Magill," in *BOMB: The Author Interviews* (New York: Soho Press, 2014), 24.

4 "Ritchie's father had been a doctor" KA, "The Gift of Disease," *Guardian Weekend*, January 18, 1987.

4 "The body remembers" KA, "Interview with Georgina."

4 "Their first session" *Ibid.*

5 "Ritchie was 'amazing'" Beth Jackson, "An Interview with Kathy Acker," KALI, 180.

5 Just before Acker died JM interview with Cynthia Carr, November 12, 2013.

5 "She could zip herself" JM interview with Johnny Golding, April 9, 2019.

5 "I'm a New Ager" Beth Jackson, "An Interview with Kathy Acker," KALI, 179.

5 "I'm basically a New Age writer" JM interview with Robert Glück, November 12, 2015.

5 She called paranormal phenomena KA, "The Gift of Disease" early draft, KAP.

6 "Fours remember abandonment in childhood" "The Re-A.N. Process," therapy session notes with Georgina Ritchie (April 10, 1995; July 7, 1995), as well as explanatory notes, KAP.

6 "Whatever happened to her" JM interview with Amy Scholder, March 26, 2015.

6 She was born, KA's natal chart, n.d., KAP.

7 she was born premature KA, *My Mother: Demonology* notebook, n.d., KAP.

7 Acker's maternal family JM interview with Pooh Kaye, November 11, 2014.

7 "We were the grandchildren" Ibid.

7 "an early draft of her novel" KA, "The Following Myth of Romantic Suffering Has to Be Done Away With," *BOMB*, April 1, 1984.

8 "Nana disdained regular clothing stores," *Variety* typescript, KAP.

8 "glad" to be Jewish Jill Bressler and Alan Kaufman, "Tattoo Jew," *Davka*, Spring–Summer 1996, 14.

8 "one childhood memory" KA, *Requiem* notebook, KAP.

8 "Constantly conscious of her weight" JM interview with Wendy Bowers, November 10, 2014.

9 "She usually dressed" KA, *Eurydice in the Underworld*, 151.

9 "She seemed bright" JM interview with Peter Gordon, November 10, 2014.

9 "I remember Claire" JM interview with Pooh Kaye, November 11, 2014.

9 "extremely conservative" JM interview with Wendy Bowers, November 10, 2014.

9 "Let me tell you" Connie Samaras, "Kathy Acker: The Birth of the Wild Heart," http://vv.arts .ucla.edu/terminals/acker/acker-4.html.

10 "His early adulthood was eventful" JM interview with Wendy Bowers, November 10, 2014; AKA, 159.

10   "described him as a 'cipher'" JM interview with Robert Acker, November 11, 2015.
11   "She gave me this name she hated" KA, "Paragraphs," *Journal of the Midwest Modern Language Association*, Spring 1995, 88.
11   "As a girl" KA, "Seeing Gender," BOW, 158.

Chapter 2

12   "she was still complaining" JM interview with Frank Malinaro, August 24, 2016.
12   "A small apartment" KA, *Requiem*, in *Eurydice in the Underworld*, 157.
13   "Among the many objects" Wendy Bowers personal papers.
14   "When Kathy was seven or eight" JM interview with Wendy Bowers, November 10, 2014.
14   "She saw Florrie" JM interview with Pooh Kaye, November 11, 2014.
15   "I'm probably concerned" KA, "Paragraphs," 90.
15   "On the one hand," Ibid.
15   "Most of it is true" JM interview with Wendy Bowers, November 10, 2014.
16   "She tallied all the above" KA, *My Mother: Demonology* notebook, KAP.
16   "I have no sense of a person" KA, *Politics*, New York: Papyrus Press, 1972.

Chapter 3

18   "The suffragette and educator Jessica Garretson Finch" "Jessica Cosgrave, Educator, Dies," *New York Times*, November 1, 1949, 27.
18   "unquestionably top-notch" JM interview with Linda Muller Vasu, March 30, 2017.
18   "her classmates included Faith Golding" *Lenox Lantern*, June 1964, New York: Birch Wathen Lenox School Archives.
19   "I was born a rich kid" Sybil Walker, "Kathy Acker," *East Village Eye*, June 1982, 28.
19   "how a great writer" KA, "The Invisible Universe," *Open Letter*, Winter 1982, 85.
19   "When I was a kid" SOF, 30.
19   "she proudly carried" JM interview with Linda Muller Vasu, March 30, 2017.
19   "The first adult authors she read" SOF, 30.
19   "Books are the only people" KA, *The Childlike Life of the Black Tarantula* notebook, KAP.
20   "They sometimes played bridge" JM interview with Susan Muller Nielsen, January 16, 2018.

Chapter 4

22   "Sometime in the summer" JM interview with Wendy Bowers, November 10, 2014.
23   "She was like a cuckoo" JM interview with Pooh Kaye, November 11, 2014.
23   "I began to think about my father" KA, *Rip-off Red Memory Experiments* notebook, KAN.
23   "living in raw mythology" Alan Moore email to JM, June 13, 2017.
24   "Kathy and Wendy wore their school uniforms" JM interview with Wendy Bowers, November 10, 2014.
24   "She started to smoke" JM interview with Pooh Kaye, November 11, 2014.
24   "the first time I remember exerting control" KA, *Rip-off Red Memory Experiments* notebook, KAN.
24   "her menstrual blood" All of these images recur in many of Acker's books, but Acker also recounts the menstrual blood in an undated letter to Glenda George, MVPP.

24 "Kathy was dating" KA to Glenda George, MVPP.

25 "he's holding me like a baby" Ibid.

25 "no recollection of these liaisons" Dale Hemmerdinger email to JM, May 19, 2015.

25 "only remembered Kathy as 'fast'" Ibid.

Chapter 5

27 "the first year Kathy published" KA, *Quill* (1960, 1962, 1963), Lenox School, courtesy of Elizabeth Marcus.

27 "Kathy's own favorite poet" P. Adams Sitney email to JM, October 27, 2014.

27 "American novelists should be considered" KA, "Writing as Magic" typescript, KAP.

27 "The language of the novel" Ibid.

28 "As a prize Daniel Schulz," "Inventarization and Creation of a Finding Aid: Kathy Acker, 1947–1997," Master's Thesis, University of Cologne, February 26, 2020, 46.

28 "the gem-like flame" Ibid.

29 "I was always imitating Shakespeare" SOF, 27.

29 "In the summer of 1963" P. Adams Sitney email to JM, October 27, 2014.

30 "He even managed to persuade" "The Impotent Decoration: An Interview with P. Adams Sitney," *Nassau Literary Review*, February 6, 2015, https://www.nasslit.com/home/2015/02/06/the-impotent-decoration-an-interview-with-p-adams-sitney.

30 "Sitney was studying Greek" PAS email to JM, October 27, 2014.

30 "She was a real live wire" JM interview with PAS, November 12, 2014.

30 "at least three Olson books" Daniel Schulz, "Inventarization and Creation of a Finding Aid: Kathy Acker, 1947–1997," Master's Thesis, University of Cologne, February 26, 2020, 51.

30 "Jonas Mekas . . . asked Sitney" JM interview with PAS, November 12, 2014.

31 "The place was cramped" Ibid.

31 "Kathy was at Lenox" KA, "Colette," BOW, 152.

31 "On that day" Ibid.

32 "Growing up as a kid" KA, "Paragraphs," 87.

33 "a story that she often" KA, unexpurgated interview with Sylvère Lotringer, SLP.

33 "used her as a secretary" PAS email to JM, October 27, 2014.

33 "one makes various compromises" Ibid.

34 "I couldn't tell" KA, "Colette," BOW, 152.

34 "fiftieth anniversary of the guild" "27 Girls Presented at Dance of Jewish Guild for the Blind," *New York Times*, November 28, 1963.

34 "At the event itself" KA to Clayton Eshelman, Clayton Eshelman Papers, Special Collections and Archives, University of California, San Diego.

34 "At some point in their relationship" PAS email to JM, October 27, 2014.

35 "she never told him" JM interview with Mel Freilicher, March 28, 2015.

35 "other people who knew Acker" JM interviews with Connie Samaras (March 31, 2015), Harris Schiff (September 24, 2015), Jill Kroesen (September 29, 2017).

35 "One can read Kathy's work" JM interview with Ron Silliman, May 10, 2017.

35 "There are things" JM interview with Carolee Schneemann, January 31, 2016.

Chapter 6

36 "The nickname is mentioned" *Lenox Lantern*, 10.

37 "When reality is up for grabs" KA, "Bodybuilding" typescript, 1991, KAP.

37 "In her senior year" *Lenox Lantern*, 10.

37 "She had her sights" JM interview with Wendy Bowers, November 10, 2014.

37 "Radcliffe was a small school" JM interview with Linda Muller Vasu, March 30, 2017.

38 "Kathy was crushed" JM interview with Wendy Bowers, November 10, 2014.

38 "she couldn't stop talking about Radcliffe" JM interview with Mel Freilicher, March 28, 2015.

38 "He clashed frequently" Abram Leon Sachar, *Brandeis University: A Host at Last* (Hanover: Brandeis University Press, 1995), 249.

38 "Art breaks open a dimension" Herbert Marcuse, *The Aesthetic Dimension* (Boston: Beacon Press, 1978), 72.

Chapter 7

43 "She was one of the beautiful ones" JM interview with Jeff Weinstein, November 11, 2014.

43 "she ditched the first roommate" KA, "Interview with Andrea Juno and V. Vale," *Angry Women*, Andrea Juno and V. Vale, eds. (San Francisco: RE/Search, 1991), 177–85.

43 "On their first day together" JM interview with Tamar Diesendruck, March 11, 2016.

43 "I remember her being kind" JM interview with Deborah Anker, March 16, 2016.

44 "On the first day of class" JM interview with Peter Gould, January 17, 2015.

44 "Do you like me?" From unpublished Peter Gould typescript, *Young Loves*, Peter Gould personal papers.

45 "Black students occupied Ford Hall" "Fighting Systemic Racism on Campus," *Justice*, February 9, 2021, https://www.thejustice.org/article/2021/02/blm-and-campus-anti-racist-policies.

45 "I didn't go down south" KA, "Interview with Andrea Juno and V. Vale."

46 "still living in the 19th century" KA, "Allen Ginsberg: A Personal Portrait" typescript, KAP.

46 "Allen Ginsberg visited the campus" JM interview with Peter Gould, January 17, 2015.

46 "I remember that they walked" KA, "Allen Ginsberg: A Personal Portrait" typescript, KAP.

47 "poetry's only rule" Ibid.

48 "The Hippies were our parents" Ibid.

48 "it was cool to fuck" KA, "Interview with Andrea Juno and V. Vale."

48 "Lusty Kathy" JM interview with Peter Gould, January 17, 2015.

48 "To Gould's chagrin" Ibid.

48 "Acker was a history major" JM interview with Robert Acker, November 11, 2015.

48 "he exclusively ate steak tartare" Acker denied all these claims, which were made in interviews with Mel Freilicher, Tamar Diesendruck, and Eleanor Antin.

48 "kicking Diesendruck" JM interview with Tamar Diesendruck, March 11, 2016.

49 "About your coming home" KA, letter to Peter Gould, n.d., Peter Gould personal papers.

50 "They thought marrying a Polish Jew" Jill Bressler and Alan Kaufman, "Tattoo Jew," *Davka*, Spring–Summer 1996, 14.

50 "I was a certain class" "Kathy Acker," *East Village Eye*, 22.

51 "I was trying to get rid of my parents" KA, *Poems 5/71–6/71*, KAN.

51 "On September 4, 1966" JM interview with Robert Acker, November 11, 2015.

51 "She was undressed" Peter Gould, *Burnt Toast* (New York: Knopf, 1971), 65.

Chapter 8

53 "The poet David Antin" David Antin lecture on KA, NYU, 2002, https://vimeo.com/4446934.

54 "When Marcuse lured his best-known student" Savannah Munoz, "Who Is Angela Davis?," *Triton*, May 6, 2019, https://tritonmag.com/who-was-angela-davis/.

54 "news of Martin Luther King's assassination" JM interview with Robert Acker, November 11, 2015.

54 "San Diego was not only" David Antin lecture on KA, NYU.

54 "I hated it" KA, "Blue Valentine" typescript, KAP.

54 "a permanent Acker" KA, *Poems 5/71–6/71*, KAN.

55 "When I speak about angels" KA, *Rip-off Red Memory Experiments* notebook, KAN.

55 "the angels are making me" KA, "Very Tired" typescript, KAN.

55 "She took courses" JM interview with Mel Freilicher, March 28, 2015.

55 "She dedicated one poem" KA, "Ode to Beautiful Women" typescript, KAN.

57 "Acker too straight" KA, "Very Tired" typescript, KAN.

58 "Melvyn and I would listen" KA, "Blue Valentine" typescript, KAP.

59 "What was going on" JM interview with Mel Freilicher, March 28, 2015.

59 "Weinstein, meanwhile, was openly gay" JM interview with Jeff Weinstein, November 11, 2014.

Chapter 9

60 "All of us come from parents" KA, "Allen Ginsberg: A Personal Portrait" typescript, KAP.

60 "The technology is language" David Antin NYU lecture.

60 "People told me" Ibid.

61 "a post-conceptual artist" Eleanor Antin, "An Autobiography of the Artist as an Autobiographer," *Journal: The Los Angeles Institute of Contemporary Art*, October 1974, 20.

61 "He was frighteningly intelligent," Robert Kushner email to JM, March 10, 2017.

61 "late adolescent expressionist poems" JM interview with David Antin, March 29, 2015.

61 "verbally more complex" Ibid.

62 "these wonderful, quickly shifting things" David Antin NYU lecture.

62 "and if you have to invent" David Antin, "What It Means to Be Avant-Garde," *What It Means to Be Avant-Garde* (New York: New Directions, 1993), 46.

63 "*this* is what a book should be" Michael Silverblatt interview with KA, *Bookworm*, KCRW, August 31, 1992, https://www.kcrw.com/culture/shows/bookworm/kathy-acker.

63 "childlike, cuddly and sweet" JM interview with Eleanor Antin, March 29, 2015.

63 "At some point in 1969" JM interview with Leonard Neufeld, May 27, 2015.

Chapter 10

65 "Dead men I don't want" KA, "Diary: Warmcatfur" typescript, KAN.

66 "Between 1966 and 1971" Peter Kihhs, "Tripled Murder Rate Here Puts Big Burden on Detective Force," *New York Times*, June 30, 1971, 26.

66 "Days and days of anxiety" KA, "Section from *Diary*, 1–2/71," KAP.

66 "One could live an interesting existence" Duncan Hannah, *20th Century Boy: Notebooks of the Seventies* (New York: Vintage, 2018), xiv.

67 "She took dance classes with Meredith Monk" All these details drawn from KAN as well as JM interview with Neufeld.

67 "... a job to me means" KA, "Section from *Diary*, 1–2/71," KAP.

67 "I've spent the last four years" KA, "Very Tired" typescript, KAN.

67 "I must at all times" KA, "Death Portraits 1.Visions, Diaries in Protection of Self Death," KAN.

68 "Within weeks of arriving" KA71, 88.

68 "I was very sick" KA to Clayton Eshleman, Clayton Eshleman Papers, Special Collections & Archives, University of California, San Diego.

68 "the city will pay for your grave" KA, *My Mother* notebook, KAP.

69 "do you love me" KA, "Diary II, Poems III," KAN.

69 "they pissed on me" KA, "Section from *Diary*, 1–2/71," KAP.

69 "there are no more parents" KA, "Very Tired," KAN.

69 "my goddamn grandmother" Ibid.

69 "extremely self-absorbed" JM interview with Diane Rothenberg, March 29, 2015.

69 "Jerry adored her" JM interview with Jerome Rothenberg, March 29, 2015.

69 "please excuse the personal stuff" KA to Jerome Rothenberg, May 8, 1971, JRP.

70 "St. Mark's Church had a long history" https://www.2009-2019.poetryproject.org/about/history/.

70 "The Poetry Project burns" https://www.artforum.com/diary/andrew-durbin-at-the-poetry-project-s-50th-anniversary-gala-68516.

70 "by reading these poems" KA, *Poems 5/71–6/71*, KAN.

71 "a succession of gasps" KA71, 631.

71 "Acker spelled out her method" KA, "Very Tired," KAN.

72 "this diary is about the destruction" KA, "Political Poems," KAN.

72 "I'm not sure what I'm doing" KA, *Jane Eyre II*, KAN.

72 "my attempt to map" KA to Alan Sondheim, n.d., KAP.

72 "Fantasy, sensorial perception" KA, *Breaking Through Memories to Desires*, KAN.

73 "in his usual depressed and ambivalent state" KA, "Death Portraits 1.Visions, Diaries in Protection of Self Death," KAN.

73 "Korevaar doesn't remember" JM interview with Wilma Korevaar, October 16, 2018.

74 "this writing is getting to be like junk" KA, "days and days of anxiety" notebook, KAN.

74 "... it's only one fucking life" KA to Peter Wollen, n.d., Leslie Dick personal papers.

Chapter 11

75 "The peeps themselves," AKA, 27.

75 "He beat his wife" Rachel Inberg, "The Peep King's Legacy: A Family Portrait," *Rumpus*, October 31, 2017, https://therumpus.net/2017/10/31/the-peep-kings-legacy-a-family-portrait/.

76 "Fink was both attracted and repulsed" JM interview with Larry Fink, December 10, 2015.

76 "Everybody had a little *vie bohème*" JM Interview with Jerome Rothenberg, March 29, 2015.

76 "Kathy was always kvetching" JM interview with Diane Rothenberg, March 29, 2015.

77 "They usually did at least six" OPT, 15.

78 "the lowest way to make the basic bread" KA, "Very Tired," KAN.

78 "I don't draw hard categories" OPT, 14.

79 "We weren't entirely joking" KA, "Blue Valentine," KAP.

79 "All writing is in fact cut-ups" William Burroughs, "Cut-Ups Self-Explained," *Evergreen Review* 32, April–May 1964.

80 "I really love doing cut up" KA to Bernadette Mayer, n.d., c. fall 1972, United Artists Records, Special Collections and Archives, University of California, San Diego.

80 "It changed my politics" KA, unexpurgated interview with Sylvère Lotringer, SLP.

81 "it's the ass-hole" KA, "Ex Libris: Morda/Diary Poems Dreams, right after: what i can remember," KAN.

81 "I admire criminals" KA, "Very Tired" typescript, KAN.

Chapter 12

82 "Acker had idolized Malanga" PAS email to JM, October 27, 2014.

82 "For Smith's very first public reading" "Patti Smith's My First Gig," YouTube, https://www.youtube.com/watch?v=tNOuHNlZwEk&t=45s.

82 "She reminded Acker" KA, "days and days of anxiety" notebook, KAN.

83 "Acker would make her own Poetry Project debut" AKA, 61.

83 "Mayer began teaching" Daniel Kane, *All Poets Welcome: The Lower East Side Poetry Scene in the 1960s* (Berkeley: University of California Press, 2003), 188.

83 "Write a soothing novel" http://www.writing.upenn.edu/library/Mayer-Bernadette_Experiments.html.

84 "While Acker never actually participated" Charles Bernstein email to JM, October 9, 2015; Ed Friedman email to JM, October 9, 2015.

84 "lively, vivid presence" JM interview with Bernadette Mayer, September 25, 2015.

85 "They thought I was some kind of pervert" KA, unexpurgated interview with Sylvère Lotringer, SLP.

85 "Waldman . . . came to consider Acker a 'hero'" Anne Waldman email to JM, February 14, 2016.

85 "During one evening" JM interview with Harris Schiff, September 24, 2015.

86 "rules which any academic poetry class" KA, "Untitled Essay Fragment," n.d., KAP.

86 "I don't know who my father was" KA, *Politics*.

86 "DOWN WITH THE FAMILY" KA, "Velvet Awareness" typescript, KAN.

86 "little prose poems" KA, unexpurgated interview with Sylvère Lotringer, SLP.

87 ". . . my desire to be seen" KA, "Section from *Diary*, 1–2/71," KAP.

87 "I didn't want to become real famous" OPT, 15.

87 "The 42nd street shit" KA to Jerome Rothenberg, May 8, 1971, JRP.

87 "I was very scared" KA, unexpurgated interview with Sylvère Lotringer, SLP.

88 "I'm getting involved" KA to Jerome Rothenberg, May 8, 1971, JRP.

89 "Concrete Poems" KA, KAN.

89 "she attended dances hosted" KA, "Diary: Warmcatfur," KAN.

89 "Liking women means liking" KA, "Death Portraits 1. Visions Diaries in Protection of Self Death," KAN.

89 "hopefully lesbians have more sense" KA, "Section from *Diary*, 1-2/71," KAP.

89 "Seeking more intellectual stimulation" As indicated by Acker's 1977 resumé, found in William S. Burroughs Papers, Ohio State University. Though her exact dates are somewhat inconsistent with other records and recollections.

90 "Neufeld had found work with Burt Lasky" JM interview with Leonard Neufeld, May 27, 2015.

90 "a very liberal guy" Ibid.

90 "I'm perpetrating the domination" KA, "The Emotions of Everyone in America" notebook, KAN.

Chapter 13

92 "I have a natural imp tendency" KA to Ron Silliman, n.d., RSP.

92 "Writers should present the human heart" KA, "A Few Notes on Two of My Books," *Review of Contemporary Fiction*, Fall 1989, 31.

92 "She's a different kind of writer" JM interview with Sylvère Lotringer, March 25, 2015.

93 "I was brought up in this poetry world" "Kathy Acker," *East Village Eye*, 22.

93 "All those novelists" Melvyn Bragg, "Kathy Acker," *The South Bank Show*, ITV, London, April 1, 1984.

93 "just churn it out" "Kathy Acker," *East Village Eye*, 22.

94 "read softly, evenly" KA, "Works Done," KAN.

94 "By the word 'Communist'" Ibid.

95 "get beyond human psychology" KA "Michael McLard," *BOMB* 1, April 1, 1981.

96 "you don't accept responsibility" KA, "Household Objects: Breaking Up, Falling In Love, Description of Life in NY," KAN.

96 "When she found out" JM interview with Jeff Weinstein, November 11, 2014.

96 "Gordon looked . . . like a giant baby" JM interview with Duncan Hannah, October 12, 2017.

96 "He was born in New York" JM interview with Peter Gordon, November 10, 2014; more background: Tim Lawrence, *Hold On to Your Dreams: Arthur Russell and the Downtown Music Scene* (Durham: Duke University Press), 74.

96 "She was fascinating" JM interview with Peter Gordon, November 10, 2014.

97 "Split w/ Lenny" KA to Harris Schiff, Harris Schiff Papers, Emory University.

97 "paradise" KA to Bernadette Mayer, n.d., United Artists Records, Special Collections & Archives, University of California, San Diego.

98 "She adopted a pseudonym" JM interview with Mel Freilicher, March 28, 2015.

98 "dance interpretively" KA71, 329.

98 "It's a nice place" OPT, 14.

98 "Through that winter" KA71, 329.

98 "'Nuff said!?!" KA, *Rip-off Red* manuscript, KAP.

99 "basically about illusion" KA to Bernadette Mayer, June 31, 1973, United Artists Records, Special Collections & Archives, University of California, San Diego.

Chapter 14

100 "David was invited" David Antin, "Talking at Pomona," *Artforum*, September 1972.

100 "That's a poem" www.tabletmag.com/sections/arts-letters/articles/talmudic-improv-david-antin.

100 "give a damn" http://writing.upenn.edu/epc/authors/antin/A-Conversation-with-David-Antin_Charles-Bernstein_Granary-2002.pdf.

101 "circumvent some of the spatial" https://assets.moma.org/documents/moma_press-release_326846.pdf?_ga=2.14666743.1742514327.1616525771-2141988142.1616525771.

101 "I consider the usual aids" http://www.columbia.edu/cu/wallach/exhibitions/Multiple-Occupancy.html

103 "Do you care whether you can *know*" KA, "Conversations," 1974, KAP.

103 "It's just another name" KA to Jackson Mac Low, n.d., JMP.

103 "everybody wore make-up" KA, unexpurgated interview with Sylvère Lotringer, SLP.

104 "Being a poet" David Antin, "What It Means to Be Avant-Garde," 46.

104 "idea of doing like a Dickens novel" KA interview with Charles Bernstein, https://media.sas.upenn.edu/pennsound/authors/Acker/04-12-1995/Acker-Kathy_01_on-publishing-her-early-work_Interview-and-Discussion-at-UB_04-12-95.mp3.

104 "Elly suggested that Acker send" JM interview with Eleanor Antin, March 29, 2015.

104 "I've never opened up to anyone" KA to Jackson Mac Low, n.d., JMP.

104 "That list in the pre-internet days" "Dear Reader: Eileen Myles on Kathy Acker," *Literary Hub*, May 2, 2019, https://lithub.com/dear-reader-eileen-myles-on-kathy-acker/.

105 "It was about setting up friendships" OPT, 14.

105 "For The Black Tarantula" Carolee Schneemann, *Cezanne, She Was a Great Painter* (New Paltz: Tresspuss Press, 1975).

106 "The only reaction against an unbearable society" KA, "Models of the Present," *Artforum*, February 1984.

106 "She never had a conventional therapist" JM interview with Mel Freilicher, March 28, 2015.

106 "saw psychological pain" Barbara Caspar interview with Peter Gordon, MVPP.

107 "the year that Flora Rheta Schreiber published *Sybil*" http://www.livingjelly.com/blog/jt-leroy-and-narratives-of-abuse.

108 "Murderers-Criminals Join Sunlight," KA, "Exercises," KAP.

109 "she went straight from an abortion" JM interview with Avital Ronell, January 25, 2016.

109 "a body I like" KA, *Portrait of an Eye*, 97.

Chapter 15

111 "there were fifty gay organizations" https://www.foundsf.org/index.php?title=The_Castro:_The_Rise_of_a_Gay_Community.

111 "anarchic, gender-bending theater troupe" https://www.diggers.org/angels_of_light_and_cockettes.htm.

112 "Basically I eat" KA to Harris Schiff, December 3, 1973, Harris Schiff Papers, Emory University.

112 "I've made the final decision" KA to Jackson Mac Low, n.d., JMP.

112 "too much of it came off as women's lib" KA, *Thesmophoriazusae* typescript, KAP.

113 "my favorite pornographer" OPT, 15.

113 "In a preview of the censorship" AII.

113 "More bothersome to her" KA to Jackson Mac Low, n.d., JMP.

114 "the title itself was a nod" OPT, 15.

115 "What an incredible fucking writer" KA to Ron Silliman, n.d., RSP.

116 "use myself changing" KA, *Nymphomaniac* notebook III, KAN.

116 "I was searching for something" OPT, 16.

118 "liberationist text" Barrett Watten, "Foucault Reads Acker and Rewrites the History of the Novel," in Scholder, Harryman, and Ronell, eds., *Lust for Life* (London: Verso, 2006), 74.

118 "Rather than drawing conclusions" Robert Glück, "The Greatness of Kathy Acker," in *Lust for Life*, 46.

118 "A mythic world opens" McKenzie Wark, *Philosophy for Spiders* (Durham: Duke University Press, 2021), 110.

118 "bloody hermit" KA to Sharon Mattlin and Jackson Mac Low, October 1, 1973, JMP.

118 "Acker stayed in touch Daniel Schulz," "Inventarization and Creation of a Finding Aid," 55.

119 "de-narrative" SOF, 24.

119 "they started hosting" JM interview with Peter Gordon, November 10, 2014; Daniel Schulz, "Inventarization and Creation of a Finding Aid," 58.

119 "It was very repressive" Loren Means, "Kathy's Genius," *Berkeley Barb*, July 4–10, 1975, 13.

120 "Kroesen loved Gordon" JM interview with Jill Kroesen, September 29, 2017.

121 "As Acker told it" KA to Alan Sondheim, n.d., KAP.

121 "At long last" Ibid; also see "Script of Untitled Tape 1," KA71, and *I Become Jane Eyre Who Rebelled Against Everyone*, KAP.

121 "On February 18" https://www.poetryproject.org/media/pages/file-library/1192053418-1605 470984/pp-readings-and-workshops-1966-1980..

122 "talked for twelve hours" KA to Alan Sondheim, n.d., KAP.

122 "exploring sexuality" KA71, 611.

122 "they ended up making two tapes" *Blue Tape*, https://ubu.com/film/acker_sondheim.html.

122 "inverse, both sexually" Ibid, 612.

122 "utter lack of self-consciousness" KA71, 614.

122 "We pushed things" KA71, 611.

Chapter 16

124 "a shit" KA to Ron Silliman, n.d., RSP.

124 she met Ron Silliman JM interview with Ron Silliman, May 10, 2017.

124 "processural" poetics Colby, *Kathy Acker: Writing the Impossible*, 28.

126 "I'm a performance artist" Schulz, ed., *Kathy Acker in Seattle*, 53.

126 "whispering 'sinisterly'" JM interview with Lynne Tillman, November 14, 2013.

126 "If she thought" JM interview with Kevin Killian, May 4, 2013.

126 "Each of us" Eileen Myles, *Inferno* (New York: OR Books, 2010), 156.

127 "It's strange" Peter Gordon to KA, n.d., KAP.

127 "the leaps of language" JM interview with Leandro Katz, November 14, 2013.

127 "old stuff seems dead to me" KA to Leandro Katz, December 11, 1974, Leandro Katz personal papers.

128 "the legend of The Black Tarantula" JM interview with Eileen Myles, January 28, 2016.

129 "she'd had an affair" KA to Ron Silliman, n.d., RSP.

129 "In one of Forti's classes" JM interview with Pooh Kaye, November 11, 2014.

129 "she had also befriended" JM interview with Constance DeJong, March 8, 2016.

131 "two hundred thousand artists" JM interview with Sylvère Lotringer, March 25, 2015.

131 "poet's district" Alan Moore with Jim Cornwell, "Local History: The Art of Battle for Bohemia in New York," in *Alternative Art New York: New York 1965–1985*, Julie Ault, ed. (Minneapolis: University of Minnesota Press), 323.

131 "there were only possibilities" Edmund White, "Why Can't We Stop Talking About New York in the Late 1970s," *New York Times*, September 10, 2015. https://www.nytimes.com/2015/09/10/t-magazine/1970s-new-york-history.html

132 "1975 is a new world" Lucy Sante, "Maybe the People Would Be the Times," in *Maybe the People Would Be the Times* (Portland: Verse Chorus Press, 2020), 19.

132 "There never was" JM interview with Sylvère Lotringer, March 25, 2015.

132 "none of it dangerous" KA to Ron Silliman, n.d., RSP.

132 "the Protestant work" Ibid.

132 "It involved befriending" Mel Freilicher email to JM, July 8, 2021.

133 "about the only job" OPT, 14.

Chapter 17

134 192 "an absolute sweetheart" JM interview with Rhys Chatham, February 23, 2017.

135 "I'd see her" JM interview with Aline Mare, March 27, 2015.

135 "I think they were utterly connected" JM interview with Betsy Sussler, May 27, 2015.

135 "It was a story" Ibid; see also IVIY, 59.

136 "fanatic" KA, "About Robert Mapplethorpe," KAP.

138 "Robbins is really" JM interview with Sylvère Lotringer, March 25, 2015.

138 "just some nut" KA to Ron Silliman, n.d., RSP.

139 "best friends" Ibid.

139 "passionate integrity" Rudy Wurlitzer email to JM, July 2, 2015.

139 "simple paragraphs" KA to Rudy Wurlizer, n.d., Rudy Wurlitzer personal papers.

140 "Hollywood bland language" KA to Jonathan Miles, n.d., Chris Kraus Collection of Kathy Acker Papers, 1971–2017, Duke University Libraries.

140 "Even a hack" KA to Ron Silliman, n.d., RSP.

Chapter 18

142 "about seventy-two thousand" JM interview with Adele Bertei, October 22, 2019.

142 "one of the nicest artists" KA to Ron Silliman, n.d., RSP.

143 "I want to do" OPT, 16.

143 "The problem of identity" KA, introduction to *Young Lust*.

143 "It was a big deal" JM Interview with Constance DeJong, March 8, 2016.

143 "I had a strong" KA, introduction to *Young Lust*.

144 "Acker was listed first" http://archive.thekitchen.org/wp-content/uploads/2015/03/Press-Release_Acker_With-Constance-de-Jong.pdf.

144 "I'll just tell you" AKA, 135.

144 "That was Kathy's first move" JM Interview with Constance DeJong, March 8, 2016.

146 "Ten Out of Many Women Writers" KA, n.d., KAP.

Chapter 19

149 "Acker found out" AKA, 141.

150 "the most documentary" "Kathy Acker," *East Village Eye*, 22

150 "a genre piece" KA to Paul Buck and Glenda George, n.d., PBPP.

151 "Kushner liked the book" Robert Kushner email to JM, March 10, 2017.

152 "some of them acquired names" IVIY, 24.

152 "In one of those toys" JM interview with Connie Samaras, March 31, 2015.

155 "I never met my father" KA, "The Killers," in *Biting the Error*, Mary Burger, Robert Glück, Camille Roy, and Gail Scott, eds. (Toronto: Coach House Books, 2004), 14.

156 "from the kind of family" Sarah Schulman, *The Gentrification of the Mind* (Berkeley: University of California Press, 2012), 75.

156 "only a partial truth" Jacki Ochs email to JM, January 31, 2017.

157 "Janey's mother had come" KA, *Blood and Guts in High School* draft, KAP.

159 "probate documents" In JM's possession. Also in Chris Kraus Collection of Kathy Acker Papers, 1971–2017, Duke University Libraries.

159 "she met with James Grauerholz" James Grauerholz calendar, in William S. Burroughs Papers, Ohio State University.

159 "didn't get her really" James Grauerholz email to JM, July 26, 2017.

159 "we try to get a lot of eroticism" Mary Ellen Strote to James Grauerholz, November 1, 1977, in William Burroughs Papers, Ohio State University.

159 "she became close . . ." the poet JM interview with Victor Coleman, May 27, 2016.

160 "They offered Acker a thousand dollars" JM interview with Fred Gaysek, May 22, 2016.

160 "The main thing I remember" JM interview with John Greyson, May 23, 2016.

160 "My least favorite," KA to Paul Buck, n.d., PBPP.

160 "What makes Kathy's adventures" Edwidge Danticat, "Preface," *Research in African Literatures* 35, 2004, vii–viii.

161 "At another reading" JM interview with Judith Doyle, July 9, 2015.

Chapter 20

162 "Goldberg tried to convince Wylie" JM interview with Jeff Goldberg, January 25, 2016.

165 "her 'editor' " "Kathy Acker," *East Village Eye*, 28.

165 "My first novels" AII.

166 "the first time" SOF, 26.

166 "In my mind" "Kathy Acker," *East Village Eye*, 22.

166 "Imagine a Lego set" JM interview with Adele Bertei, October 22, 2019.

166 "Acker loved to tell a story" KA, "Interview with Andrea Juno and V. Vale."

168 "Acker flew to Mexico" KA to Lafayette Young, n.d., KAP.

168 "It was a bad breakup" AII, 6.

169 "Every sentence this man writes" KA to Douglas Messerli, n.d., c. May 1979, Sun and Moon Press Archive, Special Collections & Archives, University of California, San Diego.

169 "She identified deeply" Teresa Rose Carmody, "On Kathy Acker: A Desk, A Disease, An Accounting," *Literary Hub*, June 19, 2019, https://lithub.com/on-kathy-acker-a-desk-a-disease-an-accounting/.

169 "described other than oedipal" KA, "A Few Notes on Two of My Books," *Review of Contemporary Fiction*, Fall 1989, 35.

169 "By the time I got" Larry Rickels, "Body Bildung," in KALI, 172.

170 "George Quasha . . . offered" KA to Lafayette Young, August 3, 1978, KAP.

170 "private backing" KA to Glenda George, n.d., Glenda George personal papers.

170 "don't be a baby" "Kathy Acker," *East Village Eye*, 22.

Chapter 21

171 "eyes of a pimp" JM interview with Sylvère Lotringer, March 25, 2015.

171 "the process by which" Sylvère Lotringer, "Press Release," in *Schizo-Culture* (Los Angeles: Semiotext(e), 2013), 8.

173 "I'm a little worried" KA to Paul Buck and Glenda George, n.d., PBPP.

174 "Acker read from 'The Persian Poems'" Adele Bertei, "Call Him Burroughs: News from the Nova Convention," *New York Rocker*, no. 17, February–March 1979, 13–15.

174 "It was the first time" KA, unexpurgated interview with Sylvère Lotringer, SLP.

174 "As opposed to construction" Ibid.

175 "He was a sexual top" JM interview with Judith Doyle, July 9, 2015.

175 "very sweet" JM interview with Sylvère Lotringer, March 25, 2015.

179 "a dispiriting estate account" Probate documents in JM's possession. Also in Chris Kraus Collection of Kathy Acker Papers, 1971–2017, Duke University Libraries.

179 "Her narrator is named Omar" JM interview with Andrew J. Paterson, June 18, 2015.

Chapter 22

181 "I hate publishers" KA letter to Paul Buck and Glenda George, n.d., c. 1980, PBPP.

181 "a little too much S&M" Ibid.

182 "like a monkey" JM interview with Duncan Hannah, October 12, 2017.

182 "I thought of her as an imp" JM interview with Betsy Sussler, May 27, 2015.

184 "It's nothing" "Kathy Acker," *East Village Eye*, 28.

185 "doing adventurous writing" Harry Hoogstraten email to JM, July 6, 2017.

185 "She was not so tough" Ibid.

186 "the fruit of a revolt" https://www.editions-laurence-viallet.com/cahier/je-est-toujours-un
-autre-par-gerard-georges-lemaire/.

186 "She was an intellectual" JM interview with Paul Buck, November 27, 2018.

186 "She was overly sensitive" AKA, 179.

186 "her grandmother broke her hip" KA to Robert Creeley, n.d., KAP.

186 "a hell hole" KA, *Variety* typescript, KAP.

187 "Blood speaks to blood" Ibid.

187 "Her estate was valued" Probate documents in JM's possession. Also in Chris Kraus Collection of Kathy Acker Papers, 1971–2017, Duke University Libraries.

188 "Acker's material was written" Joan Casademont, "Kathy Acker, The Kitchen," *Artforum*, May 1980, 79.

188 "a force" Schulz, ed., *Kathy Acker in Seattle*, 41.

188 "What I really mean" Terence Sellers to KA, n.d., Terence Sellers Papers, Fales Library and Special Collections, New York University.

188 "NYC might have got me famous" KA to Jeff Goldberg, n.d., JGPP.

189 "Her continuing ill health" Ibid.

189 "Why are you doing this?" Schulz, ed., *Kathy Acker in Seattle*, 104.

Chapter 23

191 "rewrite of Charles Dickens' novel" http://archive.thekitchen.org/wp-content/uploads/2012/01/Press-Release_Acker_Great-Expectations_2.pdf.

192 "Can you believe this person?" Gary Indiana, *I Can Give You Anything But Love* (New York: Rizzoli, 2015), 121.

193 "for emotional reasons" SOF, 30.

193 "I really felt" Ibid.

193 "You don't know any more" KA to Paul Buck, n.d, PBPP.

194 "across rational discourse" Michael Davidson, "Writing at the Boundaries," *New York Times*, February 24, 1995, 316.

194 "Vale and Acker were friendly" V. Vale email to Leslie Dick, November 13, 2018, Leslie Dick personal papers.

195 "she offered a way out" Karen Finley, *Shock Treatment* (San Francisco: City Lights, 1990).

196 "sensations of ordinary life" Dodie Bellamy and Kevin Killian, "New Narrative Beginnings 1977–1997," in *Writers Who Love Too Much: New Narrative 1977–1997*, Dodie Bellamy, Kevin Killian, eds. (New York: Nightboat Books, 2017), ix.

196 "I want to be your friend" KA to Kevin Killian, n.d., Kevin Killian personal papers.

196 "She and Denise" JM interview with Robert Glück, November 12, 2015.

197 "Fried wasn't quite so taken" JM interview with Howard Fried, November 11, 2015.

197 a "desert" KA to Glenda George, n.d., Glenda George personal papers.

197 "this animal that I hate" Ibid.

Chapter 24

199 "Even if it's death" KA to Terence Sellers, n.d., Terence Sellers Papers, Fales Library and Special Collections, New York University.

199 "*Blood and Guts* is totally unsuited" KA to Jeff Goldberg, n.d., JGPP.

199 "At some point early in" JM interview with Bette Gordon, January 25, 2016.

200 "crazy, avant-garde experimental filmmaker" Ibid.

201 "She looked up at him" Bette Gordon personal papers.

201 "Bette didn't change" KA to Peter Wollen, October 7, 1983, Leslie Dick personal papers.

203 "the most interesting new American material" JM interview with Richard Foreman, September 13, 2017.

203 "She was the first person" Neal Swettenham, *Richard Foreman: An American (Partly) in Paris* (London: Routledge, 2017), 59.

204 "postmodern quotation" JM interview with David Salle, January 29, 2016.

205 "Acker hated" JM interview with Ken Jordan, May 30, 2015.

205 "none of the actors had an inkling" www.chorusgypsy.com/avantgarde.html#Poet1.

206 "The performance certainly" Neal Swettenham, *Richard Foreman: An American (Partly) in Paris* (London: Routledge, 2017), 61.

206 "Kathy Acker's text" Ibid., 61.

207 "well-intentioned, neatly crafted mess" John Rockwell, "Opera: 'Birth of Poet,' Avant-Garde," *New York Times*, December 5, 1985, 81.

207 "What was intended" John Howell, "The Birth of a Poet," *Artforum,* March 1986, 129.

207 "I love you all" JM interview with Richard Foreman, September 13, 2017.

208 "She sent me a note" Neal Swettenham, *Richard Foreman: An American (Partly) in Paris* (London: Routledge, 2017), 63.

Chapter 25

209 "Acker found an apartment" JM interview with Pooh Kaye, November 11, 2014.

209 "large room" KA, "Property," n.d., KAP.

209 "It's the last poor section" *The South Bank Show.*

211 "But like most middle-class" JM interview with Amy Scholder, March 26, 2015.

211 "very poor" AII, 9.

212 "willful" JM interview with Fred Jordan, May 30, 2015.

213 "What I really thought" Cynthia Rose email to JM, April 25, 2019.

214 "this rather frugal art world" JM interview with Leslie Dick, March 31, 2015.

214 "would soon arrive" Cynthia Carr, *Fire in the Belly* (New York: Bloomsbury, 2012), 254.

214 "marketing concept" Carlo McCormick and Walter Robinson, "Slouching Towards Avenue D," *Art in America*, Summer 1984.

215 "no coherent aesthetic" Lynne Tillman, *What Would Lynne Tillman Do?* (New York: Red Lemonade, 2014), 235.

215 "Ultimately we were against" Indiana, *I Can Give You Anything But Love*, 165.

215 "We hung out together" KA, "Critical Languages," BOW, 82.

216 "Robert loved fun" KA, "About Robert Mapplethorpe" typescript, KAP.

Chapter 26

217 "a slick, marketing guy" JM interview with Fred Jordan, May 30, 2015.

217 "he had a brilliant instinct" Jacqueline Graham email to JM, April 23, 2019.

218 "Exactly what I want" KA to Jonathan Miles, n.d., Chris Kraus Collection.

218 "She was the kind of person" Cynthia Rose email to JM, April 25, 2019.

218 "She was a living collage" JM interview with Jonathan Miles, November 28, 2018.

219 "black Cuban voodoo candle" KA to Jonathan Miles, n.d., Chris Kraus Collection.

219 "She and Gordon would officially divorce" Divorce decree, June 23, 1983, KAP.

220 "One of Acker's greatest achievements" Chris Kraus, "Sex, Tattle, and Soul," *Guardian*, August 19, 2017, https://www.theguardian.com/books/2017/aug/19/sex-tattle-and-soul-how-kathy-acker-shocked-and-seduced-the-literary-world.

220 "favorite living writer" Matias Viegener, *2500 Random Things About Me Too* (Los Angeles: Les Figues Press, 2012), 219.

220 "I've never liked it" KA to Sylvère Lotringer, SLP.

220 "some kind of murderer" Cynthia Rose, "Punk Porn and Plagiarism," *NME*, January 22, 1983, 8, 31.

220 "She arranged the novel" "Gramercy Park Hotel Bar, NYC, Conversation with Dean Kuipers," KALI, 37.

222 "probably the most far-out" Ibid., 37.

222 "I usually admire risk-taking" James R. Frakes, "Ooh. Ooh. And Then Again, Aha," *New York Times*, January 17, 1988, 71.

222 "maybe fail and succeed" "Gramercy Park Hotel Bar, NYC, Conversation with Dean Kuipers," KALI, 37.

Chapter 27

225 "During my twenties" KA, "Bodybuilding" typescript, 1991, KAP.

226 "Nothing, not even ill health" Ibid.

226 "The gym lobotomizes me" KA to Peter Wollen, August 27, 1983, Leslie Dick personal papers.

227 "the invention of a *new insurgent* writing" Hélène Cixous, "The Laugh of the Medusa," in Keith Cohen and Paula Cohen (trans.), *Signs* (University of Chicago Press), Summer 1976, 880.

227 "If ordinary language or meanings" KA, "Against Ordinary Language: The Language of the Body," BOW, 148.

228 "a T-shirt with an image of Farrah Fawcett" Lucy Sante, "The Party," *New York Times*, October 5, 2003, https://www.nytimes.com/2003/10/05/magazine/the-party.html.

228 "dated, modified New York version" JM interview with Hanif Kureishi, November 28, 2018.

228 "Stuffed haphazardly" Dodie Bellamy, "Digging Through Kathy Acker's Stuff," in *When the Sick Rule the World* (Los Angeles: Semiotext(e), 2015), 131.

229 "Acker was taking her cues" JM interview with Leslie Dick, March 31, 2015.

229 "To grow old in New York" Roberta Fineberg, "On Exiles and Expatriates," *Books and Bookmen*, February, 1986, 28.

230 "I just couldn't live in total poverty" Mary Harron, "Lulu Comes to London," *Sunday Times*, July 7, 1985.

230 "a lot of interesting things to say" Barry Miles email to JM, June 26, 2015.

231 "a ceaseless explorer" Peter Wollen, "Kathy Acker," in *Lust for Life*, 2.

231 "Tell me everything you know about Peter" JM interview with Lynne Tillman, November 14, 2013.

233 "Coupledom is a disgusting phenomenon" KA to Amy Scholder, n.d., ASPP.

Chapter 28

234 "almost waifish" JM interview with Alan Jenkins, November 26, 2018.

235 "Acker's failure to provoke" Neville Shack, "Mistress of the Obscene," *Times Literary Supplement*, February 10, 1984.

235 "Riverside was what a university should be" Hanif Kureishi, introduction to *My Beautiful Laundrette* (London: Faber and Faber, 2014).

235 "I was a terrible person" JM interview with Simon Usher, November 29, 2018.

236 "a bit unreadable" JM interview with Hanif Kureishi, November 28, 2018.

236 "open the fucking prisons" JM interview with Simon Usher, November 29, 2018.

238 "subtle and enigmatic" Ian Mayes, "Hunter Takes a Trip," *Sunday Times*, May 27, 1984.

238 "dreadful dialogue" John Coleman, "Review of *Variety*," *New Statesman*, May 25, 1984, 29.

238 "static, uncommunicative" Janet Maslin, "Variety," *New York Times*, March 8, 1985.

239 "a bit dowdy" JM interview with Michael Bracewell, February 8, 2019.

239 "it was really weird" JM interview with Neil Gaiman, January 13, 2016.

239 "You'd go out on the lawn" JM interview with Ira Silverberg, November 14, 2013.

240 "She was a novelty act" Ibid.

Chapter 29

241 "Later I'm lyin'" Simon Usher personal papers.

242 "There was no way" Kasia Boddy, "1997: Interview with Kathy Acker," KALI, 221.

243 "to clear her mind" Ellen G. Friedman, "A Conversation with Kathy Acker," *Review of Contemporary Fiction*, Fall 1989, 13.

243 "Acker read (or re-read)" KA to Peter Wollen, September 6, 1983, Leslie Dick personal papers.

243 "her library included four" Daniel Schulz, "Inventarization and Creation of a Finding Aid."

243 "this damned world position" AII, 2.

243 "I start copying things" Ibid., 3.

244 "an incredible structuralist" Ibid.

244 "18th-century Balzacian narrative" Ibid.

244 "primitive" "Gramercy Park Hotel Bar, NYC, Conversation with Dean Kuipers," KALI, 38.

244 "If all these words" Ibid., 39.

245 "Poets are" KA, introduction to *Young Lust*.

245 "I can see why" Boddy, "1997: Interview with Kathy Acker," 225.

245 "Lots and lots of ploys" Ibid., 12.

246 "It is true" KA, "Property," KAP.

246 "All I can say" Mary Harron, "Lulu Comes to London," *Sunday Times*, July 7, 1985.

246 "this business of running away" Recording of KA and Sylvère Lotringer phone conversation, n.d., MVPP.

246 "kind of joke" Friedman, "A Conversation with Kathy Acker," 20.

246 "some great feminist ideal" http://www.marysialewandowska.com/waa/detail.php-id=4913 .html.

246 "without any reason" Friedman, "A Conversation with Kathy Acker," 20.

246 "As a woman" Helene Trespeuch, "The Feminism of Sherrie Levine Through the Prism of the Supposed 'Death of the Author,'" *Aware*, June 8, 2017, https://awarewomenartists.com/en/magazine /feminisme-de-sherrie-levine-prisme-de-pretendue-mort-de-lauteur/.

247 "I hated being defined" KA, "Interview with Andrea Juno and V. Vale."

247 "identity politics 'repulsive'" Boddy, "1997: Interview with Kathy Acker," 225.

247 "strident;" "restrictive" *ibid*, 219.

247 "There's a deep moral dislocation" Roy Hoffman, "In Short," *New York Times*, December 23, 1984, 57.

247 "Various politicians and governments exploited" Amy Scholder email to JM, November 3, 2021.

248 "I wouldn't call her a feminist writer" "Dear Reader: Eileen Myles on Kathy Acker," *Literary Hub*, May 2, 2019, https://lithub.com/dear-reader-eileen-myles-on-kathy-acker/.

248 "I didn't think of Kathy" JM interview with Leslie Dick, March 31, 2015.
248 "the S&M lesbians" KA, unexpurgated interview with Sylvère Lotringer, SLP.
248 "I'd rather be one" Boddy, "1997: Interview with Kathy Acker," 219.
248 "barking like a dog" JM interview with Robert Glück, November 12, 2015; JM interview with Ira Silverberg, November 14, 2013.

Chapter 30

249 "like Tweetie Pie" Julie Burchill email to JM, February 8, 2019.
250 "one of the writers of Reaganite America" KA, review of *Slaves of New York* typescript, KAP.
250 "tough girl aura" Alan Moore email to JM, June 13, 2017.
251 "What mattered was" Cynthia Rose email to JM, April 25, 2019.
252 "I was struck by the daring" Salman Rushdie email to JM, January 11, 2020.
252 "*Voices for Salman Rushdie*" Daniel Schulz, "Inventarization and Creation of a Finding Aid," 70.
252 "Many people, many intellectuals" KA, "A Personal View of *The Satanic Verses*" typescript, KAP.
252 "If you were an outsider" JM interview with Roz Kaveney, November 29, 2018.
253 "In England" KA, unexpurgated interview with Sylvère Lotringer, SLP.
253 "her most popular book" Based on royalty statements found in Chris Kraus Collection of Kathy Acker Papers, 1971–2017, Duke University Libraries.
253 "According to records" Julia Berner-Tobin email to JM, February 3, 2022.
254 "I got an agent" AII, 7.
254 "it's fucking capitalism" AII, 8.
255 "I probably wasn't there enough" JM interview with Anne McDermid, January 27, 2017.

Chapter 31

257 "spiritual double whammy" Amy Scholder and Ira Silverberg, introduction to *High Risk: An Anthology of Forbidden Writings* (New York: Penguin, 1991), xiv.
258 "whitewashing" KA to Ira Silverberg, June 9, 1986, ISP.
258 "our intention is merely" Ira Silverberg to KA, date June 13, 1986, ISP.
258 "I deserve better" Ibid.
259 "thinking of looking for a teaching job" Caryn James, "New York's Spinning Literary Circles," April 26, 1987, *New York Times Magazine*.
259 "yuppie culture" JM interview with Amy Scholder, March 26, 2015.
259 "might feel 'better'" KA to Amy Scholder, May 1, 1987, ASPP.
260 "a short fling Roz Kaveney," "Bodywork: The Life and Death of Kathy Acker," unpublished ms., n.d., MVPP.
260 "I have a real problem" KA to Amy Scholder, n.d., ASPP.

Chapter 32

262 "heavy metal kindergarten" Tamsin Blanchard, "Beauty Is Only Skin Deep," *Independent*, December 12, 1992.
262 "this cool chick" JM interview with Stephen Harris, January 9, 2019.
262 "had about a dozen sessions" JM interview with Dennis Cockell, May 11, 2018.

263 "a form of art," Carle VP Groome, "Kathy Acker: Making Sense of the Senseless," *Tattoo Advocate*, no. 3, 1990, 8–10.

263 "ridiculous moralists" KA, unexpurgated interview with Sylvère Lotringer, SLP.

264 "I could summarize" Brian Massumi, *The Politics of Everyday Fear* (Minneapolois: University of Minnesota Press, 1993).

265 "an astonishing writer" William Gibson to KA, n.d., KAP.

267 "she met a German cultural journalist" AKA, 226.

267 "I can't figure Rainer out" KA to Jürgen Ploog, n.d., courtesy of Daniel Schulz.

268 "Rainer . . . taught me something" IVIY, 32.

Chapter 33

269 "it's unlikely Burroughs" Barry Miles email to JM, June 26, 2015.

269 "a two-hour interview" https://ubu.com/film/burroughs_acker.html.

271 "That Kathy Acker has spawned" Eve MacSweeney, "This Disgusting World," *Times Literary Supplement*, June 17, 1988.

272 "dead country" KA to Jürgen Ploog, n.d., courtesy of Daniel Schulz.

273 "it would be best" Anne McDermid to KA, n.d., ISP.

273 "I am outraged" "Copy Write," *Daily Telegraph*, August 4, 1989.

273 "whatever she wanted" AKA, 234.

273 "What if I was in this country?" Ibid., 236.

273 "She considered cowriting" KA to Amy Scholder, n.d., ASPP.

273 "a book on vodoo" JM interview with Darius James, November 5, 2019.

274 "She received $30,000" KA to Alan Halpern, Allied Funding, March 11, 1989, KAP.

274 "initially called *Men*" KA to Amy Scholder, n.d., ASPP.

274 "a Japanese tattoo artist" KA, unexpurgated interview with Sylvère Lotringer, SLP.

274 "a fucking capitalist!" SOF, 31.

275 "I think what Faulkner does" John Carlin, "Acker Rapes Rimbaud," *Paper*, July, 1990.

275 "recover my own childhood" SOF, 31.

275 "a bit limited" KA to Amy Scholder, n.d., ASPP.

275 "too narrow and personal" SOF, 31.

275 "her favorite of her novels" Matias Viegener email to JM, August 20, 2018.

276 "The last novel of yours" Samuel Delany to KA, May 26, 1993, KAP.

276 "not so much sliding" KA to Jürgen Ploog, n.d., courtesy of Daniel Schulz.

277 "In some ways" JM interview with Cynthia Carr, November 12, 2013.

Chapter 34

280 "Years ago I lost" KA, *My Mother: Demonology* notebook, KAP.

281 "Acker is back in New York" David Trinidad, *Notes on a Past Life* (Buffalo: BlazeVOX Books, 2016), 77–80.

281 "Not only was she incredibly experimental" JM interview with Dennis Cooper, June 25, 2017.

281 "It was . . . a strange evening" Dennis Cooper email to JM, March 2, 2019.

283 "It's hard to live a life" Betsy Sussler email to JM, May 29, 2015.

283 "Hell later denied this" JM interview with Richard Hell, January 29, 2016.

284 "I did try to get on" KA to Sylvère Lotringer, March 8, 1991, SLP.

Chapter 35

289 "One of her students at SFAI" J. Myers-Szupinska and Rosa Tyhurst, eds., *Artwork for Bedrooms* (San Francisco: California College of the Arts, 2018), 33.

289 "I always got the sense" JM interview with Jenna Leigh Evans, May 7, 2018.

289 "the Net is a free zone" KA, "After the End of the Art World" typescript, KAP.

290 "Acker met Sirius first" JM interview with R. U. Sirius, November 13, 2015.

290 "obscenity in a chat room" Rosie X, "Pussy and the Art of Motorcycle Maintenance," *Geekgirl*, 1995, https://www.mhpbooks.com/deleted-material-from-kathy-acker-the-last-interview/.

290 "rattypussy LamdaMOO" registration email to KA, January 18, 1996, KAP.

290 "Whenever I'm in Webland" KA, "My Favorite Web Sites" typescript, 1997, KAP.

290 "Kathy *summoned* me" JM interview with Avital Ronell, January 25, 2016.

291 "the gayest restaurant" John Birdsall, "The Forgotten Queer Legacy of Billy West and Zuni Café," *New York Times*, May 28, 2001, https://www.nytimes.com/2021/05/28/dining/billy -west-zuni-cafe.html.

291 "she would later feed dinner" Wark, *Philosophy for Spiders*, 27.

291 "she dated a Buddhist monk" JM interview with Kevin Killian, May 4, 2013.

291 "be a complete individual person" "Ted" email to JM, August 26, 2016.

291 "a tiny little woman" Ibid.

291 "He was so small" Stephen Beachy email to JM, May 31, 2019.

292 "a rather serious alternative history" Beth Jackson, "An Interview with Kathy Acker," KALI, 179.

292 "Nobody else was that brilliant" JM interview with Frank Malinaro, August 24, 2016.

292 "a woman named Uma" JM interview with Kathy Brew, February 3, 2020.

294 "where irrationality would not" Larry Rickels, "Body Bildung," in KALI, 165.

294 "I am the backup singer" Eileen Myles, *Inferno* (New York: O/R Books, 2010), 157.

295 "certain censorships" Rickels, "Body Bildung," in KALI, 166.

296 "the dream decide" Ibid.

Chapter 36

297 "Her first course was called" Course catalogues courtesy Becky Alexander, San Francisco Art Institute.

298 "an aircraft carrier" J. Myers-Szupinska and Rosa Tyhurst, eds., *Artwork for Bedrooms* (San Francisco: California College of the Arts, 2018), 32.

298 "In her last semester" As per 1995 pay stubs in Chris Kraus Collection of Kathy Acker Papers, 1971–2017, Duke University Libraries.

299 "students were required" JM interview with Salome Milstead, November 16, 2015.

299 "Half of them come out" IVTY, 49.

299 "She doted on students," "Kathy, Queen of the Pirates," unpublished, undated ms., Jenna Leigh Evans personal papers.

299 "Only one thing's forbidden" JM interview with Jenna Leigh Evans, May 7, 2018.

300 "Acker promptly gave the woman" JM interview with Salome Milstead, November 16, 2015.

300 "She almost violently" JM interview with Anna Joy Springer, March 25, 2015.

301 "There was this little, short, butch-femme' " JM interview with Lynn Breedlove, November 12, 2015.

301 "As Springer had expected" KA, *My Mother: Demonology* notebook, n.d., KAP.

302 "hottest band" KA, "After the End of the Art World" typescript, KAP.

Chapter 37

303 "She joined Killian in a play" Kevin Killian, "Ghost Parade," in *Fascination* (Los Angeles: Semiotext(e), 2018), 207.

305 "All the critics" Richard Kadrey, "Black Tarantula," *Salon*, December 3, 1997, https://www.salon.com/1997/12/03/03media/.

305 "surprising to the end" JM interview with Kevin Killian, May 4, 2013.

305 "staccato syntax" JM interview with David Antin, March 29, 2015.

306 "Our only survival card" IVIY, 48.

307 "I read one of Sandy's books" Gary Indiana, *Rent Boy* (New York: High Risk Books, 1994), 5.

308 "I thought she would think" JM interview with Gary Indiana, January 22, 2016.

308 "After another writer" Kevin Killian, "Ghost Parade," in *Fascination* (Los Angeles: Semiotext(e), 2018), 210.

Chapter 38

309 "Fiction *remade* reality" Marita Avila and Cheryl Meier, "Consorting with Hecate: An Invocation of Literary Pirate Kathy Acker," *BUST*, 1986.

310 "Given the present political" KA, "After the End of the Art World" typescript, KAP.

310 "I don't think we know" Rosie X, "Pussy and the Art of Motorcycle Maintenance."

311 "It's not just the fear of losing" Dodie Bellamy, "In the Shadow of the Twitter Towers," *When the Sick Rule the World* (Los Angeles: Semiotext(e), 2015), 222.

312 "I'm never having a book" IVIY, 72.

313 "I was her girl" Wark, *Philosophy for Spiders*, 25.

313 "I thought she was fabulous" JM interview with Johnny Golding, April 9, 2019.

314 "she met Charles Shaar Murray" JM interview with Charles Shaar Murray, June 11, 2019.

Chapter 39

316 "Acker's doctor told her" KA, "The Gift of Disease," *Guardian Weekend*, January 18, 1987.

316 "lump diet" KA, text file on last hard drive, MVPP.

316 "I will not die" Ros Wyn-Jones, "Kathy Acker: Written on the Body," *Independent*, September 14, 1997, https://www.independent.co.uk/life-style/interview-kathy-acker-written-on-the-body-1239024.html.

317 "She was very excited" JM interview with Sheppard Powell, November 10, 2015.

317 "vast spill of bottles" Jonathan Kemp, "Kathy Acker's Houseboy," April 25, 2019, https://minorliteratures.com/2019/04/25/kathy-ackers-houseboy-jonathan-kemp/.

317 "Two weeks after the mastectomy" Matias Viegener, *The Requiem of Kathy Acker* draft ms., March 2, 2005, 2, MVPP.

318 "All three Electra accounts" KA, "BLURB-REQUIEM" text file on last hard drive, MVPP.

321 "They wanted a naked pic" KA to Ira Silverberg, November 29, 1996, ISP.

Chapter 40

325 "He sometimes fantasized" Matias Viegener, *The Assassination of Kathy Acker*, 9.

325 "He's really fun" IVIY, 110.

325 "it's torture, the whole configuration" JM interview with Carolee Schneemann January 31, 2016.

326 "I love my sister" Acker's handwritten will, MVPP.

328 "One of the last things" KA, handwritten note, November 3, 1997, KAP.

331 "I just started touching" JM interview with Connie Samaras, March 31, 2015.

Afterword

335 "selling fourteen thousand copies a year" Elaine Blair, "A Female Antihero," *New Yorker*, November 21, 2016, 42.

337 "It might just be," Tom McCarthy, "Kathy Acker's Infidel Heteroglossia," in *Typewriters, Bombs, Jellyfish: Essays* (New York: New York Review Books, 2017).

INDEX

—— × ——

Abbott, Steve, 195, 293

Acconci, Vito, 84, 104, 122, 132, 203n

Acker, Kathy
abortions of, 108–9, 241–43, 245, 294
adoptive father of, *see* Alexander, Albert
biological father of, *see* Lehman, Harry, Jr.
birth of, 6–7, 9–11
bodybuilding of, 226–27, 294, 316
books on, 335, 336
cancer of, 315–22, 323–31
cancer scare in 1977, 167, 225, 242
childhood and teen years of, xii, xxi–xxii, 6, 8, 10, 12–16, 17–21, 22–26, 27–35, 51, 86, 116, 120, 145, 191, 193, 240, 271, 275
in college, 38–39, 43–50, 53, 55, 58, 59
cremation of, 331–33
death of, xi, xix, 241, 261, 331–33
debutante ball and, 34
depressions of, 55, 108, 181–82
education and school experiences of, 17–21, 27–32, 36–39, 43–50, 53, 55, 58, 59, 90
European trip of, 185–86
exhibitions on, 336
fame of, 128, 175–76, 189, 192, 234, 238, 239, 252–53, 280, 306
family of, xii, 6–8, 12–16, 108, 221; *see also specific family members*
family photograph album of, 13–14
financial security of, 187, 209–11, 214, 236, 237, 240
first real love of, 32
first sexual experience of, 24–26
friendships of, 237
grandfather of, 7, 8, 10, 121, 153
grandmother of, 7–8, 10, 14–15, 39, 51, 69, 108, 159, 178, 179, 186–87, 192, 209, 221, 318

grant received by, 139–40, 149
Haiti trip of, 140, 149–51
half sister of, *see* Bowers, Wendy
health problems of, 37, 68, 69, 143, 167, 168, 189, 225, 226
inheritance from grandmother, 187, 209–11, 230
Jewishness of, xii, 7, 8, 50, 156, 241, 245, 252
jobs and attitudes toward employment, 67, 77, 90, 112, 133, 142, 164, 187
library of, 327, 336
mantra of, 152
marriages of, *see* Acker, Robert "Bob"; Gordon, Peter
mastectomy of, 315–17, 320, 323, 326
meditation practice of, 152, 316
memorials for, 332
in Mexico for cancer treatment, 325–33
Mexico travels of, 168
mother of, *see* Alexander, Claire
name of, 6, 11, 64, 121
nicknames of, 36, 48, 334
pelvic inflammatory disease of, 68, 143, 168, 189, 225
physical appearance and style of, xiii, xix, 3, 20, 36–37, 43, 63, 68, 112, 125, 216, 218, 227–29, 234, 291, 306
posthumous interest in, 335–38
pregnancy and contemplation of motherhood, 241–42
psychotherapy and analysis repudiated by, 106
radio shows of, 119
rivalries, grudges, and quarrels of, 144–46
sadomasochism in relationships of, 175, 181, 235, 241, 267, 283, 291

Acker, Kathy (*cont.*)
  self-care of, 291–92
  self-harm of, 55, 108
  sexual identity of, xiii, 88–90, 302
  sexual relationships of, 134–36, 167, 175, 197
  sex work of, xii, 76–81, 85, 87, 90, 98, 108, 110, 187, 191
  spiritual beliefs, practices, and healers of, 3–6, 151–52, 291–92, 310, 316–17, 319, 321, 323, 325, 332–33
  stuffed animal collection of, 152, 248, 289, 317, 328
  tattoos of, xvi, 3, 251, 262–63, 316
  teaching of, 3, 189, 195, 199, 277, 284, 289, 290, 297–302, 303, 319–20
  trust fund from grandfather, 121, 153
  will prepared by, 326–27
Acker, Kathy, writings of, xi–xxii
  abortions in, 109
  Adult Life of Toulouse Lautrec by Henri Toulouse Lautrec, The, 125, 128n, 135–38, 140, 143, 272
  "After the End of the Art World," 310
  Algeria: A Series of Invocations Because Nothing Else Works, 170, 179–80, 181–82
  "bad" writing in, xi, 86
  Birth of the Poet, The, 203–8
  Black Tarantula persona and, 24, 64, 99, 103–7, 112–14, 118, 125–26, 128, 134, 140, 159, 166, 173, 197, 306
  Blood and Guts in High School, xix, 45, 80, 109, 157–58, 161, 163–66, 168–70, 181, 189, 191, 193, 199, 203, 213, 217, 218, 235, 239, 242, 244, 247, 253, 271–73, 295, 335–38
  Blood and Guts in High School Plus Two, 218, 222, 234
  "Blue Valentine," 54
  Bodies of Work, xvii, 261, 333–34
  "Bodybuilding," 225
  "Breaking Up," 95–96
  Burning Bombing of America, The: The Destruction of the U.S., 90, 94–95, 98, 99, 169, 261
  censorship of, 113, 272–73

Childlike Life of the Black Tarantula, The, 22, 24, 34, 78, 86n, 103, 105–10, 113, 115, 116, 120, 127–28, 137, 140, 185, 186
"Concrete Poems," 89
"Dead Doll Humility," 276
Don Quixote, xi, 7, 109, 227, 242–48, 249, 254, 257–59, 263–65, 297, 318n
  dream material and maps in, 33, 79, 115, 117, 164–65, 189, 295–96, 305
Empire of the Senseless, xv, 244, 253n, 254, 263–67, 270–71, 300
Essential Acker, 261
Eurydice in the Underworld, 318, 318n, 319, 333–34
"Exercise #1: Create Music Through Repetitions of Own Sounds," 108
  first public reading in New York, 83
  first publishings of, 27–28, 92, 128
  first "real" novel, 191
Florida, 143–44, 160, 222, 272
"Gift of Disease, The," 4n, 320–21, 324n, 325
Girl Gangs Take Over the World, 166, 170, 176, 178–79, 193
Golden Woman, The, 55
Great Expectations, xi, 13, 77, 154–55, 158–59, 170, 177, 179, 182, 186–89, 191–98, 200, 204, 213, 218, 219, 221, 336
Hannibal Lecter, My Father, 87, 179, 184, 284
Household Objects, 95
I Become a Revolutionary, 127
I Dreamt I Was a Nymphomaniac!: Imagining, 74, 113–18, 124, 125, 127, 163, 188, 196
In Memoriam to Identity, xvi, 23, 109, 168, 254, 260, 268, 273–77, 280, 309
"Invisible Universe, The," 19
  journalism, 215, 249, 277, 321
Kathy Goes to Haiti, 149–51, 159–61, 162, 163, 173, 182, 194, 222, 272
"Killers, The," 155–56, 177–78
Literal Madness, 222
  literary agent relationships and, 255–56
Lust for Life, 261
Ma Vie, Ma Mort (with Foreman), 207–8, 237

"Murderers-Criminals Join Sunlight," 108
My Death My Life by Pier Paolo Pasolini,
    50–51, 136, 207, 218, 220–22, 234, 237
My Mother: Demonology, xiii, 14, 16, 28,
    32, 37, 181, 271, 280, 292–96, 297, 305,
    309, 333
myths and, 137, 264, 274, 294
New York City in 1979, 183–84, 336
"Night," 27–28
notebooks, 69–74, 77, 79, 83–86, 88, 89,
    102–3, 309
"Notes on Writing—from the Life of
    Baudelaire," 184–85
"Ode to Beautiful Women #1," 56
"Ode to Beautiful Women #2," 55
"Ode to Beautiful Women #3," 56–58
"On My Mother's Death," 178–79
"Persian Poems, The," 163, 169–70, 174
plagiarism and appropriation in, xi, xix,
    28–29, 84, 100, 103, 115, 138, 169, 193,
    242, 254, 265, 272–73, 276, 305
Poems 5/71–6/71, 26, 68, 89, 90
"Poems for Tamar 6. 7. & 8.," 58
Politics, xx, 8, 86–88, 86n, 90, 94, 97, 98,
    105, 107
"Pornographic Poems," 58
"Property," 209–10, 240
Pussy, King of the Pirates, 3, 251, 297, 303–5,
    311–12, 318, 318n, 322, 323
racialized figures in, 244
reading performances of, 126, 188, 237
Redoing Childhood spoken-word album,
    302
Requiem, xxii, 12, 16, 35, 317–18
Rip-off Red, Girl Detective, xxii, 22, 24–26,
    55, 75, 98–99, 102, 103, 108, 150, 151,
    211, 261
Rip-off Red persona and, 26, 98, 99, 112,
    127
"Scorpions, The," 161
Seattle Book, The, 189, 193
"Stripper Disintegration," 35
"Ten Out of Many Women Writers," 146
"To Peter Lee Gould," 45–46
"Variation on a Theme: Based on Romeo
    and Juliet, II, ii," 28–29

Variety, 186, 200–203, 238, 253
voice renounced in, 93
"Works Done 1968," 94
Young Lust, 150, 254, 272
Acker, Robert "Bob," 10, 48–51, 53–55, 57, 58,
    63, 75, 97
    Kathy's marriage to, 50–51, 53–55, 57, 60,
        64, 75
    Kathy's separation and divorce from, 64
Ackroyd, Peter, 317
Adams, Douglas, 217, 317
Adil, Alev, 334
Adler, Renata, 129
Aeschylus, 317
Aesthetic Dimension, The (Marcuse), 38–39
After Kathy Acker (Kraus), 4n, 213n, 335
AIDS, 3, 221, 259, 260, 279, 311, 329
Albert, Laura, 107n
Alexander, Albert "Bud" (adoptive father),
    10–11, 13, 14, 16, 22–24, 34–35, 39, 50,
    54, 60, 86, 213, 275
    death of, 157–59, 176, 178
    heart attacks of, 69, 157
    sister of, 11, 22
    trust fund and, 121
Alexander, Claire (mother), xxii, 8–11, 12–16,
    19, 22–24, 34, 37, 39, 49, 54, 60, 68, 69,
    86, 86n, 88, 108, 153, 275, 302, 318
    birth of, 8
    Bud's death and, 158–59, 176, 178
    debutante ball and, 34
    financial difficulties of, 68, 159, 178, 179
    Gould and, 47
    illness of, 9
    Kathy's father's abandonment of, 9, 10, 16,
        22–24, 156–57, 178, 318
    Kathy's marriage to Acker and, 50–51
    Kathy's reconciliation with, 176, 177,
        181
    Kathy's writing career and, 86n, 175–76
    marriage to Bud, 10, 16
    personality of, 8–9
    physical appearance and style of, 8, 9
    pregnancy with Kathy, 9, 16, 22, 23
    sexual information and, 24, 25
    in shower incident, 16, 301

Alexander, Claire (mother) (*cont.*)
  suicide of, 176–80, 181, 191, 193, 219, 221,
    275, 305, 318
  trust fund and, 121
  volunteer work of, 8–9
Algeria, 179, 244, 245, 264, 305
Ali, Muhammad, 163
Allison, Dorothy, 309
Almeida Theatre, 219
Alternative Art New York (Ault, ed.), 131
American Biologics, 326, 328
American Opera Projects, 317
Amis, Martin, 239, 252
Anderson, Laurie, 110, 118, 143, 174, 232,
    235
Anderson, Maxwell, 143–44
Anderson, Sascha, 294
Andrews, Bruce, 124
Angelou, Maya, 31
Angels of Light, 111, 112
Anger, Kenneth, 30
Anker, Debbie, 43–45
Antin, Blaise, 61, 62, 100, 241
Antin, David, 53, 60–64, 65, 69, 84, 96, 100,
    103–5, 119, 121, 124, 151, 194, 305–6,
    328, 329
  talk poems of, 100, 104
Antin, Eleanor "Elly," 60–64, 65, 69, 96, 100,
    102, 104, 105, 119, 127, 323, 328, 329
  fictional self performances of, 101
  I Dreamt I Was a Ballerina, 114
  100 Boots, 101, 104
Anti-Oedipus (Deleuze and Guattari), 174
Apfelschnitt, Carl, 279
Arbus, Diane, 76
Arendt, Hannah, 146
Argento, Dario, 292
Aristophanes, 112–13
Armah, Ayi Kwei, 244
Armantrout, Rae, 59, 124
Artaud, Antonin, 171, 195, 207, 304
Artforum, 100, 169, 188, 207, 215, 222, 245,
    257, 305
Art in America, 214, 215
Art Institute of Chicago, 304n
Artist in Society conference, 304n

Ashbery, John, 61, 70, 127
Ashley, Robert, 110, 115, 118–20, 129
A Space Gallery, 152–53, 159
Atkinson, Ti-Grace, 172
Atlantic Monthly Books, 280
Austen, Jane, 27, 146
Auster, Paul, 243
Author's Guild, 311
Avalanche, 160

Bachmann, Ingeborg, 293
Bacon, Francis, 269
Badischer Kunstverein, 336
Bailey, Rosemary, 229, 230
Baldessari, John, 53
Ballard, J. G., 194, 269
Banana, Anna, 111
Baraka, Amiri, 211
Barnes, Julian, 217
Barnes, Mary, 106
Barnet, Miguel, xvi
Barracks, Barbara, 104
Barry, Lynda, 260
Barth, John, 58, 91
Barthes, Roland, 171, 304
Basquiat, Jean-Michel, 182, 214
Bataille, Georges, 171, 186, 197, 290, 293, 294,
    300, 312
Battle of Algiers, The, 180
Baudelaire, Charles, 183–85
Baudrillard, Jean, 174, 221
Beachy, Stephen, 107n
Beat Generation, 17, 70, 111, 185, 186, 230
Beauvoir, Simone de, 95, 146
Beckett, Samuel, 211–13, 235
Bellamy, Dodie, xiii, xviiin, 195, 196, 228, 292,
    303, 309, 311, 332
Benn, Melissa, 260
Benson, Alan, 232
Benson, Steve, xii
Bergmann, Gustav, 103, 116
Bergson, Henri, 103
Berke, Joseph, 106
Berkeley Barb, 119, 140, 159
Berkson, Bill, 128, 297
Berlin, Brigid, 82

Bernstein, Charles, 70, 124, 306
Bernstein, Leonard, 38
Berrigan, Ted, 70, 162, 163
Bertei, Adele, xiii, 166, 167, 174
Bethlehem Bakery, 164
Biafra, Jello, 194
Bierstadt, Edward Hale, 103
Big Book, The (Knowles), 63
Bigelow, Kathryn, 135
Bikini Kill, 189, 190
Billy Jack, 99
Bissoondath, Neil, xvi
Blackburn, Paul, 70
Black Jacobins, The (James), 265
Black Mountain, xv, 70, 174
Blacks, The (Genet), 31
Black Sparrow Press, 87
Blake, Nayland, 301
Blake, William, 19, 27
Blanchot, Maurice, 186, 312
Blondie, 162, 163, 271
Blood in the Parlor (Dunbar), 103
Blood of a Poet Box (Antin), 61
Bockris, Victor, 162, 163, 230
BOMB, 135, 182, 215, 218
Bond, Justin Vivian, 301, 337
Booker Prize, 217, 238–39
Bookworm, xv
Boone, Bruce, 195
Boone, Mary, 206
Borden, Lizzie, 167
Borges, Jorge Luis, xi, 243, 297
Born in Flames, 167
Borowska, Emilia, 336
Boston Museum of Fine Arts, 47
Bowers, Kevin, 187
Bowers, Wendy, 9–11, 12–15, 19, 22, 24, 39,
    58, 86n, 175–76, 176n, 178, 179, 187,
    221, 326, 329–30
Bowery, Leigh, 235
Bowes, Ed, 121
Bowles, Jane, 150
Bowles, Paul, 67
Boyer, Anne, 323n
Bracewell, Michael, 238–39, 249, 269, 271
Bradbury, Ray, 114

Bragg, Melvyn, 231, 232, 250
Brainard, Joe, 67, 82
Brakhage, Stan, 30, 33
Brandeis University, 38–39, 43–50, 54, 55, 58,
    59, 75, 80
Brat Pack, 258–59
Bread and Puppet Theater, 235
Brecht, Bertolt, 82, 127
Breedlove, Lynn, 299, 301–2
Brontë, Emily, 146, 221
Brooke, Kaucyila, 228
Brooklyn Academy of Music (BAM), 206–7
Brooks, Cleanth, 46
Brooks, Rosetta, 218
Brown, Grace, 13
Brown, Trisha, 110, 129, 235
Brownmiller, Susan, 200
Buck, Paul, 160, 175, 185–89, 194, 195, 197,
    202, 203, 211, 213n
Buddies in Bad Times Theatre, 313
Bumbershoot Festival, 323
Burchill, Julie, 249
Burden, Chris, 122
Burnt Toast (Gould), 51–52
Burroughs, William S., xvii, 17, 67, 79, 80, 91,
    130, 159, 172–74, 184, 185, 194, 211,
    212, 221, 230, 257, 258, 265, 273, 274,
    291, 300, 330
    Acker and, 269–70, 320
    death of, 332
Bush, George H. W., 310
Butch Whacks and the Glass Packs, 127
Butler, Judith, 93, 248, 312
Byrne, David, 118, 143, 163

Cage, John, 61, 110, 172, 174, 205
Cain's Book (Trocchi), 167
Calle, Sophie, 199, 200
Canada, 159
    Toronto, 152, 159–61, 182
Canetti, Elias, 264
Cannon, Beth, 121
Capra Press, 114
Caravaggio, 106
Carnal Days of Helen Seferis, The (Trocchi), 113
Carr, Cynthia, xviii, 5, 214, 270, 277–78, 326

Carroll, Jim, 127
Carson, Anne, xi
Carter, Angela, 238
Carver, Raymond, 114, 217
Casademont, Joan, 188
Castle, Ted, 127–28, 152–53
CBGB, 162, 163, 182
Celan, Paul, 293
Cendrars, Blaise, 61, 115, 117
Center on Contemporary Art, 189
Cervantes, Miguel de, *Don Quixote*, 243, 244, 246
Césaire, Aimé, 149
Cezanne, She Was a Great Painter (Schneeman), 105
Chabon, Michael, xxn
Chaikin, Joseph, 235
Chance, James, 166
Change, 186
Charlesworth, Sarah, 182
Chatham, Rhys, 134–37, 142, 143
Cheng, Emily, 122
Chomsky, Noam, 297
Choukri, Mohamed, 169
Christie, Agatha, xxii, 137
City Lights Bookstore, 162, 194, 259, 260
City Lights Review, 260
City Limits, 249, 251
Cixous, Hélène, 174, 227
Clare, John, 242
Clark, Michael, 235
Clemente, Francesco, 214
Clinton, Bill, 310
Closer (Cooper), 281
Cockell, Dennis, 262–63, 266
Cockettes, 111
Cocteau, Jean, 30, 31, 203
Codrescu, Andrei, 121, 140
Coe, Sue, 260, 337
Colab, 172
Colby, Georgina, 124, 165n, 336
Coleman, John, 238
Coleman, Victor, 159
Colette, xii, 67, 239
Collective for Living Cinema, 199
Collins, Jackie, 217

Collins, Wilkie, 98
Committee for Prisoner Humanity and Justice, 124, 125
communism, 94
Conner, Bruce, 62
Contortions, 166, 167
Coolidge, Clark, 124
Cooper, Dennis, xiv, xv, 107n, 126, 248, 257, 261, 279, 281–82, 291
Coover, Robert, 58
Cornell, Joseph, 62
Cornwell, Jim, 131
Corso, Gregory, 31, 46, 185
Cortázar, Julio, 156
Cortez, Diego, 172, 173
Couples (Updike), 58
Courtney, Erin, 299
Crane, Hart, 215
Crawl Out Your Window, 59, 92, 184
Creative Artists Public Service (CAPS), 139–40, 149
Creeley, Robert, xvii, 70, 152, 160
Crisp, Quentin, 234
Crudo (Laing), 336
Cunningham, Merce, 205
Curtains, 185
Curtis Brown, 253–56
"Cyberfeminist Manifesto for the 20th century" (VNS Matrix), 310

Daily Telegraph, 273, 273n
Dallesandro, Joe, 79
D'Amato, Alfonse, 295
Dandy Dust, 314
Danticat, Edwidge, 160–61
Dartmouth College, 299
Daughters of Bilitis, 89, 111, 302
Davenport, Guy, 118
Davis, Angela, 38, 38n, 54
Davis, Lydia, 59
Dean, James, 137
deconstruction, xix, 138, 174, 229, 264, 298
DeFeo, Jay, 298
Defoe, Daniel, 303
DeFreeze, Donald, 112
DeJong, Constance, 129–31, 138, 142–45

Delany, Samuel, 276
Deleuze, Gilles, 107, 171, 172, 174, 264, 304
De Morgan, Augustus, 102
Deren, Maya, 30, 67, 146
Derrida, Jacques, 95, 171, 174
DeSana, Jimmy, 182, 279
Dial Press, 70, 87
Dick, Leslie, 126, 214, 225n, 229–31, 233, 237, 248, 249, 250, 279
Dick, Vivienne, 202
Dickens, Charles, 19, 27, 104, 188, 191, 194, 195
Dickinson, Emily, 28
Diesendruck, Tamar, 43, 48, 58
di Prima, Diane, 87, 99, 316
Diski, Jenny, 251
Dodge, Harry, 300
Dohrn, Bernardine, 200
Don Quixote (Cervantes), 243, 244, 246
Doria, Charles, 112–13
Dorn, Ed, 185
Dougherty, Cecilia, 297
Doyle, Judith, 160, 161, 175
Ducornet, Rikki, 212
Duke University, 311
du Maurier, Daphne, 194
Dunbar, Dorothy, 103
Duncan, Robert, 104, 111, 197
Dunham, Lena, 335
Duras, Marguerite, 130, 146, 211, 248
Duval, Jeanne, 183–84
Duvalier, François "Papa Doc," 149
Dworkin, Andrea, 200, 247
Dylan, Bob, 94

Eagleton, Terry, 252
Ear Inn, 129
East Village Eye, 150, 164, 214, 221
Éden Éden Éden (Guyotat), 95, 193
Edinburgh Castle, 300, 301
Edwards, Mark, 249, 271
Einstein on the Beach (Glass), 207
Eliot, George, 146
Ellis, Bret Easton, xv
Embers, 79, 85

Emergence of Greek Democracy, The (Forrest), 113
Emin, Tracey, 250
Empty Elevator Shaft, 118, 124
Empty Suitcases, 199–200
Empty Words (Cage), 172
Eno, Brian, 254
Enter Murderers (Bierstadt), 103
Ernst, Max, 30
Esquire, 139
ethnopoetics, 63–64
Evans, Jenna Leigh, 289, 299–302
Evergreen Review, 79, 211, 212
Everybody (Laing), 336
Ewert, Mark, 291
Exiles (Joyce), 242

Face, 229
Falkner, Gerhard, 294, 295
Fall, The, 235
Fanon, Frantz, 211, 265
Fanzine, xviiin
Farber, Manny, 53
Farmer, Geoffrey, 299
fashion, 228, 229, 245
Faulkner, William, xvii, 274–75
Faye, Jean-Pierre, 186
Fear of Flying (Jong), 165
Female Eunuch, The (Greer), 217
feminism, 58, 66, 80, 214, 246–48, 291, 302, 321
    riot grrrl, 190, 305, 321
Femme 100 têtes, La (Ernst), 30
Ferlinghetti, Lawrence, 61, 70
FILE, 111, 218
Film Culture, 30
filmmakers, 30–33, 62
Film-Makers' Cooperative, 31–33
Final Harvest (Dickinson), 28
Finch, Claire, 71
Finch, Jessica Garretson, 18
Finch School, 18
Fink, Larry, 76
Finley, Karen, 195, 279, 295
Firestone, Shulamith, 66
First Blood, 237

Fitzgerald, Kit, 168
Flaubert, Gustave, 189, 193
Fluxus, 31, 63, 101
Flynt, Larry, 138
Ford, Gerald, 130–31
Foreman, Richard, 131, 203–8, 258
    Ma Vie, Ma Mort, 207–8, 237
Forrest, W. G., 113
Forti, Simone, 129, 225
Foster, Marcus, 112
Foucault, Michel, 95, 171, 172, 174, 243, 297,
    304
"Foucault Reads Acker" (Watten), 117–18
Frank, Robert, 139
Franklin Furnace, 173
Frawley, Sherry, 18–19
Frears, Stephen, 235
Freilicher, Melvyn "Mel," 35, 45, 58–59, 62, 63,
    65, 73, 74, 92, 96, 97, 102, 112, 121, 132,
    142, 145, 157, 173, 175–78, 182, 191,
    210, 221, 226, 237, 267, 302, 305, 306,
    323, 326, 328, 329
Freud, Sigmund, 38, 107, 264, 294, 301
Fried, Howard, 197, 198
Friedman, Ellen G., 265
Friedman, Josh Alan, 77n
Fry, Stephen, 250
Fuller, Margaret, 59
Full Metal Jacket, xiv
Fun City, 77–79, 85, 275

Gabriel, Kay, 337
Gaddis, William, 91
Gaiman, Neil, 239, 250, 253–54, 256, 277n,
    283, 328
Gaitskill, Mary, 279, 281–82, 309
Galás, Diamanda, 261
Gaysek, Fred, 160
General History of Pirates, The (Defoe), 303
General Idea, 111
Genet, Jean, xviii, 23, 31, 80, 82, 130, 164, 167,
    169, 193, 211, 212, 245, 265, 274, 300
George, Glenda, 24, 175, 186–89, 194, 195,
    197, 203, 247
German, the, see Weber, Rainer
Gerson Clinic, 325, 326

Getty, Ann, 280
Gibson, William, 265, 290
Gill, Peter, 235
Gingrich, Newt, 310
Ginsberg, Allen, 17, 46–47, 60, 70, 142, 174,
    230, 236
    death of, 332
Ginsberg, Peter, 255, 280
Ginzburg, Carlo, 293
Giorno, John, 70, 82, 258, 328n
Girodias, Maurice, 174
Glass, Philip, 129, 130, 139, 329, 331
    Einstein on the Beach, 207
Glück, Robert "Bob," xiii, xxi, 5, 118, 195–98,
    210, 260, 261, 279, 284, 289, 302,
    309–11, 324, 332, 333, 336
Godard, Colette, 208
Godard, Jean-Luc, 93
Godspeed (Breedlove), 302
Gold, Rich, 121, 125–26
Goldberg, Jeff, 162–64, 173–75, 182, 188, 189,
    193–94, 197, 199, 206, 228, 230
Golden Boat, The, 203n
Goldin, Nan, 199, 202
Golding, Faith, 18
Golding, Johnny, xiii, 5, 313–14, 315, 320, 321,
    326
Goldkind, Igor, 250
Goldstein, Richard, 140
Gordon, Bette, 199–202, 219, 238, 260, 279
Gordon, Kim, 209
Gordon, Peter, xiii, 9, 35, 96–99, 100, 102, 104,
    106, 108–10, 111, 112, 114, 115, 118–20,
    125–28, 134, 137–40, 142–43, 151, 154,
    167–68, 176, 177, 179, 180, 188, 203,
    204, 219, 242, 284, 318, 325, 329
    in band, 127
    Birth of the Poet, The, 203, 205, 206
    Kathy's divorce from, 219
    Kathy's marriage to, 167–68, 173, 275
    radio shows of, 119
Gothard, David, 219, 235
Gould, Elizabeth, 25
Gould, Peter, 44–49, 51–52
Govinda, Anagarika, 152
Goya, Francisco, 106

Goytisolo, Juan, 118, 245, 293
Grace, Sharon, 324, 326, 332
Grafton Books, 254–55
Graham, Dan, 62, 109–10, 119, 209
Graham, Jacqueline, 217, 232
Gramercy Hotel, 271
Grauerholz, James, 159, 212, 257, 269
Gray, Spalding, 100, 200, 202
Greer, Germaine, 217
Greyson, John, 160
Groucho Club, 239, 249–51, 307, 313
Grove/Atlantic, 280
Grove Press, 94n, 95, 99, 104, 159, 162,
    211–13, 216, 217, 218, 222, 226,
    257–58, 261, 273, 274, 279, 280, 320,
    335, 337
Guardian, 252, 269, 270, 320–21
Guattari, Félix, 107, 171, 172, 174, 264
Guevara, Ché, 38
Gurdjieff, G. I., 6, 321
Guyotat, Pierre, 95, 169, 171, 186, 193, 196,
    245, 265
Guzmán, Luis, 202
Gysin, Brion, 79, 185, 211

Haiti, 140, 149–51
Hanna, Kathleen, 189–90
Hannah, Duncan, 66, 182
Harbourfront International Authors' Festival,
    xvi, xviiin
Hardy, Ed, 262, 263
Haring, Keith, 214, 279
Harmonic, Phil, 111, 115, 125–26
Harry, Debbie, 162, 271
Harryman, Carla, 124, 284, 303, 326
Harwood, Anthony, 256
Haunted Houses (Tillman), 282
Hawthorne, Nathaniel, 19
Hay, Louise, 4
Hayman, Richard "Rip," 129
Hearst, Patty, 112, 115
Hebdige, Dick, 329
Heidegger, Martin, 290
Hejinian, Lyn, 124
Hell, Richard, xiii, 163, 166, 283, 294
Hellman, Monte, 139

Helms, Jesse, 295
Hemmerdinger, Dale, 24–25, 32
Henderson, Margaret, 336
Hendrix, Jimi, 82
Heti, Sheila, xx, 335
Higgins, Dick, 31, 33, 129
High Art in Its Highest Glory, 119
High Risk Books, 260–61, 300, 307
Hillman, James, 292
Hinckley, John, Jr., 204
hippies, 47–48, 54
Hirst, Damien, 250
History of Sexuality, The (Foucault), 172
Hoch, Hannah, 165n
Hodas, Martin "Marty," 75, 77, 81
Hodder and Stoughton, 272
Hodes, Stuart, 205
Hoffman, Abbie, 38
Holby, Grethe Barrett, 317
Hollins College, 319–21
Hollywood, 199
Holzer, Jenny, 183, 209
Homes, A. M., xv
Honneger, Arthur, 119
Hoogstraten, Harry, 185
hooks, bell, 248
Hopkins, Gerard Manley, 27
Horovitz, Michael, 218
Howard, Silas, 300
Howe, Irving, 38
Husserl, Edmund, 188, 215
Huston, John, 143

identity politics, 245, 247
I Dreamt I Was a Ballerina (Antin), 114
I Love Dick (Kraus), 219, 329, 335
Independent, 262, 270–71, 316
Indiana, Gary, xiv, xv, 160, 182, 192n, 215, 257,
    261, 278, 279–81
    Acker's break with, 308
    Rent Boy, 210–11, 307–8
    Resentment, 308
Inferno (Myles), 126
Institute of Contemporary Arts (ICA), xx, 234,
    238, 239, 246, 263, 269, 336
International Times, 184

internet, 289–90, 310–11
Intersection, 118, 127
Interview, 165
Irigaray, Luce, 15, 146, 174

James, Caryn, 258–59
James, C. L. R., 265
James, Darius, 182, 273, 279
James, Henry, 98
Jane, Xylor, 298, 299
Janowitz, Tama, 250, 259
Jarmusch, Jim, 202, 203n
Jean Genet in Tangier (Choukri), 169
Jenkins, Alan, 234–35
Jewish Guild for the Blind, 8, 34, 187
John Birch Society, 53
Johnson, Mimi, 129, 143
Johnson, Ray, 62, 101, 165n
Johnson, Robert, 43
Jones, James Earl, 31
Jong, Erica, 165
Joplin, Janis, 137
Jordan, Fred, 159, 162, 206, 212–14, 217, 258, 273, 280
Jordan, Ken, 206
Journal of the Midwest Modern Language Association, 311
Joyce, James, 221, 242
"JT Leroy and the Narrative of Abuse" (Beachy), 107n

Kaddish (Ginsberg), 46
Kadrey, Richard, 290, 305
Kaprow, Allan, 53
Kastan, Denise, 196–98
Kathy Acker (Colby), 165n
Kathy Acker Reading Room, 327n, 336
Kathy Forest, xviiin
Katz, Alex, 206
Katz, Leandro, 127–28, 140n
Kaveney, Roz, 249, 250, 252, 254, 272, 273, 277n, 278
Kawabata, Yasunari, 139, 300
Kay, Karyn, 230
Kaye, Clifford, 15n, 153, 176, 209
Kaye, Lenny, 82

Kaye, Pooh, 7–8, 10, 14, 15n, 23, 129, 131, 134–35, 145, 149, 156–57, 176–78, 209, 337
Keats, John, 28
Keillor, Garrison, 100
Kelly, Robert, 31, 60
Kennedy, John F., 31
Kennedy, Robert F., 57, 61
Keep Busy, 139
Kemp, Jonathan, 317
Kern, Richard, 203n
Kerouac, Jack, 17, 185
Ketjak (Silliman), 125
Key Largo, 143–44, 160
Khashoggi, Adnan, 138
Kiefer, Anselm, 214
Killian, Kevin, 126, 142, 195, 196, 292, 300, 303, 305, 311, 326, 332
Kimmelman, Betsy, 19
Kimmelman, Milton, 19
King, Kenneth, 129
King, Martin Luther, Jr., 54, 57
Kingsley Hall, 106
Kingston, Maxine Hong, 217
Kipling, Rudyard, 27
Kipper Kids, 195
Kissinger, Henry, 137
Kitchen, the, 131, 133, 134, 135, 142–44, 188, 200, 281–82
Knowles, Alison, 63, 129
Kobek, Jarett, xx
Korevaar, Wilma, 73
Kosuth, Joseph, 62, 172, 215
KPFA, 119
KPOO, 119
Kraus, Chris, xx, 4n, 122, 165n, 213n, 219–20, 284, 294, 329, 335–36
Kristeva, Julia, 174, 293
Kroesen, Jill, 35, 119–20, 127, 142, 143, 145
Kropotkin, Peter, 115
Kruger, Barbara, 214
Kubler, George, 116
Kubrick, Stanley, xiv
Kuchar, George, 298
Kuipers, Dean, 271
Ku Klux Klan, 53

Kureishi, Hanif, xiii, 228, 235, 236, 239, 252
Kushner, Robert, 61, 151, 152, 160, 170

Lacan, Jacques, 107
Laing, Olivia, 336–37
Laing, R. D., 106, 107, 172
Lake, Suzy, 102
Landau, Nick, 250
Landesman, Cosmo, 249
Landesman, Jay, 249
L=A=N=G=U=A=G=E, 124, 184
Language poetry movement, 124, 195, 284, 290
Lasky, Burt, 90
Laure, 186, 293–95, 304
Lawler, Louise, 214
Lawson, Wayne, 257
Lear, Martha Weinman, 58
Lear, Norman, 199
Leary, Timothy, 174, 292
Leatherdale, Marcus, 234
Leduc, Violette, 113, 130, 167
Lee, Stan, 98
Leeson, Lynn Hershman, 102, 111
Lehman, Harry, 152, 153
Lehman, Harry, Jr. (biological father), 23, 121, 122, 152–57, 181, 191
    Claire and Kathy abandoned by, 9, 10, 16, 22–24, 156–57, 178, 318
    Kathy's letter to, 153–54
Lemaire, Gérard-Georges, 185–86
Lenox School, 17–19, 25, 27–28, 31, 36, 37, 113
Lerner, Max, 38
Levine, Ellen, 256
Levine, Sherrie, 214, 246
Levine, Stacey, 189
Lévy, Bernard-Henri, 135
Lew, Jeffrey, 131
LeWitt, Sol, xiii, 128n
Lichtenstein, Harvey, 206
Liebmann, Lisa, 239
LIFE, 111
Life and Times of an Involuntary Genius, The (Codrescu), 140
Lin, Tao, xx

Livingston, Jennie, 278
Locale, 129
Logan, Andrew, 228
Logie, Jim, 188–89, 191
London, 217–19, 229–33, 235–36, 238–40, 245, 246, 249, 251–53, 270, 272, 273, 276–77, 283, 284, 314, 320–22, 323
London Review of Books, 160, 211, 270
"Long Note on New Narrative" (Glück), xxi
Lorde, 335
Los Angeles Times, xv
Lotringer, Sylvère, xiii, 87–88, 92, 103, 131, 171–75, 177, 181, 186, 188, 191, 192, 219–21, 231, 241, 246, 248, 267, 269, 271, 278, 284, 294, 295, 312, 324, 325, 326, 329
Lovelace, Linda, 75
Love of Life Orchestra, 143
Lowry, Malcolm, 98
Ludlam, Charles, 127
Lunch, Lydia, 172, 194
Lust for Life (Harryman et al., eds.), xiv
Lyon, Lisa, 202, 226
Lyotard, Jean-François, 172
Lysistrata (Aristophanes), 112

Maciunas, George, 31, 66
Mac Low, Jackson, 31, 69, 104–6, 110, 111, 112, 114, 119, 120
Mad in Pursuit (Leduc), 130
mail art, 101
Mailer, Norman, 93
Maison Française, 172
Major, Eric, 272, 273n
Malanga, Gerard, 82, 127, 162, 185
Malcolm X, 45
Malinaro, Frank, 4, 6, 292, 316–18, 321–22, 324, 332–33
Mallarmé, Stéphane, 31, 169
Manguel, Alberto, xxn
Manheim, Kate, 205, 206
Mao Tse-tung, 38
Mapplethorpe, Robert, 79, 82, 202, 215–16, 218, 226, 232, 279, 289, 295
Marcuse, Herbert, 38–39, 49–50, 53–54, 59
Mare, Aline, 135, 139, 324, 326, 328

Marshall, Bertie, 313, 314, 316
Martin, Douglas, 261, 336
Marx, Groucho, 250
Marx, Karl, 38, 264, 294
Maslin, Janet, 238
Mass, Steve, 187, 191
Mattachine Society, 111
Matta-Clark, Gordon, 131
Mayer, Aline, 332
Mayer, Bernadette, 72, 80, 83–85, 94, 97, 99, 106, 108–10, 114–17, 119, 127–29, 134, 165
Mayer, Peter, 257
Mayer, Rosemary, 84
McCaffery, Larry, 274, 278
McCarthy, Alicia, 299
McCarthy, Paul, 298
McCarthy, Tom, 337
McClard, Michael, 163
McCormack, Derek, xviii
McCormick, Carlo, 214
McDermid, Anne, 253–55, 273, 273n
McEwan, Ian, 217, 238
McGrath, Patrick, 278, 279
McInerney, Jay, 258
McKinney, Casey, xviiin
McLeod, Sandy, 202
McNeil, Legs, 162
McQueen, Steve, 326
McRobbie, Angela, xx
Means, Loren, 140
Meetings with Remarkable Men (Gurdjieff), 321
Mehta, Sonny, 217, 255
Mekas, Jonas, 30–31
Mekons, 263, 311–12, 314, 322, 323
Meltzer, David, 92
Melville, Herman, 28, 156, 193, 197, 265
Melville House, 261
Memoirs of a Beatnik (di Prima), 87
Memory Play (Harryman), 303
Metaphors on Vision (Brakhage), 33
Metzger, Radley, 292–93
Mexico, 4, 164, 168, 325, 332–33
Miles, Barry, 163, 230
Miles, Jonathan, 218–19, 221
Miller, Henry, 67, 114, 211
Millett, Kate, 66

Mills College, 110, 112, 118, 119, 127
Mishima, Yukio, 139, 226
Missing Men, The (Cooper), xiv
Model, Lisette, 76
Modern Love (DeJong), 129, 131, 144
Mona Lisa Overdrive (Gibson), 265
Monde, 208
Mondo 2000, 289–90, 310
Monk, Meredith, 67, 98
Monthly Film Bulletin, 253
Moore, Alan, 23, 131, 250–51, 262, 328
Moore, Suzanne, 249
Moore, Thomas, 292
Moore, Thurston, 209
Moravagine (Cendrars), 115
Morris, Tracie, 337
Morrison, Jim, 82, 274
Motion Sickness (Tillman), 282
Mourning Becomes Electra (O'Neill), 317–18
Mudd Club, 172, 173, 182, 183, 187, 191, 192, 199, 259
Mueller, Cookie, 182, 202, 279
Muktananda, Swami, 151, 165n
Muller, Linda, 18, 20–21, 37, 38, 275
Muller, Susan, 20, 37, 38, 275
Mulvey, Laura, 230, 231
Murray, Charles Shaar, 314, 315–20
Museum of Contemporary Art, Chicago, 322
music, 66, 162–63, 166
   punk, see punk
My Beautiful Laundrette, 235
Myles, Eileen, 104, 107n, 128, 135–36, 144–45, 194, 248, 260, 294
Mythic Being, The (Piper), 101–2

Nabokov, Vladimir, 243, 297
Naked Lunch (Burroughs), 159, 257
Nares, Jamie, 167
National Endowment for the Arts (NEA), 195, 295
National Poetry Library, 249
Native Agents, 284
Negrophobia (James), 279
Neufeld, Leonard "Lenny," 63–64, 65–69, 71, 73, 75–79, 81, 87, 88, 90, 94–97, 142, 145, 302

Neuromancer (Gibson), 265
New Criticism, 46
New Narrative, 195–96, 284, 290, 303
"New Sentence, The" (Silliman), 124
New Statesman, 238, 249
Newton, Helmut, 226
New York, N.Y., 17, 32, 60, 64, 65–66, 75, 127, 128, 130–32, 183, 188, 192, 199, 209, 219, 229, 232, 234, 246, 259, 271, 272, 277–78, 284, 309, 311
    Acker's first public reading in, 83
    Acker's return to, 179–84
    art world in, 66, 131, 132, 183, 214–15, 250n, 279
    crime and violence in, 66
    downtown writing scene and magazines in, 215, 279
    East Village, 131, 142, 195, 214
    filmmakers in, 30
    gentrification in, 209, 214, 279
    music in, 66, 162–63
    Sutton Place, 12, 32, 75, 164, 175, 191, 211
New Yorker, 66, 85, 140, 335
New York Rocker, 174
New York School, 70, 72
New York State Council on the Arts, 139
New York Times, 58, 156, 194, 207, 222, 238, 247, 258, 270, 276, 335
New York University (NYU), 261
Nietzsche, Friedrich, 239, 248
Nin, Anaïs, 30, 67, 150
Nirvana, 309
Nixon, Richard, xix, 58
NME, 218, 232, 234, 239, 249, 251
North Point Press, 118
Notes on a Past Life (Trinidad), 280–81
Notley, Alice, 70, 72
Nova Convention, 173–74
Nova Express (Burroughs), 80

Oates, Joyce Carol, 137
O'Brien, Glenn, 165
Ochs, Jacki, 156
Ochs family, 156
October Gallery, 269
O'Hara, Frank, 195

Oliveros, Pauline, 53, 97
Oloomi, Azareen Van der Vliet, 335
Olson, Charles, 30, 124, 197
Onassis, Jacqueline, 137
On Certainty (Wittgenstein), 103
One-Dimensional Man, The (Marcuse), 38
100 Boots (Antin), 101, 104
O'Neill, Eugene, 317
One World Poetry Festival, 185
Only Paper Today, 77n, 159, 164
Only Prose, 164
Ontological-Hysteric Theater, 203
Opie, Catherine, 298, 301
Oresteia (Aeschylus), 317
Orlando (Woolf), xv, 93, 155
Orlovsky, Peter, 46–47
Orr, Deborah, 249
Ouloguem, Yambo, 244
Oursler, Tony, 297
Overlook Press, 257

Padgett, Ron, 70, 162
Paladin, 254
Pan Books, 217, 232
Pandora, 254, 272, 274
Pantheon Books, 280, 309
Papyrus Press, 87
Paris is Burning, 278
Pasolini, Pier Paolo, 220
Pater, Walter, 28
Paterson, Andrew J., 159–60, 179, 182
Pat Garrett & Billy the Kid, 139
Patton, Will, 202
Patty, Ann, 281–82
Peckinpah, Sam, 139
Peignot, Colette (Laure), 186, 293–95, 304
Penguin Group, 184, 196, 217, 261, 279, 318, 336
Perelman, Ron, 18, 124
Perfect Lives (Ashley), 118–20
Performance Space New York, 337
Performing Artservices, Inc., 129
Perrault, John, 104, 164, 206
Pete's Tavern, 18–19
Phillips, Anya, 182
Philosophy of Andy Warhol, The (Warhol), 141

Piaf, Edith, 31
Picador, 217–18, 232, 234, 253–55
Piper, Adrian, 101–2
Pirate, The (Robbins), 138, 272–73, 276
Plato, 113
Playgirl, 159
Ploog, Jürgen, 267, 270, 274, 284
Poe, Amos, 182
Poe, Edgar Allan, 92
Poetry Project, 70, 82–85, 90, 121, 128, 140, 162, 163, 174
Pomona College, 100
Pontecorvo, Gillo, 180
P-Orridge, Genesis, 236–37, 269, 277n, 290
postmodernism, xi, 91, 248, 272, 299
poststructuralism, xix, 298
Pound, Ezra, 30, 186
Powell, Sheppard, 316–17, 323, 326, 332
Powys, John Cowper, 27
Prince, 237
Printed Matter, 128n
processural poetics, 124
Propertius, 30, 197–98, 204
Public Intimacy, A (Buck), 185
Publishers Weekly, 276
Pulsifer, Gary, 277n
Punch, 257
punk, 162–63, 166, 217, 228, 229, 238, 239, 258, 259, 301, 302
    riot grrrl, 190, 305, 321
Purple Rain, 237
Pushcart Prize, 184
Pynchon, Thomas, 91, 137

Quasha, George, 170, 194
queercore, xv, 301
Quill, 27–28

Radcliffe College, 18, 37–38
Radical Coalition, 59
Rainer, Yvonne, 61
Random House, 280
Ransom, John Crowe, 46
Rauschenberg, Robert, 62
Ray, Rex, 300
Reagan, Ronald, xix, 121, 204, 214, 250n

Red Dora's Bearded Lady, 300–301
Reed, Lou, 82
Reich, Steve, 110, 130
Rent Boy (Indiana), 210–11, 307–8
RE/Search, 194
Resentment (Indiana), 308
Resnick, Marcia, 163
Review of Contemporary Fiction, 265
Rexroth, Kenneth, 111, 113
Ricard, Rene, 82
Ridiculous Theatrical Company, 127
Riley, Terry, 110, 119
Rimbaud, Arthur, xvii, 23, 31, 260, 274, 275, 305
riot grrrl movement, 190, 305, 321
Ritchie, Georgina, 3–6, 312, 316, 318
Riverside Studios, 218, 219, 234–36, 239, 249
Robbe-Grillet, Alain, 91, 194–95, 221
Robbins, Harold, 137–38, 140, 150
    Acker's use of passages from *The Pirate*, 138, 272–73, 276
Robinson, Walter, 214
Rodriguez, Rodrigo, 328
Rogner & Bernhard, 213n
"Roll of the Dice, A" (Mallarmé), 169
Ronell, Avital, 109, 290, 302, 303
Roots, 199
Rose, Cynthia, 213, 218, 232, 234, 251–52, 272, 304, 321, 323
Rose, The (DeFeo), 298
Rosler, Martha, 59, 63
Rosset, Barney, 104, 211–13, 257
Roth, Philip, 93, 213, 232
Rothenberg, Diane, 65, 69, 76, 104
Rothenberg, Jerome "Jerry," 60, 61, 63, 65, 69–70, 76, 83, 87, 89, 94, 104, 118, 170
Rothenberg, Matthew, 69
Rower, Ann, 294
Roy, Camille, 195
Rubinfine, David, 106
Ruh-Roh!, 291
Ruiz, Raúl, 203n
Rumour, 160
Ruscha, Ed, 104
Rushby-Smith, Uli, 255

Rushdie, Salman, xiv, 217, 238–39, 243, 250–52, 273
Ruskin, Mickey, 129
Russell, Arthur, 142, 143, 167
Russell, Stephen, 317
Rustin, Bayard, 59

Sachar, Abram, 38, 49n
Sade, Marquis de, 113, 119, 164, 211
sadomasochism (S&M), 77n, 220, 228, 248, 302
    in Acker's relationships, 175, 181, 235, 241, 267, 283, 291
St. Mark's Church-in-the-Bowery, 70, 72, 82–85, 90, 122, 127, 128, 132, 134, 140, 176
St. Pierre, Jean, 28
Salle, David, xiii, 204–7, 214, 232
Samaras, Connie, 331
Sand, George, 146
Sanders, Ed, 159
Sand Dollar, 118
San Diego, Calif., 53–54, 60, 64, 65, 75, 97, 110
    University of California at, 49–50, 53–54, 58, 59, 60–63, 80, 96, 105, 110
San Diego Free Press, 59
San Francisco, Calif., 3, 111–12, 118, 119, 128, 195–97, 259, 284–85, 289–92, 309, 311, 321–22, 324, 333
San Francisco Art Institute (SFAI), 197, 324
    Acker as teacher at, 3, 189, 195, 199, 277, 284, 289, 297–302, 303
Sante, Lucy, xiv–xv, 92, 132, 228
Sappho, 45
Saroyan, Aram, 162
Sarraute, Nathalie, 91
Sartre, Jean-Paul, 95, 116, 193
Satanic Verses, The (Rushdie), 252
Satyagraha (Glass), 129
Scheirl, Ashley Hans, 314
Schiff, Harris, 35, 85, 94, 97, 112, 114
Schiff, Stephen, 276
Schiffrin, André, 280
Schizo-Culture conference, 171–73
Schnabel, Julian, 214

Schneemann, Carolee, 31, 35, 61, 104, 105, 170
    cancer of, 325–26
Scholder, Amy, 6, 95, 211, 259–61, 262, 263, 267, 268, 271, 277, 284, 290–91, 302, 307–8, 328, 329, 332, 333
Schreiber, Flora Rheta, 107n
Schulman, Sarah, 156, 157, 260, 337
Screens, The (Genet), 169
Seattle, Wash., 188–89, 191
Seattle Times, 304
Seaver, Richard, 212
Seedbed (Acconci), 122
Selby, Cecily, 18, 37
Sellers, Terence, 182, 188, 209
Semiotext(e), 171–73, 185, 199, 218, 219, 284, 294
"September" (Vallejo), 168, 169
Serpent's Tail, 260–61, 276
Serra, Richard, 135, 139
Serrano, Andres, 295
Shafransky, Renée, 201
Shakespeare, William, 28, 29
Shape of Time, The (Kubler), 116
Sharp, Willoughby, 160
Shepard, Sam, 82
Sherman, Cindy, 214
Shoemaker, Jack, 118
Shoot (Burden), 122
Siddha Yoga, 151
Siegle, Robert, 279
Signs and Meaning in the Cinema (Wollen), 230
Silliman, Ron, 35, 77n, 104, 124–25, 128, 130–33, 135–39, 142, 144, 149, 152, 181, 306
Silverberg, Ira, 107n, 212n, 240, 253, 256, 257–58, 260, 267, 269, 280, 297, 307, 317, 320, 321, 323, 325, 326, 328, 332, 337
Silverblatt, Michael, xv
Simon, Kate, 258
Sinatra, Frank, 137
Sinclair, Iain, 251
Singer, Isaac Bashevis, 91
Siouxsie Sioux, 166, 313
Sirius, R. U., 289, 290, 292, 305, 312, 326

Sischy, Ingrid, 215
Sitney, P. Adams, xiii, 29–35, 37, 39, 45, 62, 66, 67, 78–79, 81, 104, 179, 197, 206
Skelley, Jack, 335
Slaves of New York (Janowitz), 250
Slow Fade (Wurlitzer), 140
Small Press Traffic (SPT), 196
Smith, Jack, 30, 31, 33
Smith, Kiki, 182, 215
Smith, Lindzee, 183
Smith, Patti, xi, 66, 82–83, 162, 174
Socialist Review, 124
Sondheim, Alan, xiii, 72, 121–23, 124
    Acker's videotapes with, 122–23
Sonic Youth, 209, 306
Sontag, Susan, 191–92
Soul II Soul, 251
SOUP, 293
South Bank Show, The, 231–32, 238, 239, 253, 271
Speedboat (Adler), 129
Spero, Nancy, 165n
Spice Girls, 309–10, 321
Spicer, Jack, 111
Spiegel, 267
Springer, Anna Joy, 299–302, 305
Sprinkle, Annie, 203n
Stain, The (Ducornet), 212
Stallone, Sylvester, 237
Station Hill Press, 170, 194
Stein, Chris, 271
Stein, Gertrude, xi, xvii, 84, 89, 91, 117, 130, 146, 203, 300, 330
Steinberg, Leo, 206
Steir, Pat, 172
Sterne, Laurence, 330
Stevens, Marc, 79
Stevenson, Robert Louis, 303–4
Stone, Robert, 217
Stonehill, 170, 181
Story of the Eye, The (Bataille), 300
Strachan, Elizabeth, 187
Stranded, 92
Strote, Mary Ellen, 159
"Structuralist, The" (Antin), 104
student activism, 44–45, 57, 59

Students for a Democratic Society (SDS), 38, 44, 45, 59, 94
Styrene, Poly, 166
Sun and Steel (Mishima), 226
Sunday Times, 238
Sussler, Betsy, 135–36, 177, 182–83, 206, 283
Swamp Thing (Moore), 250
Swift, Jonathan, 59
Sybil (Schreiber), 107n
Symbionese Liberation Army (SLA), 112, 115

Tarantino, Quentin, 301
Tattoo Advocate, 263
tattoos, 263, 265–67, 284
    of Acker, xvi, 3, 251, 262–63, 316
Taubin, Amy, 238
Tea, Michelle, 301
Telegraph Books, 162
Thatcher, Margaret, xix, 217, 240, 251
Thérèse and Isabelle (Leduc), 113
Thesmophoriazusae (Aristophanes), 112–13
Thief's Journal, The (Genet), 169
Third Mind, The (Burroughs and Gysin), 79n
Thomas, Dylan, 27
Thomson, Virgil, 146
Throat, 300
Throbbing Gristle, 236
Thurman, Judith, xii
Tillman, Lynne, xv, 126, 131–32, 182, 199, 214–15, 231, 261, 268, 277, 279–83, 294, 328, 337
    Acker's rift with, 282
Times Literary Supplement (TLS), xiv, 234–35, 257, 271, 334
Tin Pan Alley, 134
Titan Books, 250
Todd, Kim, 160
Tomb for 500,000 Soldiers (Guyotat), 95
Top Stories, 144, 184
Toronto, 152, 159–61, 182
Toulouse-Lautrec, Henri de, 137
Transformations (Lake), 102
transgressive literature, xv, 171
Traveler's Digest, 162, 163, 188
Treasure Island (Stevenson), 303–4
Tree, 92

Tribe8, 301, 302, 310, 321
Trinidad, David, 280–81
Trinity College, 29–30
Tristram Shandy (Sterne), 330
Trocchi, Alexander, 99, 113, 167
Trollope, Anthony, 27
Turyn, Anne, 144, 184
TVRT (Vanishing Rotating Triangle Press), 127–28, 137, 140, 152, 185
Twain, Mark, 265
21-C, 320
Twitter, 311
Two Accounts of a Journey Through Madness (Barnes and Berke), 106
Two-Lane Blacktop, 139
Tyler, Parker, 31
Tyranny, "Blue" Gene, 111, 115, 143
Tyson, Cicely, 31

Undying, The (Boyer), 323n
University of California at San Diego (UCSD), 49–50, 53–54, 58, 59, 60–63, 80, 96, 105, 110
University of Cologne, 327n, 336
University of Toronto, 270
Unwin, Robin, 272
Unwin Hyman, 254, 272, 273n
Up, Ari, 166
Updike, John, 58, 93
Urizen Books, 170
Usher, Simon, 235–38, 240, 241–42, 244, 249

Vale, V., 194
Valitsky, Ken, 317
Vallejo, César, 127, 168, 169
Van Gogh, Vincent, 137
Vanishing Rotating Triangle Press (TVRT), 127–28, 137, 140, 152, 185
Vanity Fair, 257
van Paemel, Monika, xvi
Van Tieghem, David, 143
Vasu, Linda Muller, 18, 20–21, 37, 38, 275
Velvet Underground, 58, 66, 98, 253–54
Verlaine, Paul, 274
Verso Books, 261
Vertigo, 200

Viegener, Matias, 220, 228n, 318n, 323–33, 336
Viegener, Valentin, 327–28
Vietnam War, 44, 50n, 53, 57, 98, 124, 245
Viking Penguin, 318
Vile, 111
Village Voice, 43, 75, 102, 140–41, 144, 159, 207, 215, 238, 270
Viper's Tongue, 140n
Virgil, 32
Virilio, Paul, 171
VNS Matrix, 310
Vogue, 239
Volcano, Del LaGrace, 314
Vollmann, William, 300

Wakoski, Diane, 69, 70
Waldman, Anne, 70, 72, 83–85, 129, 159, 174, 185
Wallace, David Foster, xiv, 309
Wallis, Brian, 279
Warhol, Andy, 30, 33, 57, 58, 66, 79, 82, 141, 163, 207
Wark, McKenzie, xvi, 118, 268, 291, 306, 312–13, 325, 335–37
Warsh, Lewis, 129
Watson, Don, 249, 271
Watten, Barrett, 117–18, 124, 284, 303
Way of the White Clouds, The (Govinda), 152
Weather Underground, 66, 94, 115, 199–200
Weber, Rainer ("the German"), 267–68, 271, 275, 283, 312
Wegman, William, 128n
Weidenfeld, George, 280
Weil, Simone, 80
Weiner, Hannah, 124
Weiner, Lawrence, xxi, 62, 104, 119, 128n, 142, 215
Weinstein, Jeff, 43, 58, 59, 65, 96, 164, 175, 206–7, 215, 228, 312
Weird Fucks (Tillman), 126
Weill, Albert (grandfather), 7, 8, 10, 121, 153
Weill, Florence "Florrie" (grandmother), 7–8, 10, 14–15, 39, 51, 69, 108, 159, 178, 179, 186–87, 192, 221, 318
death of, 187, 209

Weisz, Rachel, 250
Western Front, 159
"What It Means to Be Avant-Garde" (Antin), 62
White, Edmund, 131, 169, 260
Who's Afraid of Kathy Acker?, 335
Wiggins, Marianne, 252
Wilde, Oscar, 239
Wildroot Hair Tonic Company, 121, 152, 153
Wiley, Kehinde, 298
William Morris Agency, 256
Willner, Hal, 302
Willis, Ellen, 66
Wilson, Martha, 173
Wilson, Robert, 207
Winnie the Pooh (Milne), 165n, 189
Winograd, Garry, 76
Winters, Robin, xiii, 151
Winterson, Jeanette, xv, 300, 328
Without Falling (Dick), 233
Wittgenstein, Ludwig, 103, 221
Wizard of Oz, The, 28
Wojnarowicz, David, 260, 279
Wolf, Christa, 146
Wolfe, Bob, 75–76

Wolinsky, Stephen, 6
Wollen, Peter, xiii, 74, 225n, 230–31, 233, 242, 243, 246, 250, 267, 279, 328
Women Against Pornography (WAP), 200
Woolf, Virginia, xv, 67, 93, 130, 155, 171
Working Title Films, 235
Wright, Andrew, 55
Writers in Conversation, xx
Wurlitzer, Rudolph "Rudy," xiii, 139–40, 258
Wuthering Heights (Brontë), 293, 296, 333
Wylie, Andrew, 162

Yeats, W. B., 28, 113
Yoshitoshi, Taiso, 274
Young, Lafayette, 151, 165
Young, Noel, 113–14
Yuknavitch, Lidia, xiii, 335

Zambreno, Kate, 335
Zap Club, 311
Zappa, Frank, 174
ZDF, 200
Zedd, Nick, 203n
ZG, 218
Zorn, John, 203n

ABOUT THE AUTHOR

JASON McBRIDE'S writing has appeared in *The New York Times Magazine*, *New York* magazine, *The Believer*, *The Village Voice*, *The Globe and Mail*, *Hazlitt*, and many others. He lives in Toronto. *Eat Your Mind* is his first book.

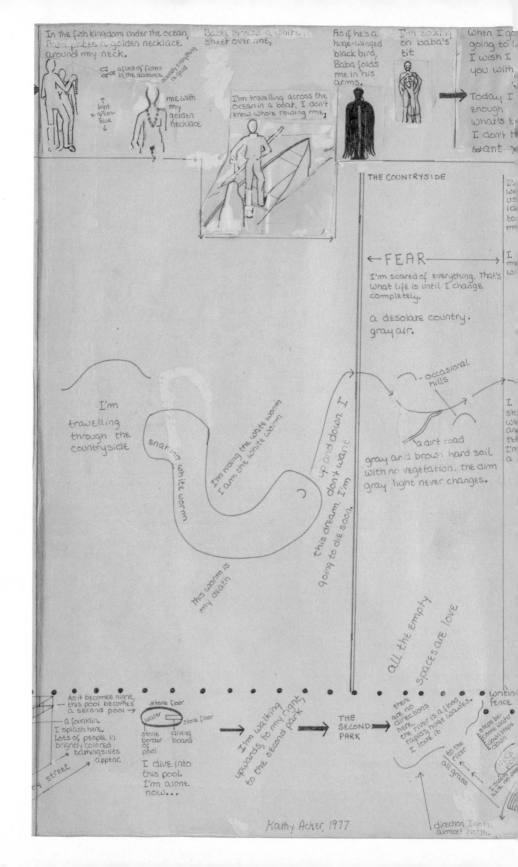

In the fish kingdom under the ocean, Baba places a golden necklace around my neck.

a flock of fishes in the distance

actually everything is gold

light green-blue

me with my golden necklace

Baba throws a white sheet over me,

I'm travelling across the ocean in a boat. I don't know who's rowing me.

As if he's a huge-winged black bird, Baba folds me in his arms.

I'm sucking on baba's tit

When I go going to l I wish I you with

Today I enough What's e I don't t want

THE COUNTRYSIDE

←—FEAR—→

I'm scared of everything. That's what life is until I change completely.

a desolate country. gray air.

I'm travelling through the countryside

snaking white worm

I'm riding the white worm I am the white worm

this worm is my death

up and down. I don't want this dream. I'm going to die soon.

— occasional hills

a dirt road
gray and brown hard soil with no vegetation. the dim gray light never changes.

ALL THE EMPTY SPACES ARE LOVE

As it becomes night, this pool becomes a second pool →

a fountain. I splash here. Lots of people in brightly colored bathingsuits appear.

street

stone floor
water stone floor
stone border of pool diving board

I dive into this pool. I'm alone now...

I'm walking upwards, to my right, to the second park

THE SECOND PARK

there are no directions here. the river is a flood rapids huge boulders. I love it.

writin fence

steps be- come steps down steps down

to the river all grass

deep pool I sudde come hole no wa

direction I go in almost North.

Kathy Acker, 1977